Theology for International Law

Theology for International Law

Esther D. Reed

B L O O M S B U R Y

LONDON • NEW DELHI • NEW YORK • SYDNEY

Bloomsbury T&T Clark

An imprint of Bloomsbury Publishing Plc

50 Bedford Square	1385 Broadway
London	New York
WC1B 3DP	NY 10018
UK	USA

www.bloomsbury.com

Bloomsbury is a registered trademark of Bloomsbury Publishing Plc

First published 2013

© Esther D. Reed, 2013

British Library Cataloguing-in-Publication Data

A catalogue record for this book is available from the British Library.

ISBN: HB: 978-0-567-62150-4
PB: 978-0-567-26206-6
ePDF: 978-0-567-40065-9
ePub: 978-0-567-00139-9

Library of Congress Cataloging-in-Publication Data

A catalog record for this book is available from the Library of Congress.

Design by Newgen Knowledge Works (P) Ltd., Chennai, India
Printed and bound in Great Britain

CONTENTS

ACKNOWLEDGEMENTS

This book would not have been possible without the kindness and assistance of many. I am grateful especially to Dr William Storrar, Director of the Center of Theological Inquiry in Princeton, for the invitation to join the Theology and International Law Working Group 2007–10. Members of the Working Group included Jeremy Waldron (Co-Director, New York University and All Souls College, Oxford), Mary Ellen O'Connell (University of Notre Dame), Amanda Perreau-Saussine (University of Cambridge), Nick Grief (Bournmouth University), Roger Alford (Pepperdine University), David Hollenbach S. J. (Boston College), Robin Lovin (Co-Director, Southern Methodist University), David Gushee (Mercer University) and Christiane Tietz (University of Mainzy). It is with great sadness I record Amanda Perreau-Saussine's death in 2012.

I am grateful to the attendees of a colloquium at Westminster Abbey in February 2012, organized by the Network for Religion in Public Life, University of Exeter. This colloquium, entitled *The Use of Force, Drones and Jus Cogens Norms*, Colloquium was led by Mary Ellen O'Connell. In addition to two senior military personnel, attendees included Nigel Biggar (University of Oxford), Rosemary Durward (King's College London), Richard Harries (Member of the House of Lords), Caroline Kennedy-Pipe (University of Hull), Steve Hucklesby (Public Issues Team, Baptist, Methodist and URC), Anatol Lieven (King's College London), James Page (United Nations Assistance Mission Afghanistan), Anicée Van-Engeland (University of Exeter now SOAS), Vernon White (Westminster Abbey), John Williams (Durham University).

I further acknowledge extremely helpful conversations among the working group on the report about armed unmanned aerial vehicles ('drones') prepared by the Joint Public Issues team of the UK Baptist, Methodist and URC churches. Members included Steve Hucklesby (Joint Public Issues Team), Peter Lee (Department for

Defence Studies and Kings College), Paul Morrison (Joint Public Issues Team) and Paul Schulte (Kings College London).

Earlier versions of chapters, or sections thereof, appeared in 'International Law and the Question of Authority: Natural Law Reasoning between Dystopia and Empire', *Jurisprudence* 2 (2010); 'Refugee Rights and State Sovereignty: Theological Perspectives on the Ethics of Territorial Borders', *Journal of the Society of Christian Ethics* 30:2 (2010); 'Nation-States and Love of Neighbour: Impartiality and the *ordo amoris*' in *Studies in Christian Ethics* 25:3 (2012); 'Responsibility to Protect and Militarized Humanitarian Intervention: When and Why the Churches Failed to Discern Moral Hazard', *Journal of Religious Ethics* 40:2 (2012) and 'Responsibility to Protect and Militarized Humanitarian Intervention: A Reply to Glanville', *Journal of Religious Ethics* 41:1 (2013). I am grateful to be able to reprint some of this material in my book.

My greatest debts are to family, colleagues and friends, not least Rachel Davila for copy-editing prior to submission.

ABBREVIATIONS

ESV English Standard Version

NKJV New King James Version

RSV Revised Standard Version

All citations are from the *ESV* unless indicated otherwise.

1

Introduction

Christian ethics and political theology is familiar with questions about the relation of church and state, divine and human law. Yet relatively little attention has been devoted to questions of international law. Much has been written on issues of ecology and the environment, the world economy, debt relief and development, refugee rights, the possibility of a global ethic, reconciliation after conflict and more, but far less on the history and jurisprudence of international law, the sources and norms of international law, its Christian heritage, the responsibilities of major world religions for collaboration with respect to particular issues in international law and such like. Many Christian people raise money for the relief of famine and otherwise support humanitarian-relief organizations and international non-governmental organizations. Fewer pay detailed attention to the rules, principles and concepts that govern relations between nation-states. As Jeremy Waldron has observed: 'Theology has never neglected law as such. . . . But international law has been much less thought about in the tradition of Christian theology, and the neglect of international law has left Christian theologians fairly tongue-tied so far as responding to the jurisprudential crisis of international law is concerned.'[1]

An aim of this book is to move issues of international law higher up the agenda of Christian theology, ethics and moral reasoning. At its most general, the book seeks to elucidate the theological resources available to Christian people for thinking through the ethics of a range of issues in international law. More specifically,

---

[1] Jeremy Waldron, 'A Religious View of the Foundations of International Law', Charles E. Test Lectures, Princeton, NJ, March 2011, p. 10 http://ssrn.com/abstract=1823702 [accessed 10 February 2013].

it attempts to offer a restatement of natural law reasoning for the twenty-first century in Protestant Thomist perspective – that is, an ecumenically viable and strongly Christological restatement of natural law reasoning for our global age, open to dialogue with major world religions and diverse secularist discourses. Themes running throughout the book include theological perspectives on:

- the contested meaning in the international arena of 'the rule of law';
- whether and/or how it is meaningful to speak of international common good;
- the sources and authority of international law;
- the meaning of 'universality';
- ways forward for Christian people in colloquy about human rights with those of other faiths, especially the Abrahamic;
- what should characterize the service of Christian ethics and political theology to international politics and jurisprudence;
- what moral significance to attach to national borders when attempting to love one's neighbour 'near' and 'far';
- where and why fresh thinking about the classic traditions of just war reasoning is necessary for the present day.

The book advocates peace through law while recognizing that the place and purpose of human law with divine providence is ambiguous. Divine justice exceeds all human law and puts in question every human attempt at attaining peace through law. Human hope does not reside in the advent of constitutionalism on the global level, stronger democratic processes, more effective international courts or the promise of a post-national society. Despite advocating peace through law, we do not get far before encountering the inherent violence of human law and the inseparability of law and injustice. No human law of any kind can effect perfect or complete justice before God or neighbour. *Nevertheless* there remains upon every human community a responsibility to strive after justice (Gen. 9.5; Ps. 10.18; Ps. 33.5; Ps. 106.3; Is. 1.17; Is. 28.17; Jer. 5.1; Ezek. 45.9; Amos 5.15). This book is written at the point of the *nevertheless* between the injustice and violence of human law, and the responsibility upon all humanity to strive after justice and peace through law.

A perceived crisis in international law

More specifically, the book grew from my involvement with the Theology and International Law Project based at the Center of Theological Inquiry (CTI), Princeton – which, in turn, arose from discussions at Princeton Theological Seminary about torture and detainee abuse. Uppermost in our minds throughout our time together were the so-called torture memos prepared by lawyers in the administration of US President George W. Bush. These memos claimed, in effect, that the President had the legal authority to permit the use of torture during interrogation.[2] The immediate occasion for our discussions was a perceived crisis in international law, stemming from an apparent shift towards unilateralism on the part of the United States and repudiation of the role of international institutions and many of its obligations under international law in regard to the response to terrorist attacks and the invasion and occupation of Iraq. For the CTI Working Group, attempts to ignore or circumvent international humanitarian law and human rights law in the treatment of detainees in the war on terror could not be so dismissed.

Aware of the pull towards unilateralism on the part of the United States, the CTI Working Group was concerned also about the new realities of an increasingly integrated yet loosely governed world and the limits of nation-states in the face of global challenges. Risk regulation in environmental law, the need for economic regulation, food security concerns, the legality of the use of force against states that attack their own peoples, questions about the scope of human rights protection and the prosecution of war crimes, international dispute settlement, violations of the right to seek asylum and international conventions relating to the status of refugees, persistent racial discrimination and discrimination against women, the disposal of hazardous waste and so much more, all put questions to our existing framework of international laws, institutions and other global arrangements. The effects of poverty

---

[2] I refer especially to 'Standards of Conduct for Interrogation under 18 U.S.C. §§2340–2340A', 1 August 2002; 'Military Interrogation of Alien Unlawful Combatants Held outside the United States', 14 March 2003. See Jack Goldsmith, *The Terror Presidency: Law and Judgment inside the Bush Administration* (New York: Norton, 2009), pp. 142–43.

in nations far away from the United States and Western Europe spill over in ways that increasingly affect us all. Nuclear proliferation and the need for environmental protection cannot be handled by early modern models of tolerance and power-balancing between nations. Pressing issues such as environmental degradation, disease transmission and weapons proliferation challenge the de facto interdependence of nations and demand new responses that cut across national borders.

That there is an existent, functioning system of international law is not to be downplayed amidst talk of new challenges and the changing character of complex global governance. None of us could travel between countries without the routine functioning of civil air transport regulations or the lawful freedom of maritime traffic. NGOs could not examine the role of states and international institutions in response to forced migration and the denaturalization of forced migrants without legal or quasi-legal frameworks provided by UN conventions and related reporting arrangements. China and the United States could not dispute each country's right to place duties on goods from the other without reference to rulings by the World Trade Organization about fairly traded imports, export subsidies and anti-dumping measures. Diverse treaties, conventions regulating the use of force and the procedures for peaceful settlements in disputes, the law of the sea, international criminal law, international environmental and economic law regulate international relations from day to day. Hence the phrases 'crisis of international law' and 'crises of international jurisprudence' were challenged by some of the Working Group's dialogue partners as tripping from our tongues too easily.

In some respects such commentators are correct. One need only note the increasing numbers of public international law firms providing legal services not only in the domestic law of nations around the world but also dispute resolution and regulatory cases in an international context, as well as legal advice on international issues, to remind ourselves that the processes by which public international law is shaping decisions by nation-states and penetrating into national legal orders are ongoing. From the perspective of the CTI Working Group, however, the 'torture memos' exemplified a scepticism about the moral and political force of international law and institutions such as the United Nations, and a resurgence of strongly realist views of international order, that warrant the description 'crisis of international law' and 'crises of international jurisprudence'. The subsequent increase in targeted killings outside recognized battlefields, questions about secret detention and rendition flights, the massive incidence of avoidable severe poverty and violation of the rights of the global poor and so on, reinforce this sense of urgency and the need for theological engagement with the jurisprudence and politics of international law. It is in this context of resurgent awareness of the need for global governance and the complexities of what this will entail that Christian people, and the religions more generally, have a role to play in questioning attitudes and approaches to international law.

Theoretical contexts

John Paul II's call for the renewal of the international legal order

Pope John Paul II spoke shortly before his death of the need for a 'profound renewal of the international legal order', similar to that which occurred after the Second World War.[3] John Paul II's challenge was not of the moment of emergency but more deeply rooted – namely, that individuals and nation-states learn afresh 'the "grammar" of the universal moral law'.[4] His vision was not for an empirically observed or philosophically constructed global ethic but for a rediscovery of the various aspects of international law that are rooted in natural law. From the sixteenth century onwards, he wrote, jurists, philosophers and theologians, were engaged

---

[3]John Paul II, 'An Ever Timely Commitment: Teaching Peace', World Day of Peace, 1 January 2004 www.vatican.va/holy_father/john_paul_ii/messages/peace/documents/hf_jp-iI_mes_20031216_xxxvii-world-day-for-peace_En.html [accessed 3 February 2013]; John Paul II, *Centesimus Annus* (1991), §52 www.vatican.va/holy_father/john_paul_ii/encyclicals/documents/hf_jp-iI_enc_01051991_centesimus-annus_En.html [accessed 22 February 2013].

[4]John Paul II, 'Do Not Be Overcome by Evil but Overcome Evil with Good', World Day of Peace, 1 January 2005 www.vatican.va/holy_father/john_paul_ii/messages/peace/documents/hf_jp-iI_mes_20041216_xxxviii-world-day-for-peace_En.html [accessed 3 February 2013].

in developing the various headings of international law and 'in grounding it in the fundamentals of natural law':

> This process led with increasing force to the formulation of universal principles which are prior to and superior to the internal law of States, and which take into account the unity and the common vocation of the human family.[5]

His plea, as in the 1987 encyclical *Sollicitudo Rei Socialis* (On Social Concern), was for 'a *greater degree of international ordering*'.[6] His simple (naïve?) reminder was that respect for the law is necessary for the maintenance of peace in the new international order that we inhabit today; 'law favours peace'.[7] Following John Paul II's direction, I agree that the time is, indeed, ripe for renewed engagement with this 'grammar' of moral law around questions of the authority of international law. At issue is whether the pontiff's hopes for the direction of international law scholarship can make headway in the present-day context, and what is required to hasten such a renewal.

I cite more of this message for the celebration of the World Day of Peace 2004 because the methodological sections of this book offer proposals as to what learning afresh 'the "grammar" of the universal moral law' might entail with reference to the meaning of 'the rule of law' and international common good:

> Peace and international law are closely linked to each another: *law favours peace*. . . .
>
> Today international law is hard pressed to provide solutions to situations of conflict arising from the changed landscape of the contemporary world. . . .
>
> International law must ensure that the law of the more powerful does not prevail. Its essential purpose is to replace 'the material force of arms with the moral force of law' . . .

---

[5]John Paul II, 'An Ever Timely Commitment', §5.
[6]John Paul II, *Sollicitudo Rei Socialis* 30 December 1987, §7 (emphasis in original) www.vatican.va/holy_father/john_paul_ii/encyclicals/documents/hf_jp-iI_enc_30121987_sollicitudo-rei-socialis_En.html [accessed 3 February 2013].
[7]John Paul II, 'An Ever Timely Commitment', §5.

[I]n . . . 1997, I observed that *international law* is a primary means for pursuing peace: 'For a long time international law has been a law of war and peace. I believe that it is called more and more to become exclusively a law of peace, conceived in justice and solidarity. And in this context morality must inspire law. . . .'[8]

John Paul II urged leaders of the nations, jurists and all teachers of the young to recognize the temptation at times of friction and dispute to resort to the law of force rather than the force of law, and paid tribute to the work of the United Nations in bringing about a renewal of the international legal order after the horrors of the Second World War, and also of the role of non-governmental organizations in furthering respect for human rights. Respect for the rule of law is necessary for the maintenance of peace in the international order that we inhabit today.

John Paul II assumed the bishopric of Rome in 1978 and spoke within a year about respect for the rule of law in 1979. Speaking to participants in the 9th World Conference on Law, he asserted that the rule of law in no way implied a rigid immobility and did not ignore the tensions that arise from life, 'nor the aspects of truth contained in the protests and contestation of those people which a given legal system refuses to recognize as legitimate aspirations'.[9] Redolent of his support for the Polish trade union Solidarity, he looked to the law for an ordered structure in human society but did not assume the law in force always to be just. The law must change and develop; it will be forged according to the traditions of different nations, and support the devising and creating organized systems appropriate to the needs of the international community. His characterizing of the 'rule of law' as fluid and developing is noteworthy. John Paul II stood in the tradition of Leo XIII, who encouraged the international community to engage in drafting and ratifying international agreements that led to the Hague conferences in the late nineteenth and early twentieth centuries, and also of Pius XII, who reiterated in 1940 and 1941 the importance of international law and the

---

[8]John Paul II, 'An Ever Timely Commitment', §§5, 8, 9.
[9]John Paul II, address to the 9th World Conference on Law, Madrid, 24 September 1979, www.vatican.va/holy_father/john_paul_ii/speeches/1979/september/documents/hf_jp-iI_spe_19790924_ix-conference-on-law_En.html [accessed 3 February 2013].

significance of treaties in maintaining peace.[10] Of particular interest for our purposes, however, is the immense importance that John Paul II attached to juridical institutions and an awareness of 'the good that the law can accomplish and the mischief into which it can venture'.[11] *Sollicitudo Rei Socialis* again raised the theme of the rule of law in the context of human development, inequitable political systems, corruption, dictatorship and authoritarianism, and the inalienable dignity of every person.

Today we cannot use the phrase 'the rule of law' without hesitation. Many, myself included, think it necessary to repeat Judith Shklar's observation that the rule of law serves typically as an enforcement mechanism within a particular ideology: 'legalism . . . is the ethical attitude that holds moral conduct to be a matter of rule following, and moral relationships to consist of duties and rights determined by rules.'[12] Many are uncomfortable using the phrase. Friedrich Hayek, for example, understood 'the rule of law' as too narrow to be a protection for individuals against arbitrary decisions by government officials,[13] whereas in Philip Pettit's more recent *Republicanism: A Theory of Freedom and Government*, it is associated exclusively with the equal status of citizens under the law, thereby delimiting debate.[14] Many are aware that Michael Trebilcock and Ronald Joel Daniels have exposed how 'the rule of law' has become a mantra in international development studies while remaining elusive in meaning and operation.[15] Utopian projects

---

[10]This is noted by Robert John Araujo, S. J., 'John Paul II and the Rule of Law: Bringing Order to International Disorder', *Journal of Catholic Legal Studies* 45:2 (2007), pp. 293–319, at p. 299. See Pius XII, 'Conditions for a New World Order', Christmas message 1940, reprinted in *The Major Addresses of Pope Pius XII*, 2 vols., ed. Vincent A. Yzermans (St. Paul, MN: North Central Publishing, 1961), p. 33.

[11]Araujo, 'John Paul II and the Rule of Law', p. 304.

[12]Judith N. Shklar, *Legalism: Law, Morals, and Political Trials* (Cambridge, MA: Harvard University Press, 1964), p. 1.

[13]The rule of law means that 'the government is bound in all its actions by rules fixed and announced beforehand so that it is possible to foresee with fair certainty how authority will use its coercive powers in given circumstances and to plan one's individual affairs on the basis of this knowledge' (Friedrich A. Hayek, *The Road to Serfdom* [London: Routledge, 1944], p. 39).

[14]Philip Pettit, *Republicanism: A Theory of Freedom and Government* (Oxford: Oxford University Press, 1997), pp. 174–75.

[15]Michael J. Trebilcock and Ronald Joel Daniels, *The Political Economy of Rule of Law Reform in Developing Countries* (Cheltenham: Edward Elgar, 2009). On the

reinforced by appeal to 'the rule of law' have blighted much Christian involvement in world politics. An inescapable issue for Christian people thinking about law and governance remains why so many were silent when the Nazi regime used the rhetoric of law and order as a cover for anti-Semitism and other atrocities.

Yet this elusive, manipulable and contested phrase 'the rule of law' can still serve as a meeting point for discussion about the ethical ends and political objectives of the law. Heedful of John Paul II's emphasis on the rule of law as fluid, open to change and development, in service of human dignity and a creative force built on lasting human values, I want to emphasize that talk of the rule of law (in the singular) multiplies into talk of laws, rulings, rights and judgements (in the plural) as the discussion gets practical. Precisely because of this phenomenon, which the Pope described with regard to the human search for truth in diverse social contexts and not 'some harmful form of relativism', the 'rule of law' in the international arena remains an important idea that may be approached in terms of international order – international law being a mode of ordering among nations, peoples, transnational corporations and individuals.[16]

Post-1945 political realism

In 1948, Hans J. Morgenthau listed in *Politics among Nations* what he saw as the main problems of international law: its 'primitive', that is, decentralized character, which was the inevitable result of the decentralized structure of international society; the vagueness that surrounds the status of international legislation with respect to its binding force; problems with respect to judicial function and enforcement; the problem of the veto under the provisions of the UN Charter, which 'eliminates for all practical purposes' actions to restrain the great powers.[17] International law, he argued, was unable to escape the axiom of the legal self-sufficiency of states.

---

different meanings of 'the rule of law' in the liberal and republican traditions, see Christian List, 'Republican Freedom and the Rule of Law', in *Politics, Philosophy and Economics* 5 (June 2006), pp. 201–20.
[16] John Paul II address, 24 September 1979.
[17] Hans J. Morgenthau and Kenneth Thompson, *Politics among Nations: The Struggle for Power and Peace*, 6th edn (New York: McGraw-Hill, 1985), p. 303.

International law was complied with when, and only when, it served the needs of sovereign states to know, for instance, where the frontiers of their own and other states were on land and on sea, the conditions under which ships may sail, the authority that a state had over citizens of other states abroad. Existing international law had been observed during the 400 years of the modern era, he remarked, only to the extent that it served the balance of powers.[18] Law was subordinate to political power and, in effect, no more than a means of promoting state interests.[19]

For Morgenthau, the story of international law is one of progress cast in terms of national interest; a politically constructive and peaceable idea that arose from the last phases of the European Wars of Religion, troubled relations between the Netherlands and Spain, and the need for law to mediate rivalries between colonial powers. He cast the jurisprudence arising from this progress in terms of national interest. His theoretical context was still largely determined by Grotius's application of Aquinas's and other medieval natural law teachings to the shaping of modern international law with respect to the sea, the air and the moon in the name of common interest, as part of 'the great political transformation that marked the transition from the Middle Ages to the modern period of history'.[20] His realism is not amoral but a working acceptance that international law must be based on ethico-legal principles outside of the law itself if it is to function for the civil society from

---

[18]Morgenthau and Thompson, *Politics among Nations*, p. 273. Morgenthau's indebtedness to Reinhold Niebuhr might be mentioned here. Their friendship has been said by Morgenthau's biographer Christoph Frei to have given him access to the prophetic dimension of the Judeo-Christian scriptures, including their hope of justice (*Hans J. Morgenthau: An Intellectual Biography* [Baton Rouge, LA: Louisiana State University Press, 2001], p. 166).
[19]Hans J. Morgenthau, *Dilemmas of Politics* (Chicago: University of Chicago Press, 1958), p. 229.
[20]Morgenthau and Thompson, *Politics among Nations*, p. 271. In similar vein, Hedley Bull described Grotius's significance as follows: 'The work of Grotius is cardinal because it states one of the classic paradigms that have since determined both our understanding of the facts of interstate relations and our ideas as to what constitutes right conduct therein. This is the idea of international society: the notion that states and rulers of states are bound by rules and form a society or kind of community with one another, of however rudimentary a kind' ('The Importance of Grotius in the Study of International Relations', in *Hugo Grotius and International Relations*, ed. Hedley Bull et al. [Oxford: Clarendon Press, 1990], p. 71).

which it originates. Hence his criticism of legal positivist notions that locate the identity and authority of law in ad hoc exercises of power: 'The foundation of the binding force of "positive" law can logically be found, not in this "positive" law itself, but only outside it.'[21] Positivism fails as a basis of legal authority not only because of the philosophical weaknesses of any appeal to textual authority without explanation of the grounds and methods of interpretation but also because the rules of national and international law must start from recognition of the social mechanisms that it is designed to enable if it is to have chance of success, and receive validity from subsequent enactment in legal instruments. Enforcement requires that international law functions by means of political agreements, treaties, alliances, arbitration and consultation.

It is important to be clear that this book is not a rant against Morgenthau-type realism but is intended, rather, as a serious questioning of *the kind of realism* that the international community needs today, given the unfruitful tension in much relevant theory of statism versus cosmopolitanism. There is, potentially at least, common ground between theological realism and the refusal of Morgenthau and others to gloss over or distort the tragic contradictions of moral existence that require those in authority to choose between evils.[22] Theologians have reason be grateful to Morgenthau and his successors for bearing witness to what Orthodox theologians call ancestral sin. Morgenthau and his successors are undoubtedly correct that there is often no alternative but to accept that the validity of the rules of international law falls victim to conflicting national interests.[23] As Morgenthau says, this is not because they wish it this way or 'the result of the whims of statesmen or an ephemeral historic situation' but because it is of the nature of things.[24] His basic point for our purposes is that international

---

[21]Morgenthau, *Dilemmas of Politics*, p. 219.
[22]Hans J. Morgenthau, 'The Evil of Politics and the Politics of Evil', *Ethics: An International Journal of Social, Political and Legal Philosophy* 56 (January 1945), p. 17.
[23]Frei notes that Morgenthau's friendship with Niebuhr gave him access to the prophetic dimension of the Judeo-Christian scriptures, including their hope of justice (*Hans J. Morgenthau*, p. 166).
[24]Hans J. Morgenthau, *Political Theory and International Affairs: Hans J. Morgenthau on Aristotle's 'The Politics'*, ed. Anthony F. Lang, Jr (Westport, CT: Greenwood, 2004), pp. 36–7.

law is dependent for its functioning upon a balance of power among the most powerful nations, or groups of nations, on earth: 'Where there is neither community of interest nor balance of power there is no international law.'[25] The twentieth-century theologian Reinhold Niebuhr shared Morgenthau's conviction that morality is needed not to overturn the balance of power mechanism as the best approximation to peace that human society is likely to achieve but to tame and control temptations to hubris and pride.[26] Robin Lovin, the foremost theological expositor of Niebuhr's realism today, was a member of the CTI Working Group who reminded us continually of Morgenthau's insight.

At the least, post-1945 political realism reminds us that the modern experience of nations and nationhood is plagued by ambiguity, violence and strife.[27] The need for a 'balance of powers', said Morgenthau, is as true of mothers-in-law and new husbands as it was of the Cold War: 'You have the intention to subvert my autonomy and I have the intention to subvert yours.'[28] The moral responsibility of all concerned is not to disrupt or supersede this relationship but ensure that the balance of power is even. Morgenthau's sense of humour might not be to everyone's taste but he set an agenda in international law jurisprudence that resonates today. My concern is not, broadly speaking, to dispute the historical diagnosis by Morgenthau and others of the problems that have beset international law since the seventeenth century, or to denounce the 'balance of powers' realism of the Cold War era but, rather, to point to new post-Cold War realities that have multiplied power bases and which urge reconsideration of aspects of Western tradition that talk about the relation between self- or national-interest, reasonability, custom and the virtues.

---

[25]Hans J. Morgenthau, *Dilemmas of Politics*, 'Positivism, Functionalism, and International Law', *The American Journal of International Law*, 34(2):260–84 (260).

[26]For a highly regarded account of Niebuhr's realism, see Robin W. Lovin, *Reinhold Niebuhr and Christian Realism* (Cambridge: Cambridge University Press, 1995), esp. pp. 36–38.

[27]E. J. Hobsbawm, *Nations and Nationalism since 1780: Programme, Myth, Reality* (Cambridge: Cambridge University Press, 1990); Hugh Seton-Watson, *Nations and States: An Inquiry into the Origins of Nations and the Politics of Nationalism* (London: Methuen, 1977); Ernest Gellner, *Nations and Nationalism*, 2nd edn (Oxford: Blackwell, 2006).

[28]Morgenthau, *Political Theory and International Relations*, p. 27.

In the new global order after the end of the Cold War era, Niebuhr was increasingly sensitive to how the central concern of political realism was no longer the need for balance between two major powers but the management of diverse competing interests for which no more than a tolerable solution could typically be sought: 'This global order is not a new way of balancing states against one another, but a new way of relating the governments of states to everything else in an increasingly global system.'[29] Today there is even greater need for explicit engagement with Morgenthau's position with respect to human goods being achievable only inside the state.[30] The effects of a budget deficit in one country can ricochet around the globe. Core banking systems are international. Issues of biodiversity cross national borders. International agricultural agreements are crucial to a country's food security.[31] The challenge is to get beyond outdated dismissals such as 'nations have no moral obligation to comply with international law' and to rethink a new realism for the new global order.

The theologian must surely welcome Morgenthau's grappling with the realities of sin, selfishness, pride, self-deception, ideological concealment and so on, when commenting directly on the human tendency to become morally blind in the face of necessity. Yet he set a predominantly negative tone for discussion of international law in the hugely influential textbook *Politics among Nations*:

An increasing number of writers express the opinion that there is no such thing as international law. A diminishing number of observers hold that international law, if duly codified and extended to regulate the political relations of states, could become through its own inner force, if not a substitute for, at

---

[29]Robin W. Lovin, *Christian Realism and the New Realities* (Cambridge: Cambridge University Press, 2008), p. 178.

[30]'Man cannot achieve his *telos* outside the state. So the state is essential for the individual's ability to achieve his purpose in life' (Morgenthau, *Political Theory and International Affairs*, p. 28). Morgenthau is not uncritical of this tradition of political philosophy which, he says, can become an ideology of the status quo and justification for keeping the lower classes in their place. Subsequent lectures are devoted, inter alia, to equality, law and government, and the common good.

[31]World Health Organization, 'Food Security', World Food Summit, Rome, 13–17 November 1996 www.who.int/trade/glossary/story028/en/ [accessed 3 February 2013].

least a restraining influence upon, the struggle for power on the international scene.[32]

International law, he argues, is unable to escape the axiom of the legal self-sufficiency of states. 'The result', as Mary Ellen O'Connell summarizes so aptly, 'was that by the 1990s, international law was increasingly being mischaracterized as weak, unimportant or even dangerous – nothing that should fetter the superior American state. And Bush officials were able to find in the Constitution support for a strong-man leader above the law in wartime.'[33]

We should note, of course, that the memos advising the Bush Administration on the use of 'enhanced interrogation techniques' were reviewed and withdrawn by Jack Goldsmith during his time as head of the Office of Legal Counsel (October 2003–June 2004) on the grounds that they were legally defective. Goldsmith raises an eyebrow of surprise at the March 2005 Department of Defense *National Defense Strategy of the United States,* which stated that 'our strength as a nation state will continue to be challenged by those who employ a strategy of the weak using international fora, judicial processes, and terrorism':[34] comparing international organizations and judicial systems with terrorism goes too far. Yet Jack L. Goldsmith and Eric A. Posner are clear that international law exerts no moral force independent of content that derives from the actions of states to maximize self-interest.[35] Their 'new sovereigntist' theory casts jurisprudence in terms of national interest, approaches international law via a behavioural approach to the interest-oriented actions of states, supposes the authority of international law to arise from the consent of the international community to certain rules of custom, and dismisses customary international law as weak, vague and fragile.[36]

---

[32]Morgenthau and Thompson, *Politics among Nations,* p. 253.
[33]Scott Horton, 'Six Questions for Mary Ellen O'Connell on the Power of International Law', *Harper's Magazine,* 6 December 2008 www.harpers.org/archive/2008/12/hbc-90003966 [accessed 3 February 2013].
[34]US Department of Defense, *National Defense Strategy of the United States of America,* March 2005, p. 5 www.defense.gov/news/Mar2005/d20050318nds2.pdf [accessed 9 January 2013], cited by Goldsmith, *The Terror Presidency,* p. 53.
[35]Jack L. Goldsmith and Eric A. Posner, *The Limits of International Law* (New York: Oxford University Press, 2007), p. 30 and *passim.*
[36]Goldsmith uses the term 'new sovereigntist' when describing how his work has been received (*The Terror Presidency,* p. 21).

Post-2001 new cosmopolitanism

Versions of the new cosmopolitanism vary considerably in their philosophical and/or religious outlook. Most agree with sociologist Ulrich Beck, however, who observes that the so-called national outlook is coming under increasing scrutiny:

> It fails to grasp that political, economic and cultural action and their (intended and unintended) consequences know no borders. . . . The cosmpolitan outlook is a prerequisite for analyzing the real process of overcoming boundaries that trigger the neonational reflex to re-erect fences and walls.[37]

'Cosmopolitanization', writes Beck, crosses frontiers like a stowaway. The point is not simply, however, that tastes in popular music and some foods are increasingly global, that climate change, terrorism and financial crises all cross borders, and that global trade, information technology, the transfer of viruses and the like all demand a revision of the syntax and grammar of Westphalian notions of territorial boundaries. The call from Peter Singer, Thomas Pogge, Kwame Anthony Appiah and others is for a new international grammar that starts from the connectedness of all people and reconceptualizes our transnational interdependence.[38] Thus Robert Fine criticizes Beck for according too much significance to the 'methodological nationalism' that resulted from nineteenth-century European politics and theories of the state propounded by Hegel and other thinkers.

For some, cosmopolitanism means putting one's faith in the moral benefits that result from the benefits of commerce (Michael Doyle, David Held, Darrel Moellendorf); or in the progress of international relations towards reasonability and the constitutionalization of law (Jürgen Habermas, Seyla Benhabib, Amartya Sen); or in the rejection of national sovereignty as the

---

[37]Ulrich Beck, *The Cosmopolitan Vision* (Cambridge: Polity Press, 2006), p. 19.
[38]Fine's own project is to take the 'ism' out of cosmopolitanism decouples political theory from a teleological philosophy of history that hopes for 'a cosmopolitan age to come' and concentrates instead on the practical ways in which contemporary cosmopolitanism can be decoupled from doctrinal baggage; hence his interest in international law, human rights and political norms that nurture international society (Robert Fine, *Cosmopolitanism* [London: Routledge, 2007], p. 4).

touchstone of international law in favour of the international protection of human rights (Allen Buchanan). If we are to believe some of the more moderate cosmopolitans, then Immanuel Kant's conception of cosmopolitan law remains the destiny of the human race. All humanity belongs to a single moral community; we share a common humanity. States are sovereign but should unite as a federation in covenant around international law. We are all citizens of a universal state of humankind – citizens of the earth. Cosmopolitan law deals with relations across borders. The constitution of every state should be republican and based on principles of freedom of its members; the laws of nations shall be founded on a federation of free states: 'Cosmopolitan Right shall be limited to the conditions of Universal Hospitality.'[39] Hospitality means 'the right of a stranger not to be treated with hostility when he arrives on someone else's territory'.[40] He talks of a right to hospitality. This is *not* a right to be treated as a guest. A state has the right to deny a visit, as long as it does so non-violently. Individuals have the right to *present themselves,* not the right actually to visit with others, since the others are free to decline the request. The right is to approach, not to enter.

Today there is considerable variation among theorists concerned with these issues. Whereas Singer specifies positive obligations upon all persons to relieve the suffering of others, Thomas Pogge calls for the recognition of negative responsibilities to stop collaborating with the maintenance of systems, economic and political, that keep the poor in poverty, thereby perpetuating the affluent life-styles of those in richer countries.[41] Whereas Singer argues that states do not have legitimate grounds for the exclusion of foreigners and should maintain open borders, Kwame Anthony Appiah's philosophy of contamination seeks only cross-cultural exchange and presupposes the continuation of nation-states with territorial borders.[42] David Held's politically astute 'layered cosmopolitanism' allows for

---

[39]Immanuel Kant, 'Perpetual Peace: A Philosophical Sketch', in H. S. Reiss (ed.), *Kant: Political Writings* (Cambridge: Cambridge University Press, 1991), p. 105.
[40]Kant, 'Perpetual Peace', p. 105.
[41]Thomas Pogge, *World Poverty and Human Rights,* 2nd edn (Cambridge: Polity Press, 2008), p. 502.
[42]Kwame Anthony Appiah, *Cosmopolitanism: Ethics in a World of Strangers* (Princeton, NJ: Princeton University Press, 2007), ch. 7.

principles of equal worth and dignity, avoidance of harm and so on that apply universally to be interpreted in local contexts.[43] Committed to the challenge of sharing global goods more justly but critical of the idealism that supposes that humanity can be educated to fraternity, the book treats at several points why a Christian theology of international law cannot be a sacralized version of secularist cosmopolitanism.

International law in Christian (Protestant Thomist) perspective

Against the backdrop of these theoretical contexts, I attempt to write from the perspective of what has been called 'Protestant Thomism'. Broadly speaking, the phrase refers to Protestant thinkers shaped by Barthian sensibilities and yet experiencing the renewed influence of Aquinas's account of the natural law and approach to practical reasoning.[44] Some Protestant Thomists emphasize with Roman Catholic colleagues the need to press forward the theological developments of Vatican II.[45] Some want to read Barth with a 'revisionist' Aquinas in mind and to show that differences between them are more apparent than real.[46] I understand the phrase to refer to Protestant thinkers shaped by Barthian sensibilities and yet experiencing a renewed influence of Aquinas's account of the natural law. The effort is to read these major figures in Christian tradition together without caricature, and in ways that move beyond simplistic dismissals of Aquinas's as suggesting that humans have some sort of independent knowledge of God through reason as opposed to revelation. Protestant

---

[43]David Held, 'Principles of Cosmopolitan Order', in Gillian Brock and Harry Brighouse (eds), *The Political Philosophy of Cosmopolitanism* (Cambridge: Cambridge University Press, 2005), p. 18.

[44]John Bowlin, 'Contemporary Protestant Thomism', in Paul van Geest, Harm Goris and Carlo Leget (eds), *Aquinas as Authority* (Leuven: Peeters, 2002), pp. 235–51; Eric Gregory, 'The Spirit and the Letter: Protestant Thomism and Nigel Biggar's "Karl Barth's Ethics Revisited"', in Daniel L. Migliore (ed.), *Commanding Grace: Studies in Karl Barth's Ethics*, (Grand Rapids, MI: Eerdmans, 2010), pp. 50–59.

[45]See Gregory, 'The Spirit and the Letter', p. 58.

[46]Bowlin, 'Contemporary Protestant Thomism', p. 243.

Thomism takes into account Jean Porter's observation that aspects of Barth's challenge to the scholastics fail because they never claimed to speak of 'unaided natural reason' outside of a Christian theological context; contemporaries of Aquinas never intended natural law to be understood as an alternative to belief in the incarnation and the saving grace of God; natural law was always 'a theological concept . . . grounded in a particular reading of Scripture'.[47] The scholastics affirmed natural reason but their approach rarely fell outside of affirmations of God as creator and redeemer. The distance between Aquinas and Barth's critique of a natural law ethic is not as great as sometimes supposed.

Answerability before God and the international community

At its simplest, the Protestant Thomism that I advocate takes from Karl Barth a central emphasis on the dynamic of the Word of God that speaks and is answerable in human affairs, and from Thomas Aquinas an emphasis on common good and the relation within divine providence of the one to the many. When I talk about 'natural law reasoning in Protestant Thomist perspective', these central emphases are implied. Many difficulties are likely to beset such an attempt to hold together these emphases from both Barth and Aquinas, and many notes of caution must be sounded in due course. There need be no gulf, however, between an ethic centred on the command of God and an account of moral reasoning in which important features of human agency are considered. I broadly support Porter's urging of Barthian scholars to look again at the theological commitments that enabled the scholastics to affirm natural reason from their reading of the scriptures,[48] and acknowledge indebtedness to the revival

---

[47]Jean Porter, *Natural and Divine Law: Reclaiming the Tradition for Christian Ethics* (Grand Rapids, MI: Eerdmans, 1999), pp. 169–70. See also Jean Porter, *Natural as Reason: A Thomistic Theory of the Natural Law* (Grand Rapids, MI: Eerdmans, 2004), pp. 41–45, for an assessment of openings for rapprochement between traditional Roman Catholic and Protestant approaches to the natural law.

[48]Porter's account of Barth's challenge is as follows: 'any moral system (whether pre-reflective or philosophical) that claims to offer clear, systematic and self-contained guidance on matters of good and evil is fundamentally an expression of pride. It presupposes a degree of independent discernment that the human person

of interest recently in points of contact between Barth's theology and creation and ethics.[49] To claim human beings are capable of distinguishing good from evil and are subject to divine judgement whether or not they acknowledge the lordship of Christ does not equate to asserting that there is, or can be, unaided natural reason outside of Christ. To speak of God is to speak about goodness. Humanity knows of the goodness of God pre-eminently in Jesus Christ; it is because of this truth and not despite it, however, that the believer affirms that 'good is to be done and pursued and evil is to be avoided' (*bonum faciendum, malum vitandum*).[50] Even in our sinfulness, the divine command addresses every human person who, despite the effects of sin, remains capable in their willing, judging and acting to do the good and to refrain from evil.[51]

Chapter 2 looks in more detail at how to avoid old and unfortunate caricatures between Barthian and Thomist approaches to human law. The witness from Barth especially is that God's Word is answerable. Humanity's vocation is to communion with God and obedience to the divine Word. This takes different form in different times and places, but the answerability of the divine Word is intrinsic to the human power of speech and linked to our rational nature.[52] Answerability entails both accountability to the prior reality of the divine Word and responsibility to one another

---

cannot attain, and it reflects the human desire to attain justification and security independently of God, over against God. And since the only way the human person can stand over against God is through the separation of sin, therefore, ethics is itself the fruit of sin – even, as Barth suggests at one point, the original sin' (*Natural and Divine Law*, p. 170).

[49]John Webster has described Barth's construal of Christian ethics as 'a diverse pattern of correspondences or analogies, of similarities and dissimilarities, between the actions of God and human actions' (*Barth's Moral Theology: Human Action in Barth's Thought* [Edinburgh: T&T Clark, 2004], p. 177). Paul T. Nimmo has drawn attention to the telic aspects of Barth's ethical vision, as well as its noetic and ontic aspects, in explicating points of contact between Barth's theology of creation and ethics (*Being in Action: The Theological Shape of Barth's Ethical Vision* [Edinburgh: T&T Clark, 2011], ch. 8).

[50]Thomas Aquinas, *Summa Theologiæ* (*ST*), 60 vols. (London: Eyre & Spottiswoode, 1963–74), I–II, q. 94, a. 2, sed contra.

[51]Aquinas, *ST*, I, q. 79, a. 13, c.

[52]'The task of theological ethics is to understand the Word of God as the command of God. . . . Ethics has first to attempt with an upward look as it were, in relation to the divine action' (Karl Barth, *Church Dogmatics* [*CD*], 13 vols., ed. G. W. Bromiley and T. F. Torrance [Edinburgh: T&T Clark, 1956–75], III/4, p. 4).

for obedience to its command. Answerability is always a response to
divine initiative; the absolute need for response to the divine Word
constitutes both the possibility and the substance of our ethical
concern. The answerability of the nations before the Son of Man
(Matt. 25.31–35; Ps. 96.10–13; Is. 2.4; Is. 25.6; Jer. 25.9; Zech.
8.22; Mic. 4.3) implies something provisionally significant about
mutual answerability between the nations for actions with respect
to the global common good. This answerability is at the heart of
our concern and is understood primarily with reference to Matt.
25.31–35 and the other biblical texts referred to above. God is our
judge and lawgiver. The event of judgement eschatologically is the
condition of answerability; all answerability is before another and
ultimately before the Almighty and the Lamb. This is the impetus
for our ethico-political consideration of the answerability of the
nations, one to another for the global common good, in the context
of international law.

The word 'answerability' is at the heart of what I seek to
achieve in the proposed theological restatement of natural law
reasoning in Protestant Thomist perspective. Theologically, this
concern derives from the eschatological vision for the nations of
the earth – which is a vision of judgement when all peoples and
nations will be summoned before the throne of God at the end of
time. All the peoples, multitudes, tribes, nations and languages of
the earth will witness the adulation of the Lamb before the throne
of heaven.

Look! He is coming with the clouds;
every eye will see him,
even those who pierced him;
and on his account all the tribes of the earth will wail.
So it is to be. Amen. (Rev. 1.7)[53]

---

[53]The word *phylē* refers both to all the persons descended from the 12 tribes of Jacob
and to all the nations or peoples of the earth. Similarly, Revelation 17.15 says: 'The
waters that you saw, where the whore is seated, are peoples (*laoi*) and multitudes
(*ochloi*) and nations (*ethnē*) and languages (*glōssai*).' All terms are in their plural
form, and the rhetorical effect of their repetition is to drive home the point that not
only every single eye but every possible grouping of humanity will be present to
witness the events of the eschaton. The peoples, multitudes, nations and languages
of the earth will be seated with the great whore (*pornē*) who represents Babylon and/
or Rome. On this, see Richard Bauckham, *The Theology of the Book of Revelation*
(Cambridge: Cambridge University Press, 1993), p. 126.

This witness to the end times includes reference to the 'glory' (*doxa*) and 'honour' (*timē*) that the kings of the earth will bring into the city (Rev. 21.24). Thus our thinking about earthly nations cannot be entirely negative. The predominant biblical witness is, however, to the existence of nations as a work of divine wrath.[54] Human beings belong to nations, peoples and nation-states only provisionally, temporarily and in a disposition of judgement.

I emphasize the point because much contemporary theological writing focuses on individual, personal answerability before divine judgement and not that of the nations. Answerability before God bears upon every person's unique, unrepeatable position before God. Answerability is actualized in the uniqueness and irreplaceability of every person for all of their actions. There is, to use Mikhail Bakhtin's phrase, a 'non-alibi in Being' [Rus. *ne-alibi v bytii*]. No one can escape their own unique answerability in their own unrepeatable place in Being. Humanity-in-general has no meaning apart from acknowledgement of the never-repeatable, irreplaceable uniqueness of personal being as experienced relation to the similarly once-occurrent answerability of our fellow-beings. Significantly, in Christian tradition, however, this answerability extends to the nations. The answerability of all humanity before divine judgement extends not only to individuals standing before their creator but to peoples, communities and nations too. New Testament witness is that the Son of Man will judge the nations against several requirements:

> When the Son of Man comes in his glory, and all the angels with him, then he will sit on his glorious throne. Before him will be gathered all the nations, and he will separate them one from another as a shepherd separates the sheep from the goats ... Then the King will say to those at his right hand, 'Come, O blessed of my Father, inherit the kingdom prepared for you from the foundation of the world; for ... I was a stranger and you welcomed me ...' (Matt. 25.31–35 RSV)

As eschatological judge, the Son of Man assumes a role that normally belongs to God himself.[55] 'Coming with "all the angels"',

---

[54] Barth, CD, III/4, §54, p. 313.
[55] Craig S. Keener, *A Commentary on the Gospel of Matthew* (Grand Rapids, MI: Eerdmans, 1999), p. 602. Keener cites Jewish eschatological texts from the

writes New Testament scholar Craig S. Keener, 'alludes to Zechariah 14.5 . . . where God is in view.'[56] In other words, the Son of Man is deemed worthy of the accolades due to the divine being. Like the judgement alluded to in Zechariah, the Son of Man's judging of the nations is based on the good or evil they have done. Imperatives familiar to readers of the Old Testament (Deut. 10.19; Ps. 146.9) are taken up into this vision of the Son of Man's judgement when he comes in glory.[57] Matthew 25.31–35 implies not only that individual persons will be judged against their reception of the gospel and fulfilment of the law in these respects but also that the nations or peoples of the earth (*ta ethnē*) will appear before his throne.[58]

Old Testament Pseudepigrapha in support of this claim – for example, Sibylline Oracles 4.183–84; 1 Enoch 9.4; 60.2; 62.2; Testament of Abraham 14A.

[56]Keener, *Commentary on Matthew*, pp. 602–603.

[57]See also David Wenham, 'When Will These Things Happen? A Study of Jesus as Judge in Matthew 21–25', *Journal for the Study of the New Testament* 28 (July 2006), pp. 53–54; Ulrich Luz, 'The Final Judgment (Matt. 25.31–46): An Exercise in "History of Influence" Exegesis', in David R. Bauer and Mark Allan Powell (eds), *Treasures New and Old: Recent Contributions to Matthean Studies* (Atlanta: Scholars Press, 1996), p. 308; idem, 'The Son of Man in Matthew: Heavenly Judge or Human Christ', *Journal for the Study of the New Testament* 15 (October 1992), pp. 3–20.

[58]The tension between the representative role of the nations and the personal responsibility of members of the nations is maintained in the anonymous patristic text *Incomplete Work on Matthew*, which speaks of every person acting according to their faith and being judged according to the type of their souls (Manlio Simonetti, (ed.), *Ancient Christian Commentary on Scripture, New Testament 1b: Matthew 14–28* [Downers Grove, IL: Intervarsity Press, 2002], pp. 46–47). Wicked and righteous persons are intermingled, and the Son of Man will distinguish the merits of each. Even so, witness in Christian tradition to the subjection of the nations to the Son of Man's judgement is strong. John Chrysostom speaks of Jesus raising the sights of his hearers to the final judgement seat, 'with all the world gathered around him' (*Nicene and Post-Nicene Fathers*, ed. Philip Schaff, series 1, vol. 10: *St. Chrysostom: Homilies on the Gospel of Saint Matthew* (Grand Rapids,MI: Eerdmans, 1952), p. 475). The lowliness of Jesus' earthly ministry is contrasted with his appearance in glory to confront, reproach and pass judgement on the entirety of humanity gathered as nations before him. Epiphanus the Latin wrote in the late fifth- or early sixth-century CE that every people on earth will see him: 'All nations will be gathered together by the angels from the foundation of the world, beginning first with Adam and Eve down to the last person on earth'. [Epiphanus the Latin, *Interpretation of the Gospels*, 38 in A. Hamman, (ed.), *Patrologia Latinae Supplementum* (Paris: Garnier Frère, 1958), 33, p. 899. Cited in Simonetti, (ed.), *Ancient Christian Commentary*, p. 231.]

INTRODUCTION 23

Answerability and the international common good

The witness from Aquinas is, inter alia, his account of the ordering within divine providence of the relation between the good of 'the whole' and that of 'the part' within the hierarchical government of the whole cosmos. Because God's goodness is the ultimate end of every 'part' and 'whole', the good of each is found in God without threat to the good of another. The highest good, which is God, is the common good:

> Just as it belongs to the good to produce a good, so it belongs to the sovereign good to make a thing best. Now God is the sovereign good . . . Therefore, it belongs to Him to make all things best. Now it is better that the good bestowed on someone should be common to many, than that it should be proper to one: since the common good is always considered to be more godlike than the good of the one only. But the good of one becomes common to many, if it flows from the one to the other: and this can only be when the one, by its own action, communicates it to the others: and if it has not the power to transmit it to others, that good remains its own property. Accordingly, God communicated His goodness to His creatures in such wise that one thing can communicate to another the good it has received. Therefore it is derogatory to the divine goodness to deny things their proper operations.[59]

God, who is the supreme good – the *Summum Bonum* – whom all other goods are derived, is the ultimate end of the entire universe. All goods are related to the *Summum Bonum*, who is above and anterior to them all, holding all within a cosmic, metaphysical and ontological unity of divine purpose.[60] God's absolutely transcendent unity of being and purpose, which is mirrored in the unity and order of creation, draws all created things towards concord and fulfilment;

---

[59]Thomas Aquinas, *Summa Contra Gentiles*, Book Three: *Providence*, part I, trans. Vernon J. Bourke (Notre Dame: University of Notre Dame Press, 1975), ch. 69.
[60]See O. J. Brown, *Natural Rectitude and Divine Law in Aquinas: An Approach to an Integral Interpretation of the Thomistic Doctrine of Law* (Toronto: Pontifical Institute of Medieval Studies, 1981), pp. 74–84.

'it belongs to Him to make all things best'. This 'best-ness' is found in the universal order and beauty to which the Bible testifies. It cannot be reduced to an arithmetical aggregation because it has a transcendent and God-oriented character. Every good belongs within a cosmic continuity and is drawn towards both higher things and its 'best'. In this sense, 'the common good is always considered to be more godlike than the good of the one only'. 'The common good' is greater than 'the good of one only' because it reflects more perfectly the oneness and order of the divine plan; it is closer to God's own unity in relation.[61]

Within Aquinas's worldview, it is fundamental that law should be framed for the community rather than for the individual per se. Consider his response to the following objection to his vision of human law in relation to the common good:

> It would seem that human law should be framed not for the community, but rather for the individual. For the Philosopher says (*Ethics* v. 7) that 'the legal just . . . includes all particular acts of legislation . . . and all those matters which are the subject of decrees', which are also individual matters, since decrees are framed about individual actions. Therefore law is framed not only for the community, but also for the individual.[62]

The hypothetical objector makes the point that human acts are about individual matters. Presupposing previous teaching that good has varying degrees (it can be more or less perfect or imperfect), Aquinas appeals to the 'principle of direction' that relates cases of individual justice to the common good. If every human good enjoys a graced participation in God's absolute goodness, and if human law extends beyond individual acts because it directs their actions towards a common end, then Aquinas sees no reason to compromise on the assertion that law should be framed for the common good:

> Whatever is for an end should be proportionate to that end. Now the end of law is the common good; because, as Isidore says (*Etym* v. 21) that 'law should be framed, not for any benefit,

---

[61]Aquinas, *Summa Contra Gentiles*, vol. 3, bk I, ch. 17.
[62]Aquinas, *ST*, I–II, q. 96. a. 1, obj. 1.

but for the common good of all the citizens'. Hence human laws should be proportionate to the common good.[63]

His response becomes more sophisticated in the light of Aristotle's distinction between different kinds of legal justice (general laws, private laws and those which have application only to particular cases) and the need to amend unjust laws that place disproportionate burdens on particular individuals. The main point is simple enough, though. It belongs to the notion of human law to be framed for the common good because individual and common good belong successively within a single trajectory. Divine Wisdom places individual and common good within a single continuum: 'a certain order is to be found in those things that are apprehended universally.'[64] This Wisdom, in which human goods participate, directs all actions and movements towards their proper end; 'a principle of direction should be applicable to many'.[65]

Of interest for our purposes is whether and/or how renewed appreciation of Aquinas's approach to order and the common good, the mutual ordering of discrete parties in peace and harmony, custom and conditions of accountability and more, can yield a more sustainable approach to the twenty-first-century problem of legitimacy and the authority of international law than some politically realist dismissals of customary and other international law. It is a long way in many respects from Aquinas's *Summa Theologiæ* and the Treatise on Law to the present day, but John Paul II was clear about points of connection. In every generation, he said, renewal of the international legal order requires attention to the common good of nation-states within the common vocation of the human family where international law serves primarily as a pledge of peace.[66] Pursuit of the common good of a single political community is realized most fully as integral to the common good of humanity.[67] Today, as complex networks of interdependence

---

[63]Aquinas, *ST*, I–II, q. 96. a. 1, c.
[64]Aquinas, *ST*, I–II, q. 94. a. 2, c.
[65]Aquinas, *ST*, I–II, q. 96. a. 1, ad. 2.
[66]John Paul II, 'An Ever Timely Commitment', §§5, 9.
[67]John Paul II, '"Peace on Earth for Those Whom God Loves!"' World Day of Peace, 1 January 2000 www.vatican.va/holy_father/john_paul_ii/messages/peace/documents/hf_jp-iI_mes_08121999_xxxiii-world-day-for-peace_En.html [accessed 3 February 2013].

pertain in trade and finance, the environment, electronic media and more, the international community can no longer draw sharp distinctions between national and international interests.[68] Of interest for our purposes are comparisons between Thomist realism and some versions of Morgenthau-type political realism, notably Goldsmith and Posner's rational choice thesis, advancing the claim that Thomist realism offers a potentially more viable model than their purportedly comprehensive explanatory theory that fails to account for so much.

What is asked of Christian ethics and political theology?

It is not a demand upon Christian ethics or political theology necessarily to pronounce on every issue of international law or international relations that arises, prescribing ways forward in minute detail that might be outdated in a matter of weeks. Such is the labour of specialists and professionals – not least the many disciples of Christ Jesus who live out vocations in government, with NGOs, the United Nations, academia or other policy-drafting contexts and the like. It is not the business of Christian ethics or political theology to draft proposals for the enhancement of international institutions or the reform of international law. Yet a witness at the heart of Christian tradition is that the universality of the gospel of Christ transcends national borders and is worldwide in scope. Jesus taught his disciples to pray that God's will be done 'on earth as it is in heaven' – not simply in the lives of individuals or the church but everywhere on earth. From the opening verses of the Bible (Gen. 1.1–2.9), which confess that God created the heavens and the earth, humanity and all other creatures, to the closing vision of a new heaven and a new earth (Rev. 21.1), the Bible testifies to the history of salvation in global perspective.

This global perspective does not equate to secularist accounts of cosmopolitanism but asks believers not to delimit their thinking about the implications of the Christian vision to the local and

---

[68]David Hollenbach, S. J., *The Common Good and Christian Ethics* (Cambridge: Cambridge University Press, 2002), p. 52.

national, or to neglect questions about how to love and serve the neighbour far away. 'There is one Maker for all, one law, and one judgement', according to Gregory of Nazianzus.[69] The entire worshipping life of the church is carried out in the context of the universal reach of the saving grace of God, thereby placing an obligation on all Christian people to stand against injustice in any part of the world and participate consistently in efforts to achieve peace. To be a creature means to be prepared for the place where God's honour dwells.[70] There can be no delimitation of divine activity to the sphere of the church or paucity of outlook concerning the generative work of divine grace throughout the created order. Christ, the New Adam, is 'man for man, for other men, His fellows'.[71] God's election in Christ of all humanity is the ground of the believer's hope that human history is held open to the possibility of choosing good rather than evil because the destiny of the creature is in Christ and not damnation. At its broadest, therefore, the theological question is about salvation and that for which the believer may hope and strive because of Christ. More contentiously, we ask why and how the obligations of just laws proceed from and to God.

Sensible of these limits and challenges, I attempt in Chapter 2 to explicate further how insights from both Barth and Aquinas can be held together within a so-called Protestant Thomist approach to natural law reasoning. The chapter begins to unpack what might be entailed in a strongly Christological restatement of natural law reasoning for the twenty-first century within the limits of Karl Barth's 'Nein', that is, resisting any notion of the natural law as something like a body of knowledge to be specified with reference to the revealed laws of God, explained and applied in diverse contexts, times and places, and yet taking seriously the practical demands of lawmaking and enforcement. At the heart of the chapter is the understanding that human justice is an *impossible* demand but a *demand* nevertheless because of the resurrection. In proclaiming the resurrection, Paul proclaims that conscience forms

---

[69]Quoted in John of Damascus, *The Sacred Parallels*, in Jacques Paul Migne (ed.), *Patrologia Graeca* (Paris: Garnier Frères et J.-P. Migne, 1864), 95: 1373C.
[70]Barth, *CD*, III/1, p. 364.
[71]Barth, *CD*, III/2, p. 208, quoted in Tom Greggs, *Barth, Origen, and Universal Salvation: Restoring Particularity* (Oxford: Oxford University Press, 2009), p. 82.

part of the rational aspect of the human soul and functions in ways complementary to the judgement of God, from which nothing is hidden (1 Cor. 4.4).[72] The crucifixion of Jesus is the ultimate instance of the injustice of human justice that still shocks to the core. Human justice stands in contrast to the justice of God, and human law to the law of God. *Nevertheless*, human law remains a necessity implied by divine justice that is before and beyond the law. Human law is practiced in answer to, or before, another law that functions as a kind of limit or 'beyond' before which complex interactions of answerability are lived.[73] The chapter describes natural law reasoning as a hermeneutic endeavour in which context-specific interpretation of the requirements of morality are integral to the practice or art of judgement-making. With respect to the law, the chapter considers how best to aim at the requirements of peace and good order through the mediation of the appropriate institutions.[74]

Chapter 3 picks up these issues more specifically in relation to the *jus cogens* norm against torture. It asks whether the Christian may (or should) hold that existing legal norms, for example, *jus cogens* norms, are somehow the direct application in international affairs of natural law principles and, if not, then how the question of normative law might be addressed. At issue are the grounds on which Christian people may engage the debate

---

[72]On the dangers of interpreting Paul's theology of conscience in the light of Augustine and Luther's struggles with their introspective consciences, see Krister Stendahl, 'The Apostle Paul and the Introspective Conscience of the West', in idem, *Paul among Jews and Gentiles and Other Essays* (Philadelphia: Fortress, 1976), pp. 78–96.

[73]An Orthodox icon with which I try to think about such matters is *Christ before Pontius Pilate: The Voluntary Humiliation of Our Savior* in the Church of the Holy Virgin Mary and St Pishoy, a Coptic Orthodox church in Los Angeles, California (http://theotokos.org/church-icons/crucifixion.html [accessed 4 December 2012]). It is a modern icon (reminiscent of the famous fifteenth-century icon *Christ Standing before Pilate* from the Rostov School) in which Jesus stands in the judgement hall of Pontius Pilate accused of political crimes, not least 'corrupting the nation' (Lk. 23.2), and is condemned by both religious and imperial law in the name of preserving order. (This second icon may be viewed at Ministry of Culture of the Russian Federation, Russian Icons http://iconrussia.ru/eng/icon/detail.php?ID=1345 [accessed 4 December 2012].)

[74]Ethical intention defined as '*aiming at the "good life" with and for others, in just institutions*' (Paul Ricoeur, *Oneself as Another* [Chicago: University of Chicago Press, 1995], p. 172 [emphasis in original]).

about normativity. The question is whether and/or why talk of the international common good is not moralizing baloney but necessary to the flourishing of all, and how this might bear upon international prohibitions against torture. Concluding sections recognize the legitimacy of national interests which conflict with both the international common good and other national interests; it is unavoidable that nation-states will seek after certain goods not in conformity with the common good. The claim from Thomas, however, is that the function of authority is inter alia to express the requirements of the (international) common good. Attention is drawn to Aquinas's understanding of the relation between custom, consent and political authority in order to expose some of the limits of present-day statism, and to suggest that Thomistic natural law reasoning is, potentially at least, better able to cope with the intractable disagreement that characterizes twenty-first-century global relations than some forms of neo-Kantian jurisprudence.

Chapters 4 and 5 treat contested issues pertaining to peacemaking, just war and international law. Chapter 4 reviews why increasing numbers of theorists today think that the 'fit' between the classic just war tradition and the complexities of so-called fourth-generation warfare has become untenable, before identifying different streams of just war thinking in the modern era and a drift in the meaning of 'war' from classic, narrowly penal definitions – pertaining to the overcoming of injustice – to looser conceptions of armed conflict for political ends, constrained mainly by *jus in bello* criteria. Working with Richard Tuck's broad distinction between the narrow, theological tradition and secularist, humanist traditions, the chapter investigates changing meanings of 'just' or justifiable war (from an exceptional measure resorted to only when there is a failure of 'ordinary means' to deal with injustice and wrongs committed, to an exercise of the right of collective self-defence, or even armed conflict for the promotion of democracy and human rights). It argues that the classic narrow, overtly theological just war tradition is not exhausted and that fourth-generation warfare is precisely the context in which to reclaim well-established and widely understood principles.

Chapter 5 addresses the moral hazards associated with the emerging doctrine of the Responsibility to Protect (RtoP). It reviews the broad acceptance by the Vatican and the World Council of Churches of the doctrine between September 2003 and September

2008, and attempts to identify grounds for more adequate investigation of the moral issues arising. The themes pursued include changing notions of sovereignty, the authority that can approve or refuse the use of force, when the discourse of humanitarian ethics becomes problematically politicized, and which tests might still usefully be applied when assessing the necessity of military force.

Chapter 6 is about humanity's division into nations and how this reality bears upon the evangelical imperative to love one's neighbour near and far. The primary dialogue partner is Peter Singer and his preference utilitarian approach to moral reasoning wherein the challenge is to count the welfare of individuals impartially, regardless – or at least with far less regard than is often given – of divisions into nation-states. The claim is made that, despite the considerable and proper challenges from Singer and other so-called new cosmopolitans, it remains possible and indeed necessary at the present time for Christian people to work with an account of nation and nationhood as permitted within divine providence. This claim is cast in terms of traditional Christian teaching about the order of love (*ordo amoris*).

Chapter 7 persists with the question of normative law but with reference to the concept of universality in human rights discourse. Gramsci's theory of hegemony is employed in attempting to distinguish between the role that human rights standards perform beneficially in encouraging the implementation of internationally agreed standards and as a dominant global ideology, given content by liberal Western philosophy and backed by the massive superstructures of the major world powers. The aim of this chapter is to investigate where claims to universality with respect to human rights are emerging as overblown, ideological notions that hinder rather than help the protection of religious freedom, and where the Abrahamic faith traditions, including the churches, are being swept up into self-protective positions and ideological game-play at the expense of focus on those whose freedom of religion or belief are violated.

Chapter 8 offers a summary of the theological findings of this book and framework for future discussion.

2

Towards a Restatement of Natural Law Reasoning

Methodologically, it is impossible to begin a project of this kind from scratch. As Rowan Williams has said: 'the theologian *is* always in the middle of things. There is a practice of common life and language already there.'[1] Diverse Protestant and the Roman Catholic traditions have grappled with questions about the relation of divine and human law, the responsibilities of human governance, peacemaking through law and much more, over many generations. Yet new situations and unforeseen crises call for fresh engagement with familiar questions. Today's crises in international law and challenges with respect to the proper role of the churches and the religions more generally in the international arena demand creative thinking around the purpose of law, normativity, obligations to obey or resist, the possibilities of critique and more. Of interest is how to frame this kind of engagement in ways that might yield theoretical and practical ways forward; how to think rigorously and well about what this challenge entails, how to hold in tension the many criss-cross lines between the disciplines, the minutiae of specialist questioning and the panoramic scope of the potential range of concern.

The broad claim in what follows is that classically theological traditions of natural law reasoning are not exhausted and that a restatement of natural law reasoning in strongly Christological terms is possible for the twenty-first century, in ways that will inform

---

[1] Rowan Williams, *On Christian Theology* (Oxford: Blackwell, 2000), p. xii.

and learn from present-day engagement with issues of international law. To this end, it is necessary to fight on three fronts:

1   Against those who suppose that there is only one tradition of natural law/natural law reasoning rather than many.[2] This seemingly obvious point warrants mention because clusters of errors arise when differences between theological and non-theological are either exaggerated or minimized. There is no single natural law tradition in Western philosophy that stretches from Sophocles through seventeenth-century accounts of natural rights that further develop into the 1948 UN Declaration of Human Rights, thereby suggesting some kind of quasi-evolutionary progress in which the march of reason triumphs in the present day. There is no single tradition that starts with Antigone's 'unwritten laws' before moving to Diogenes Laertius' accounts of Zeno of Citium's famous description of the end as 'life in agreement with nature';[3] and on to Cicero's claim that 'the law of nature is divine and that it fulfils its function by enjoining what is right, and forbidding what is wrong; we cannot understand'; and beyond.[4] Any notion of a single natural law tradition in Western philosophy fails to recognize significant differences between pre-modern and modern ethical thought, notably between 'natural right' and 'natural rights' and between 'natural right' or action that accords with the demands of right reason and 'natural

---

[2]Among authors of the copious literature on this topic is Heinrich Rommen, who clarifies the differences between traditional natural law as represented in the writings of Cicero, Aquinas and Hooker and the revolutionary doctrines of natural rights espoused by Hobbes, Locke and Rousseau (Heinrich Rommen, *The Natural Law: A Study in Legal and Social History and Philosophy*, trans. Thomas R. Hanley [1936; rpt Indianapolis, IN: Liberty Fund, 1998]). See also Knud Haakonssen, *Natural Law and Moral Philosophy: From Grotius to the Scottish Enlightenment* (Cambridge: Cambridge University Press, 1996); Alexander Passerin d'Entrèves, *Natural Law: An Introduction to Legal Philosophy*, 3rd ed. (New Brunswick, NJ: Transaction, 1994); Richard Tuck, *Natural Rights Theories: Their Origin and Development* (Cambridge: Cambridge University Press, 1982).
[3]In J. von Arnim, *Stoicorum VeterumFragmenta*, 4 vols. (Leipzig: Teubner, 1905–34), vol. I, pp. 179a, 552. See Jason L. Saunders, (ed.), *Greek and Roman Philosophy after Aristotle* (1966; rpt New York: Free Press, 1994), p. 111.
[4]Cicero, *On the Nature of the Gods*, transl. Francis Brooks (London: Methuen, 1896), Bk 1, p. 14.

law' as that which derives goodness from conformity to
a universal law, and would downplay questions about
whether the notion of natural law is defensible on rational
grounds or whether its claim to universal acceptability
is dependent ultimately upon theological claims.[5] It fails
to recognize also how, in the modern era, there were
major shifts from natural law understood in term of the
conception of 'right order', that is, the plan by which
creation is ordered and humanity participates in the eternal
law,[6] to a general rule of reason whereby every man ought
to endeavour peace,[7] to the subjective rights of individual
human beings as the starting point of the natural state;[8]

---

[5]Aristotle's notion of the natural law as reason independent of human desire and
positive law, but universal, permanent and changeless, is different from the varying
Stoic notions of living in willing acceptance of life according to nature and governed
by virtue. There is little textual evidence in the classical Western tradition until
Cicero of the doctrine of natural law supposing a morally lawful universe in which
all evils are eventually set straight. Cicero was arguably the first to furnish natural
law with specific moral and political content, and there are marked differences
in his understanding of a divinely sanctioned moral law to which are attached
appropriate rewards and punishments as compared to the absence in Sophocles
and Plato of any law of the cosmos certifying that justice will necessarily prevail in
human affairs. See Ernest L. Fortin, *Collected Essays*, vol. 2: *Classical Christianity
and the Political Order: Reflections on the Theologico-Political Problem*, ed. J. Brian
Benestad (Lanham, MD: Rowman & Littlefield, 1996), p. 201.
[6]Aquinas, *ST*, I–II, q. 91, a. 1.
[7]Thomas Hobbes, *Leviathan*, ed. Richard Tuck (Cambridge: Cambridge University
Press, 1996), ch. 14.
[8]Several studies have been devoted to this question. Michael Villey's *Questions de
saint Thomas sur le droit et la politique* (Paris: Presses universitaires de France,
1987) drew a sharp distinction between Aquinas's notion of natural right and
modern conceptions of subjective, individual right, arguing that the latter was
rooted in the nominalist philosophy of the fourteenth century. William of Ockham
(c. 1287–1347), he claimed, inaugurated a new way of thinking about natural right
that facilitated its transition into subjective powers or claims. Ockham moved
beyond classical thought in which, typically, a right was an incorporeal thing within
a given set of metaphysical premises. The ancient Greeks and Romans, Villey claimed,
could speak of each person being entitled to a just share, or their just due, within a
particular set of social relationships – the point being that this classical perspective
fits ill with modern conceptions of rights inhering in persons as such; Ockham did
something new. Ernst L. Fortin agrees: 'The passage from natural law to natural
rights and, later, human rights, represents a major shift – arguably *the* paradigm
shift – in Western understandings of justice and morality' (*Collected Essays*, vol. 3:
Human Rights, Virtue, and the Common Good: Untimely Meditations on Religion

2   Against those Protestants so accustomed to the displacement
    of natural law in twentieth-century Protestant theology that
    they neglect rich seams of biblical and traditional teaching
    thereby leaving Christian people unnecessarily ill-equipped
    to speak about the implications of the gospel for social and
    political moral judgements. There have been attempts recently
    to move beyond caricature to a more nuanced appreciation
    of natural law teaching in Protestantism. Stephen J. Grabill's
    *Rediscovering the Natural Law in Reformed Theological
    Ethics* warrants mention especially because of its detailed
    account of how Reformed theologians, notably not only
    John Calvin but also Peter Martyr Vermigli, Johannes
    Althusius, Francis Turretin and others drew upon the
    natural law teaching of the medievals. Against a backdrop
    of Karl Barth's rejection of any idea of natural law as setting
    the terms for grace by giving some kind of independent
    ontological status to the natural apart from God and apart
    from salvation history, Grabill rediscovers a richer theology
    of natural knowledge of the creator than often supposed
    by neo-Barthians. His (convincing) contention is that a gap
    in historical knowledge has begun to correct the paucity of
    Protestant treatments of natural law/natural law reasoning;[9]

---

and Politics, ed. J. Brian Benestad [Lanham, MD: Rowman & Littlefield, 1996],
pp. 20–22). Brian Tierney takes issue, however, with the weight that Villey puts
on the novelty of Ockham's theory of quasi-subjective rights and argues that the
whole western tradition stretching back before Ockham to the ancient world is more
diverse than Villey and Fortin allow (Tierney, *The Idea of Natural Rights: Studies on
Natural Rights, Natural Law and Church Law 1150–1625* [Atlanta, GA: Scholars
Press, 1997]).

[9] For our purposes, a study of Calvin could yield an account of natural law reasoning
in light of the revelation of the judgments and purposes of God that would enable the
believer to move between confession of the gospel and earthly systems of international
law. It would be possible to explicate his theology of the international as a basis for
a constructive engagement today with the moral foundations of international law.
The *Commentary on Isaiah* warrants particular reconsideration for what it says of
the relation between divine law, natural law and international law. Calvin's theology
of law consists of three parts: the doctrine of life; threatenings and promises; and
the covenant of grace (John Calvin, *Commentary on Isaiah* [Grand Rapids, MI:
Christian Classics Ethereal Library, 1958], vol. 1, p. 16 www.ccel.org/ccel/calvin/
calcom13.toc.html [accessed 16 February 2013]). The doctrine of life teaches that
the order of nature is nothing other than obedience rendered to God in every part
of the world. This order of life extends to plant life yielding its fruit, the seas not

3   Against those who reduce the faith commitments of
    diverse communities to a singular, abstract entity without
    dissociation from lived practice. It is difficult for members
    of diverse faith traditions to engage across disciplines
    from the non-place that is 'religion'. The term is 'the most
    barren and desert-like of all abstractions'.[10] Its use typically
    assumes the reduction of religion to a natural human
    phenomenon.[11] Jacques Derrida makes the point most
    clearly when linking the question of religion to the sickness
    or deracination of abstraction and suggests that, today,

---

flowing beyond its boundaries, the sun, moon and stars remaining in their courses
(p. 26). These are the laws that the Creator has transcribed for the natural order.
So too is the care of children by parents, the absence of cruelty amongst animals to
their own species, and the requirements of the law specified to Moses. The law, says
Calvin, is not to be taken in a limited sense; it does not mean only bondage (p. 64)
but may be understood as the Word of God that is water for the whole world: 'for the
law formerly proceeded out of Mount Sinai (Exodus 19.20), but now it proceeded
out of Zion . . .' (p. 65). God's Word of creation and re-creation are the same: 'the
doctrine of God is the same, and always agrees with itself' (p. 65). The gospel does
not repeal the law which extends to all people. All know 'the common law of nature
and humanity' that makes for brotherly harmony: '[I]t is founded on the common
law of nature and humanity, the Prophet indirectly insinuates that the hungry and
thirsty are defrauded of their bread, when food is denied to them' (vol. 2, p. 72).

[10]Jacques Derrida, 'Faith and Knowledge: The Two Sources of "Religion" at the
Limits of Reason Alone', in *Acts of Religion*, ed. Gil Anidjar (London: Routledge,
2002), p. 42.

[11]David Hume's posthumously published *The Natural History of Religion*
(1757/1779) and complementary *Dialogues Concerning Natural Religion* (1776)
mark something of a beginning in the story of the reduction of religion to a natural
human phenomenon. Hume's sceptical method merged a scientific approach to
ethnology and anthropology with a psychological approach to the philosophy of
religion. This, in effect, made human experience the true object of the study of
religion. Most starting points and end points in philosophico-historical movements
can be disputed. Arguably, however, this particular history of modern discourse
about religion burnt itself out in John Hick and Paul F. Knitter, (eds), *The Myth
of Christian Uniqueness: Toward a Pluralistic Theology of Religions* (Maryknoll,
NY: Orbis Press, 1987), in which the truth of the myth was measured as a kind
of practical truth consisting in the appropriateness of the attitude it evokes. The
plurality of religions was deemed to undermine the credibility of the truth-claims
of any. Questions about truth claims were deemed inappropriate. Instead, Hick
drew upon Wilfred Cantwell Smith's book *The Meaning and End of Religion*
(Minneapolis, MN: Fortress Press, 1962), in which the latter encouraged members
of religious communities to see their faith 'as an outsider', that is, to see their own
piety and faith, obedience and worship, as abstract and impersonal patterns of
behaviour.

the question of religion is emerging in a new and different light. The abstraction 'religion' cannot be reckoned, he warns, in contextless and impersonal ways but only in an idiom inseparable from lived experience, 'from the political, familial, ethnic, communitarian nexus, from the nation and from the people . . . from the ever more problematic relation of citizenship and to the state'.[12] To think religion adequately is to think the name(s) of God as well as patterns of observable behaviour. With Derrida, this chapter warns against grouping too quickly under the one category 'religion' all that is connoted by Athens, Jerusalem, Rome, Byzantium, Graeco-Roman Christianity, Islam, Islamicism, fundamentalisms of varying description and so much more, while holding open the possibility of colloquy.[13] To speak of 'religion' in the singular as significant again in the public arena and yet unknown in its abstractness risks reinforcing the prejudice that this unknown still requires the 'lights' of enlightenment if new wars of religion are not to be unleashed over all the earth.[14]

Given these pitfalls, this book does not propose a particular 'idea' of international law, theory of natural law for jurisprudence, theory of international relations, blueprint for reform of the United Nations, proposals for development of the International Criminal Court, or anything representing a quasi-political manifesto. The primary calling of Christian ethics and political theology is not to draft policy or prescribe jurisprudence but bear witness to Christ crucified and risen. Oliver O'Donovan makes the point when warning theologians against trying to give content to the vision of the New Jerusalem because no one can guard adequately against the corruptibility of our imaginations when proclaiming the gospel of work and the eschatological hope of transformation. Better to describe offences against God's law in what he terms 'the ministry of condemnation' than transpose our own prejudices and biases into the eschatological vision.[15] The church's ministry is not to

---

[12]Derrida, 'Faith and Knowledge', p. 44.
[13]Derrida, 'Faith and Knowledge', p. 45.
[14]Derrida, 'Faith and Knowledge', p. 61.
[15]Oliver O'Donovan, *The Ways of Judgment* (Grand Rapids, MI: Eerdmans, 2005), p. 88.

outline policy for government engagement with international law but to render judgement on actual wrongs, harms done or that will perhaps be done to future generations. '[I]n an act of political judgment', says O'Donovan, 'it is the right that is indeterminate, the wrong determined.'[16]

With O'Donovan, I affirm that the primary calling of the church and the academic theological endeavour is not to devise theory or describe good working practices for other professionals but to focus theologically on divine kingship, law and judgement and to stand against sin exposed by the revealed judgements of God (Rev. 15.4). The purpose of this book is not to devise a theory of international law but to think theologically about whether, and if so, how the authority of human law pertains to the normative order given to creation by God, to which human practices tend naturally. Reflecting on the answerability of the nations before divine judgement, it highlights areas of concern where policies consequent upon particular conceptions of international law are likely to result in decreasing constraints on the use of force, decreasing human rights protections, increasing poverty, increasing militarization, attacks on the rule of law, harm to the natural environment and suchlike. Natural law reasoning is understood more in terms of human capacities for rationality than conformity to a set of precepts..

Avoiding old caricatures

Old caricatures abound with respect to differences between Protestant and Thomist approaches to human law. Witness the insightful if exaggerated description by Sergii Bulgakov, the Russian Marxist philosopher who took holy orders in the Russian Orthodox church, of both the Roman Catholic aim to clericalize the world, or 'tendency to seek for ecclesiastical domination of the social order', as compared to Protestant neutralization of questions about the secular or 'passive acceptance of a corner within the secular and pluralistic marketplace'.[17] Bulgakov's caricature presents us with a picture of Roman Catholic clerical guardianship of the civil and

---

[16]O'Donovan, *The Ways of Judgment*, p. 58.
[17]Rowan Williams, *Sergii Bulgakov: Towards a Russian Political Theology* (Edinburgh: T&T Clark, 2000), p. 270.

political order, according to human laws derived from the natural law, in stark contrast to Protestant indifference to the affairs of national and international law and deference to positive law. The former seeks a major political role in addition to its spiritual responsibilities. The latter evades questions about the civil and political order under the pretext that Jesus' teaching 'Render to Caesar the things that are Caesar's, and to God the things that are God's' (Mk 12.17) more or less leaves the state to its own affairs.

As with most caricatures, there is more than a grain of truth in the representation.[18] A thread of contention throughout Western Christianity concerns earthly government as 'either/or' or 'both/ and' (i) a consequence of sin and (ii) integral to the state of nature before the fall and directive towards the good. Unfortunately, the Latin West did not always hold these two meanings (or ministries) of government together adequately and tended to fall into dichotomized ways of thinking with far-reaching consequences for relations between the Church and earthly powers.

Augustine, and some later Protestant traditions, tended to view earthly government and lawmaking as comprising measures to curtail the corruption of human nature, essentially coercive, law-based, focused on punishment and restraint of the wicked and hence not a proper object of human love. Augustine construes earthly government as a consequence of sin and consisting of checks against violence, bulwarks to secure society against disintegration, provisions for temporal peace and so on. Humankind was created to live peaceably and co-operatively with all creation and to be governed by none but God; humankind is naturally sociable but

---

[18]Nor has Eastern Orthodoxy always negotiated these tensions well. Its theology of government is sometimes difficult to disentangle from a complex history of the supremacy of the state over the church – exemplified by the subordination of the Russian Orthodox Church to the state in the eighteenth and nineteenth centuries, beginning with the reforms of Peter the Great. The concept of *symphonia*, however, that is, a mutuality of submission and co-operation, remains a guiding aspiration. Emperor Justinian's Sixth Novella of 535 spoke of the blessings of both as flowing from the same divine source. The *Epanagoge* or legal compendium of the Byzantine era, written probably by Patriarch Photius I in the ninth century, described this *symphonia* of priestly and imperial earthly government as comparable to the harmony of body and soul. This relationship never existed in a pure form. At the least, however, and in similarity to aspects of Augustinian and Thomist theology, it offers a way of conceiving of the tension between coercive and directive modes of government.

not naturally political.[19] The consequences of anger and lust must be checked and restrained by wisdom and 'this is accomplished only by compulsion and struggle (*cohibendo et repugnando*): it is not a healthy, natural process (*ex natura*), but, thanks to guilt, 'a weary one'.[20] The need for political dominion and the force of law arose with the need to find temporal peace and felicity amidst resentment, murder and destruction.[21]

Aquinas, and some later Roman Catholic traditions, tended to view earthly government and lawmaking as, potentially at least, an expression of human nature in its goodness. Arguing from final causes, Aquinas emphasizes the true role of earthly government as directive, in the sense of ordering those governed towards the ultimate end (*telos*) of created existence in God:

> For as 'it belongs to the best to produce the best', it is not fitting that the supreme goodness of God should produce things without giving them their perfection. Now a thing's ultimate perfection consists in the attainment of its end. Therefore it belongs to the Divine goodness, as it brought things into existence, so to lead them to their end: and this is to govern.[22]

The aim of the common good necessitates political dominion. The natural order as established by God in the universe requires this directive influence. That Aquinas drew frequently upon Augustine indicates that differences between them are not as deep as sometimes implied.[23] John Calvin later insists that the tasks and burdens of civil government are necessitated by sin *and* integral to the 'order established by God'.[24] Yet the contrast recalls much about the politics of Western Christianity in the Middle Ages, notably the power struggles between the papacy and the Holy Roman emperors in the eleventh and twelfth centuries about the investiture of bishops and popes – which were ultimately struggles over whether the Pope

---

[19] Augustine, *The City of God against the Pagans*, trans. R. W. Dyson (Cambridge: Cambridge University Press, 1998), bk XII, ch. 28; bk XIV, ch. 10.
[20] Augustine, *City of God*, bk XIV, ch. 19.
[21] Augustine, *City of God*, bk XV, chs. 3–4.
[22] Aquinas, *ST*, I, q. 103, a. 1, sed contra.
[23] Aquinas, *ST*, I, q. 96, a. 4.
[24] John Calvin, *Institutes of the Christian Religion*, ed. John T. McNeill, 2 vols. (Louisville, KY: Westminster/John Knox Press, 2001), bk 4, ch. 20, §1.

had the power to depose the Catholic rulers of medieval Europe –
and 'two realms' or 'two swords' theologies that tended to separate
church and state.

It would be easy to get mired in these old caricatures and
enmeshed in debates about whether Christian theology can specify
what all people, Christian and non-Christian, share morally
in common, whether to interpret the Decalogue as minimalistic
norms by which all humanity will be judged, what it means to
affirm that the natural law is part of the law of Christ, and more.
The strategy in this book is to resist getting stuck in old ruts by
attempting to draw from and fuse commitments derived from
Barth and Aquinas respectively, namely, answerability before
God and the (international) common good. A practically oriented
engagement with questions about the rule of law, the meaning of
universality, promotion of the common good through international
law, the proper self-interest of nation-states, the ethics of territorial
borders and more often cuts across or works through many of
these issues. To this end, a working assumption is that Roman
Catholics and Protestants share concern about good governance
and the purpose of human law. For me as a Protestant, the question
of what it means to affirm for theological reasons the obligation
upon all human beings that 'good is to be done and pursued and
evil is to be avoided' is as much my question as it is a question for
Catholic social ethicists. Conversely, questions about how the truth
of natural law is found in Christ are as much questions for the
Roman Catholic as the Protestant.

Three moments in the task: Confession, critique, construction

More needs to be said, however, about the shared theological
ground upon which this kind of collaboration is possible. To this
end, I find it helpful to think in terms of three interrelated and yet
distinguishable moments in an ongoing spiral: confession, critique
and construction. Each moment is found variously in the writings
of Barth and Aquinas as well as in much wider swathes of Christian
tradition. Attention to these moments helps to cut across besetting
caricatures.

The *telos* of law in God

First, the Christian community confesses that the *telos* of human law is in God. Earthly government is at no time unrelated to the history of redemption because all history is oriented towards divine judgement. International affairs are of concern to Christian ethics and political theology for the same reasons that any issues of justice and injustice, poverty and oppression, good order and the overcoming of wrongdoing, governance and judgement, are of concern – namely, because God incarnate, the Word made flesh, became truly human in order that humans might share in the divine life. No part of creation was left void of the Word at creation. Therefore, no part was excluded when the Word assumed humanity and shared our human life:

> He 'delivered' to Him [the Son] man, that the Word Himself might be made Flesh, and by taking the Flesh, restore it wholly. For to Him, as to a physician, man 'was delivered' to heal the bite of the serpent; as to life, to raise what was dead; as to light, to illumine the darkness; and, because He was Word, to renew the rational nature.[25]

Because of what God has done in Christ, the natural movement of all creation is towards God. That the Word of God became truly human and shared every aspect of human existence in all its physicality and pain, needfulness and disorder, means that no ethical sphere of human life is beyond the concern of Christian ethics.

Today, Roman Catholic and Protestant traditions enjoy an increasing degree of convergence with respect to explicitly Christological accounts of natural law. As the Vatican has led the way in theological renewal, so Protestant scholars have been recovering the natural law in theological ethics and seeking Christologically focused ways of construing both 'the natural' and 'natural law reasoning' in relation to God's ordering of human affairs. The Christological focus of natural law teaching is expounded in the papal encyclical *Veritatis Splendor*, which finds

---

[25]Athanasius, *On Luke X. 22* (Matt. XI. 27), in *Nicene and Post Nicene Fathers*, series 2, ed. Philip Schaff and Henry Wace, vol. 4: *Athanasius: Selected Works and Letters* (Edinburgh: T&T Clark, 1891), p. 87.

the truth of the natural law in Christ.[26] Likewise, the concluding chapter of a document drawn up by a papal commission in 2009 was entitled 'Jesus Christ, the Fulfilment of the Natural Law'.[27] Through the light of natural reason, humanity is able to examine the intelligible order of the universe, to discover the expression of the wisdom and beauty of the Creator – but only because the Logos, the Word of God, the 'image of the invisible God' (Col. 1.15–17), is before all things and in all things. 'The *Logos* is therefore the key of creation' who did not come to abolish the law but fulfil it (Matt. 5.17).[28] The plan of salvation from eternity 'is realized by the mission of the Son who gives humanity the new Law, the law of the Gospel . . . but at the same time takes up and realizes the natural law in an eminent manner'.[29] Natural law is thus deemed the foundation of a universal ethic from which to reflect on our common human nature. The end of the natural law is found in Christ, the living law.

Conversely, recent Barth scholarship has been open to ecumenical dialogue and has revisited questions about Barth's approach to questions of 'the natural'. Recent Barth scholarship has clustered variously around his orientation to the use of language (Graham Ward, Walter Lowe, William Stacey Johnson), his affinity with so-called post-modern thinkers in his critiques of Enlightenment modes of reasoning (Bruce McCormack, Neil MacDonald) and his openness to ecumenical dialogue (Carl E. Braaten, Joseph L. Mangina, Amy Marga). Marga finds significant common ground between Barth and Catholicism in mutual commitment to the objectivity of divine revelation.[30] Drawing attention to Barth's comments on 'law as gospel', Mangina highlights the significance of Barth's theology of creation and divine command for Christian

---

[26]John Paul II, *Veritatis Splendor*, 6 August. 1993 www.vatican.va/holy_father/john_paul_ii/encyclicals/documents/hf_jp-ii_enc_06081993_veritatis-splendor_En.html [accessed 11 February 2013].

[27]International Theological Commission (ITC), *In Search of a Universal Ethic: A New Look at the Natural Law* (2009) www.vatican.va/roman_curia/congregations/cfaith/ctI_documents/rc_con_cfaith_doc_20090520_legge-naturale_En.html [accessed 11 February 2013].

[28]ITC, *In Search of a Universal Ethic*, §103.

[29]ITC, *In Search of a Universal Ethic*, §102.

[30]Amy Marga, *Karl Barth's Dialogue with Catholicism in Göttingen and Münster* (Tübingen: Mohr Siebeck, 2010).

ecumenism and reminds readers of how, because of the doctrine of the divine command, Barth interprets the law as a form of the gospel.[31] The problem of 'general ethics' remains the endeavour to reason ethically without reference to the divine self-communication of reconciling grace; when humans set themselves up in the place of God, they sin. Nevertheless, to affirm that people who 'do not have the law' (Rom. 2.14) can still do what the law requires by virtue of their natural reason does not, of itself, valorize 'general ethics' or presuppose that existence independent of Christ is possible.[32] It is simply to affirm that nothing of natural reason falls outside the grace of God.

Battista Mondin made similar points in the 1960s when arguing that Aquinas's doctrine of *analogia entis* and Barth's teaching of the *analogia fidei* are not as far apart from one another as is often imagined to be the case:

> It is true that Barth insists more than Aquinas on the *sola gratia* but not to the point of eliminating nature and reason. On the other hand, it is true that Aquinas insists more than Barth on the relative autonomy of nature but not to the point of forgetting its subordination to revelation and grace.[33]

Mondin drew attention to how Aquinas warns constantly against any use of analogy that threatens the qualitative difference between God and humankind when looking for some kind of logic by which to order theological discourse about God. When attending to formal likenesses in respect of the properties appertaining to the

---

[31]Joseph L. Mangina, *Karl Barth: Theologian of Christian Witness* (Aldershot: Ashgate, 2004), p. 146.

[32]'The problem of ethics generally – the law or good or value which it seeks as a standard by which human action and modes of action are to be measured, and according to which they are to be performed, the problem of the truth and knowledge of the good – is no problem at all in the ethics immanent in the Christian conception of God, in the doctrine of the command of God. For in virtue of the fact that the command of God is the form of His electing grace, it is the starting-point of every ethical question and answer. It is the starting-point which is already given and to that extent presupposed and certain in itself, so that it can never be surpassed or compromised from any quarter' (Karl Barth, *Church Dogmatics (CD)*, 13 vols., ed. G. W. Bromiley and T. F. Torrance [Edinburgh: T&T Clark, 1956–69], II/2, § 36, p. 519.

[33]Battista Mondin, *The Principle of Analogy in Protestant and Catholic Theology* (Leiden: Martinus Nijhoff, 1963), p. 171.

Creator and creation, his main concern always is to find modes of predication that neither endanger divine absoluteness nor threaten to devalue the perfections of creatures as given by God alone. When speaking of *analogia attributionis intrinsecae*, as distinct from *analogia attributionis extrinsecae*, the point is that creatures possess qualities that are 'natural' or intrinsic to them by virtue of the fact that they have been given by God. There is no suggestion that the nature of the creature can be compared intrinsically with the Creator in any sense that compromises the uniqueness of the divine being; any and every perfection that belongs to the creature naturally, as given by grace and perceived in faith:

> For their being creatures depends only on God, who does not fail to communicate to each one of them, intrinsically, the perfections required by their own being. Therefore 'good', 'being', etc., are predicates of creatures by intrinsic denomination.[34]

Barth and Aquinas both reject illegitimate modes of predication that signify a quantitative correspondence between God and humankind. Mondin's claim (which I echo) is that Barth and Aquinas in their teachings about nature and grace differ more in emphasis than in substance.[35] Both agree that human logic alone is not enough to speak of divine salvation; the concept of the *analogia fidei* is useful but no guarantee against apostasy.[36]

Against this backdrop, we may look again at what Barth says about the *telos* of human law in God, and the 'inward and vital connection' between human law and order and the order of the Kingdom of God, as not excusing from but directing the believer in the ethical task. While it is clear that, for Barth, no earthly legal system or government constitutes an ideal to be sought, and that the relation between divine and human law – which is always viewed 'from above' or from the perspective of the 'last things' in which sense the Church's witness to Christ – is always strange or

---

[34]Aquinas, *ST*, I, q. 45, a. 5. Barth, *CD*, 2/1, p. 234; Mondin, *The Principle of Analogy*, pp. 26, 153–55.

[35]See also Eberhard Mechels, who traces the development of Barth's treatment of this question in *Analogia bei Erich Przywara und Karl Barth: Das Verhältnis von Offenbarungstheologie und Metaphysic* (Neukirchen-Vluyn: Neukirchener Verlag, 1974).

[36]Barth, *CD*, 4/1, pp. 634–35.

alien to the politics of human governance, there remains an ethical task for the believer. At its simplest, this task is nothing more than pointing towards divine judgement and bearing witness to the hope of redemption in Christ. Christians are called to proclaim the God who redeems from sin and bestows renewing gifts of grace on all creation. Significantly, however, the simplicity of this witness does not excuse the believer from the ethical task but casts the responsibility in eschatological terms: '[T]he ethical problem possesses an eschatological tension; otherwise it is not ethical.'[37] 'In the eschatological knowledge about the actual end of the world, the present world is proclaimed in its true character as the creation of God's word.'[38] The divine origin and destiny of earthly government and human law obligates Christian people to pray for its peace and order, and for its rulers, and explains the service that the church renders to the state by its witness to the judgement of Christ and call to faith. The 'inward and vital connection' between human law and order and the order of the earthly governance is found in God.

For our purposes, this means that the endeavour is to engage questions arising from the practice and theory of international law in terms not only of the worshipping life of the church as such but also in what may be described as a 'political' service of God – a service of God which, to borrow Barth's words, 'would consist in the careful examination of all those problems which are raised by the existence of human justice, of law, or rather, which would consist in the recognition, support, defence and extension of this law – and all this, not in spite of but because of divine justification.'[39] The saving work of God in Christ is the real focus of all theological engagement with questions of human reason and human law, in their many modes and formats; our questions are about how concerns regarding human law that belong to the proper autonomy of the secular may be conceived also as belonging ultimately within the transforming influence of the gospel, and situated within a dynamic in which grace not sin is determinative. Consequently, there can be no delimitation of divine activity to

---

[37]Karl Barth, *The Epistle to the Romans*, trans. E. C. Hoskyns (1933; rpt Oxford: Oxford University Press, 1968), p. 430.
[38]Karl Barth, *Church and State*, trans. G. Ronald Howe (London: SCM, 1939), p. 40.
[39]Barth, *Church and State*, p. 2.

the sphere of the church, or narrowness of outlook concerning the generative work of divine grace throughout the created order, because Christ, the New Adam, is 'man for man, for other men, His fellows'.[40] God's election in Christ of all humanity is the ground of human hope that history is held open to the possibility of choosing good rather than evil, because the destiny of the creature is in Christ, and not damnation. The church attests the death and resurrection of Christ Jesus as the beginning and end of all things, his presence in and lordship over all things, his saving power throughout the earth. At no point can any of our questions about human law and common good be divorced from confession of God the Creator and Redeemer. Conversely, questions about the relation of divine and human law, the affairs of the international community, the injustice of human justice, are to be addressed with reference to the coming reign of Christ and the eternal law of God, wherein true justice is found.[41]

To the extent that Protestant Thomism represents a single outlook or perspective, I suggest in what follows that Aquinas and Barth share a formal and material understanding that the context of all human action is the created order and inclusion of all humanity in Christ. For each, albeit in their different ways, challenge is to discern the shape of an account of human law within this ontology of creation, redemption and eschatological hope. Confession of God the origin and end of law, the judge of all human law, whose revelation in Christ Jesus is the measure of normativity and reason for the church's engagement with questions of law, will be determinative somehow for our purposes of engagement between theology and international law. With both, we may suppose that the divine origin and destiny of earthly government and human law obligates Christian people to pray for its peace and order, and for its rulers, and explains the service that the church renders to the state by its witness to the judgement of Christ and call to faith. All normative concepts are defined in terms of their theological foundation in Christ, in whom 'all things . . . things in heaven and things on earth' are united (Eph. 1.10).

---

[40] Barth, quoted in Tom Greggs, *Barth, Origen, and Universal Salvation: Restoring Particularity* (Oxford: Oxford University Press, 2009), p. 82.

[41] 'Now this eternal law of Jesus Christ constitutes precisely the content of the message of justification, in which, here and now, the task of the Church consists' (Barth, *Church and State*, p. 47).

The injustice of human law

Second, the injustice of human law that is integral to the fallen human state prevents any idealism with respect to that for which the believer can hope with respect to human law. Jesus' crucifixion exposes *par excellence* that both religious and imperial law produce injustice rather than justice. Nevertheless, despite its impossibility and injustice, human law still obliges the conscience. That earthly government is at no time unrelated to the history of redemption entails what Barth calls the dialectic of 'positive possibilities' and 'negative possibilities' in human affairs. This dialectic between so-called positive and negative possibilities is concerned fundamentally with the relation between law and gospel, whereby the realities of grace and sin are spoken of together. The two (seemingly opposing) positions with respect to the possibilities and impossibilities of human law are held together because of the paradoxical nature of divine truth: Jesus is fully human and fully divine; human obedience to the divine will is impossible yet possible; the gospel is both affirmative and destructive of the possibilities of human law.

The moment that Barth calls 'positive possibility' or recognition that the truth of God constitutes a negation of this world because all human possibilities are perishable and imperfect.[42] For our purposes, this concerns why, despite its impossibility, human law still normally obliges the conscience, and why the injustice of the cross – on which the Jesus condemned by religious and Roman law – was crucified, is the locus of both the impossibility and the necessity of human law. Hence the section below on 'The Injustice of Human Law' considers that which negates the affairs of this world before God in their violence and injustice. The moment of 'negative possibility' is more obviously practical and begins to consider what might be willed and done 'congruous to the *transformation of this world*' to disrupt injustice and testify to divine judgement in the concrete details of daily life.[43] (The section below entitled 'Reasoning about Human Law' picks up Barth's concern with those things that may be willed or done that do not render evil for evil but bear witness to the truth of the resurrection amidst the everyday, and concerns how to reason about human law for good ends.)

---

[42]Barth, *The Epistle to the Romans*, pp. 450–60.
[43]Barth, *The Epistle to the Romans*, pp. 460–65.

'Properly speaking, "Positive Ethics" belong only to the volition and action of God.'[44] Nothing of human law achieves true justice. Recognition of this reality is not novel. Habakkuk, one of the 12 minor prophets of the Hebrew bible, lamented the weakness of the legal system in Jerusalem in the mid-to-late seventh-century BCE, shortly before the Babylonians laid siege to the city and captured its inhabitants.

> O LORD, how long shall I cry for help,
>   And You will not hear?
> Even cry out to You, 'Violence!'
>   And You will not save.
> Why do You show me iniquity,
>   And cause me to see trouble?
> For plundering and violence are before me;
>   There is strife, and contention arises.
> Therefore the law is powerless,
>   And justice never goes forth.
> For the wicked surround the righteous;
>   Therefore perverse judgment proceeds.
>
> But the LORD is in His holy temple.
>   Let all the earth keep silence before Him.
>
>   Hab. 1.2–4; 2.20 NKJV

Habakkuk's point is not merely that human legal systems could do better. Where faith is interpreted as the acknowledgement of divine justice beyond human law, divine justice necessarily exceeds, questions and destabilizes the human law's provisional legitimacy. The justice of human law is always a process of becoming and thinking of justice 'outside, beyond, and even against law'.[45] Similarly for Paul, human law and divine justice are distinguished qualitatively from any human formulation of the meaning of 'justice before the law' or 'rule of law' (Rom. 1.18; Rom. 2.9; 2 Cor. 5.10). The 'impossibility' of human justice before God introduces an instability into claims made for the justice of any and all human law, while demanding nevertheless that human

---

[44]Barth, *The Epistle to the Romans*, p. 451.
[45]Theodore W. Jennings, Jr, *Reading Derrida/Thinking Paul: On Justice* (Stanford, CA: Stanford University Press, 2006), p. 19.

law is law only by reference to the 'beyond' of justice which takes the form of a call upon humans in their sociality. Human law is unable to produce true justice and can, indeed, say little more than 'the LORD is in His holy temple / Let all the earth keep silence before Him' (Hab. 2.20).

True justice lies beyond human law. Grace abrogates and suspends the possibility of human justice and the prospect of a good conscience. Even so, the claims of human justice are not set aside but affirmed. '[G]race, so far from suspending the claim of justice, actually renders that claim effective, actually "grounds" that claim in a way that law could not do'.[46] As fifth governor of the Roman province of Judaea, Pilate was responsible for ensuring that this rebellious people acquiesced to Roman rule.[47] His abnegation of ethical responsibility with respect to Jesus' death and overriding concern for the security situation in Jerusalem at the time has been vilified through the centuries but does not alter the fact, says Barth, that 'this power was really given him "from above"'.[48] Pilate deflected the course of justice and exposed the power-hungry, true face of the Roman Empire, thereby contradicting his true function. He could not, however, separate himself from the divine work of redemption; it was in the exercise of power given by God that Jesus was executed.[49]

This seemingly paradoxical recognition that the truth of God constitutes a negation of this world and that *nevertheless* earthly rulers have responsibilities before God is explicated by Theodore Jennings in *Reading Derrida/Thinking Paul,* which juxtaposes Derrida's deconstructive approach to the seeming inconsistencies and contradictions in Paul's writings. Jennings's book is of particular note because it attempts to think through some ethical and political implications of Christian belief with respect to the need for stable legal regimes, while, simultaneously, provoking disquiet about confidence in human law as justice.[50] It

---

[46]Jennings, *Reading Derrida/Thinking Paul,* p. 86.
[47]See Helen K. Bond, *Pontius Pilate in History and Interpretation* (Cambridge: Cambridge University Press, 1998), p. 2.
[48]Barth, *Church and State,* p. 21.
[49]Ernst Käsemann, *Commentary on Romans* (Grand Rapids, MI: Eerdmans, 1980), p. 354.
[50]Jennings, *Reading Derrida/Thinking Paul,* ch. 2, esp. p. 25.

draws our attention to how the qualitative gap between human law and divine justice includes recognition not only of the need for human law but that it is exercised by the sword (Rom. 13.4) or with force. Derrida's deconstructive approach to the multiple and seemingly conflictual meanings of a text does not downplay Paul's political realism and recognition that those in authority are avengers who carry out God's wrath on wrongdoers. '[L]aw is always an authorized force, a force that justifies itself or is justified in applying itself.'[51]

Derrida's observations on Walter Benjamin's account of the violence of law make the point: 'There is, first, . . . the founding violence, the one that institutes and posits law (*die rechtsetzende Gewalt*) and the violence that preserves, the one that maintains, confirms, insures the permanence and enforceability of law (*die rechtserhaltende Gewalt*).' Enforceability is not an optional extra to human law but is implied in the very concept of *justice as law*. Human law is not law without performative force. Justice lacks justice if not enforced. Paul reckons head-on with one of the names of death, which is law.[52] Huge slippages occur between human law and the justice demanded by the prophets. Paul is the destroyer of what Badiou calls 'the law's transcendent neutrality' as it touches human affairs.[53] There is no place for dewy-eyed with optimism with respect to instantiation in positive law of the requirements of divine justice.

---

[51]Jacques Derrida, 'Force of Law: The "Mystical Foundation of Authority"', in Gil Anidjar (ed.), *Acts of Religion*, p. 233. We may understand Derrida's deconstructive approach to be a mode of analysis whereby the various components of a text are taken apart, or undone, in order to hear the differing voices within a text. As literary theorist Barbara Johnson explains, 'If anything is destroyed in a deconstructive reading, it is not the text, but the claim to unequivocal domination of one mode of signifying over another. A deconstructive reading is a reading which analyses the specificity of a text's critical difference from itself' ('Deconstruction', in J. A. Cuddon, *A Dictionary of Literary Terms and Literary Theory*, 3rd ed. [London: Blackwell, 1991], p. 189). To use Derrida's own words, we are dealing with the displacement of oppositional logic, which starts by 'destabilizing, complicating, or recalling the paradoxes of values . . . and of all that follows from these', and looking instead for the insights that emerge from paradox and opposition, and a questioning through and through of the relation of human law to justice. Derrida, 'Force of Law', p. 235.
[52]Alain Badiou, *Saint Paul: The Foundation of Universalism*, trans. Ray Brassier (Stanford, CA: Stanford University Press, 2003), p. 74.
[53]Badiou, *Saint Paul*, p. 9.

Similar to Derrida in this respect, writes Jennings, is atheist philosopher Alain Badiou's treatment of Paul as 'a monumental figure of the destruction of all politics'.[54] Badiou discerns in Paul's Letter to the Romans especially an account of Roman empire and law as figures of death, drawing attention to how Paul describes civil magistrates as those 'of no account' (*exouthenou;* see 1 Cor. 6.4) in the church, earthly government as 'doomed to perish' (1 Cor. 2.6) and Jesus Christ is as an anti-Caesar – the promise of whose coming again in glory carries a huge political charge, and seems at times to delegitimize rather than legitimize earthly government. Badiou reads these texts as distinguishing between a legalizing subjectivity, which is a power of death, and 'a law raised up by faith, which belongs to the spirit and to life'.[55] He posits another law of love, a 'nonliteral law', another law, that universalizes the subject and orients each one towards *agapē.*

He rediscovers the living unity of thinking and doing. This recovery turns life itself into a universal law. Law returns as life's articulation for everyone, path of faith, law beyond law.[56]

Whether in Mosaic or Roman terms, faith in Christ expands the believer's concern with human from subjectivity and adherence to legal prescriptions to seeing afresh that life is a possibility for everyone. This is not to decry the subject dimension of Christian living. 'The word is near you, on your lips and in your hearts' (Rom. 10.8). Rather, it is to realize that the law of love connects a person to all for whom Christ died. 'Faith prescribes a new possibility, one that, although real in Christ, is not, as yet, in effect for everyone.'[57] 'Law returns' as a demand of love. The resurrection reduces the multiplicity of legal prescriptions to the single, affirmative norm of love. Love is made possible by the resurrection because it means that neither self nor neighbour are given up to death. Despite being a self-confessed non-believer himself, Badiou gets to the heart of how, for Paul, because of Christ, law returns as a question or demand or love for believer and non-believer alike. Conscience

---

[54]Badiou, *Saint Paul*, p. 7.
[55]Badiou, *Saint Paul*, p. 87.
[56]Badiou, *Saint Paul*, p. 88.
[57]Badiou, *Saint Paul*, p. 88.

is not an inner voice that advises quietude and compliance but a means by which God addresses humanity and puts all human law under question.

Badiou and Derrida both remind readers that, for Paul, justice lies always beyond the human law and yet demands adherence to human law. Human justice is an *impossible* demand but remains a *demand* nevertheless because of the resurrection. Christ is the end of the law (Rom. 10.4), both Mosaic and Roman. Divine justice is destructive of human justice, while reserving the possibility of the latter at the very point of its denial.[58] Derrida describes the injustice of human law before true justice as follows:

> These two regimes of law, of *the* law and the laws, are thus both contradictory, antinomic, *and* inseparable. They both imply and exclude one another simultaneously.[59]

We are dealing, he says, with the displacement of oppositional logic, which starts by 'destabilizing, complicating, or recalling the paradoxes of values . . . and of all that follows from these', and looking instead for the insights that emerge from paradox and opposition, and a questioning through and through of the relation of human law to justice.[60] The rupture between divine and human justice is exposed most clearly on the cross. Jesus was condemned by religious law (the laws of Moses) and state law (the laws of the Roman empire). Neither could effect justice and Jesus was executed as a threat to law and order.

In other words, Derrida's deconstructive reading draws our attention to how the qualitative gap between human law and divine justice includes recognition not only of the need for human law but that it is exercised by the sword (Rom. 13.4) or with force. Those in authority are avengers who carry out God's wrath on wrongdoers. '[L]aw is always an authorized force, a force that justifies itself

---

[58]Decades previously, Barth also related conscience to the co-knowledge (*conscientia*) that all humans have of their conduct with reference to the goodness of God, emphasizing the expansiveness and flexibility of personal responsibility within the framework of the divine ordering of creation (Karl Barth, *Ethics*, trans. G. W. Bromiley [Edinburgh: T&T Clark, 1981], p. 476).
[59]Jacques Derrida, *Of Hospitality* (Stanford, CA: Stanford University Press, 2000), p. 79.
[60]Derrida, 'Force of Law', p. 235.

or is justified in applying itself.'[61] Every exercise of human justice carries 'an explicit reserve' or warning to the effect it will entail injustice, violence and arbitrary force.[62] This is the tragedy of the human condition. Every instance of the framing and enacting of human law is unstable in the sense that it knows little of truth, is effected through force and political intrigue, and must always be distinguished from the justice of God or true justice. *Nevertheless*, Paul affirms the place of human lawmaking and enforcement within divine providence.

This seemingly impossible tension has caused some representatives of the recent trend in New Testament scholarship away from post-Reformation readings of Romans and towards political readings to find ways around the literal meaning of Romans 13.1–7. Taken at face value, says T. L. Carter, these verses can be seen as 'an embarrassingly unqualified endorsement of the political *status quo*'.[63] Only an ironic reading makes sense of Paul's seeming affirmation of the institutions of human justice. The problem of the crucifixion of Jesus under religious and Roman law as the instance par excellence that shows human justice not to be true justice relieved by construing these verses as pregnant with the rhetoric of irony such that Paul was really intending to say the opposite of what he actually says, thereby expose the corruption and oppressive authority structures of the Roman empire. When the straightforward meaning of the text is implausible and unacceptable, says Carter, an ironic reading best captures the underlying sense of an otherwise crass commendation of the authorities that would have alienated his audience.[64] Paul employs irony elsewhere as a rhetorical device and in mock self-disparagement, and so it would be unwise to dispense entirely with the possibility that Paul writes ironically in Romans 13.1–7.[65] If there is a hint of irony in the passage, however, it does not relax but reinforces the tension between the claims of divine and

---

[61]Derrida, 'Force of Law', p. 233.
[62]Derrida, 'Force of Law', p. 234.
[63]T. L. Carter, 'The Irony of Romans 13', *Novum Testamentum* 46 (2004), p. 209.
[64]Carter, 'The Irony of Romans 13', p. 215.
[65]Carter draws attention to the following: M. D. Nanos, *Irony in Galatians* (Minneapolis, MN: Augsburg/Fortress, 2002); A. B. Spencer, 'The Wise Fool (and the Foolish Wise): A Study of Irony in Paul', *Novum Testamentum* 23 (1981) pp. 349–60; K. A. Plank, *Paul and the Irony of Affliction* (Atlanta, GA: Scholars Press, 1987); G. Holland, 'Paul's Use of Irony as a Rhetorical Technique', in *The*

human justice, the witness of conscience and the inherent violence of political power. An exclusively ironic reading does not cope with the high premium that Paul places on the testimony of conscience (*suneidesis*), through which believers should submit themselves to the ruling authorities, not only from fear of the wrath they might unleash but because they are instruments on earth for good. Paul's teaching elsewhere about conscience does not bear the telltale signs of irony but is used consistently as a witness in the heart that can both accuse and excuse (Rom. 2.15), and whose proper sensitivities concern the purposes of the heart (1 Cor. 4.5).

While it is true that this ironic reading of 13.1–7 lessens the oddity of verses, given the radical nature of Paul's challenge to the imperial cult, it leaves unanswered the question of how best to negotiate the further tension between Paul's instruction to 'be subject to the governing authorities' because they are 'God's servants', the need for human law and reality that the power of the state and requires force.[66] Paul's instruction to 'be subject to the governing authorities' because they are 'God's servants' sits uneasily with texts that appear to designate earthly governors as destroyers of the earth set themselves for destruction (Rev. 4.2–11; 5.6–10). But I find the ironic solution to this tension textually implausible and opt for a reading that does not resolve but persists with the impossibility of the tension between the injustice and yet demand before God for operative legal systems. As compared to ironic readings of Romans 13.1–7 that undermine the literal sense of this verse by implying

---

Rhetorical Analysis of Scripture: Essays from the 1995 London Conference, ed. S. E. Porter and T. H. Olbricht (Sheffield: Academic Press, 1997), pp. 234–48.
[66]Other New Testament texts also affirm the need for earthly government to deal with wrongdoers, and to be subject to rulers and authorities (e.g. Titus 3.1; 1 Pet. 2.13–19). In the gospels, Jesus' reply to the Pharisees and Herodians about the payment of taxes implies that some kind of earthly rule is part of the universal human experience of divine providence: 'Render to Caesar . . .' (Mk 12.17). Jesus gives little ground to the Zealot politics of violence (Jn 18.11; see Lk. 22.35–38), implying rather that earthly government and lawmaking has a justifiable place within divine providence. He appears to accept the right of government to expect its citizens to meet certain obligations for the sake of good order. The saying in Mark 12.17 depends for its effectiveness on a distinction between the limited jurisdiction of earthly government and the supreme authority of God. Others call for the churches to oppose the 'beast rising out of the sea' (Rev. 13.1) and the harlot of Babylon (Rev. 19.2) – figures commonly understood to represent the political tyranny and economic exploitation of Rome.

that the governing authorities wreak injustice and the effects of their own wrath, Derrida reminds readers that every exercise of human justice carries 'an explicit reserve' or warning to the effect it will entail injustice, violence and often arbitrary force.[67] This reading, more than Carter's ironic reading, seems better to express Paul's account of this particular tragedy of the human condition. It provides both the rationale and the space for critical engagement with the justice and injustice of human law.

Reasoning about human law

There is no place for Christian ethicists and political theologians to be idealistic about the achievements of and prospects for human law. Yet the critical space between what Barth calls 'negative' and 'positive' possibilities, however, is where questions can be asked about these achievements and prospects, mindful of the judgement of God from which nothing is hidden (1 Cor. 4.4). Of interest in this section is how curiously similar Aquinas and Barth are with respect to what this constructive work of moral reasoning entails – specifically in maintaining a gap between the general principles of the natural law and the command of God, respectively, and the practicalities of reasoning about human law. Neither suggests a simple process of deduction that extracts meaning from the Bible and tradition to be applied to everyday contexts. Each maintains a space within which reasoning about human affairs, including the law, is to take place. Neither supposes that the task of Christian living is to chase certainty in moral reasoning by deducing principles or analogies from biblical texts or looking for what Hans-Georg Gadamer calls 'the phantom of a historical object', but to think and ask questions within a given tradition about how best to aim at that which good order requires, intrinsic to the requirements of common good, through the mediation of the appropriate institutions.[68] Neither supposes that the challenge for Christian living is that of an exercise in formal logic, whether deduction or induction, but what is entailed in living out the story of salvation,

---

[67]Derrida, 'Force of Law', p. 234.
[68]Hans-Georg Gadamer, *Truth and Method*, 2nd edn, rev., trans. Joel Weinsheimer and Donald G. Marshall (London: Continuum, 2004), p. 299.

continually rediscovering and reinterpreting anew the call to answerability before God and neighbour, understanding how we are always involved in our own knowing, trying to acknowledge our presupposition and pre-judgements, grappling with how human communities are conditioned by time and circumstance, and living out to the creative, conflictual and performative aspects of interpretation. Hence the importance in what follows of explicating natural law reasoning as a task of hermeneutics.

A criticism levelled often against Barth's ethics has been that of abstraction and failure to offer sufficiently concrete advice to be useful to the churches.[69] Significantly for our purposes, however, it is not only Barth but Aquinas also who fails to yield a reliable method for moral reasoning.[70] Neither holds that moral reasoning is effected through logical processes but more complex and diffuse interactions. Human law is rarely, if ever, conceived by either as the instantiation of an a priori standard but, rather, an interpretation of what God's law requires amidst the disorder and contingency of everyday affairs. There is no channel between the general principles of the natural law and the proper conclusions of practical reason that does not entail at least potential human disagreement; no legal norms can be said to derive directly from natural law, as secondary

---

[69]A summary of this debate is given by Paul T. Nimmo, *Being in Action: The Theological Shape of Barth's Ethical Vision* (Edinburgh: T&T Clark, 2011), pp. 74–78.

[70]Recent scholarship has contested this accusation with responses to the effect that Barth was a contextual thinker whose scholarship emphasized the shape of Christian living in ways that yield surprisingly practical guidance but only when engaged with actively. Paul Nimmo has drawn attention to the telic aspects of Barth's ethical vision, as well as its noetic and ontic aspects, whereas John Webster describes Barth's construal of Christian ethics as 'a diverse pattern of correspondences or analogies, of similarities and dissimilarities, between the actions of God and human actions'; and David Clough argues that criticisms of abstraction against Barth often fail to understand his appreciation of the space for human agency that the divine command opens, and in which it is encountered. See Nimmo, *Being in Action*, pp. 167–70; John Webster, *Barth's Moral Theology: Human Action in Barth's Thought* (Edinburgh: T&T Clark, 2004), p. 177; David Clough, *Ethics in Crisis: Interpreting Barth's Ethics* (Aldershot, Hants: Ashgate, 2005), p. 114. In keeping with the spirit of these endeavours, a challenge for this project is to address some of these questions within the discipline of theological ethics and political theology within the limits set by Barth, while not neglecting the responsibilities of humankind before God for the rule of law and exercise of justice.

principles that follow directly from first principles because there can be no compromise between 'nature' as a sphere of revelation and the revelatory activity of God in Christ.

It is especially important to be clear that Aquinas did not suppose there to be any direct route from the general principles of the natural law to human law but, rather, supposes there to be a gap between these general principles and the proper conclusions of practical reason. Aquinas's teaching on the natural law in this respect is far less determinate than often assumed. As R. A. Armstrong explains: '[W]hen we speak of a precept "following" or being "derived" from another, we are not suggesting a procedure in any way analogous to the strict deductive system employed by Euclid.'[71] Aquinas's practical reasoning does not involve a chain of logical syllogisms, beginning with a highest moral principle, followed by more specific moral principles and finally ending with a practical syllogism, the conclusion of which is an action.[72] Rather, Aquinas's indication of the tendency of human obligation towards common good and very broad description of the moral principles that emerge from life's experiences are not deduced strictly from general principles. There is no strict logical relation between the highest moral principles and how a legislator should decide in a given situation.

Consider Aquinas's answer to the question whether the natural law is the same for all people.[73] His, perhaps surprising, answer is that with regard to the specifics of how to act, we can know little or nothing about the content of the natural law:

The practical reason, on the other hand, is busied with contingent matters, about which human actions are concerned: and consequently, although there is necessity in the general principles, the more we descend to matters of detail, the more frequently we encounter defects. Accordingly then in speculative matters truth is the same in all men, both as to principles and as to conclusions: although the truth is not known to all as

[71]R. A. Armstrong, *Primary and Secondary Precepts in Thomistic Natural Law Teaching* (Leiden: Martinus Nijhoff, 1966), p. 134.
[72]Scholarship on this point is divided. James Fieser argues the opposite in 'The Logic of Natural Law in Aquinas's "Treatise on Law"', *Journal of Philosophical Research* 17 (1992), pp. 147–64.
[73]Aquinas, *ST,* I–II, q. 94, a. 4.

regards the conclusions, but only as regards the principles which
are called common notions. But in matters of action, truth or
practical rectitude is not the same for all, as to matters of detail,
but only as to the general principles: and where there is the same
rectitude in matters of detail, it is not equally known to all.[74]

Aquinas distinguishes between speculative and practical reason.
The former means simply the use of the intellect in order to
understand and reason about the truth of things.[75] The term
'speculative' does not have an Hegelian or otherwise modern
sense. For Aquinas, speculative reason gives rise to mathematics
and other intellectual disciplines. Practical reason concerns human
acts in the interplay between intellect, the will and the passions. It
is governed by the first principle of the natural law: 'Good is to be
done and evil avoided.' Later in this article, Aquinas refers also to
how the natural law is fulfilled in those actions whereby 'everyone
is commanded to do to others as he would be done by' (ad 1). Of
central interest, however, is the gap between the general principles
of the natural law and the proper conclusions of practical reason.
Aquinas devotes several lines to an exposition of the differences
between speculative reason, which yields necessary results with
respect to the angles of a triangle, and practical reason, which
does not. Consider, he says, the proposition that goods entrusted
to another should be restored to their owner. In the majority of
cases, he says, it is likely to be reasonable that they should indeed
be restored. Yet there could be cases where this course of action
would be injurious. Of significance is the observation that no
particular, practical decisions can be deduced from the natural law
in any manner expected to be binding upon all persons. Aquinas
does not make this claim and is thus a different kind of thinker
from the generations of neo-Kantian theorists.

    Aquinas has in mind chiefly the applications of natural law to
particular cases. He is speaking of the gap between general principles
and the specifics of decision-making due to the contingencies of
daily existence. Even so, says Jean Porter, Aquinas's concession to
contingency is substantive: 'he . . . leaves open the possibility that

---

[74]Aquinas, ST, I–II, q. 94, a. 4c.
[75]R. J. Henle, S. J., The Treatise on Law: ST, I-II, qq. 90–97 (Notre Dame, IN:
University of Notre Dame Press, 1993), p. 262.

this diversity with respect to "rectitude" – that is to say, with the normative substance of the natural law – might be reflected as a communal level, and not just at the level of particular applications.'[76] In other words, Aquinas's theology of the natural law is more like a set of capacities, requirements and responsibilities than something to which reference can be made in a fixed way. Consider his answer to the question whether there is natural law in us:

> it is evident that all things partake somewhat of the eternal law, in so far as, namely, from its being imprinted on them, they derive their respective inclinations to their proper acts and ends. Now among all others, the rational creature is subject to Divine providence in the most excellent way, in so far as it partakes of a share of providence, by being provident both for itself and for others. Wherefore it has a share of the Eternal Reason, whereby it has a natural inclination to its proper act and end: and this participation of the eternal law in the rational creature is called the natural law.[77]

Here again we see that, for Aquinas, the essence of law is something pertaining to reason; law has a necessary reference or relation to reason. It 'is the essential use in which law is in the reason, functioning as regulating something else'.[78] It is important to disaggregate the different definitions of law. For any human instance of law to have the true nature of law, however, it must have some participation in reason. Human laws command, guide or forbid, to the extent that they participate in reason, which, in turn, derives from God's law or the divine *ratio*. Human law never ceases to be *human* law because the operation of human reason never becomes divine; it may never be pronounced God. By grace, the capacity to reason is given by God and may be drawn towards faith, and mingled with God's self-disclosure. At its best, human law is both proper to reason and potentially at least a participation in the divine understanding.

In addressing the question whether there is natural law in us, Aquinas's answer includes the specification of moral norms, but not

---

[76]Jean Porter, *The Recovery of Virtue: The Relevance of Aquinas for Christian Ethics* (Louisville, KY: Westminster/John Knox Press, 1990), p. 57n.
[77]Aquinas, *ST*, I–II, q. 91, a. 2.
[78]Henle, *The Treatise on Law*, p. 120n.

in a manner specific or concrete enough to yield guidance as to conduct. While committed to holding that specific requirements of the natural law are rationally justifiable, for example, that good is to be sought and evil avoided, he comes much closer to saying that the natural law is experienced in the anxieties of positive lawmaking rather than as some kind of reality outside of the mind in an ahistorical, fixed 'idea' or realm of facts to which humans should seek to correspond. The natural law, that is, participation by created beings in uncreated wisdom, yields universal norms.[79] There is a considerable gap, however, between these norms and specific instances of decision-making. 'The practical reason', writes Aquinas, 'is concerned with practical matters, which are singular and contingent: but not with necessary things, with which the speculative reason is concerned.'[80] Even supposing, therefore, that the law of nations is derived from the law of nature as conclusions are derived from premises, this is unlikely of itself to yield many specific principles of law. Moral reasoning is always contextual and embedded, requiring an element of improvisation because every agent is somehow confronted with novel circumstances and dilemmas.

Natural law reasoning as critique

This element of improvisation in natural law reasoning may be described as the critical endeavour of moving from confession, to critique and construction.[81] Broadly speaking, I take from both Barth and Gadamer that the temporal distance between ancient (including biblical) texts and the present day need no longer be conceived primarily as a gulf to be overcome because it separates past from present, but as filled with the continuity of theological engagement: 'time . . . is actually the supportive ground of the

---

[79]Aquinas, *ST*, I, q. 41, 3.
[80]Aquinas, *ST*, I–II, p. 91, a. 3, ad 3.
[81]Paul Ricoeur speaks of the movement 'from knowledge to critique' – his point being that no claim to knowledge is unmediated but that critique is possible nevertheless. See 'Hermeneutics and the Critique of Ideology', in *From Text to Action: Essays in Hermeneutics II*, trans. Kathleen Blamey and John B. Thompson (Evanston, IL: Northwestern University Press, 1991), ch. 13, pp. 270–306.

course of events in which the present is rooted.'[82] What Gadamer calls the effect (*Wirkung*) of a living tradition allows 'sacred time' in the present moment.[83] I broadly accept that Gadamer's hermeneutics treatment of 'effective history' (*Wirkungsgeschichte*) creates theoretical space in which to encounter Paul's engagement in various New Testament texts with issues of (Mosaic and trans-ethnic) law. In Gadamer's terms, we may reject 'the abstract anti-thesis between tradition and historical research, between history and the knowledge of it' and 'concretize' the moral import of biblical texts by reinterpreting their accounts of the divine command for own day.[84] Amidst all our questions about the modern entanglement in historical investigations, the inspired and holy status of the Bible remains a source of divine self-communication to us: 'A grammar of faith must deal with what actually happens when the call of God's word is heard.'[85] As Gadamer says of legal interpretation: 'The interpreter . . . finds his point of view already given, and does not choose it arbitrarily. Thus it is an essential condition of the possibility of hermeneutics that the law is binding on all members of the community in the same way.'[86] As the jurist bears a given relation to the law, so the believer operates within certain limits of faith and practice that are given in the tradition and cannot be chosen or abandoned arbitrarily.

There is no escaping the duality in thinking throughout biblical teaching and Christian tradition about the natural law as both something contained in the Decalogue and other biblical and traditional witness, and natural law as practical reasoning or a theory of action or speech. On the one hand, witness to the content of the natural law echoes down the centuries in Paul's words 'therefore you have no excuse' (Rom. 2.1). In every human situation, the injustice and violence of human law is inescapable but does not detract from the theological reality that all are guilty before God. The laws given to the world via Noah are valid for all and obligatory upon everyone because they issue from God (Gen. 9.4–6). Rom. 1.18–23 roars out the wrath and condemnation of

---

[82]Gadamer, *Truth and Method*, p. 297
[83]Gadamer, *Truth and Method*, p. 120.
[84]Gadamer, *Truth and Method*, pp. 283–84.
[85]Gadamer, *Truth and Method*, p. 525.
[86]Gadamer, *Truth and Method*, p. 325.

God upon the wickedness of all. None can plead ignorance, because for Jew and Gentile 'what can be known about God is plain because God has shown it to them' (Rom. 1.19). The availability of this knowledge renders guilty every person who turns away from it and follows senseless reasoning into the darkness of unbelief (Rom. 1.20–24). Paul relies on something like a doctrine of natural law to show that all people are guilty before God, and that all, both Jew and Gentile, are in need of salvation.[87]

On the other hand, Jesus asks why the people do not judge for themselves what is right (Lk. 12.15) and refers to civil rulers as God's servants for the good (Jn 19.11; see Rom. 13.1; 1 Pet. 2.13). Those who 'do not have the law' (Rom. 1.24) can still do what the law requires by virtue of the powers of their natural reason. Irenaeus picks up the subject of the natural law via a doctrine of creation. Arguing against any notion of God creating in accordance with pre-existent 'ideas', he affirms *creatio ex nihilo* and God's implantation in humans of reason, including the knowledge of good and evil.[88] Civil government in all its diversity among various peoples is a requirement for the correction to sin.[89] Clement of Alexandria taught that God created the world with a moral order.[90] Justin Martyr condemned the doctrine of relativity in morals because God begot from the beginning a rational power, the Logos, proceeding from himself.[91] Human reason is Christ in man; the universality of human rationality is explained with reference to God.[92] Clement of Alexandria taught that reason, which is found in all rational beings, is the natural moral law.[93] For Origen, reason is a 'footprint' of the divine will in humanity.[94] The Logos is the source of reason and knowledge of good.

---

[87]Subsequently, Irenaeus appears to have identified or treated as coterminous the Decalogue and the natural law (*Against Heresies,* in *Ante-Nicene Fathers* [ANF], ed. Philip Schaff, vol. 1: *The Apostolic Fathers with Justin Martyr and Irenaeus,* bk IV, ch. 15, §1). Clement of Alexandria taught that God created the world with a moral order (*Exhortation to the Heathen,* in *ANF,* vol. 2: *Fathers of the Second Century,* ch. 6). The Epistle of Barnabas spoke of the world's having a moral framework (*ANF,* vol. 1, chs. 19–20).

[88]Irenaeus, *Against Heresies,* bk IV, ch. 4, § 4.

[89]Irenaeus, *Against Heresies,* bk V, ch. 24, §§ 1–3.

[90]Clement of Alexandria, *Exhortation to the Heathen,* ch. 6.

[91]Justin Martyr, *Dialogue with Trypho, ANF,* vol. 1, ch. 61.

[92]Justin Martyr, *The First Apology, ANF,* vol. 1, chs. 6, 13, 15.

[93]Clement of Alexandria, *The Paedagogus, ANF,* vol. 2, chs. 2, 3, 7.

[94]Origen, *De Principiis,* bk I, ch. 1, §8; bk 1, ch. 5, §§1–5; bk II, ch. 9, §4.

Emphasis on the former recognizes that the natural law is something like a body of knowledge that may be specified with reference to the revealed laws of God, and explained and applied in diverse contexts, times and places. Emphasis on the latter conceives of natural law more like the activity of speech realized in the act or art of discursive practice. Without seeking to resolve this tension – between the general principles of the natural law and the command of God, respectively, and the practicalities of reasoning about human law, natural law reasoning understood in this project as less like adherence to a set of precepts that can be transposed into a system or theory than a set of requirements and responsibilities – the proposal to consider natural law reasoning as critique shifts the centre of gravity away from 'natural law' as a set of precepts and toward 'natural law reasoning' as more like a set of requirements and responsibilities. Without downplaying the tension between the natural law as having content and as being a responsibility that demands performance, the attempt to speak more about 'natural law reasoning' rather than 'the natural law' is intended to indicate the problems with any attempt to objectify and thence potentially instrumentalize the content of the natural law.

While heeding the divergence noted above, I hold that the natural law comprises for neither Barth nor Aquinas a set of precepts that yields clear notions about what kinds of legal institutions and juridical constitutions might be desirable. There can be no compromise on this point. Protestant Thomists still properly have Barth's '*Nein!*' ringing in their ears.[95] Instead, I suggest that we are urged by both Barth and Aquinas towards what, today, we might describe as a kind of hermeneutic reasoning that is not simply a matter of rewriting biblical texts but of thinking with scripture and tradition amidst historical, contextualized processes in which interpreter(s) ask about how to live in witness to the gospel of salvation. The task is not to chase certainty in moral reasoning by deducing principles or analogies from biblical texts or looking for what Gadamer calls

---

[95]Whether or not we contend that Barth misheard or misunderstood Emil Brunner, or hold that Barth's theology of incarnation requires him to say something about a point of contact between divine revelation and human capacity, the dangers that he flagged with respect to sources of 'natural' authority and knowledge of God's will outside of Christ are too serious to be forgotten. See Trevor Hart, 'The Barth-Brunner Debate Revisited', *Tyndale Bulletin* 44 (1993), p. 305.

'the phantom of a historical object'.[96] There can be no simple process of deduction that extracts meaning from the Bible and tradition that does not entail interpretation. Hence the emphasize on the performative nature of natural law reasoning, natural law reasoning as an act of human endeavour, casting the meaning of natural law in performative terms as reasoning that has to be done. All natural law reasoning is interpretation because the concerns of serious hermeneutic inquiry are integral to the practice or art of judgement-making. The task is to think about how best to aim at that which peace and good order requires, intrinsic to the requirements of common good, through the mediation of the appropriate institutions.

With Barth in particular, I understand Christian ethics and political theology to be a striving 'to understand the Word of God as the command of God', the effort of which is to discern how the divine command is directed to humanity.[97] Christian ethics and political theology can only proceed in the framework of 'the event of God's command and man's concrete obedience or disobedience'.[98] The Protestant Thomism that I advocate shares Barth's conviction that Christian ethics is concerned with God incarnate, the Word made flesh, before it is concerned with anything else, and is alert to his warning against 'the attempt to establish and justify the theologico-ethical inquiry within the framework and on the foundation of the presuppositions and methods of non-theological, of wholly human thinking and language'.[99] From Aquinas, I take questions about the relation of the good of 'the one' to 'the many', what it means to understand law as an ordinance of reason for the common good, commonality of intention with respect to the ends of law, substantive consideration of the common good, and more. Both assume that the Word of God has practical content but recognize also the gap between the natural law and the command of God, respectively, and the conclusions of practical reason.

More specifically, approaching natural law reasoning as critique, or a critical exercise in hermeneutics, entails exploring what it might mean with Aquinas to hold that law pertains to reason in these two

---

[96]Gadamer, *Truth and Method*, p. 299.
[97]Barth, *CD*, III/4, p. 4.
[98]Barth, *CD*, III/4, pp. 15–16.
[99]Barth, *CD*, II/2, p. 520.

ways. He writes that law pertains to reason: 'First, as in that which measures and rules: and since this is proper to reason, it follows that, in this way, law is in the reason alone. Secondly, as in that which is measured and ruled.'[100] All human things are subject to the eternal law.[101] Moreover, human law has the nature of law insofar as it participates in right reason.[102] Unjust laws that do not partake of right reason, says Aquinas, have the nature not of law but of violence. The sinful reality of the human condition means that there is no reliable way of attaining knowledge of when and how human law participates in right reason. All ways of so doing 'are imperfect, and to a certain extent destroyed'.[103] Humanity's basic inclination to good is impeded, darkened and weakened by sin. The working supposition nevertheless is that good human law participates in reason and tends away from violence.

My proposal is that (at least) three limits or tests should guide moral reasoning in Christian tradition with respect to international law: just peacemaking, good order, and common good. The obvious questions arise: are these limits or tests descriptive or normative? If descriptive, then have they been evidenced adequately by appropriate historical investigation? If normative, then on what authority? Such questions cannot all be treated in advance and will reoccur in subsequent chapters. The three proposed limits or tests – that is, 'the just peacemaking requirement', 'the good order requirement', and 'the common good requirement' – are not intended as comprehensive. I am not interested in providing a representatively Christian, let alone a comprehensive, map of what theological engagement with international law should entail. Put simply, I try to think with questions that attract sustained witness within scripture and tradition about the emergencies of today, some of which threaten the well-being of future generations.

Peacemaking

Just peacemaking is at the heart of Christian witness and tradition, not a bolt-on extra. The people of Israel were enjoined to 'depart

---

[100]Aquinas, *ST*, I–II q. 90, a. 1. ad. 1.
[101]Aquinas, *ST*, I–II, q. 93, a. 6.
[102]Aquinas, *ST*, I–II, q. 93, a. 3, ad. 2.
[103]Aquinas, *ST*, I–II, q. 93, a. 3, c.

from evil and do good; seek peace and pursue it' (Ps. 34.14). Isaiah foretells the time when the Prince of Peace will reign and 'of the increase of his government and peace, there will be no end' (Isa. 9.6–7). God's will for all creation is for peace. The believer's calling is to live in anticipation of the day when 'nation shall not lift up sword against nation, neither shall they learn war any more' (Isa. 2.4b). 'Blessed are the peacemakers, for they shall be called the children of God', says Jesus (Matt. 5.9). Peace is a characteristic of the kingdom of God (Rom. 14.17), the gift of God (Rom. 15.13) and a fruit of faith (Gal. 5.22), says Paul. The mysterious peace that the redeemed have with God through our lord Jesus Christ can, and must, be distinguished from human attempts at peacemaking. True justice and peace is found in Christ Jesus alone (Jn 14.27), whose reign of not of this world (Jn 18.36). Yet the unbridgeable distance between divine justice and peace, and frail human efforts at both, does not leave us without hope or responsibility.

I draw especially in what follows on Barth's refusal to normalize political violence, notably the treatment of war as part of a reflection on the sixth commandment: 'you shall not murder' (Heb. *ratsach*). Barth wrote presciently in 1960:

> [I]n a way very different from previous generations we can and should realize that the real issue in war, and an effective impulse toward it, is much less man himself and his vital needs than the economic power which in war is shown not so much to be possessed by man as to possess him, and this to his ruin, since instead of helping him to live and let live it forces him to kill and be killed.[104]

Christian ethics cannot insist too loudly, says Barth, that slaughter might well be murder, and therefore 'this final possibility should not be seized like any other, but only at the very last hour in the darkest of days'.[105] Christian ethics must insist that war is 'an *opus alienum*' for the state.[106] Killing is not necessarily integral to the role of state, not its *opus proprium*, as given by God to governing authorities as servants for good (Rom. 13.1–7). Christian ethics must insist that

---

[104]Barth, *CD*, III/4, p. 452.
[105]Barth, *CD*, III/4, p. 456.
[106]Barth, *CD*, III/4, p. 456.

killing is alien to the good functioning of a state. For this reason, it is appropriate that Christian ethics and the churches should have the effect of delaying the state's decision to kill: 'The Church and theology have first and supremely to make this detached and delaying movement.'[107] This does not mean that they will always assert that war is wholly unacceptable but that they will be in no position authentically and authoritatively to say this unless they have previously thrown their weight on the side of non-violence.[108] Today, this delaying movement on the part of Christian ethics and the churches might take many and diverse forms. At the least, it should mean critical exposure of attempts to decrease constraints on the use of force.

Against a political and legal backdrop where legal positivism is predominant, Barth's reminder is that moral responsibility with respect to military force lies with every citizen and not merely politicians and generals: 'To-day everyone is a military person, either directly or indirectly. . . . everyone participates in the suffering and action which war demands. . . . Each individual is himself . . . the people, the state; each is himself a belligerent.'[109] Gone are the days when the monarchy, nobility and military classes took such decisions to themselves. Liberal democracy means that there is no such thing as an uncommitted spectator. Regardless of the important criticisms voiced by radical democrats about the failings of current democratic practices and their identification of the need to restore political power to the people by fostering new ways in which new voices might speak, welcome diversity, find ways of broadening the spectrum of political engagement, etc.,[110] it remains true nevertheless that every member of a democratic society – especially though not exclusively those of an age to vote – is involved morally in the actions of government. Barth writes:

> war is an action in which the nation and all its members are actually engaged in killing. All are involved in this action either as those who desire or as those who permit it, and in any case as those who contribute to it in some sector. All are directly

---

[107]Barth, CD, III/4, p. 456.
[108]Barth, CD, III/4, p. 457.
[109]Barth, CD, III/4, p. 457.
[110]Chantal Mouffe, On the Political (London: Routledge, 2005) p. 88.

responsible in respect of the question whether it is commanded killing or forbidden murder.[111]

By 'commanded killing', Barth means that which the individual must see as the will of God that he should not on any account contradict.[112] He does not mean, I suggest, that every individual has direct access to the mind of God with respect to particular human affairs; such knowledge is beyond the reach of finite minds. Rather, every individual be confident that the terrible reality of killing is a responsible act and necessary for true peace. Every individual is asked whether they are working for 'the righteous inner peace which cannot lead to war, or whether he is contributing to a rotten and unjust peace which contains the seeds of war'.[113]

Good order

The second proposed limit or test concerns why and how the question of the authority and normativity of international law may be addressed in terms of what good order requires – this because the authority of human law pertains somehow to the normative order given to creation by God, to which human practices tend naturally. In the beginning, the Spirit of God brought forth order from the world which was without form and void (Gen. 1.1–2). 'For God is not a God of disorder but of peace' (*akatastasia* – meaning disorder, disturbance, instability or confusion; see 1 Cor. 14.33 NIV). The Spirit of God raised up wise leaders to govern his people with justice (Num. 11; Judg. 2.16–23). Consequently, the importance of (national and) international law in Christian tradition may be understood in terms of what order entails.

Augustine wrote in *De Ordine*, his response to a trilogy of dialogues by Cicero, about the divine ordering of the world and why human problems living in the world are the result of failure to comprehend rather than God's lack of design. Understanding what order entails, he writes, is one way in which human beings can come to God: 'order is that which will lead us to God, if we

---

[111]Barth, *CD*, III/4, p. 454.
[112]Barth, *CD*, III/4, p. 465.
[113]Barth, *CD*, III/4, p. 465.

hold to it during life'.[114] Calvin spoke of the 'order of nature' as nothing else than obedience to the divine will, the authority of which shines forth before heaven and earth.[115] Aquinas's jurisprudence informed traditions of international law (Vitoria, Grotius, Suarez, Pufendorf and more) that tended to defend an account of moral judgement as a rational process that attends to the relation between the good of 'the whole' and that of 'the part'. The requirement for order in human life, including relations of appropriate authority, lawmaking, enforcement and sanction, are necessary elements in the social life of rational animals. Judgements about what this ordering entails inevitably involve significant degrees of contingency, fallibility and diverse specification of positive law, but the natural human desire for order and well-being requires communally shared deliberation and adequate structures for social life. Nevertheless, the question of the authority and normativity of international law may be approached in terms of the requirements of good order.

By implication, the 'rule of law' in the international arena may be understood in terms of international order; international law being understood as a mode of ordering among nations, peoples, transnational corporations and individuals. The inevitable and unavoidable reality, of course, is that the requirements of 'order' are rarely capable of being set against a set of clearly identifiable precepts but must be instantiated amidst the disorder and contingency of international affairs. Good order is rarely to be measured against an a priori standard but must be effected every day to the best of human capability. Ethical responsibilities are always contextual and embedded and thus require an element of improvisation because every agent is somehow confronted with novel circumstances and dilemmas.[116] Even so, what we may call the 'good order requirement' is fundamental.

---

[114]Augustine, *On Order*, trans. Silvano Burruso (Chicago: St Augustine's Press, 2007), bk 1, First Debate, §§5–6, pp. 16–20; Second Debate, §9, p. 30.

[115]John Calvin, *Institutes*, vol. 1, p. 25.

[116]Moral improvisation has been considered recently by Martha Nussbaum, Barbara Herman and Cora Diamond, and Sam Well, among others; see Martha C. Nussbaum, *Love's Knowledge: Essays on Philosophy and Literature* (New York: Oxford University Press, 1990), p. 91. Nussbaum unpacks the metaphor of theatrical improvisation further on p. 94.

Common good

Third, the question of the authority and normativity of international law may be addressed in terms of human obligation towards common good. An implication is that, unlike the legitimacy-based argument propounded by Goldsmith and Posner, and other theorists who empty all aspects of the question of authority into the exercise of democracy, the question of answerability (in Protestant Thomist perspective) is not satisfied by the exercise of democracy alone. I shall argue instead that, in addition to an account of the authority of law that appeals only to the intrinsic value of democratic procedure, it is necessary to ask whether democratic procedure(s) make good decisions. Instead of focusing exclusively on the conditions required to ensure emancipative, communicative reason, appropriate procedures and fora for the processes for the formation of rational opinion and reasonable public discourse, it is necessary to concentrate also on questions of what constitute the *telos* of democratic procedure. Hence I shall argue that the question of democratic deficit is not paramount in consideration of the authority of international law. While there must be appropriate institutions and systems at the international level to facilitate efficient and effective argumentation between nations, the question of good law is not exhausted by the provision of equitable procedures or enhanced democratic accountability but also requires justification with reference to the proper ends of lawmaking.

Given that the weight of attention in jurisprudence and political theory has fallen in recent years on questions of procedure (Rawls, Habermas, Benhabib), I devote energy in this book to the 'common good requirement' of good law in addition to the 'procedural requirement', with its questions of democratic legitimacy and more. Both are important, but I do not want to ease the tension between the common good requirement and the procedural requirement of good law but, rather, to concentrate on the former because this is where overtly theological voices are likely to be able to contribute most. The requirements of procedural justification are important and necessary but do not exhaust the requirements of good law because it belongs to the notion of human law to be 'ordained to the common good', that is, oriented towards the common *felicitas*.[117] Most attention in Christian tradition has been devoted to the requirements of the common good at relatively local or national levels but the realities of globalization now demand more. David Hollenbach wrote in 2002 of 'the birthpangs of a transnational common good' and asked what kind of normative considerations were required.[118] This book may be located with reference to, and understood as a continuation of, Hollenbach's initiative.

Lawmakers and politicians concerned to exercise their democratic duty appropriately are likely to be concerned to ensure that laws and other normative standards will make claims of both kinds; that is, they will be both procedurally legitimate and oriented towards the common good. Nevertheless, international law is plagued by this deep-seated tension especially. Hence the need to look at the relationship between procedure and *telos* in reference to the question of global common good, and to move between the two approaches to accountability. The potential criticism is that any such concern for two approaches to accountability will inevitably vacillate unstably between each; it is not possible to effect a system that offers a unified conception of the authority of law. This tension is unavoidable and ineradicable, not because these theses are connected to divergent theories (ancient or medieval versus modern) but because it is at the heart of fallible human lawmaking.

---

[117]Aquinas, *ST*, I–II, q. 95, a. 3, sed contra.
[118]David Hollenbach, S. J., *The Common Good and Christian Ethics* (Cambridge: Cambridge University Press, 2002), p. 212.

3

Jus Cogens Norms and the Impurity of Natural Law Reasoning

'On no subject of human interest, except theology . . . has there been so much loose writing and nebulous speculations as on international law.'[1] Hans J. Morgenthau cites these words of John Chipman Gray in the opening pages of an essay on international law in the widely influential collection of essays, *Dilemmas of Politics*. His point is that international law is beset by vagueness with respect to the binding force of its instruments and riddled with problems pertaining to enforcement and judicial function, not to mention the problem of the veto under the provisions of the UN Charter which 'eliminates for all practical purposes' actions to restrain the great powers.[2] His implied point is that theology tends towards the platitudinous and speculative. When brought together, there is a double risk of nonsense! Whether amused or incensed by Morgenthau's style, his quip asks theologians and others interested in international law to think hard about reasonability, normativity, legitimacy, enforceability and more. What characterizes the rational nature of law? What kinds of norms are created and sustained in international law? Why are they binding? What kinds of argument might be employed when a nation-state wishes to ignore or circumvent a particular law? What accounts for the legal, moral

---

[1]Hans J. Morgenthau, *Dilemmas of Politics* (Chicago: University of Chicago Press, 1958), p. 216.
[2]Morgenthau, *Dilemmas of Politics*, p. 303.

and/or theological 'ought' of the law's normative force? Why should a major world power meet obligations that do not appear to be in its interests?

On the reasonability of law

Of interest in this chapter are questions about the reasonability of law, and what it means to advocate natural law reasoning in the context of realist claims that inter alia international law need not be heeded when contrary to short- or medium-term national interests, and lacking the legitimacy of democratic process. The two main arguments for the justification of so-called torture memos authorizing controversial interrogation techniques were the legal self-sufficiency of states and the democratic deficit of international law. Together these arguments were plied so effectively that, as O'Connell summarizes aptly, 'by the 1990s, international law was increasingly being mischaracterized as weak, unimportant or even dangerous – nothing that should fetter the superior American state. And Bush officials were able to find in the Constitution support for a strong-man leader above the law in wartime'.[3] Of interest in this chapter are the kinds of response that might be deemed reasonable. More specifically: Why might the believer and their dialogue partners claim it reasonable to maintain a default position in favour of adherence to international norms that prohibit torture? Can international common good be considered substantively as having content shared by all or merely as the pursuit by nation-states of national goods, that is, as the aggregate of individual goods?

Discussion is focussed on the status of *jus cogens* norms – especially the prohibition against torture – and the status of such norms if/when not originating in a treaty or other inter- or multi-state similar agreement. Here challenges from realists along the lines of Morgenthau that the normative standards of international law (especially the vagueness of customary international law which includes *jus cogens* norms) can or should be overridden by national

---

[3]Scott Horton, 'Six Questions for Mary Ellen O'Connell on the Power of International Law', *Harper's Magazine*, 6 December 2008 www.harpers.org/archive/2008/12/hbc-90003966 [accessed 10 June 2010].

interest are especially potent. We concentrate on *jus cogens* norms especially because they represent aspects of international law that political realists find most lacking in intelligible meaning. The challenge from Goldsmith and Posner et al., is that *jus cogens* norms are especially beset by vagueness, and lack either treaty-based or democratic legitimacy. Any association of these norms with moral claims is risible. What is especially nonsensical about international law, *jus cogens* norms in particular, for Morgenthau and his successors is not that its various precepts and rules can serve the national interest but that some people suggest that it has moral force. Suggestions to this effect smack typically, say Goldsmith and Posner, of 'moral or religious rhetoric' used to persuade citizens of a non-existent responsibility.[4] International law cannot be about morality but the balance of power between nations and the pursuit of national interests. Hence they apply rational choice theory to decisions affecting the long term, and frame policy discussions with reference to hypothetical games such as the Prisoner's Dilemma, in which decisions are evaluated according to the optimal outcome for the isolated 'I' (or nation).[5]

The political realist notion of morality is, however, far narrower and more limited than Aquinas's understanding of the relation of the good of 'the part' or 'the one only' to the good of 'the whole'. At its most basic, Aquinas's political realism entails the recognition that the good of every living creature on planet earth is somehow tied to the good of every other. Virtuous living is not solely other-regarding. Self-interest does not necessarily equate to self-centredness but is to be addressed in its proper relation to wider, collective goods. Natural self-love is for Aquinas the drive to preserve life. Subsequent forms of self-interest are judged according to how they participate in rationality. 'Even the lower appetitive powers are called rational, in so far as "they partake of reason in some sort"'.[6] The truest self-love consists in turning oneself towards God in search of the *visio Dei*. Aquinas's focus is less on how morality can be saved from consideration of self-interest than on how self-interest is guided by reason's command; reason's striving after human fulfilment;

---

[4]Jack L. Goldsmith and Eric A. Posner, *The Limits of International Law* (Oxford: Oxford University Press, 2005), p. 184.
[5]Goldsmith and Posner, *The Limits of International Law*, p. 13.
[6]Aquinas, *ST*, I–II, q. 24, a. 1, citing Aristotle's *Nicomachean Ethics*.

reason's directedness towards the truth, the common good and thus to God. Of interest in this comparison of different types of realism is the (un)reasonability of law in relation to common good.

Debate about whether and/or why nations have a moral obligation to comply with international law is often construed in terms of tension between Morgenthau-type realism and neo-Kantian discourse-oriented cosmopolitanism. Hence, later sections of the chapter look also at problems of legitimate law as discussed by Jürgen Habermas and related thinkers. While, from one direction, political realists raise questions about national interest and democratic deficit, neo-Kantian cosmopolitans raise different questions from another direction about why and how the legitimacy of the *ius cosmopoliticum* resides in democratic process. The claim is that Thomistic natural law reasoning is, potentially at least, better able to cope with the intractable disagreement that characterizes twenty-first-century global relations with respect to the power and purpose of international law than some realist sceptics allow, especially as this concerns normative standards that derive from elsewhere than treaty or democratically achieved consensus. A restatement of Thomist natural law reasoning is potentially more realistic – in that it better relates the good of the one to the many – and hence better able to cope with today's global uncertainties than prominent modes of secularist political realism (e.g. Goldsmith and Posner), and more adequately cosmopolitan than selected examples of neo-Kantian approaches to the legitimacy and constitutionalization of international law through democratic process.

These potentially vast areas of discussion crystalize theoretically, for our purposes at least, around whether primacy belongs to the intellect or will. This question of whether primacy belongs to the intellect or will is an old scholastic question that might seem outdated in the twenty-first century but underlies many significant present-day debates, including whether nations have no moral obligation to comply with international law because of its supposed democratic deficit, or whether torture is to be accepted if/when a majority votes in support. When we are told that laws instituted in liberal democracies are binding because they express the will of the people, we might be satisfied with the practical significance of these words merely because the law is born of the sovereign will of the people, or we might want to determine further whether the laws in question can also be arrived at rationally. At issue is whether the sheer fact that the laws instantiate the will of the people is enough to exclude them from other tests of reasonableness. Does a law need no other ground than that it has been chosen by a sovereign will? Or is something to be gained by reclaiming a teleological perspective on the reasonability of law? More specifically: Is it reasonable for a nation-state to ignore or circumvent *jus cogens* norms that prohibit torture when, seemingly, not in its immediate interests? It is reasonable to include the democratic deficit of international law in this complaint? How much should it matter that *jus cogens* norms do not typically have a treaty-based status in international law? What if a democratic majority were to support state-sponsored torture?

Legal prohibitions against torture

It might be helpful to comment briefly on legal prohibitions against torture. Article 5 of the UN Declaration of Human Rights states: 'No one shall be subjected to torture or to cruel, inhuman or degrading treatment or punishment.' Article 4 of the 1984 UN Convention against Torture, to which the United Kingdom is a party, criminalizes 'an act by any person which constitutes complicity or participation in torture'. The 1998 Rome Statute of the International Criminal Court extends criminal responsibility where military commanders and civilian superiors 'should have known' that international crimes were being committed but 'failed to take all necessary and reasonable measures within his or her power to prevent or repress their commission'.[7] The Declaration of Human Rights is technically not legally binding but was ratified by proclamation by the General Assembly on 10 December 1948 with a count of 48 votes to none, with only eight abstentions. The Convention against Torture and Rome Statute are open for signature by all states. In addition to these measures that invite obvious and explicit consent from nation-states are *jus cogens* norms that, traditionally, have not been contracted for or agreed explicitly.

---

[7]Philippe Sands, QC, summarizes international law on torture in 'Rules Did Nothing to Stop Detainee Abuse', *The Guardian*, 18 June 2009.

Few legal textbooks say much more than that *jus cogens* norms exist and that certain human rights standards – for example, the right to life – are *jus cogens*. Nor have they been derived customarily from written or otherwise positive laws. Something higher (or deeper) than the agreement of states or individuals, positive law whether national or international, has given rise to these norms that have somehow attracted, and continue to attract, widespread accord. They function differently from positive legal norms, even when enshrined in constitutional frameworks. There is no unbroken line of development of *jus cogens* norms in international law from Cicero or Grotius to the present day. Recent debate tends to begin with reference to Article 53 of the 1969 Vienna Convention on the Law of Treaties, which states that treaties in conflict with peremptory norms are void.[8] This is not to say that *jus cogens* norms were not operative international law prior to 1969 but that this treaty drew together and codified the wealth of customary law and treaties that were typically recognized between states.[9] Karl Zemanek, a member of the Austrian delegation to the conference that drafted the Vienna Convention, noted that the rules of interpretation given in Articles 31 and 32 'are teleological elements which militate against a narrow literal construction of treaty texts'.[10] Article 31 reads:

Recourse may be had to supplementary means of interpretation, including the preparatory work of the treaty and the circumstances of its conclusion, in order to confirm the meaning resulting from the application of article 31, or to determine the meaning when the interpretation according to article 31:

(a) leaves the meaning ambiguous or obscure; or

(b) leads to a result which is manifestly absurd or unreasonable.

---

[8]Alexander Orakhelashvili, *Peremptory Norms in International Law* (Oxford: Oxford University Press, 2008).

[9]"It is noteworthy that the International Court of Justice stated in the Judgment on the Arbitral Award of 31 July 1989 that ". . . [a]rticles 31 and 32 of the Vienna Convention on the Law of Treaties may in many respects be considered as a codification of existing customary international law . . ." (*I.C.J. Reports 1991*, pp. 69–70, para. 48' (Karl Zemanek, *Introduction*, Vienna Convention on the Law of Treaties, 23 May 1969 http://untreaty.un.org/cod/avl/ha/vclt/vclt.html [accessed 17 February 2013]).

[10]Zemanek, *Introduction*, p. 2.

We return below to the complex relationship between teleology and deontology that cannot be allowed to rigidify into opposition, or a tragic dilemma, if practical reasoning is to remain possible.

The Vienna Convention defined a peremptory norm as 'a norm accepted and recognized by the international community of States as a whole as a norm from which no derogation is permitted and which can be modified only by a subsequent norm of general international law having the same character.'[11] This, says Alexander Orakhelashvili, is a clear example of the hierarchy of norms in international law where peremptory norms prevail not because the States involved have so decided but because these norms are intrinsically superior to the positive law of states. Orakhelashvili adopts a particular stance with respect to *jus cogens* norms. He holds that these norms function as so essential to the international community for its welfare and even survival that they must be regarded as inderogable. This contrasts with, for instance, Ulf Linderfalk, who denies the very existence of *jus cogens* norms in positive international law.[12] Mindful of these differences, we note that for the Vienna Convention, *jus cogens* norms are deemed to be mandatory and imperative in all circumstances; they are to apply whatever the will and attitude of individual states and cannot be modified or excluded.

Consider further the Third Restatement of US foreign relations law. This work of a group of scholars is not binding law but is nevertheless widely regarded as 'an authoritative and prominent interpretation' and exerts great influence as a summation of the customary international law and international agreements to which the United States is a party.[13] Issued in 1987, the Third Restatement

---

[11]Orakhelashvili, *Peremptory Norms in International Law*, p. 8.

[12]Ulf Linderfalk, 'The Effect of Jus Cogens Norms: Whoever Opened Pandora's Box, Did You Ever Think about the Consequences?' *European Journal of International Law* 18 (2007), p. 871 www.ejil.org/pdfs/18/5/248.pdf [accessed 17 February 2013].

[13]I acknowledge my indebtedness in this section to Mary Ellen O'Connell and am grateful for permission to cite her work. I draw heavily upon her insights but remain responsible for any errors. I also draw from Mitsue Inazumi, *Universal Jurisdiction in Modern International Law: Expansion of N Jurisdiction for Prosecuting Serious Crimes under International Law* (Utretcht: G. J. Wiarda Institute, 2005), pp. 75–76.

specifies the following list of human rights norms that are widely accepted as customary law and from which no derogation is permitted:

Customary International Law of Human Rights

A state violates international law if, as a matter of state policy, it practices, encourages or condones

  a. genocide,
  b. slavery or slave trade,
  c. the murder or causing the disappearance of individuals,
  d. torture or other cruel, inhuman, or degrading treatment or punishment,
  e. prolonged arbitrary detention
  f. systematic racial discrimination.[14]

The prohibition against torture is especially interesting because it demonstrates that the law is not static in terms of what is and is not widely recognized as *jus cogens*.

The prohibition against torture has not always been treated as *jus cogens* but relatively recently has been recognized as such. The list of core *jus cogens* rights, now commonly recognized by a number of authorities in international law, includes the right to be free from aggression, genocide and mass killing, slavery, torture, cruel, inhuman and degrading treatment (CID) and widespread racial discrimination. So, for instance, the International Court of Justice in the 1970 *Barcelona Traction* case cited all of these, except torture and cruel, inhuman and degrading treatment, as belonging in a special category:

When a State admits into its territory foreign investments or foreign nationals, whether natural or juristic persons, it is bound to extend to them the protection of the law and assumes obligations concerning the treatment to be afforded them. These obligations, however, are neither absolute nor unqualified. In

---

[14]American Law Institute, *Restatement of the Law, Third: The Foreign Relations Law of the United States*, vol. 2 (1987), §702, p. 161, cited in Henry J. Steiner et al., *International Human Rights in Context: Law, Politics, Morals*, 3rd ed. (Oxford: Oxford University Press, 2008), p. 172.

particular, an essential distinction should be drawn between the obligations of a State towards the international community as a whole, and those arising vis-à-vis another State in the field of diplomatic protection. By their very nature the former are the concern of all States. In view of the importance of the rights involved, all States can be held to have a legal interest in their protection; they are obligations *erga omnes*.

Such obligations derive, for example, in contemporary international law, from the outlawing of acts of aggression, and of genocide, as also from the principles and rules concerning the basic rights of the human person, including protection from slavery and racial discrimination. Some of the corresponding rights of protection have entered into the body of general international law . . . others are conferred by international instruments of a universal or quasi-universal character.[15]

Today, international lawyers agree readily that the ban on torture and cruel, inhuman and degrading treatment is *jus cogens*. I cite a paper by Mary Ellen O'Connell:[16]

In 1984, torture and CID were absolutely prohibited by the Convention against Torture, which entered into force 1987 and today has 140 states party. The Geneva Conventions with 192 parties also prohibit torture and list the infliction of torture and cruelty among the Conventions' 'grave breaches'. The International Criminal Tribunal for Yugoslavia called the ban on torture a *jus cogens* norm that is superior to contrary national law. The *Restatement* has included torture and CID among the human rights that are also *jus cogens* norms since 1987.

Other norms may also reflect sufficient consensus to be *jus cogens* norms. In addition to the norms listed in the *Barcelona Traction* case and the ban on torture and CID, the *Restatement* also includes 'murder or causing the disappearance of individuals' and 'prolonged arbitrary detention'. The Inter-American Commission on Human Rights has found a *jus cogens*

---

[15]*Barcelona Traction, Light and Power Co., Ltd. (Belg. v. Spain)*, I.C.J. 3, 14 (5 February 1970), §§ 33–34.
[16]Mary Ellen O'Connell, 'Affirming the Ban on Harsh Interrogation', *Ohio State Law Journal* 66 (2005), pp. 1231–67.

norm prohibiting the use of the death penalty to punish crimes committed by juveniles. A European Court of Justice court of first instance has indicated that the arbitrary taking of property by the state violates *jus cogens*. Greek and Italian courts have found *jus cogens* violations committed by Germany for forced labor during the Second World War. As a consequence, those courts have lifted Germany's sovereign immunity from civil liability claims for over sixty-year-old offenses. Germany has brought a case against Italy in the International Court of Justice challenging the legality of lifting immunity. The International Court of Justice is likely, therefore, to hear its first case squarely considering the implications of violating *jus cogens* norms on secondary principles of international law, in particular, sovereign immunity.

Identified clearly is a growing acceptance within the international legal system that the prohibition against torture and cruel, inhuman and degrading treatment is *jus cogens*. Analogous to Aquinas's comments on whether the natural law can be changed, O'Connell's observation is that a change in *jus cogens* norms is permitted by way of addition but not subtraction.[17]

Is it then reasonable for a nation-state to ignore or circumvent *jus cogens* norms that prohibit torture when, seemingly, not in its immediate interests, and is it reasonable to include the democratic deficit of international law in this complaint? Goldsmith and Posner, for instance, do not hesitate to affirm international law as 'endogenous' to national interest and legitimated somehow within a democratic system but dismiss that which is merely an 'exogenous' restriction.[18] Most nation-states heed the requirements

---

[17]Aquinas, *ST,* I–II, q. 94, a. 5, c.

[18]Goldsmith and Posner, *The Limits of International Law,* p. 13. See also Anne van Aaken, 'To Do Away with International Law? Some Limits to "The Limits of International Law"', *European Journal of International Law* 17 (2006), pp. 289–308. Goldsmith and Posner are more interested in how law circumscribes the possibilities of actions rather than how a precept or prohibition came to be law. International law is self-evidently both endogenous to state interest and an exogenous restriction when obeyed in instances when not immediately and obviously in a given state's interest. The distinction here is between law obeyed because it accords with a state's interest and law obeyed for fear of sanction or respect for international norms. A second premise they advance is that there is no duty to engage in the strong cosmopolitan actions.

of international law most of the time. Their point, however, is that none should be required to intend the common good materially considered through international law.

The problem of democratic deficit

In their rational choice approach to international relations, Goldsmith and Posner understand the nation-state to be the central political actor in the international political system, and hold the nation-state responsible only for acting in a rational manner to maximize possible gains for its citizens.[19] The model of rationality employed is bounded by these constraints; international law is thought to promote co-operation between nation-states only under the restrict conditions of rational functionalism.[20] Witness how

---

[19]On this, see Beth A. Simmons and Lisa L. Martin, 'International Organizations and Institutions', in ed. Walter Carlsnaes, Thomas Risse and Beth A. Simmons (eds), *Handbook of International Relations* (London: Sage, 2001), pp. 195–96.

[20]Morgenthau's comments in 1965 about the 'crisis' of the United Nations are illuminating in this respect. Reviewing Richard N. Gardiner's *In Pursuit of World Order*, he echoed Gardiner's concern that the United States, the most powerful nation in the world, was less able to employ its power alone, in pursuit of national ends, than at any previous point in history. He further supported Gardiner in positing that debate about the United Nations needs to move beyond the dichotomy of emotional proponents versus opponents of international organization: 'What we really need is to accept the fact that international organizations are here to stay and to turn to the much more difficult question of how we can use them better to promote our national interest. We need to discuss the U.N. and other international organizations in operational rather than in symbolic terms' (Hans J. Morgenthau, 'The UN in Crisis', *The New York Review of Books*, 25 March 1965). Morgenthau's point was not that the United Nations cannot serve the international common good but that this does not require that every nation know and desire the same object(s). The common good may be understood as co-existence in mutual national interest without necessary regard to those nation-states or others who are not party to these interests. Thus Morgenthau's approach to international common good does not include the proposal of shared, substantive deliberation as a necessary or sufficient cause. This deficiency as compared to Aquinas's account of the reasonability of law is a major point of tension between the two approaches. This does not mean that Morgenthau can be categorized as a legal voluntarist for whom the will of the nation is the sole or fundamental agency or principle in law. This would be a mistake; his writings are often seen as mitigating the extreme voluntarism of Karl Schmitt and others (see Michael C. Williams, 'Why Ideas Matter in International Relations: Hans Morgenthau, Classical Realism, and the Moral Construction of Power Politics', *International Organization* 58 [October 2004], pp. 633–65). As Morgenthau saw

Goldsmith and Posner argue throughout *The Limits of International Law* to the effect that 'nations have no moral obligation to comply with international law' because of its democratic deficit.[21] They posit that international law has (or should have) no moral force comparable to the moral force of domestic law, which is subject to democratic procedure, and thus the former has no democratic pedigree or epistemic authority:

> The reason that [international law] can exert no moral force comparable to the moral force of domestic law is that it has no democratic pedigree or epistemic authority; it reflects what states have been doing in the recent past and does not necessarily reflect the moral judgments or interests or needs of individuals.[22]

Goldsmith and Posner recognize that it is almost always in the long-term interest of the United States to comply with international law. As the torture memos debacle demonstrates, however, leading politicians and theorists recognized only practical reasons for compliance. The normativity of international law was held to be conditional upon its being in the interest of their country to comply. For Goldsmith and Posner too, there are practical and political reasons why it is good to comply with international law in most instances but no reasons beyond this. They transpose the question of the authority of international law into the question of democratic legitimacy within a given state and conclude that, because of the democratic deficit of international law: 'International legality does not impose any moral obligations.'[23]

Goldsmith and Posner are interpreted (approvingly) by one reviewer as arguing that international law conflicts with the higher principle of democratic sovereignty: 'as a normative principle, when such law interferes with a state's (especially a liberal democratic

---

with clarity: 'The foundation of the binding force of "positive" law can logically be found, not in this "positive" law itself, but only outside it' (*Dilemmas of Politics*, p. 219).

[21] This is Goldsmith and Posner's own summary in 'The New International Law Scholarship', *Chicago Public Law and Legal Theory Working Paper*, no. 126 (May 2006), University of Chicago Law School, p. 463 www.law.uchicago.edu/files/files/126.pdf [accessed 17 February 2013].

[22] Goldsmith and Posner, *The Limits of International Law* , p. 199.

[23] Goldsmith and Posner, *The Limits of International Law*, p. 197.

state's) own interests, that law does not need to be followed.'[24] If it is supposed that the highest law for the United States is the Constitution, the question arises as to the authority of international law. If elected representatives in a democracy make the law, then the law that they produce carries sufficient higher moral weight than international law. Put simply, asks Lieutenant Colonel Walter M. Hudson, what if the majority of the population of a given nation does not want the state to enforce a set of international standards? If the electorate votes for a candidate who supports waterboarding, that carries more moral weight than the prohibition under international law of torture and other cruel, inhuman or degrading treatment or punishment. When combined with the paralysis that often besets the United Nations, and a growing sense of the importance of the flexible use of force in international affairs, the seeming democratic deficit of international law is seen by some as placing not only the legal but also the moral authority of international law under question.[25]

At base, Morgenthau, Goldsmith and Posner operate with an understanding of politics derived from the will of sovereign states. They offer a version of legal voluntarism in which law is primarily an act of sovereign will and might, at the extreme, be an arbitrary expression of an absolute, irrational will. For Morgenthau, legal validity can be achieved only inside the state: 'Man cannot achieve his *telos* outside the state. So the state is essential for the individual's ability to achieve his purpose in life.'[26] This reality is not, he says, because he wishes it this way or an ephemeral historic situation but because it is of the nature of things. 'Where there is neither community of interest nor balance of power there is no international law.'[27] Morgenthau affirms that law demands rules that are rational in character but understands this to mean that nation-states are able to employ their power, including legislative power, in pursuit

---

[24]Walter M. Hudson, review essay, *The Limits of International Law* by Jack Goldsmith, *The Army Lawyer*, pamphlet 27–50–400 (September 2006), p. 32 www. loc.gov/rr/frd/Military_Law/pdf/09–2006.pdf [accessed 20 April 2011].

[25]On other challenges to the legitimacy of international law, see Allen Buchanan, 'The Legitimacy of International Law', in John Tasioulas and Samantha Besson (eds), *The Philosophy of International Law* (Oxford: Oxford University Press, 2010), pp. 85–7.

[26]Morgenthau, *Dilemmas of Politics*, p. 28.

[27]Morgenthau, *Dilemmas of Politics*, p. 274.

of national ends. Morgenthau and his successors reject traditional notions of customary international law in favour of a relatively unrestricted pursuit of national interest.

Nor are they alone in expressing frustration at the uncertainty and lack of clarity that besets aspects of international law. Hans Kelsen described customary international law as 'unconscious and unintentional law-making'.[28] Antonio Cassese describes the uncertainty that besets the processes by which custom develops to become normative: 'custom is made up of two elements: general practice, or *usus* or *diuturnitas*, and the conviction that such practice, reflects, or amounts to, law (*opinio juris*) or is required by social, economic, or political exigencies (*opinio necessitatis*).'[29] Anthony d'Amato elaborates upon this tension by positing that there is no way of separating the *opinio juris* from the rule of international law itself because a rule cannot be accepted before it has arisen.[30] No rule in international law can be dependent, he says, upon subjective intent or a feeling that international jurists might have about whether a law is binding; such vagueness amounts to nonsense in the international arena. Only treaty-based international law – often agreed after conflict or dispute – is intellectually and politically robust enough to meet standards of legitimacy.

The problem of vagueness

At the international level, the implications are at least twofold. The first implication is that international law is deemed inferior to domestic law and does not command the same levels of conformity because of its democratic deficit. The second is that only treaty-based international law is regarded as intellectually and politically robust enough to demand adherence; treaty-based law has a basis in consent, whereas the legitimacy of customary international law is more vague and therefore less deserving of respect. One of

---

[28]Hans Kelsen, *Principles of International Law* (1952; rpt Clark, NJ: The Lawbook Exchange, 2003), pp. 307–8.
[29]Antonio Cassese, *International Law*, 2nd edn (Oxford: Oxford University Press, 2005), p. 156.
[30]Anthony d'Amato, 'Customary International Law' (2009), Audiovisual Library of International Law, UN Office of Legal Affairs http://untreaty.un.org/cod/avl/ls/D-Amato_IL.html [accessed 17 February 2013].

Goldsmith and Posner's complaints against standard accounts of customary international law is their lack of clarity with respect to how customary laws have been formed over time. Their point concerns the uncertainty that surrounds the process whereby customs are recognized as reflecting or amounting to law, and also the process whereby a custom becomes law: 'There is no convincing explanation of the process by which a voluntary behavioral regularity transforms itself into a binding legal obligation.'[31] It is not clear, for instance, how the uneasy relation of *usus* (customary law confirmed through the action of states) and *opinio juris* (the expressed opinion of states that certain actions have a basis in law) would be negotiated for new standards of behaviour to be recognized in, for instance, environmental law.

Their associated claim is that customary international law, as traditionally understood, has little explanatory power: 'The international behaviors said to constitute [customary international law] are actually disparate and changing practices that follow different logics depending on the interaction of state interests in particular contexts.'[32] No one, they suppose, can rightfully claim to know the best way to arrive at a substantive concept of international common good, and so nation-states should be allowed to choose freely depending on the interaction of diverse interests in particular contexts. No individual or institution is capable of describing the content of an n-state public or common good created through multilateral co-operation. The costs of attempting to co-ordinate interests are high and rise exponentially with the number of states. '[Customary international law] norms that have apparent universal scope are in fact the result of coincidence of interest, coercion' or some other interaction.[33] States might act consistently in adherence to international legal norms because 'they receive payoffs when other states successfully rely on their actions', because they are coerced or adherence otherwise benefits their interests, but '[s]tates can also benefit from reputations for

---

[31] Jack L. Goldsmith and Eric A. Posner, 'A Theory of Customary International Law', *John M. Olin Law & Economics Working Paper*, no. 63, 2nd ser. (November 1998), University of Chicago Law School, pp. 6–7 www.law.uchicago.edu/files/files/63. Goldsmith-Posner.pdf [accessed 17 February 2013].
[32] Goldsmith and Posner, 'A Theory of Customary International Law', p. 3.
[33] Goldsmith and Posner, 'A Theory of Customary International Law', p. 21.

toughness or even for irrationality or unpredictability'.[34] All of this, say Goldsmith and Posner, causes embarrassment to traditional accounts of customary international law and supports their claim that it should exert no independent and exogenous influence on national behaviour.[35] Only treaty-based international law – often agreed after conflict or dispute – is intellectually and politically robust enough to meet standards of legitimacy.[36]

Goldsmith and Posner posit adherence to international law in terms of rational choices that maximize national interests. Governments do not preoccupy themselves with questions about the origins, nature or validity of international law but restrict their objectives to examining the utility of given decisions in specific political, economic or other contexts. Goldsmith and Posner's definition of state interest turns on assessment of the expected utility of a given course of action without reference to any default assumption that nation-states should comply with international law; they exclude from their calculation the assumption that a nation-state should operate with a default commitment to adhere to international law and opt instead to assume that a successful theory of international law should show at every point why compliance is preferable.[37] Hence the denial that there should be a default position in favour of adherence to international law.

For the Protestant Thomist, the claim is that the long-term flourishing of both individual nation-states and the international community is more likely to emerge from law characterized by habitual virtue than a narrow, introspective statism.[38] Aquinas's focus on the relationship between the good of 'the part' or 'the one only' to the good of 'the whole' is not an over-easy moralizing but a deeply realistic engagement with the recognition that the good of every living creature are interrelated. At a time when challenges of globalization are not only new but potentially subversive of political reasoning that assumes an overly simple Westphalian order of nation-states, the really prudent realist needs a far more complex and subtle appreciation of the relation

---

[34]Goldsmith and Posner, 'A Theory of Customary International Law', pp. 27, 28.
[35]Goldsmith and Posner, 'A Theory of Customary International Law', p. 90.
[36]Goldsmith and Posner, *The Limits of International Law*, p. 226.
[37]Goldsmith and Posner, *The Limits of International Law*, p. 9.
[38]Aquinas, *ST,* I–II, q. 91, a. 3.

between the good of 'the one' and 'the many' than is offered by any narrowly statist thinker. Aquinas's challenge is to get beyond outdated dismissals such as 'nations have no moral obligation to comply with international law' and to rethink a new realism for the new global order. His ethical naturalism, and its related understanding of the interconnections between custom, consent and political authority, provides guidance and encouragement in the specification of reasons that should be communicable and cogent to non-Christian or otherwise non-religious audiences because good moral and jurisprudential thinking is rational in its character.[39] Today, whether or not one accepts the theological convictions behind his reasoning, Aquinas's challenge is to be realist enough both to accept the evidence that Morgenthau and others present with respect to the motivations of state action, and to know when realism requires more than a balance of power mechanism or actions to protect short-term state interest.

What if the consensus supports torture?

For those theorists who eschew the statism that prioritizes survival and self-help, more promising ways forward are often seen as propounded by discourse theorists of law and democracy. Such thinkers typically make no plea for the revival of interest in natural law but focus on the performance and extension of deliberation among all relevant parties (including NGOs and multinationals) about the requirements of good law. Here the issue is not that of vagueness as described by Morgenthau and his successors, and lack of democratic deficit, but what to say when the consensus supports torture. The old scholastic question of whether primacy belongs to the intellect or the will acquires new significance as proceduralist theorists risk prioritizing the will of the people and democratic legitimacy over all other considerations.

---

[39]This phrase is from Jean Porter, *Moral Action and Christian Ethics* (Cambridge: Cambridge University Press, 1995), p. 44.

The problem of legitimacy

The immediate theoretical background to this supposed crisis of authority with respect to international law in this alternative, neo-Kantian cosmopolitan perspective is large and complex. Briefly, in the mid-twentieth century, even secularist conceptions of natural law were written off by broad sweeps of opinion because of the plurality of modern and post-modern conceptions of the good. As Max Weber wrote, it was no longer assumed that there was a shared rational foundation for moral and legal judgement. In a supposedly post-metaphysical and godless age, ethical and legal norms were no longer held to be written in nature and no metaphysic could integrate what the plurality of worldviews with respect to basic and social goods. No one could say any longer what the law ought to be. The theories of legal positivism (which arose in opposition to classical natural law theory) were seen to have a tendency towards circularity of argument, describing validity in terms of either what a sovereign pronounces to be valid or what was believed to be valid by most people, legitimacy having been defined previously in terms of either sovereignty or convention. Similarly, the so-called command theories (Jeremy Bentham and John Austin) and social convention theories (Hans Kelsen and H. L. A. Hart) were no longer acceptable because, as the direct expression of will, they lacked integration in the politics of the day. Such theories told us what the law ought to be but tended in their application towards the amoral, apolitical and atheoretical. It was not enough to achieve order by either the force exercised by a sovereign or that implicit in convention. The pyramid of traditional, ethical and social hierarchies that gave authority to law had been replaced by a trampoline on which the legitimacy of the governments of individual states goes up and down depending upon their performance in the eyes of the electorate or the extension of democracy to new groups.[40]

Max Weber gave classic expression in the early twentieth century to modern liberal approaches to the legitimacy of law in his analyses of the beliefs, attitudes and willingness of individuals in a given society to assume the disciplines and burdens required for membership.[41] The key issues were also summarized by Jürgen

---

[40]Agnes Heller, *Can Modernity Survive?* (Cambridge: Polity Press, 1990), p. 148.
[41]See Max Weber, *Economy and Society: An Outline of Interpretive Sociology* (New York: Bedminster Press, 1968), pp. 212ff.

Habermas in *Legitimationsprobleme im Spätkapitalismus*, a book which popularized the term 'legitimation crisis'. A response to the crises that shook advanced capitalist societies in 1968 and afterwards, with the resurgence of neo-Marxist ideologies and industrial action, it examined economic theories emerging from the Marxist tradition, together with the systems theories of Niklas Luhmann and others, trying to identify crisis tendencies within advanced capitalism, notably economic crises and crises of rationality, legitimation and motivation.[42] The term 'legitimation' referred to the ways in which governments and legislators claim legal status or authorization for their existence and power, and 'crisis' referred to situations in which various tensions and strains have reached such a point that the whole system is likely to implode. As early as 1973 Habermas denied any source of legitimacy outside the processes of democracy, and this commitment to democratic procedure has remained constant in his work. In a more recent book, subtitled *Contributions to a Discourse Theory of Law and Democracy*, he argued that discourse constitutes the conceptual or inherent relation between the rule of law and democracy in post-metaphysical, sociologically disenchanted democratic societies.[43] The crisis of legitimacy in lawmaking and legal interpretation – that is, the lack of consensus on answers to essential questions regarding the nature of law – is overcome through the performance and extension of democracy. Transcendence consists in the recognition that the conditions of linguistic subjectivity are greater than and beyond any individual or social grouping; higher-level constructions, namely theories about the procedures of discourse, transcend tradition-specific norms. No metaphysical grounds of authority or legitimacy can carry sufficient warrant in a pluralistic society; the goods of reason are found in political process rather than metaphysics or teleology.

Alternative secularist trends of anti-foundationalism include the legal formalism or legal voluntarism advocated by Ernest Weinrib and Stanley Fish. In contrast to Habermas's discursive approach, these so-called post-modern theories of jurisprudence react against the reduction of law and legal interpretations to political games (as happens in much liberal democracy) and posit law as the

---

[42]Jürgen Habermas, *Legitimation Crisis* (London: Heinemann, 1976).
[43]Jürgen Habermas, *Between Facts and Norms: Contributions to a Discourse Theory of Law and Democracy* (Cambridge: Polity Press, 1996), p. 449.

self-contained practice of making judgments in a court. Stanley Fish's approach, for instance, has been described as a new formalism because the practice and doctrine of the law produce decisions that demand compliance.[44] His formalism is compatible with his post-modern convictions about the ceaseless flow of semantic meaning and law. To paraphrase Winston Churchill's observation that history is just one damn thing after another, Fish's new formalism (as distinct from the old formalisms of Platonic idealism or positivism which established the meaning of justice with reference to metaphysics, the will of a sovereign or some 'plain meaning' of legal language) is just one damn legal interpretation after another. Crises of legitimacy find resolution in the continuous process of making legal doctrine and the enforcing of (arbitrary?) decisions. Nothing internal to law is properly ethical; extra-legal norms and processes are required in order to determine juridical relations and, consequently, a new legalism is gaining ground. In some similarity to Goldsmith and Posner's game-theory approach, law is analogous to a game of chess – except that the decisions made in the courtroom will influence other practices outside.[45] Meaning is made through the force of rhetoric, and the link between law and justice means may mean nothing outside of the game. The result is a gap between law and justice, in the sense that any element of universality is denied and alternative visions of links between law and justice suppressed. As discussed above, this perspective was criticized by Morgenthau as insufficiently able to distinguish the rule of law from the arbitrary exercise of power.

To cynical observers of modern Western jurisprudence, such tensions might seem predictable and expected. In the early nineteenth century, Hegel accused Kant of 'empty formalism', condemning his approach to practical reason as producing an empty concept of community: 'the essence of pure will and pure practical reason is to be abstracted from all content.'[46] The accusation was overly simplistic, but Hegel made the point that external regulation is inadequate for the building of community. Today, the loss of faith in natural law and recognition of the susceptibility of positivism to

---

[44]Michael Rosenfeld, *Just Interpretations: Law between Ethics and Politics* (Berkely, LA: University of California Press, 1998), ch. 2.
[45]Rosenfeld, *Just Interpretations*, p. 151.
[46]G. W. F. Hegel, *Natural Law* (Philadelphia: University of Pennsylvania Press, 1975), p. 76.

arbitrariness is giving rise to worrying new types of voluntarism and formalism that separate ethics and law, while legal positivism and fictional delusions of the individualized state are denounced by others as an insufficient basis for the international community to address satisfactorily the many practical needs that confront our leaders and the relation between law, ethics and morality. The dissolution of teleology in the dominant social-contract legal theories of the nineteenth and twentieth centuries and the metaphysics-free alternative of 'discourse theory' promote accounts of international law largely undirected by the belief commitments that sustained the older jurisprudence of natural law. Stephen Hall summarizes: 'We are sceptical as to the natural law's capacity, or certain of its incapacity, to replace the rotting timbers of legal positivism. In reaction we cling tenaciously to the wreckage of positivism. We also increasingly seek to salvage positivism by grafting it onto one or other of the 'social sciences' – especially sociology, political science, international relations or economics – in the vain hope that a firm basis of, or functional substitute for, legal authority and obligation can be found there.[47] Recourse to the old *ius gentium* and appeals to the natural law are seen by many to be an inadequate medium through which to engage the discipline. Over against such trends, in which grand narratives are rejected and it is assumed that there can be no common *telos* or eschatology, the work of jurisprudence is emptied into game theory, the practicalities of discourse and/or procedural reason.

An interesting example of this new approach focused on the practicalities of discourse and/or procedural reason is Robert McCorquodale's favourable reception of the type of deliberative theory advanced by Habermas. '*Once upon a time*', he writes, 'there was an idea called international law'.[48] It was a flexible, open and inclusive idea that applied to actions between governments, by indigenous peoples, corporations, individuals and communities.

---

[47]Stephen Hall, 'The Persistent Spectre: Natural Law, International Order and the Limits of Legal Positivism', *European Journal of International Law* 12 (2001), p. 306.

[48]Robert McCorquodale, 'International Community and State Sovereignty: An Uneasy Symbiotic Relationship', in Colin Warbrick and Stephen Tierney (eds), *Towards an International Legal Community? The Sovereignty of States and the Sovereignty of International Law* (London: British Institute of International and Comparative Law, 2006), p. 241 (emphasis in original).

It acknowledged and included some conception of international community. The idea was fragile, and 'its potential power was recognized and seized upon by a few influential people to strengthen the emerging notion of the individualized State.' This notion of international law was ridiculed and dismissed by the actions of a few, mainly colonialist states that favoured closed and restrictive rules only applicable by and for states, and was replaced by legal fictions of state sovereignty that excluded other participants in the international community. Even the Preamble to the UN Charter, which spoke of 'We the Peoples of the United Nations', was interpreted in ways that merely reinforced the idea that international law is limited to the activities of states. So, in this international legal story, '[s]tates live happily ever after as the creators of all international law for their own international community'.[49]

McCorquodale's scenario is a familiar but dark one in which he puts the question of the authority of international law in a particular way. A state-based system in which international law is reduced to the drafting and negotiating of agreements between states, forecloses possibilities in international relations and dangerously ignores much of what is actually happening in the international community. Traditional renditions of the authority of international law framed in terms of the natural law are barely mentioned but the source of the problem is traced to the nineteenth-century new doctrine of legal positivism which downplayed international law and traditions of natural law in jurisprudence, thereby introducing an initial fissure between positivist jurisprudence and international law and developing the idea of the individualized state. The 'Dark Ages' of the idea of international law gave rise to the hegemony of states on the international stage, which McCorquodale predicts will end shortly as international law develops into a matrix of relationships of states with states *and* with other parties. The artificial constraints and current slowing of the international legal system result from limitations in its operative concept of sovereignty. This crisis is to be overcome through more inclusive claims to normative recognition and the practice of discursive reason.

McCorquodale's purpose is to call for a different story of international law to be heard in which non-state actors – for example,

---

[49]McCorquodale,'International Community and State Sovereignty', p. 242 (emphasis in original).

non-governmental organizations, transnational corporations and individuals – have a role. He makes no plea for the revival of interest in natural law but opts for an approach that looks similar to Jürgen Habermas's discourse theory of law and democracy. The crisis of authority with respect to international law comes in many shapes and sizes. The way forward is not a rethinking of natural law but via a procedural-rationalist approach to lawmaking in which legitimation depends upon the performance and extension of democracy. This reconstructive approach to law through discourse and procedural reason urges that the participation of all legal subjects in the common exercise of political autonomy should be oriented towards agreement about justified interests and standards of behaviour.[50] The norms recognized by political legislatures and the international community must prove their 'rationality' by means of procedures and communicative presuppositions.

McCorquodale – one of the most probing questioners of authority in international law that contemporary secularist philosophy and jurisprudence offers – places his hope in discursive resolution of the tension between ideas of international law as something exhibiting moral value or integrity and as an inherently value-free social phenomenon, something morally neutral and empirically descriptive of the hegemony of nation-states rather than morally substantive in nature because of an association with metaphysics. International law is no longer synonymous with the natural law as it had been prior to the nineteenth century, when it was supplanted by the new legal positivism.[51] Natural law was part of what Habermas calls 'the clamp' that held the different components of social order together in medieval Europe and which sprang open in the early modern period with ideas of self-realization and self-determination.[52] Today, legitimacy is a project or fallible process in which the only dogmatic core is the idea of individuals as autonomous agents who must obey the laws they make for themselves through democratic structures of recognition and accountability at every level of society as a whole. The way forward that he sees is, in effect, through analysis of the presuppositions of rational discourse and ensuring that the conditions of communicative reason are met.

---

[50]Habermas, *Between Facts and Norms*, p. xlii.
[51]See Hall, 'The Persistent Spectre', p. 271.
[52]Habermas, *Between Facts and Norms*, p. 95.

The problem of prioritizing democratic will over reason

Habermas's position with respect to international law is laid out most clearly in the essay 'Does the Constitutionalization of International Law Still Have a Chance?' in which the agenda is to distinguish the realism of Hans Morgenthau and Carl Schmitt from the legacy of hope left by Kant's now-famous essay 'Perpetual Peace'.[53] The question posed in the former essay is 'Kant or Schmitt?' – with a note to the effect that Schmitt and Morgenthau share the belief that states cannot do anything wrong in a moral sense and that justice between states is not a viable goal.[54] Habermas contrasts the realism of a 'balance of powers' approach with the Kantian idealism that regards human rights and international law as the medium for realizing the goals of peace among nation-states, and as a law-governed freedom in which commerce replaces wars of aggression; discourse is constitutive of the free association of parties and is achieved through the medium of law, which then acquires legitimate organizing and coercive power. The immediate political focus of this essay, published in 2004, is to call the United States back to international law: 'For the Kantian project can only continue if the US returns to the internationalism it embraced after 1918 and 1945 and once again assumes the role of pacemaker in the evolution of international law toward a "cosmopolitan condition".'[55]

---

[53]Jürgen Habermas, 'Does the Constitutionalization of International Law Still Have a Chance?' in Ciaran Cronin (ed.), *The Divided West* (Cambridge: Polity Press, 2006), pp. 115–93. See also Habermas's previous essay 'Kant's Idea of Perpetual Peace: At Two Hundred Years' Historical Remove', in Ciaran Cronin and Pablo De Greiff (eds), *The Inclusion of the Other: Studies in Political Theory* (Cambridge, MA: MIT Press, 1998), pp. 165–202. In the earlier essay, Habermas was relatively optimistic with respect to the Kantian vision being realized through the realization of the democratic ideal and legitimate government. The later essay is looser with respect to how the democratic ideal might be realized and place more emphasis on diverse publics and civil society.
[54]Habermas, 'Does the Constitutionalization of International Law Still Have a Chance?' p. 188.
[55]Habermas, 'Does the Constitutionalization of International Law Still Have a Chance?' p. 117.

By law, Habermas means 'the process of legal pacification for which Kant prepares the ground with his work "Perpetual Peace"'.[56] The 'cosmopolitan condition' is specified in terms of international constitutions, organizations and procedures, based on the assumption that law remains an appropriate medium for realizing the declared goals of peace, security, democracy and the recognition of human rights throughout the world. The *ius cosmopoliticum* is distinct from classical international law in that the source of law is not sovereign states that recognize no secular authority above themselves but the ideal of ensuring the equal liberties of every individual under universal law. This ideal is not to the exclusion of the bounds of national sovereignty. Domestic law continues to function within national boundaries; cosmopolitan law deals with relations across borders. Habermas's re-reading of Kant's 'Perpetual Peace' seeks a way beyond both legal positivism and the descent of international law into sterile debate about the foundations of its supposedly binding force;[57] it begins from the problem of individual (state) solipsism as the problem of self-interest transposed onto the supranational level. This space for dialogue is, in effect, that which Kant identified beyond the international law centred exclusively on states, in the cosmopolitan order of world citizenship where the democratic, republican manner of government subordinate to 'the idea of reason' is extended to the international community.[58]

For Habermas, the legitimacy of law (including international law) is found in the transcendence of linguistic conditions. He argues that discourse for post-metaphysical societies constitutes the conceptual or inherent relation between the rule of law and democracy.[59] The legitimacy of transcendence consists in the recognition that the conditions of linguistic subjectivity are greater than, and beyond any, individual or social grouping. The 'ideal' communication community is projected above the vagaries of human particularity. The legitimacy that matters in today's democratic societies is very different to that of previous generations because no single perspective can be privileged above

---

[56]Habermas, 'Kant's Idea of Perpetual Peace', p. 165.
[57]Morgenthau, *Dilemmas of Politics*, p. 219.
[58]Habermas, 'Does the Constitutionalization of International Law Still Have a Chance?' p. 115.
[59]Habermas, *Between Facts and Norms*, p. 449.

others; legitimacy is grounded in difference. No faith can make the pretence of being 'right' when this has political implications for unconsenting others: 'only those norms are valid that meet (or could meet) with the approval of all affected in their capacity as participants in a practical discourse.'[60] The only truth that will suffice has passed through the fires of argumentation and is therefore a form of knowledge rather than belief.

The question of legitimacy is addressed appropriately, according to Habermas, when democratic governments make possible a discursively structured legislature within which none has special privileges for arcane historical reasons. Validity claims connected with norms of action, upon which commands or 'ought' sentences are based, can, analogously to truth claims, be redeemed discursively. It is not enough for any interest group to ask, What is good for us? or even, How can we act for the good of others? without being willing to subject possible answers to the wider discourse community. Lawmaking is interwoven with the formation of communicative power. Communicative power depends upon self-understanding and 'enlightened resolutions' in which ethical discourses (which may include discourses shaped by identity-influencing traditions) are examined and tested according to the 'comprehensive perspective of an unlimited communication community'.[61] In 1973 Habermas denied any source of legitimacy outside the democratic procedure, and this commitment to democratic procedure has remained a constant in his work.[62]

---

[60]Habermas, *Between Facts and Norms*, p. 107.
[61]Habermas, *Between Facts and Norms*, p. 162.
[62]Habermas, *Between Facts and Norms*, p. 449. Critical voices have warned that the universal conditions of possibility of rationally justifying norms of actions or evaluation as supposed by Habermas have themselves a normative character. Extended discussion of this point is not possible here. Suffice to note that some question the assumptions hidden in the claim that the norms of discourse are valid or, at least, potentially valid, for all people. Chantal Mouffe's related concern is to maintain antagonism in politics without destroying political association. Her book *On the Political* is, in part, a reaction against Habermas's claims for the potential universality of liberal democracy. (*On the Political: Thinking in Action* [London: Routledge, 2005], p. 88). See also Michael Hardt and Antonio Negri, *Empire* (Cambridge, MA: Harvard University Press, 2000), p. 34. While welcoming aspects of Habermas's philosophy as anti-authoritarian and oriented towards human freedom and justice, Richard Rorty questions his idea that inquiry about the meaning and purpose of law is bound somehow to converge to a single point (*Philosophy*

But what if the democratic processes make state torture normative? What is really being asked for our purposes is whether the role of the will in the constitution of the law is primary or subordinate.[63] As Simon writes: 'the first question . . . is whether, in order to have the character of a rule and a measure of human action, the thing called law should be primarily a work of the reason or a work of the will'.[64] Reason can awaken the will and prompt it to action but the will of the lawgiver should be directed and regulated by reason. Reason has primacy as the regulator of action and the will.[65] That every law requires an act of will is not at issue. Whether the will of the prince in medieval societies, or 'the act of the general will' as described by Rousseau, or the expression today of the democratic will of the citizens of a nation state, that every law involves an act of will is taken for granted. At issue is not that law entails an expression of will per se (this is not, of itself, a problem) but whether the role of the will in the constitution of law is primary or subordinate.[66]

If the will is reasonable, if it follows the reason, it is to the reason that primacy belongs; but if the will is held to enjoy primacy, it

---

and Social Hope [London: Penguin, 1999], p. 238). International relations theorist Patricia Owens contrasts Habermas's account of the public sphere as the political awakening of the bourgeoisie with Hannah Arendt's identification of the political rule of the bourgeoisie with imperialism. Arendt, she says, was intensely alert to how Habermasian-type visions of the political emancipation of the bourgeoisie are linked typically to a distinctive configuration of economic interests and market function. Owens speaks of a model of 'a bourgeois debating and coffee drinking public' ('Hannah Arendt and the Public Sphere: Model for a Global Public?', paper presented at a conference of the International Studies Association, New Orleans, 24–27 March 2002, p. 44). Her note of satire points to links between the kind of political emancipation envisaged by Habermas and the free-market economy. The scope of Habermas's civil society increases as markets become globalized and as liberal values are accepted; the norms of legitimation within Habermas's communicative ethic are not neutral a priori but have been produced within a particular economic and institutional system.

[63]The issue is formulated in this way by Yves R. Simon, *The Tradition of Natural Law: A Philosopher's Reflections* (New York: Fordham University Press, 1965), p. 71.

[64]Simon, *The Tradition of Natural Law*, p. 72.

[65]R. J. Henle, S. J., *The Treatise on Law: Summa Theologiae, I–II, qq. 90–97* (Notre Dame, IN: University of Notre Dame Press, 1993), p. 123.

[66]Simon, *The Tradition of Natural Law*, p. 71.

is also held to be free from reasonableness, from agreement with the reason, from direction by the reason. Such will is arbitrary, and the most adequate way to convey the rationality of the law may be to say that such a will is lawless.[67]

Good law demands rules that are rational in character. Teleologically ordered attention is required to questions such as, What is law?, What is law for? and, By what criteria do we judge between good and bad law? In the twenty-first century, these questions may be addressed through the performance and extension of democracy but have also been addressed through other political means in earlier periods of history. The point is not that law may be enacted through the exercise of will, democratic or otherwise sovereign, but whether the exercise of will (whether of a medieval prince or democratic electorate) is reasonable in character or arbitrary. Even if a democratically elected leader deems their electorate to support the limited use of state torture, that does not mean necessarily that laws to permit the limited use of state torture are reasonable if these laws undermine the international order and tend away from peace.

On the *telos* of law

In advocating a Protestant Thomist approach to natural law reasoning, I am seeking to affirm the primacy of a teleological perspective on thinking about international law over the game theory approach of some political realists, social contract legal theories or discourse theory. This approach is analogous to the kind of primacy asserted by Paul Ricoeur of ethics over morality, an Aristotelian heritage where ethics is characterized by a teleological perspective over a Kantian heritage where morality is defined by the obligation to respect the norm:

> I propose to establish . . . (1) the primacy of ethics over morality, (2) the necessity for the ethical aim to pass through the sieve of the norm, and (3) the legitimacy of recourse by the norm to the aim whenever the norm leads to impasses in practice . . . In other words, according to the working hypothesis I am proposing,

---

[67]Simon, *The Tradition of Natural Law*, p. 80.

morality is held to constitute only a limited, although legitimate and even indispensable, actualization of the ethical aim, and ethics in this sense would then encompass morality . . . a relation involving at once subordination and complementarity, which the final recourse of morality to ethics will ultimately come to reinforce.[68]

For Ricoeur, ethics is teleologically oriented but not necessarily in conflict with deontologically determined or other modes of morality. At least potentially, these various commitments are complementary, not incompatible. Ricoeur exposes the limits of deontology when viewed in the light of Aristotelian *phronesis*. In broad similarity, I maintain the need for questions about the ethics or aim of international law as the framework in which to consider how the law serves national and other interests. There is no attempt to decry the proper consideration of national and other interests but to rediscover ways of thinking that permit at once 'subordination and complementarity'.[69] The challenge is to keep questions about the telos of law in play and, indeed, to find ways in which the aims of law with respect to just peace, good order and common good function as the final recourse in situations of impasse and lack of consensus.

Regarding the relation of subordination and complementarity between an Aristotelian (or for our purposes Thomist) heritage where ethics is characterized by a teleological perspective over a Kantian heritage where morality is defined by the obligation to respect the norm, I affirm what Ricoeur calls 'the obligation to respect the norm' as demanding attention with Morgenthau, Goldsmith and Posner and others to the issues of democratic deficit and vagueness surrounding *jus cogens* norms, and with Habermas to finding discursive ways forward around the requirements of good law. With Ricoeur, however, the intention is to establish the primacy of questions about the telos of law over questions about questions of procedure, democratic deficit, vagueness and more. Natural law reasoning as critique, or a critical exercise in hermeneutics, attempts to probe in diverse situations what is

---

[68]Paul Ricoeur, *Oneself as Another*, trans. Kathleen Blamey (Chicago: University of Chicago Press, 1992), pp. 170–71.
[69]Ricoeur, *Oneself as Another*, pp. 170–71.

required for peacemaking, good order and common good, and to clarify how the teleological orientation of this kind of questioning both has primacy over and bears upon other kinds of reasoning.

More specifically, Aquinas offers a way of thinking about the relation of 'the one' to 'the many' that remains persuasive, especially if interpreted in terms of an ethic whose centre is answerability. Of interest is the relation for Aquinas between the legal self-sufficiency and self-interest of states and the common good of the international community, whether and how the question of answerability features, and whether his account of the relation between custom, consent and political authority speaks to the supposed problem of the democratic deficit of international law. We consider law as a work of reason and not merely the will (whether the will of a medieval prince or democratic electorate) when it is 'an ordinance of reason for the common good, issued by the one who has care of the community, and promulgated'.[70] Of interest is how, for Aquinas, legal justice is the justice that orders the actions of individuals (or nations) towards the common good: 'It is the presence of this goal which distinguishes law from mere command' and makes law primarily a work of reason rather than the will.[71] The referring of law to the common good is a test of right reason that may coincide with the will of those in power and/or the consent of the many, but is not to be identified with either. The issue is not an opposition of the authority of law terms of natural law reasoning versus modern approaches to legitimacy, but how to reconnect the problem of legitimacy to teleologically oriented questions of what constitutes good law.

Reading Aquinas in context

It is important to be clear at this point that Thomist realism does not propose a political hierarchy above the princedom or nation with authority residing by nature in the various gradations of level.[72] Aquinas says nothing about the good of the entire community of

---

[70]Aquinas, *ST*, I–II, q. 95, a. 3; see also I–II, q. 90, a. 2.
[71]M. S. Kempshall, *The Common Good in Late Medieval Political Thought: Moral Goodness and Political Benefit* (Oxford: Clarendon Press, 1999), p. 112.
[72]A similar point is made by Mark C. Murphy, 'Consent, Custom, and the Common Good in Aquinas's Account of Political Authority', *The Review of Politics* 59 (Spring 1997), p. 324.

the universe – *tota communitas universi* – residing in some kind of personal, world authority where the active power of authority is a person 'who has care of the community' and exercises this care through command and coercion.[73] Accepting Isidore's division between the law of nations, the civil law and the natural law, Aquinas distinguishes between the law of nations and the civil law not on the grounds of their respective jurisdictions (the one much larger than the other) but on the different procedures by which each is related to the natural law – the former by means much more closely related to quasi-philosophical deduction and the latter by the more complex processes of day-to-day determination.[74] Aquinas adopts the tripartite division adopted from Ulpian and Isidore of the law of nations (*jus gentium*), the civil law (*jus civile*) and the natural law (*jus naturale*). He 'preserves the view of Ulpian and Isidore that the law of nations is common to all nations and that the civil law is peculiar to a certain community'.[75] The few explicit comments that he makes on political authority, consent and custom apply to the civil law and not the law of nations; the precepts of the law of nations are derived from the first principles of natural law, whereas the civil law is determined by local communities according to what is suitable to them: 'The distinction between the law of nations and the civil law, then, corresponds to the distinction between those precepts which are derived from the natural law by way of logical deduction and by way of determination, respectively.'[76]

Recognizing this distinction in Thomist writings between the 'law of nations' and civil law, I am not proposing a straightforward transposition of Aquinas's teaching about civil law to the international level. I do not suggest that Aquinas offers a template

---

[73]Aquinas, *ST,* I–II, q. 91, a. 1; I–II, q. 90, a. 4.

[74]The example that he gives of what may be derived from the law of nations by way of logical deduction, as distinct from the more particular, historically rooted ways of moral determination, is the conclusion that 'one must not kill' derived as a conclusion from the principle that 'one should do harm to no-one' (*ST,* I–II, q. 95, a. 2, c.). The law of nature has it that the evil-doer should be punished but does not specify how; that is a determination of the particular community or nation: 'The general principles of the natural law cannot be applied to all men in the same way on account of the great variety of human affairs: and hence arises the diversity of positive laws among various people' (I–II, q. 95, a. 2, ad. 3).

[75]See Murphy, 'Consent, Custom, and the Common Good', p. 333, commenting on Aquinas, *ST,* I–II, q. 95, a. 4.

[76]Murphy, 'Consent, Custom, and the Common Good', p. 333.

for good governance at the local and national levels that may simply be writ large for the international community. There is no suggestion that the international order is to be governed by a single, personal authority, or that Thomist realism equates somehow to a universalist cosmopolitanism. Having embarked upon a restatement of Thomist realism that is critical of the kind of statism advanced by Morgenthau, there is a risk that this critique could be cast as a version of the new *ius cosmopoliticum;* I want to be clear that attempting to restate the possibilities of Thomist natural law reasoning for international law jurisprudence today, not least Aquinas's treatment of the common good of the political community in terms of the inclusive imagery or 'the part' and 'the whole', need not equate to some kind of universalist cosmopolitanism.[77] Nevertheless, Aquinas raises for us the question of whether and/or to what extent the international common good can be considered substantively.

Nor does Aquinas discuss the personal character of authority at the international level because the political authority that exists by the law of nations pertains at the level of the state: 'What Aquinas means by saying that political authority exists by the law of nations, then, is that it is such a straightforward implication of the natural law that political authority be instituted and exercised that such institutions of governance are features of almost every known human community.'[78] The few explicit comments that he makes on political authority, consent and custom apply to the civil law and not the law of nations. This is because the natural law supposes that

---

[77]There are, of course, many types of cosmopolitanism, some of which are compatible with Thomist realism. The Jesuit political theologian David Hollenbach, a co-member of the CTI Working Group, writes that the Christian cosmopolitan may have strong affinities with secularists who hold that the global community has moral priority over narrower communities defined by ethnicity, religion or suchlike: 'In this approach, the common humanity of all people is seen as the basis of a worldwide moral community' (David Hollenbach, S. J., (ed.), *Refugee Rights: Ethics, Advocacy, and Africa* [Washington, DC: Georgetown University Press, 2008], p. 184). The international community, he says, can no longer draw sharp distinctions between national and international interests: 'This leads to confusion about when and where pursuit of realistic self-interest can promote the good life today' (p. 52). I agree broadly with Hollenbach's deepening sense that shared global goods cannot be reduced simply to the private goods of individuals or the discrete goods of states but am concerned to distance this account of Thomist cosmopolitanism from some secularist versions that are as utopian as Goldsmith and Posner fear.
[78]Murphy, 'Consent, Custom, and the Common Good', p. 334.

each person and the relevant authorities promote the common good in their own communities: 'it belongs to the notion of human law, to be ordained to the common good of the state.'[79] The common good of the state requires personal authority: 'it belongs to the notion of human law, to be framed by that one who governs the community of the state.' The common good is dependent on the institution and exercise of personal and political authority. By contrast, the common good of the international community depends upon the proper ordering of relations between nation-states. Similarly, I do not suppose that we should treat the common good of the international community in directly analogous ways to the good of the community or state. There is no suggestion in either Aquinas or what follows that the common good of the international community depends upon the exercise of personal authority analogous to the nation state, or any hint of a world government held together by some form of monarchy or equivalent. It remains to be settled, however, whether teleologically ordered attention is still required to address the fundamental questions above which we have been circling in this chapter: What is law? What is it for? By what criteria do we judge between good and bad law?

Telos, custom and consent

Significant again in this respect is that Aquinas's *Treatise on Law* is an integral part of his ethical naturalism, according to which every species adds to the perfection of the universe, and perfection is marked by diversity and order. Until very recently, as Porter observes, the importance attached by Aquinas and other scholastics to what is natural, that is, to what extent humans share non-human animal sensation and appetites and how this helps us to understand human activity, would have been dismissed as the most outdated and least attractive aspect of their account of natural law reasoning.[80] Today, as climate change and environmental crises remind us of multiple lines of continuity between human and non-human animals, natural law reasoning is ripe for revival because, inter alia,

---

[79] Aquinas, *ST*, I–II, q. 95, a. 4.
[80] Jean Porter, *Nature as Reason: A Thomistic Theory of the Natural Law* (Grand Rapids, MI: Eerdmans, 2005), p. 54.

it has nature at its roots. For Aquinas, humans share a multiplex commonality with all other creatures.[81] Some animals judge only by instinct and inclination. Humans have additional competences but share a range of characteristics and competences with non-human animals.[82] As for all other animals, the *telos* of every human is their own proper perfection, according to their kind and in a relationship of interdependence with all others. Aquinas's fundamental notion of goodness is that which all animals and all creation pursue.[83] The roots of morality and good law lie in links between the pre-rational nature and reason. And here is the rub for our purposes. Humans from different economic and cultural contexts can, potentially at least, attain agreement about moral norms due *not only* to the balancing of powers or to tacit assumptions of universal validity integral to the conditions of discourse, but to the fact that humans are one animal among many, creatures among creatures, all of whom pursue their own good.[84]

Consider Aquinas's treatment of whether custom can obtain the force of law:

it is evident that by human speech, law can be both changed and expounded, in so far as it manifests the interior movement and thought of human reason. Wherefore by actions also, especially

---

[81]Aquinas, *ST,* I, q. 47, a. 1, c.

[82]On this see John Berkman, 'Towards a Thomistic Theology of Animality', in Celia Deane-Drummond and David Clough (eds), *Creaturely Theology: On God, Humans and Other Animals* (Norwich: SCM Press, 2009), ch. 1.

[83]Aquinas, *ST,* I–II, q. 94, a. 2.

[84]There is no need at this point to re-open older criticisms, notably David Hume's claim about the fact/value dichotomy and G. E. Moore's formulation of the naturalistic fallacy. John Finnis has shown convincingly that neither Aristotle nor Aquinas ever suggested that 'ought' could be deduced from 'is' in the sense suggested by Hume (*Natural Law and Natural Rights* [Oxford: Clarendon Press, 1980], p. 33). Both Aristotle and Aquinas, Finnis says, would have rejected Hume's claim that the precepts of natural law were moral in the modern sense. For Aristotle and Aquinas, the precepts of natural law are pre-moral; they are principles concerned with the self-evident relations of conformity or disconformity to human nature. As such, they precede the mores of particular societies; they are trans-cultural and universal. Finnis's distinction between basic goods and practical reasonableness is also widely accepted as circumventing the so-called naturalistic fallacy of assuming that good is identical with some natural fact. See also Nicholas C. Bamforth and David A. J. Richards, *Patriarchal Religion, Sexuality and Gender: A Critique of New Natural Law* (Cambridge: Cambridge University Press, 2008), p. 4.

if they be repeated, so as to make a custom, law can be changed and expounded; and also something can be established which obtains force of law, in so far as by repeated external actions, the inward movement of the will, and concepts of reason are most effectually declared; for when a thing is done again and again, it seems to proceed from a deliberate judgment of reason. Accordingly, custom has the force of a law, abolishes law, and is the interpreter of law.[85]

In this passage, Aquinas offers a remarkably flexible account of the relationship between custom and civil law, why some laws fail and why human laws will be different in different places. Of particular interest is that, for Aquinas, it would be nonsensical to deny a moral obligation to obey the customary law because of the embeddedness of the authority of law in customary practice exercised for the common good; an obligation to obey the customary law is likely to serve one's personal and wider interests because of reason's orientation towards a hierarchy of goods. Of course, a custom can become 'vicious' or detrimental to the common good. There is no guarantee of practical wisdom in human affairs because of the sinful nature of the human will. Yet the customary basis for law counts for more than the authority of the sovereign because it represents the free consent of the people.[86]

Aquinas's comments on political authority are few. He is clear, however, on two points. First, natural law requires that political authority be established and exercised: 'law should take account of many things, as to persons, as to matters, and as to times. Because the community of the state is composed of many persons; and its good is procured by many actions; nor is it established to endure for only a short time, but to last for all time by the citizens succeeding one another, as Augustine says.'[87] The institution and exercise of laws are required for the achievement of the common good. Second, the consent of free people to customary laws is generative of political authority: 'For if they are free, and able to make their own laws, the consent of the whole people expressed by a custom counts far more in favor of a particular observance, than does the authority

---

[85]Aquinas, *ST,* I–II, q. 97, a. 3.
[86]Eleanore Stump, *Aquinas* (London: Routledge, 2003), p. 314.
[87]Aquinas, *ST,* I–II, q. 96, a. 1, c.

of the sovereign, who has not the power to frame laws, except as representing the people.'[88] The specifics of lawmaking for a given community are not deducible directly from the natural law because the circumstances of communities differ and change; human laws sometimes fail to protect against evil or their utility is exhausted. In the main, however, he is surprisingly clear that the consent of the community for whom certain rules apply is constitutive in the making of political authority.

Here the gap between Aquinas's medieval period and our own matters most. Legal theorists today are unlikely to hear Aquinas's words without reflecting on the long history of contention about the sources of international law, complex relations between international custom and consistent state practice, tension between general principles of law and unexpected judicial decisions, requirements that operate at a high level of generality and regional tribunals, 'hard' as distinct from 'soft' developments in international law and more.[89] It is not possible in this essay to trace historically the extension of customary law to the international community by those jurists and legal scholars who drew upon Aquinas (Vitoria, Suárez, Grotius and others) for whom the relation between custom, consent and political authority was vital. My contention remains, however, that Aquinas's attention to the relationship between custom, consent and political authority might yet inform present-day discussion about the limits of statism. His teaching yields little overtly with respect to the relation between custom, consent and political authority in the international community. Conceptually, however, Aquinas orients us towards a restated account of natural law reasoning in which the authority of law is likely to include but will not be exhausted by consent through democratic legitimacy. The authority of law is measured by its power to restrain evil and cause an increase in the commonweal.

'Virtue', says Aquinas, 'is that which makes its possessor good, and his work good likewise.'[90] By this he means that a person (and, by extension, a nation) has virtue when their reason has learned

---

[88]Aquinas, *ST,* I–II, q. 97, a. 3, ad. 3.
[89]For these terms, see Hilary Charlesworth and Christine Chinkin, *The Boundaries of International Law: A Feminist Analysis* (Manchester: Manchester University Press, 2000), pp. 71–77.
[90]Porter, *Moral Action,* p. 55.

to will with ease what is according to the truth, and according to reason. Humankind, says Aquinas, does not possess the perfections of the angels but does have the inferior perfection of a rational soul. When the power to reason virtuously is perfected in a person, it may be called a habit. The acts of a perfected power or habit can then be described as a person's second nature. Habitual virtue is the *ultimum potentiae* or the perfection of a power; the perfection of the power of willing that which is directed to the good. Both as a moral and political category, virtue is a disposition that forms passions and/or creates habits. Personal moral virtue and political virtue (i.e. excellence or strength) are movements of the powers of the soul and habits directed towards the good of human flourishing as appointed by reason. Personal and political action inclined habitually to the good of reason belong to the field of moral virtue, which is identical with practical wisdom. When a person (or, by extension, a society or nation) acts contrary to virtue they do not lose their habit of virtue immediately because a habit does not proceed from one single act: 'and one sinful act does not destroy a habit of acquired virtue, since it is not an act but a habit, that is directly contrary to a habit.'[91] Yet the strength or excellence of the agent, and the necessarily customary basis of society or international community, is weakened.

Law is, as Simon expounds, a premise or work of reason having the character of a proposition upon which an argument is based or from which a conclusion is drawn.[92] The relation between premise and conclusion is not that of logical deduction; there are no reliable middle terms that permit unquestionable demonstration of a conclusion but there are inclinations that tend towards differing directions: 'That a conclusion is always necessary as the antecedent is almost a definition of a strictly logical connection. But the antecedents may be divided into those which do not and those which do involve a contingent condition.'[93] Like all other questions about human law, the question of why torture is wrong involves contingent conditions between the premises concerning the requirements of justice and a conclusion. What matters are the kinds of measure and/or direction by which a law is both measured

---

[91]Porter, *Moral Action*, p. 63.
[92]Simon, *The Tradition of Natural Law*, p. 129.
[93]Simon, *The Tradition of Natural Law*, p. 151.

and by which it measures human action. Aquinas's *Treatise on Law* posits:

> Since law is a kind of rule and measure, it may be in something in two ways. First, as in that which measures and rules: and since this is proper to reason, it follows that, in this way, law is in the reason alone. Secondly, as in that which is measured and ruled. In this way, law is in all those things that are inclined to something by reason of some law: so that any inclination arising from a law, may be called a law, not essentially but by participation as it were. And thus the inclination of the members to concupiscence is called 'the law of the members'.[94]

Law has to do with reason both with reference to how it is measured and to how it measures. The 'law in my members' about which Paul spoke in Romans 7.23, and to which the objection that Aquinas counters alludes, makes plain that law of itself is not the power of reason. The law or that which regulates the passions may or may not participate in reason. When the law leads to sin (*fomes peccati*) it has nothing to do with reason. Yet law may still be spoken of as 'a rule and measure of acts' that binds one to act, because law properly directs to those things that are inclined to by reason.[95]

Aquinas's first article on this subject is concerned with the final cause, end or purpose of law, and his second with how law is properly ordered to the common good:

> Consequently, since the law is chiefly ordained to the common good, any other precept in regard to some individual work, must needs be devoid of the nature of a law, save in so far as it regards the common good. Therefore every law is ordained to the common good.[96]

Laws may deal with relatively small, particular matters or particular ends. The example often given is traffic regulations. It does not really matter whether a nation's cars drive on the left or the right

---

[94]Aquinas, *ST*, I–II, q. 90, a. 1, ad. 1.
[95]Aquinas, *ST*, I–II, q. 90, a. 1, c.
[96]Aquinas, *ST*, I–II, q. 90, a. 2, c.

of the street but it does matter that the law sets a general rule for traffic, for the sake of the common good:

> Actions are indeed concerned with particular matters: but those particular matters are referable to the common good, not as to a common genus or species, but as to a common final cause, according as the common good is said to be the common end.[97]

The general requirement of law is that it is ordained or directed towards the common good which, in turn, is constituted by good order and just peace. To ask whether a law is reasonable is to ask about how it is relative to the common good which enjoys primacy over the particular good.

The rules of custom are not moral niceties or pieties but ordinances of reason for the common good; they are norms of action generated by teleologically oriented reason. Laws that come into custom 'by reason of utility' have been sanctioned 'by fear and reverence for the law'.[98] Moreover, the rules of custom are not expected to be solely other-regarding. Self-interest (and, analogously, state interest) does not equate necessarily to self-centredness but is to be understood in relation to wider, collective goods. Natural self-love is for Aquinas the drive to preserve life. Subsequent forms of self-interest are judged according to how they participate in rationality. 'Even the lower appetitive powers are called rational, in so far as "they partake of reason in some sort".'[99] The truest self-love consists in turning oneself towards God in search of the *visio Dei*. Aquinas's focus is less on how morality can be saved from consideration of self-interest than on how self-interest is guided by reason's command; reason's striving after human fulfilment; reason's directedness towards the truth, the common good and thus to God. The theological components of Aquinas's *Treatise on Law* cannot be excised from his practical philosophy without damage to the whole. Aquinas's primary concern is to relate the natural law to the eternal law. Any

---

[97]Aquinas, *ST*, I–II, q. 90, a. 2, ad. 2.
[98]Charlesworth and Chinkin, *The Boundaries of International Law*, pp. 91–3.
[99]Aquinas, *ST*, I–II, q. 24, a. 1 (quoting Aristotle's *Nichomachean Ethics*, bk 1, ch. 13).

theology-lite reading of Aquinas because it risks (mis)representing him as a practical philosopher whose notion of integral human fulfilment or this-worldly happiness is detachable from its theological roots; Thomist realism is rooted in a theologically motivated account of the relation of the good of 'the part' or 'the one only' to the good of 'the whole'. This said, the suggestion is that Aquinas's realism still speaks to self-interested people (and states) in societies where the accommodation of significant individual interests to the good of the many is rarely easy yet neglect of the commonweal could be disastrous for all concerned.

My purpose is not to place a Thomist approach to natural law reasoning in unqualified conflict with Habermasian-type notions of legitimacy. Others have shown it possible to read Habermas and Karol Wojtyla (Pope John Paul II) together as highly compatible theorists of liberal democracy, and that they can be allies in the development of strong international institutions and the protection of fundamental rights.[100] In many respects, Habermas and Wojtyla share common concerns and objectives. Similarities can be noted as to how each grounds their social and political critiques on congruent analyses of intersubjectivity. The debate is more subtle. In the opening sections above, the debate concerning Goldsmith and Posner's statism was cast more-or-less in terms of how to keep their present-day realism realist enough in the face of twenty-first-century global uncertainties. Here, the question about the meaning of legitimacy versus authority in selected neo-Kantian versions of cosmopolitanism is about how to keep the debate sufficiently cosmopolitan and adequately reasonable. The challenge from Aquinas is that customary law, which arises from political action inclined habitually to the common good' is still potentially better able to serve the interests of all than short-term action for state interest, and that lacking ethical orientation towards a common good that exceeds the conditions of legitimate law. Following Aquinas, the point is that a law which is the expression of democratic will may have formal legitimacy but its authority is unwarranted unless the import of the law bears reference to the common good.

---

[100]Celestino Perez, 'Jürgen Habermas and Pope John Paul II on Faith, Reason and Politics in the Modern World', PhD thesis, Indiana University, Bloomington, 2008 http://gradworks.umi.com/33/19/3319921.html [accessed 24 February 2013].

Can international common good be known and advanced?

A theoretical point of tension throughout this chapter has been whether, to have the character of a rule and measure of human action, a law should be primarily the work of reason or the will. Writing in Protestant Thomist perspective, I have advocated the primacy of reason over will and followed Aquinas in affirming that law is primarily the work of reason. Analogous to Ricoeur's affirmation of the primacy of ethics over morality but yet complementarity of the two approaches, there is no attempt to substitute one for the other but merely describe the orientation of reasoning about human law. Political will (whether of a sovereign, president and/or a democratic people) is arbitrary and potentially lawless unless also reasonable. Hence the need to ask in what capacity law is a work of reason.[101] 'Sound method requires that we should consider first that which is ultimate in the system of practical reason, that is, the fully determinate judgements which apply to the action immediately.'[102] Thinking with Aquinas, the suggestion has been that all practical matters pertaining to diverse contingent scenarios and particular situations require a primary orientation towards the proper ends of law, and subordinate considerations with respect to moral norms; good law is premised or based on the orientation of reason towards the proper ends of law. The reality of human politics is that actual laws participate unequally in the reasonable character of law.[103] Nevertheless, the critical work required concerns whether the laws in question are so ordered and should therefore be regarded as binding.

The main applied point of tension has been the *jus cogens* norm against torture that some sought to circumvent when adherence to it was deemed not to be in a nation's short-term interests. Our question has been whether it is 'nebulous speculation', to borrow Morgenthau's phrase, to hold that law is a rule of reason, relative to the common good, that proceeds from the community, or whether (international) law may still be considered properly as an ordinance

---

[101]Simon, *The Tradition of Natural Law*, p. 82.
[102]Simon, *The Tradition of Natural Law*, p. 82.
[103]Simon, *The Tradition of Natural Law*, p. 86.

of reason for common good. In the context of international law, to ask about this understanding of normativity and when a law is binding is to ask whether the international common good has primacy over the political will of a given nation. As Simon is clear: 'To ask whether this understanding of law is warranted is the same as to ask whether the common good has primacy over the private good.'[104] It is to ask whether international common good is something more than the aggregate of individual interests pursued autonomously. Can international common good function as an object of practical knowledge? Can international common good be known and advanced? Or is it best served through the discrete, independent and autonomous pursuit by nation-states of respective national interests?

These questions are familiar in liberal democracies at the level of the nation. Michael Novak, for instance, claims that it is possible to bridge the gap between Aquinas's treatment of the common good in the medieval era and present-day practices of liberal democracy but that this bridge will lead to a thin, formal concept of the common good as a conceptual standard to be distinguished sharply from any material conception of what that the good entails. The three features of liberal democracy central to Novak's revised concept of the common good are the distinction between the state and society, the need to restrict political authority and the realization that the modern social order is typically tripartite, consisting of economic, political and moral-cultural systems.[105] Novak's work is useful as indicative of a consensus position that nothing a priori prevents this kind of dialogic engagement between Aquinas's socio-economic and political context and our own. He supposes, however, that Aquinas's concern for the common good can be met with a Rawlsian-type supposition (which, for our purposes, is shared by Goldsmith and Posner) that both individuals and nation-states are to determine for themselves in what the common good consists – analogous in economic terms to the operations of the free market. For Novak, the common good is striven for among plural and fundamentally

---

[104]Simon, *The Tradition of Natural Law*, p. 87.
[105]See Michael Novak, *Free Persons and the Common Good* (New York: Madison Books, 1989), pp. 41–73. For a summary, see Thomas R. Rourke, 'Michael Novak and Yves R. Simon on the Common Good and Capitalism', *The Review of Politics* 58 (Spring 1996), p. 231.

free persons who decide for themselves in what the common good consists; again, no one can say in what the common good consists substantively.

At the international level, the question is still whether, following Aquinas, it is possible for a natural law reasoner to argue convincingly today that something more than the discrete, autonomous pursuit of individual or national interest is required for adequate consideration of common good. In more applied terms, does claiming normativity for international law (*jus cogens* norms especially) with reference to morality, religion, higher universal norms, or indeed, anything beyond national self-interests, stray into nebulous and irresponsible speculation or to advocate a position that is reasonable? Can the completeness that determines the common good of the international arena still be persuasive when set against thinner, liberal conceptions of common good as comprising the aggregate of discrete national goods? If so, the issue becomes whether permitting state-sponsored torture contributes to good international order, just peace in the international arena and the international common good. Whether such questions tend the leaders of nation-states towards 'nebulous speculation' and/or peaceable co-existence is the question that remains.

4

Peacemaking through Law: Ambivalence, Violence and Answerability

'Peacemaking is at the heart of the teaching of Jesus, not an optional extra.'[1] So too is the love of enemies. Consequently, the only valid reason for going to war in the classic, theologically oriented tradition of just war reasoning was the restoration of peace after the doing of injustice. Today, at a time of changing definitions of 'war' and 'armed conflict', and amidst suggestions that the classic just war tradition is exhausted because it cannot meet the challenges of new modes of armed conflict against non-state parties and terrorist groups, Christian people are faced with difficult questions about how to bear continuing witness to the evangelical imperatives to seek peace and love one's enemy.

Peacemaking through law has many dimensions. I have written elsewhere about the need for accountability in contexts where the laws of armed conflict apply, how insufficient information is often available in order for appropriate standards of answerability to be met, about issues of transparency and accountability concerning civilian casualties and other effects of

---

[1]See the report produced jointly by the Methodist Church and the United Reformed Church, *Peacemaking: A Christian Vocation* (London: Trustees for the Methodist Church and the United Reformed Church, 2006), p. 24. I was a member of the working party that wrote this document and am grateful to all colleagues for conversation and mutual learning.

weaponry in remote areas, and more.[2] Normative standards demand
that prior procedural requirements are met. Hence it is troubling
that the repeated witness of UN Special Rapporteurs has been that
procedural requirements are being avoided.[3] Legal theorist Nils
Melzer makes the point as follows:

> While it may be permissible and even necessary to periodically
> challenge the adequacy of the law in force, it would be a
> catastrophic failure of civilization to allow the demise of the
> fundamental principle according to which collective power and
> authority must be exercised in accordance with predictable,
> reliable and generally binding rules.[4]

If the rule of law has normative content that remains vitally important in safeguarding the international community from descent into
arbitrariness and uncontrolled use of brute force, then the call to
accountability is of pressing concern. For engagement to be possible
with the normative content of the rule or *ruling* of law with respect
to the laws of armed conflict, preliminary procedural requirements
of answerability must be met. Where nation-states are reluctant to

---

[2]Esther D. Reed: '"Let All the Earth Keep Silence": Law, Religion and Answerability
for Targeted Killings', *Oxford Journal of Law and Religion* 1 (2012), pp. 496–509.
[3]In a report to the UN General Assembly human rights committee in October
2010, Philip Alston's successor Christof Heyns called for a halt to CIA-directed
drone strikes on al-Qaeda and Taliban suspects in Afghanistan and Pakistan until
serious concerns about violations of international human rights and humanitarian
law could be investigated (Patrick Worsnip, 'U.N. Urged to Set up Panel on Ethics
of Robot Weapons', 22 October 2010 www.reuters.com/article/2010/10/22/us-un-
rights-robots-idUSTRE69L5RL20101022 [accessed 10 December 2011]). There
is widespread recognition of issues concerning transparency and accountability
relating to difficulties of obtaining accurate information about civilian casualties
and other effects of armed unmanned aerial systems in remote areas. Counter-
terrorism experts David Kilcullen and Andrew Exum estimate that, in early 2009,
drones were killing 50 people for every intended target, and speak of how the
United States has used the CIA for such operations because it is not part of the
armed forces and therefore not bound by the Uniform Code of Military Justice to
respect the laws and customs of war. See Mary Ellen O'Connell, 'Unlawful Killing
with Combat Drones: A Case Study of Pakistan, 2004–2009', Notre Dame Legal
Studies Research Paper, no. 09–43, 9 November 2009, p. 7 http://papers.ssrn.com/
sol3/papers.cfm?abstract_id=1501144 [accessed 4 December 2011].
[4]Nils Melzer, *Targeted Killing in International Law* (Oxford: Oxford University
Press, 2008), p. 420.

submit to minimum levels of international accountability, thereby evading the procedural requirements of the compliance of states with international law, normative standards cannot be applied.

Non-international and international armed conflict

I remain concerned about these issues of transparency and accountability but concentrate in this chapter on the status of the enemy and the implications of a trend under way away from law enforcement as the conventional paradigm for addressing terrorism towards a lowering of the threshold at which international humanitarian law (IHL, otherwise referred to as LOAC or the law of armed conflict) applies.[5] At issue especially are attitudes to enemies of the state and the targeted killing of individuals outside of lawfully recognized battlefields, and the increasing prevalence of the idea that governments have a right to kill citizens who are senior leaders in al-Qaeda or affiliate groups who pose an imminent threat of attack against the United States, and whose capture is not feasible.[6] More specifically, the legal issue is which body of law should be applied: international humanitarian law, or human rights and law enforcement legislation? The matter turns on where the threshold is to be drawn between international and non-international armed conflict. If the threshold is deemed to be

---

[5]'Armed conflict' is generally viewed as being broader than the traditional concept of 'war', but the modern international law of war is now called the law of armed conflict or 'international humanitarian law'.

[6]I understand targeted killings to be 'the intentional, premeditated and deliberate use of lethal force, by States or their agents acting under colour of law, or by an organized armed group in armed conflict, against a specific individual who is not in the physical custody of the perpetrator'. I take this definition from Philip Alston, UN Special Rapporteur 2004–10, and refer especially to his concerns about the 'highly problematic blurring and expansion of the boundaries of the applicable legal frameworks – human rights law, the laws of war and the law applicable to the use of inter-state force' and 'the displacement of clear legal standards with a vaguely defined licence to kill, and the creation of a major accountability vacuum' (addendum to the Report of the United Nations Special Rapporteur on Extrajudicial, Summary or Arbitrary Executions, 28 May 2010 www2.ohchr.org/english/bodies/hrcouncil/docs/14session/A.HRC.14.24.Add6.pdf [accessed 4 December 2011]).

low, then international humanitarian law is triggered by insurgency and terrorist attacks classified as non-international armed conflicts. If the threshold is maintained at the higher level of international armed conflict, international humanitarian law does not apply, but law enforcement and human rights law do.[7]

The matter is of the highest international import, and it is contentious:

> The definitions of international and internal armed conflict are of considerable importance. Neither term is defined in the Geneva Conventions or other applicable agreements. Whereas there is an extensive literature on the definition of 'war' in international law, armed conflict has always been considered a purely factual notion and there have been few attempts to define or even describe it.[8]

As surprising as it might seem, international law does not yield a definition of armed conflict that attracts broad-based consensus.[9] Article 51 of the Charter of the United Nations recognizes the inherent right of individual or collective self-defence if an armed attack occurs against a member of the United Nations 'until the Security Council has taken measures necessary to maintain international peace and security'. Historically, such attacks have most commonly been made by one nation-state against another, and international humanitarian law is applicable.[10] 'The traditional position is that IHL provides *lex specialis* in non-international armed conflict.'[11] Since the attacks of 11 September 2001, however,

---

[7] See Anthony Cullen, 'The Threshold of Non-International Armed Conflict', in idem, *The Concept of Non-International Armed Conflict in International Humanitarian Law* (Cambridge: Cambridge University Press, 2010), pp. 117–57.

[8] Christopher Greenwood, 'The Development of International Humanitarian Law by the International Criminal Tribunal for the Former Yugoslavia', *Max Planck Yearbook of United Nations Law* 2 (1998), p. 114 www.mpil.de/shared/data/pdf/pdfmpunyb/greenwood_2.pdf [accessed 19 February 2013].

[9] For an account of the Report on the Meaning of Armed Conflict issued by the International Law Association in 2008 to address this need, see Mary Ellen O'Connell, 'Defining Armed Conflict', *Journal of Conflict and Security Law* 13 (2008), pp. 393–400.

[10] Article 51, Charter of the United Nations, 26 June 1945 www.un.org/en/documents/charter/ [accessed 19 February 2013].

[11] Christine Gray, 'The Meaning of Armed Conflict: Non-International Armed Conflict', in Mary Ellen O'Connell (ed.), *What is War? An Investigation in the Wake of 9/11* (Leiden: Martinus Nijhoff, 2012), p. 78.

the issue of whether international humanitarian law is applicable in armed responses to non-state actors has become pressing.

Academic, legal and political opinion is divided.[12] The Obama Administration was clear that non-international armed conflict against non-state actors such as al-Qaeda and its affiliates triggers international humanitarian law.[13] Its policy on the use of armed unmanned aerial vehicles (drone warfare) and targeted killing was based on the opinion that international humanitarian law rather than human rights or international criminal law applies even if the action takes place in a territory outside a *de jure* armed conflict. There is a sufficient level of violence and it is being conducted with sufficient organization and duration to cross the threshold into what is, in effect, an international armed conflict governed by IHL. Consequently, the question of where the armed conflict is taking place, or why, is replaced by the question of the identity of the actor. Whether or not the target is a member of the armed conflict becomes the primary legal question rather than whether he is a combatant in a field of battle. Different laws then apply. In a field of battle, for instance, an unarmed combatant running away from the site of an exchange of fire may be targeted and shot. They are an enemy combatant and thus a lawful target. Outside a field of battle, where human rights and international criminal law applies, the target must be treated on the basis of their actions rather than their identity. The rationale is that, given the nature of international terrorism, the conflict must follow whether the terrorist attacks happen; the identity of the target (whether or not they are a terrorist) is the more appropriate issue than where the conflict is taking place, or why.

Those concerned about the implications of a low threshold for triggering international humanitarian law ask whether the global war against al-Qaeda and its affiliates has been appropriately dubbed a 'war' or armed conflict because this, in effect, justifies the killing of targets anywhere in the world and the detention without trial of

---

[12]See Sandesh Sivakumaran, *The Law of Non-International Armed Conflict* (Oxford: Oxford University Press, 2012).

[13]See Harold H. Koh, US Department of State, 'The Obama Administration and International Law', paper presented at the annual meeting of the American Society of International Law, Washington, DC, 25 March 2010 www.state.gov/s/l/releases/remarks/139119.htm [accessed 20 February 2013].

persons designated enemy combatants. If the United States is not lawfully at war with al-Qaeda and its affiliates under international law, then recent killings of terrorist suspects and associated claims by the Obama Administration look suspiciously like a claimed right to use military force in states experiencing instability when there is no international legal right to exercise military force on this basis. If the United States is not lawfully at war but is ordering targeted killings in Somalia, Yemen and elsewhere, the question is whether we are dealing with a vaguely defined executive licence to kill and a major 'accountability vacuum'.[14] Related issues arise concerning violations of the *jus cogens* norm against arbitrary killing, and whether any such violations are tantamount to a supposed right to kill.[15]

Consider the high-profile case of Anwar al-Awlaki, a radical American-born Muslim cleric who is widely reported as having become a leading figure in al-Qaeda's affiliate in Yemen.[16] He was killed in Yemen on 30 September 2011 by a missile fired from an American drone. There is little doubt that al-Awlaki was a prominent English-speaking advocate of violent jihad against the United States. It is widely reported that his preaching was broadcast over the internet. *The New York Times* has also reported evidence of incriminating contact with convicted terrorists. This case raises many vexed issues including whether and/or on what grounds such killing is justified by the administration, whether this kind of action is properly dubbed an 'executive power to kill',[17] and whether the United States can regard an American citizen as an enemy combatant. The journalist Charlie Savage reported that a roughly 50-page memorandum prepared by the Justice Department's Office of Legal Counsel, completed around June 2010, 'concluded that Mr. Awlaki could be legally killed, if it was not feasible to capture him, because intelligence agencies said that he was taking part in the war between the United States and Al Qaeda and posed a significant

---

[14]Philip Alston, Report of the United Nations Special Rapporteur.
[15]O'Connell, 'Unlawful Killing with Combat Drones', p. 7
[16]'Anwar al-Alawki', *New York Times*, 19 October 2012 http://topics.nytimes.com/topics/reference/timestopics/people/a/anwar_al_awlaki/index.html [accessed 20 February 2013].
[17]David Cole, 'Killing Citizens in Secret', *New York Review of Books* blog, 9 October 2012 www.nybooks.com/blogs/nyrblog/2012/nov/28/its-time-stop-killing-secret/ [accessed 20 February 2013].

threat to Americans, as well as because Yemeni authorities were unable or unwilling to stop him.'[18]

As Savage noted, several news reports before June 2010 had quoted anonymous counter-terrorism officials as saying that al-Awlaki had been placed on a kill-or-capture list around the time of the attempted bombing of a Detroit-bound airliner on 25 December 2009. Al-Awlaki had been accused of helping to recruit the attacker for that operation. The Justice Department, said Savage, concluded that Awlaki was covered by the authorization to use military force against al-Qaeda that Congress enacted shortly after 11 September 2001 – the implication being that the Obama Administration had not breached the Fifth Amendment's guarantee that the government may not deprive a person of life 'without due process of law'. It would not have been feasible to capture him and, in any case, the Yemen authorities reportedly permitted the drone attack. The issue, of course, is that al-Awlaki was not on the battlefield; he was in Yemen. While it is not necessarily illegal to kill a citizen without trial in warfare, the definition of 'war' against al-Qaeda and its affiliates remains contested. There is a strong case to be answered that what the memorandum advocates what is, in effect, an executive power to kill. Even though al-Awlaki was alleged to be a leader of al-Qaeda in the Arabian Peninsula (AQAP), an organization in Yemen founded long after the 11 September attacks, he had never been tried, 'much less convicted, for any terrorist crime'.[19]

In March 2012 the US Attorney General, Eric Holder, relied on a Second World War legal case to assert that citizenship did not protect a US national from the consequences of his belligerency. In *Ex parte Quirin,* the Supreme Court had held that 'citizenship in the United States of an enemy belligerent does not relieve him from the consequences of a belligerency which is unlawful because in violation of the law of war.'[20] Speaking at Northwestern University School of Law, Holder proceeded to distinguish between 'due

[18]Charlie Savage, 'Secret U.S. Memo Made Legal Case to Kill a Citizen', *New York Times,* 8 October 2011 www.nytimes.com/2011/10/09/world/middleeast/secret-us-memo-made-legal-case-to-kill-a-citizen.html?pagewanted=all&_r=0 [accessed 20 February 2013].

[19]Cole, 'Killing Citizens in Secret'.

[20]Stephanie Hessler, 'Presidential Power to Kill? Obama's Assassination Orders Deface the Constitution', *Washington Times,* 16 March 2012 www.washingtontimes.com/news/2012/mar/16/presidential-power-to-kill/ [accessed 20 February 2013].

process' and 'judicial process', laying out the 'due process' now
followed by the United States before carrying out the kind of strikes
that killed Anwar al-Awlaki and his 16-year-old son:

A 'thorough and careful review' determines the individual poses
an 'imminent threat' of violent attack against the United States.

Capture is not feasible.

The operation is carried out in a manner consistent with the law
of war.[21]

Mr Holder's speech is noteworthy for its emphasis on the United
States's track record in prosecuting terrorists:

Over the past three years, we've built a remarkable record of
success in terror prosecutions. For example, in October, we
secured a conviction against Umar Farouk Abdulmutallab for
his role in the attempted bombing of an airplane traveling from
Amsterdam to Detroit on Christmas Day 2009. . . .

In addition to Abdulmutallab, Faizal Shahzad, the attempted
Times Square bomber, Ahmed Ghailani, a conspirator in the
1998 U.S. embassy bombings in Kenya and Tanzania, and three
individuals who plotted an attack against John F. Kennedy
Airport in 2007, have also recently begun serving life sentences.
And convictions have been obtained in the cases of several
homegrown extremists, as well. . . .

. . . Although far too many choose to ignore this fact, the previous
Administration consistently relied on criminal prosecutions in
federal court to bring terrorists to justice. John Walker Lindh,
attempted shoe bomber Richard Reid, and 9/11 conspirator
Zacarias Moussaoui were among the hundreds of defendants

---

[21]Attorney General Eric Holder, speech at Northwestern University School of
Law, Chicago, 5 March 2012 www.northwestern.edu/newscenter/stories/2012/03/
attorney-general-holder.html [accessed 20 February 2013]. See also Tom Parker,
'Eric Holder Unveils "The Cake Doctrine"', Human Rights Now blog, Amnesty
International, 6 March 2012 http://blog.amnestyusa.org/us/eric-holder-unveils-the-
cake-doctrine-2/ [accessed 20 February 2013]; Kevin Johnson, 'Holder: Constitution
Doesn't Cover Terrorists', USA Today, 3 March 2012 http://usatoday30.usatoday.
com/news/washington/story/2012–03–05/eric-holder-killing-us-citizens-terrorist-
threat/53374776/1 [accessed 20 February 2013].

convicted of terrorism-related offenses – without political controversy – during the last administration.[22]

He draws attention deliberately to the use of the courts to effect judgement while contending simultaneously that the process outlined above is sufficient to meet the 'due process' standard in the Fifth Amendment.

The case of al-Awlaki is peculiar in that he was an American citizen. The choice before the Obama Administration has been which set(s) of law to apply and where to set the threshold at which IHL applies in the context of counter-terrorism.[23] 'The US administration admits that the laws of war require "translation" in order to be applied in the context of counter-terrorism.'[24] History will judge whether this was a choice that made for peace or not. So, for instance, on 1 May 2012 the BBC reported that John Brennan, chief adviser on counter-terrorism to President Barack Obama, addressed this issue in a televised speech to a Washington think tank. Nothing in international law, he said, prohibits the United States from using lethal force against US enemies outside of an active battlefield, 'at least when the country involved consents, or is unable or unwilling to take action against the threat'. Targeted strikes are ethical: 'Without question, the ability to target a specific individual, from hundreds or thousands of miles away, raises profound questions.' But it is useful, said Brennan, 'to consider the use of such strikes against the basic principles of the laws of war that govern the use of force. Targeted strikes conform to the principle of necessity; the requirement that the target have definite military value. In this armed conflict, individuals who are part of al-Qaeda or its associated forces are legitimate military targets.'[25] But opinion is divided. Hina Shamsi, director of the American Civil Liberties Union, told the BBC's World Today programme that Mr Brennan's speech showed the US administration believed its authority went 'far beyond what has been recognized under international law'. Few things are as dangerous, she said, as the proposition that 'the

[22]Holder, 5 March 2012.
[23]Koh, 'The Obama Administration and International Law'
[24]Koh, 'The Obama Administration and International Law'.
[25]BBC World News (video clip), 1 May 2012 (my rendition of television footage) www.bbc.co.uk/news/world-us-canada-17901400 [accessed 20 February 2013].

government should be able to kill people anywhere in the word, including citizens, on the basis of legal standards and evidence that are never submitted to the court either before or after the fact.'[26]

Just war criteria stretched to breaking point?

The character of international terrorism in our own time leads some to challenge the continuing relevance of traditional just war criteria. As expounded in a now famous *Marine Corps Gazette* article of October 1989, fourth-generation warfare (4GW) is nonlinear, possibly to the point of having no delineated battlefields or fronts; it is dispersed and largely undefined.[27] The distinction between 'civilian' and 'military' may disappear as lines also become blurred between other types of responsibility and active 'mission'. The typical scenario is not democracies at war because, to cite Terry Terriff, Aaron Karp and Regina Karp, virtually no states with respected governments of any stripe fight one another; rather, war has become associated with 'ever more nebulous events'.[28] Warfare is no longer focused at a contested frontier between lands controlled by opposing forces, as at the Western Front during the First or Second World Wars, but is conducted on the streets and in commercial aircraft. The distinction between war and peace is blurred. Hence the *Marine Corps Gazette* article predicted: 'Major military facilities, such as airfields, fixed communications sites, and large

---

[26]Hina Shamsi comments in 'White House in First Detailed Comments on Drone Strikes', BBC World News, 1 May 2012 www.bbc.co.uk/news/world-us-canada-17901400 [accessed 20 February 2013].

[27]William S. Lind et al., 'The Changing Face of War: Into the Fourth Generation', in Terry Terriff, Aaron Karp and Regina Karp (eds), *Global Insurgency and the Future of Armed Conflict: Debating Fourth-Generation Warfare* (London: Routledge, 2008), pp. 13–20. Lind's co-authors were Col. Keith Nightengale (USA), Capt. John F. Schmitt (USMC), Col Joseph W. Sutton (USA) and Lt Col Gary I. Wilson (USMCR). The sequence of 'generations' of warfare is summarized by Greg Wilcox and G. I. Wilson as follows: 1GW – up to and including the Age of Napoleon: armies along battle lines, bronze cannon, muskets; 2GW – the Age of Firepower (American Civil War, First World War); 3GW – the Age of Manœuvre and Ideas (Second World War, Korean War, Gulf War) including technological advantages that enable forces to strike targets from greater distances; 4GW – the Age of Asymmetric Warfare: small independent action cells.

[28]Terriff et al., (eds), *Global Insurgency*, p. 3.

headquarters will become rarities because of their vulnerability; the same may be true of civilian equivalents, such as seats of government, power plants, and industrial sites (including knowledge as well as manufacturing industries).'[29] While all of these elements are present in third-generation warfare, characterized by the manœuvering of battleships, aircraft, military personnel and ideas, fourth-generation warfare accentuates them considerably. The enemy uses methods that differ substantially from their opponent's usual mode of operation and seeks disproportionate psychological and political advantage as compared to the 'asymmetric' investment.

Hence the supposed problem that traditional just war criteria are stretched to breaking point: 'Just War Theory now faces problems its framers never expected, dragging it far beyond ethical assessments of separately identifiable state ventures of organised military-on-military violence.'[30] This is Paul Schulte's summary of the experience of many that it has become increasingly difficult to match just war theory to 'war' or 'armed conflict' in the years following the attacks of 11 September 2001. Schulte's working understanding of just war theory is that given by General Lord Charles Guthrie of Craigiebank, Chief of the Defence Staff 1997–2001, and Sir Michael Quinlan, Permanent Under-Secretary of State 1988–92, in *Just War: The Just War Tradition; Ethics in Modern Warfare*.[31] This slim volume gives an overview of the roots of this tradition in Roman law and the writings of Augustine and Aquinas, and states clearly the criteria that are now accepted as falling into two groups: 'the right to fight' and 'how to fight right'.[32] Briefly stated, under *jus ad bellum* these criteria are just cause, proportionate cause, right intention, right authority, reasonable prospect of success, last resort and, under *jus in bello*, treat discrimination and proportionality.[33] The book proceeds to explicate their meaning

[29]Lind et al., 'The Changing Face of War', p. 20.
[30]Paul Schulte, 'Going off the Reservation into the Sanctuary: Cross-Border Counter-Terrorist Operations, Fourth Generation Warfare and the Ethical Insufficiency of Contemporary Just War Thinking', in David Fisher and Brian Wicker (eds), *Just War on Terror? A Christian and Muslim Response* (Farnham, Surrey: Ashgate, 2010), pp. 151–74.
[31]Charles Guthrie and Michael Quinlan, *Just War: The Just War Tradition; Ethics in Modern Warfare* (London: Bloomsbury, 2007).
[32]Guthrie and Quinlan, *Just War*, p. 11.
[33]Guthrie and Quinlan, *Just War*, pp. 11–15.

in practice with admirable clarity and brevity, and with reference to conflicts including the Second World War, the Soviet invasions to suppress freedom in Hungary in 1956 and Czechoslovakia in 1968, the 1990–91 Gulf conflict, NATO action in Kosovo in 1998 and the invasion of Iraq in 2003. Schulte's point is not only that inadequate engagement is offered in this book (which he takes as representative of the literature) with respect to the realities of armed conflict today, but that attempts at such engagement are unlikely to be fruitful.

Briefly stated, the issue of *proportionate cause* dissolves into what an electorate will stomach, and how to negotiate strategic alliances with other nations. It is difficult, if not impossible, says Schulte, for today's political and military leaders to weigh the question of proportionate cause when the emotions of an electorate are running high and the pertinent question – How significant is the threat? – is not capable of easy answer. The question of *right authority* is difficult to address at a time when the UN Security Council is viewed by many as an ice pack that typically freezes out decisive action when most needed. 'There is deep disagreement about which authority can give sufficient legitimacy today to authorise these actions.'[34] Only the Security Council? Or regional organizations such as NATO (as in its 1999 armed intervention over Kosovo)? Or perhaps, in future, the African Union? The principle of *last resort* is increasingly difficult to employ in moral and political thinking about fourth-generation warfare because few cross-boundary interventions will be an absolute or literal last resort; '[t]here will generally be other, varyingly effective, Lines of Operation'.[35] Many lines of operation will not work alone, or at all. Some might anyway be pursued 'synergistically in parallel – often on back channels'.[36] It is increasingly unclear what might count as a *reasonable prospect of success*. Outright victory, analogous to that achieved against the Nazi regime at the end of the Second World War, is impossible. What, then, might meet this criterion? Would improvement of the geopolitical balance be adequate under classical formulations of the central concerns of the just war tradition? What about eliminating a significant proportion of the insurgent leadership and arsenal or

---

[34]Schulte, 'Going off the Reservation', p. 157.
[35]Schulte, 'Going off the Reservation', p. 162.
[36]Schulte, 'Going off the Reservation', p. 163.

achieving a more satisfactory *'hurting stalemate'*?[37] What about degrading the will of the enemy organization – or its 'civilian' supporters? What should count as 'reasonable', and to whom? How much security is enough? None of these questions is capable of ready answer. Hence Schulte's point that just war tradition is increasingly likely to be sidelined.

Schulte is not alone in his observations. General Sir Rupert Smith's widely read *The Utility of Force: The Art of War in the Modern World* makes broadly similar observations:

- The ends for which we fight are changing from the hard objectives that decide a political outcome to those of establishing conditions in which the outcome may be decided.

- We fight among the people, not on the battlefield.

- Our conflicts tend to be timeless, even unending.

- We fight so as to preserve the force rather than risking all to gain the objective.

- On each occasion new uses are found for old weapons and organizations which are the projects of industrial war.

- The sides are mostly non-state, comprising some form of multi-national grouping against some non-state party or parties.[38]

Schulte and Smith both question whether the just war tradition supplies the necessary answers to low intensity but long-running and seemingly intractable conflicts against terrorists. It is increasingly difficult, they imply, to address questions of *just intent* and *proportionate cause* in the terms bequeathed by the just war tradition when predicted harms include suicide bombers in city streets, the shooting down of aircraft by portable missile systems, and effective and deployable chemical, biological, radiological and nuclear weapons. During so-called 4GW operations, *discrimination*

---

[37]Schulte, 'Going off the Reservation', pp. 159–60 (emphasis in original). Schulte explains the term: frequently encountered in conflict resolution analysis, it is connected with the notion of 'ripeness' – that stage in a conflict when both sides might be willing to consider concessions to escape from a mutually intolerable situation.

[38]Rupert Smith, The Utility of Force: The Art of War in the Modern World (London: Penguin, 2005), p. 269.

between combatant and non-combatant is notoriously difficult to achieve because terrorists locate themselves within civilian communities. Insurgents are indistinguishable from the people. They aim to create and exploit menace, uncertainty, an atmosphere of discord, doubt, chaos and mistrust; and operate typically by aiming to 'sever moral bonds that bind people to existing regime'.[39] *Proportionality* calculations are thrown into disarray, as forward-looking calculations are increasingly necessary but difficult to make.

On the changing definition of war

International law supposes a fundamental distinction between peace and armed conflict. Different sets of laws apply in the two conditions. Of particular concern is the delimitation of lethal force to a lawfully recognized, active battlefield. Hence the significance of the language of 'war' as used by the Bush and Obama administrations against 'terror' and 'al-Qaeda, the Taliban and their known affiliates' respectively. President George W. Bush, speaking to the nation in the aftermath of 11 September 2001, used the phrase 'war on terror':

> On September the 11th, enemies of freedom committed an act of war against our country. Americans have known wars – but for the past 136 years, they have been wars on foreign soil, except for one Sunday in 1941. Americans have known the casualties of war – but not at the center of a great city on a peaceful morning. Americans have known surprise attacks – but never before on thousands of civilians. All of this was brought upon us in a single day – and night fell on a different world, a world where freedom itself is under attack. . . .
>
> Our war on terror begins with al Qaeda, but it does not end there. It will not end until every terrorist group of global reach has been found, stopped and defeated.[40]

---

[39]John R. Boyd, 'Patterns of Conflict' (1982) www.dnipogo.org/fcs/pdf/4GW_wilson-wilcox_boyd_conf_2002.pdf [accessed 20 February 2013].
[40]George W. Bush, address to Joint Session of Congress, 20 September 2001 http://georgewbush-whitehouse.archives.gov/news/releases/2001/09/20010920–8.html [accessed 20 February 2013].

This war would not be like previous wars, he said. The war against Iraq a decade before had been swift and with a clear conclusion. This war would not look like the air war above Kosovo, where no ground troops were used and not a single American was lost in combat. But America was at war, said Bush. 'Freedom and fear are at war' against terror.

The vagueness of this language is remarkable. How can a nation fight against a concept? The implications of its usage are significant. Is international humanitarian law to be suspended outside legally recognized battlefields? Are sovereign borders not to be recognized? Are terrorists to be regarded not as criminals but soldiers? Are those murdered by terrorists the victims of war? Are we supposed to believe that there is a battlefield solution to terror?[41] There have been repeated denunciations of the phrase 'war against terror' by leading politicians, lawyers and security service officers. It was reported on 28 December 2007 that the phrase 'war on terror' would no longer be used by the British government to describe attacks on the public. The then Director of Prosecutions was cited as saying: 'The people who were murdered on July 7 were not the victims of war. The men who killed them were not soldiers.'[42] Lady Eliza Manningham-Buller, the former head of MI5, used her Reith Lectures as an opportunity to indicate that she had long decried use of the phrase.[43] Use of the phrase 'war on terror' remains worryingly in common parlance even today.

In the years following the attacks of 11 September 2001, however, not only politicians were guilty of using this dangerous

---

[41]'The worst thing that happened was the words, "We are at war". September 11 was not war, it was murder. You want to arrest murderers. As soon as the words "We are at war" were said, it gave Bin Laden what he wanted. It made him a warrior. Before that, he was a murderer. Islamic people also abhor murder. And if we had kept the language within that range we would have had a better chance at securing the cooperation we needed from people who could actually do something' (Homiletics Online interview: Stanley Hauerwas, 'Bonhoeffer: The Truthful Witness' (2011) www.homileticsonline.com/subscriber/interviews/hauerwas.asp [accessed 20 February 2013].

[42]'Britain Drops "War on Terror" Label', *Daily Mail*, 28 December 2007 www.military.com/NewsContent/0,13319,159067,00.html [accessed 20 February 2013].

[43]Richard Norton-Taylor, 'MI5 former chief decries "war on terror"', *The Guardian*, 2 September 2011 www.guardian.co.uk/uk/2011/sep/02/mi5-war-on-terror-criticism [accessed 29 January 2012].

rhetoric. Jean Bethke Elshtain's 2003 book *Just War against Terror: The Burden of American Power in a Violent World* did not use a question mark after the phrase 'Just War against Terror' but argued that the use of force was justified against the act of aggression inflicted on the body politic in these attacks. Elshtain elided the language of 'war' and military force at the behest of right authority, and cited with approval the historian of war Caleb Carr's conclusion that 'war can *only* be answered with war'.[44]

As a renowned advocate of the just war tradition, Elshtain addressed the 'war against terror' announced by President George W. Bush after 11 September in the terms of the tradition – *causus belli*, last resort, prospect of success, proportionality and discrimination – but with relatively little attention paid to whether the use of force in this context is justifiably deemed to be 'war' or the moral and legal conditions that should be met before military intervention in another state is justified. The point that America had been attacked and had the right to defend itself was made starkly and unambiguously. Moreover: 'As the world's superpower, America bears the responsibility to help guarantee . . . international stability, whether much of the world wants it or not.'[45] Given the typical prevarications of the UN Security Council, America bore a responsibility to defend its own people and others around the world who cannot defend themselves. She glossed over whether the use of force in this context is justifiably deemed to be 'war'.

President Obama has been more circumspect in his language, choosing to speak of 'armed conflict' with al-Qaeda, the Taliban and their known affiliates. State Department advice under Obama has been that 'as a matter of international law, the United States is in an armed conflict with al-Qaeda, as well as the Taliban and associated forces, in response to the horrific 9/11 attacks, and may use force consistent with its inherent right to self-defense under international law.'[46] He has further defended the use of drones for targeted killings in an hour-long video 'hangout' on Google's social

[44]Jean Bethke Elshtain, *Just War against Terror: The Burden of American Power in a Violent World* (New York: Basic Books, 2003), p. 59, citing Caleb Carr, *The Lessons of Terror* (New York: Random House, 2002), pp. 13–14.
[45]Elshtain, Just War against Terror, p. 169.
[46]Koh, 'The Obama Administration and International Law'.

network, Google Plus, which was also streamed live on YouTube.[47] When asked about the large number of civilians killed by these drones since he took office, Obama answered:

> I want to make sure that people understand that drones have not caused a huge number of civilian casualties. For the most part, they have been very precise, precision strikes against al-Qaeda and their affiliates. And we are very careful in terms of how it has been applied. And so I think that there is this perception somehow that we're just sending in a whole bunch of strikes willy-nilly. This is a targeted, focussed effort at people who are on a list; active terrorists who are trying to go in and harm Americans, hit American facilities, American bases and so on. It is important for everyone to understand that this thing is kept on a very tight leash.[48]

Obama's comments were made in response to questions arising from the London-based Bureau of Investigative Journalism, which found that between 282 and 535 civilians, including 60 children, have been reported as killed as the result of drone attacks since Obama took office.[49] The intention was clearly to indicate that all such actions are necessary and proportionate. The matter turns, however, on whether it is legally and morally defensible for the United States to regard itself as 'at war' with al-Qaeda and its affiliates thereby potentially justifying capture or 'kill lists', or whether the fact that the United States is not at war in many of the places where American strikes have been taking place means that the laws of armed conflict do not apply but only the more restrictive international human rights law – in which case these strikes are unlawful, extra-judicial executions.

---

[47]'Obama Defends US Drone Strikes in Pakistan', BBC World News, 31 January 2012   http://dissenter.firedoglake.com/2012/01/30/president-obama-says-us-must-be-judicious-in-drone-use/ [accessed 20 February 2013].

[48]'Your Interview with the President', 30 January 2012; this is my rendering of a portion of the video www.whitehouse.gov/blog/2012/01/30/watch-live-president-obama-answers-your-questions-google-hangout [accessed 20 February 2013].

[49]The Bureau of Investigative Journalism reports breakdowns of figures on CIA drone strikes in Pakistan from 2004; US covert action in Yemen from 2002; US covert action in Somalia from 2007 www.thebureauinvestigates.com/2012/02/04/a-question-of-legality/ [accessed 12 December 2012].

I cannot emphasize too strongly that terrorism would be inherently, irremediably illegal as a way of war if accorded the honour of being dubbed 'war'. As military theorist Davida E. Kellogg spells out: 'It is impossible to conduct terror warfare without intentionally committing criminal breaches of the Geneva Conventions.'[50] The attacks of 11 September 2001, the Mumbai bombings in 2003, the Madrid train bombings in 2004, the London transport bombings in 2005, the attack against a Pakistani police academy in 2006 and many subsequent suicide bombings in Pakistan, suicide bombings in Yemen and so many more violate international laws of war and should be denounced as both immoral and illegal forms of warfare. The question, however, is whether terrorist attacks should be dubbed warfare, thereby triggering the laws of war rather than the criminal and human rights law that protects more rights. We should be clear that, when terrorism is treated as warfare, human rights standards such as the right to life, the right to a trial and the right to respect for private property that prevail outside of war may be suspended.

The legality of the use of armed unmanned aerial vehicles outside legal battlefields has not been tested in an international court. There is, as yet, no international agreement delimiting the use of these weapons-delivery systems. The matter is disputed but it seems likely that, at the time of writing and during the period covered in this chapter, the United States and United Kingdom have been involved in armed conflict (war), as defined in international law, in one place only: Afghanistan. If so, then, at issue legally is what, if any, laws of war apply and whether, if not, these attacks amount to state-sanctioned extra-judicial executions. Harold Koh, a legal adviser at the US Department of State, has claimed that the use of advanced weapons systems for lethal operations is in accordance with all applicable law and with principles of distinction and proportionality. Koh told an audience of lawyers that '*U.S. targeting practices, including lethal operations conducted with the use of unmanned aerial vehicles, comply with all applicable law, including the laws of war.*'[51] What we are witnessing, however, is a shifting of questions from the location and delimitation of lawful battlefields

---

[50]Davida E. Kellogg, 'International Law and Terrorism', *Military Review* (September–October 2005), pp. 50–57, esp. pp. 50–51.

[51]Koh, 'The Obama Administration and International Law' (emphasis in original).

to the setting of the threshold at which international humanitarian law applies anywhere in the world, and a propensity to opt for the 'extraordinary' means of targeted killings with drones and other remote means rather than the slower, perhaps more difficult for a variety of reasons, 'ordinary' building up of internationally recognized and authoritative mechanisms of law enforcement.

Questions about the kind of international legal regime necessary for the delimiting of war and setting the conditions for peace are ultimately political rather than legal.

Whether or not an international or non-international armed conflict is part of the 'global war on terror' is not a legal, but a political question. The designation 'global war on terror' does not extend the applicability of humanitarian law to all events included in this notion, but only to those which involve armed conflict.[52]

Hence the need for critical engagement at points of tension between what might be deemed just war and political violence. Of concern in this chapter are both the increasingly expansive definitions of war or armed conflict and the slippage towards a new type of just war reasoning that appears to sanction a claimed right to kill without judicial process on the supposition – not tested judicially – that the named persons are members of a militant group. This slippage is due primarily to political rather than legal reasons but results in a seeming rush to the 'extraordinary' means of armed conflict where the Geneva Conventions and international humanitarian law supposedly apply but in situations where it is far from clear that an armed conflict is actually taking place in terms recognized by international law. Of interest in the remainder of this chapter are some of the cultural and philosophical influences that lie behind these shifts.

A brief historical survey

My concern especially is with the seeming rush in recent years to the 'extraordinary' means of war or non-international armed

---

[52]International Committee of the Red Cross, 'The Relevance of IHL in the Context of Terrorism', 1 January 2011 www.icrc.org/eng/resources/documents/misc/terrorism-ihl-210705.htm [accessed 20 February 2013].

conflict such that basic human rights are suspended by executive decision for those whom governments (not only the United States) deem to be a threat to national security, and the blurring of the traditional distinction between two legal situations: armed conflict and peace. The following brief historical survey attempts to track changes in the tradition(s) of just war reasoning that help to explain some of the differences between these diverse traditions and some of the (problematic) justifications for lowering of the threshold at which international humanitarian law applies. Not all just war reasoning is the same. Distinction is drawn between the narrowly penal classic just war tradition that tended to have theological roots (notably Ambrose, Augustine, Aquinas, Gratian, Isidore of Seville, the canon lawyers of the eleventh and twelfth centuries and the Salamancan school of moral theology) and what Richard Tuck dubs the modern humanist tradition (Gentili, Grotius, Hobbes, Pufendorf through to Walzer and Rawls).[53] At the heart of differences between the narrow, theological tradition and the looser secularist, humanist tradition is the progressive reduction of natural law reasoning to an extremely narrow set of rights and the single, normative principle of national self-defence, together with a compensatory focus on jus in bello criteria and increasing attention to the identity of the enemy rather than wrong doing actually committed. I identify a shift away from the traditional just war criteria that remain focused on the question of whether wrong has been committed towards political violence on ideological grounds.[54]

For some Christian people, of course, there is no valid distinction between just war and political violence. The case for Christian pacifism has been advanced most powerfully in recent years by Stanley Hauerwas, including his recent essay 'Why War is a Moral

---

[53]Richard Tuck, *The Rights of War: Political Thought and the International Order from Grotius to Kant* (Oxford: Oxford University Press, 2001).
[54]The noted legal scholar Ingrid Detter writes: 'Distinguishable from the thus largely obsolete *jus ad bellum* are the rules of warfare and the humanitarian rules that apply within a war, the *jus in bello*. It may appear that since the right to war has been abolished there would not be any need for rules in war. However, it is clear that given the number and intensity of present-day conflicts, both international and internal, that there is a great need for the regulation of humanitarian issues' (*The Law of War*, 2nd edn [Cambridge: Cambridge University Press, 2000], pp. 157–58). Her description of *jus ad bellum* as 'largely obsolete' is explained in part by reliance in international law on 'individual or collective self-defence' following an armed attack (UN Charter, Article 51) and/or UN authorization.

Necessity for America'.[55] His point is not only that the churches have been inextricably linked to the war-driven politics of the United States and governments in Europe but that war is linked to sets of political goods, sustains a nation's belief in its peculiarly moral standing, fuels the rebirth of national identities through ritual and notions of sacrifice, and perpetuates the idea that killing and dying have redemptive purpose. I am not pacifist in the sense advocated by Hauerwas but sympathetic to, among other things, how he exposes the confusions that have beset some recent Christian thinking about the war on terror. In a comment on Jean Bethke Elshtain's *Just War against Terror*, Hauerwas's point was that fighting a *war* against terror is impossible: 'If one of the crucial conditions of a just war is for the war to have an end, then the war against terrorism clearly cannot be just because it is a war without end.'[56] I am heedful also of his biting critique of those who gloss the intention of going to war with expressions of love for the enemy; his appraisal must never be far from our thoughts when dealing with the topic in question. Supposing with Oliver O'Donovan, however, that pacifism is not simply a refusal to a refusal to enact judgement, that is, not only a disagreement about the means that may be used to defend peace but a disagreement about the nature of worldly peace before Christ's kingdom comes, the question is where the main points of slippage occur between 'just war' fought for the restoration of peace and for the protection of national security, and what is entailed in this distinction.

'Ordinary' and 'Extraordinary' judgement

The distinction between 'ordinary' and 'extraordinary' judgement was not peculiar to theological theorists but foundational to Roman accounts of the rights of war. Witness Livy's comments on the justifiability of avenging the unpunished maltreatment of a herald to another city-state.[57] Every city-state was responsible

---

[55]Stanley Hauerwas, *War and the American Difference: Theological Reflections on Violence and National Identity* (Grand Rapids, MI: Baker Academic, 2011), ch. 3.
[56]Hauerwas, *War and the American Difference*, p. 26.
[57]Titus Livius, *Livy's History of Rom*, ed. Ernest Rhys (London: Dent, 1905), vol. 2, bk 9, §11 http://mcadams.posc.mu.edu/txt/ah/livy/livy09.html [accessed 5 February 2012].

for redeeming injuries done to foreigners by its citizens. When a city-state defaulted on this responsibility, the other city-state had a right to punish it by war. 'Denial of justice became the primary cause of a just war seen as an extraordinary legal process.'[58] According to Cicero, no one is permitted by Nature's laws to injure his neighbour for his own advantage. The fellowship which the gods have established between human beings demands that the law deals with such practices 'as far as it can lay its strong arm upon them'.[59] Expediency is not sufficient justification for contending shamefully with enemies. Cicero presupposed a clear violation of the pre-existing rights of the injured party in all wars deemed just; a just war was limited in its aims to securing redress of grievance and compensation for loss.[60] Augustine echoes Cicero in supposing that a just war avenges injuries *'iusta bella ulciscuntur iniuria'*.[61] War is justified when a people or a city neglects to punish wrongs done by its members or to restore what it had unjustly seized.

The distinction is expounded further in Aquinas and Gratian. Just cause is linked by Aquinas to violent acts against the innocent and the avenging of wrong:

> [A] just cause is required, namely that those who are attacked, should be attacked because they deserve it on account of some fault. Wherefore Augustine says: 'A just war is wont to be described as one that avenges wrongs, when a nation or state has to be punished, for refusing to make amends for the wrongs inflicted by its subjects, or to restore what it has seized unjustly.'[62]

---

[58]Frederick H. Russell, *The Just War in the Middle Ages* (Cambridge: Cambridge University Press, 1977), p. 5.
[59]Cicero, *De Officiis*, trans. Walter Miller (Cambridge, MA: Harvard University Press, 1913), bk III, chs. 5, 17.
[60]Cicero, *De Officiis*, bk III, ch. 22.
[61]'Iusta autem bella ea definiri solent quae ulciscuntur iniurias, si qua gens vel civitas quae bello petenda est, vel vindicare neglexerit quod a suis inprobe factum est, vel reddere quod per iniurias ablatum est' (Augustine, *Quaestiones in Heptateuchum in Corpus Scriptorum Ecclesiasticorum Latinorum* [Wien: Verlag der Österreichischen Akademie der Wissenschaften, 1872], bk VI, ch. 10 (cited by Russell, *The Just War in the Middle Ages*, p. 18).
[62]Aquinas, *ST*, II–II, q. 40, a. 1, c.

Aquinas recalls Augustine's sermon on Matthew 5.38–42 which includes Jesus' teaching on not repaying evil with evil, and turning the other cheek. This should always be borne in mind, says Aquinas, because the Christians may refrain from resistance or self-defence. Nevertheless, it is necessary sometimes for the common good to act otherwise by refraining a person from sin or punishing them 'with a kindly severity'.[63] His representation of a just cause for war is narrowly judicial and penal. Aquinas emphasizes the similarity between a judicial process and the just war. So too does Gratian in his selections from the earlier tradition and particular emphasis on the need for patience of the heart in dealing with such matters. Gratian speaks of the 'secret of a spirit of patience with good will' (*secreto animi patiencia cum beniuolentia*) and observes that, unless a judge decide justly, there is no justice in the decision.[64] War is not to be undertaken except in the interest of justice, which may include the avenging of wrongs or rescuing the neglected and those who have been improperly injured.[65] To be condemned in war is desire to hurt or revenge, and the lust of power. Wars are to be 'peaceful events'.[66]

These emphases persist in Grotius's writings. War is potentially admissible only in those conditions where 'judicial procedure ceases to be available either temporarily or continuously'.[67] When undertaken in the absence of appropriate judicial procedure, it must nevertheless 'be carried on with not less scrupulousness than judicial processes are wont to be'.[68] Grotius makes the point – about the conditions of war being met only if recourse to a judge or other lawful authority is not available – with reference to private rather than public war, that is, by those 'private' individuals who do not have lawful authority. Public war is prohibited also, however, except

---

[63]Aquinas, *ST*, II–II, q. 40, a. 1, c.

[64]Gratian, Decretum, Causa XXIII, q. 1, ch. II (Iure autem disceptare est iuste iudicare. Non enim est iudex, si non est iusticia in eo ['By the Law of debate, however, is to judge justly']); Decretum Magistri Gratiani, ed. Emil Friedberg, in Corpus Iuris Canonici (1879; rpt Graz: Akademische Druck- u. Verlagsanstalt, 1959), vol. 1 www.columbia.edu/cu/lweb/digital/collections/cul/texts/ldpd_6029936_001/index. html [accessed 20 February 2012].

[65]Gratian, *Decretum*, q. II, ch. II.

[66]Gratian, *Decretum*, q. II, ch. IV; q. II, ch. VI.

[67]Hugo Grotius, *The Law of War and Peace*, trans. Francis W. Kelsey (Indianapolis, IN: Bobbs-Merrill, 1925), bk 1, ch. 3, §II.

[68]Grotius, *The Law of War and Peace*, Prolegomena, §25.

where wrong has been done and reparation or punishment has not otherwise been effected.[69] Preliminary questions about the justice or otherwise of war turn what is required for the restoration of justice and maintenance of the social order through the exercise of judgement in the face of wrong. Grotius cites, inter alia, the Roman fetial college appeal to Jupiter, as preserved by Livy, to the effect that war is justified only in consequence of an unjust act, such as a direct invasion or breach of treaty, for which no restitution has been made: 'I call you to witness that that people is unjust and does not do what is right in making restitution,'[70] and finds support in Augustine's observation that injury of the opposing side 'occasions just wars'.[71]

After Grotius, the development of modern natural law reasoning (John Locke, Thomas Hobbes, Benedict de Spinoza, Samuel Pufendorf) became markedly detached from Christian confession of the law of nature implanted in humans and revealed by God and more associated with secularist rationalism. Hobbes affirms a natural law of self-preservation, pursuant upon his discussion of the laws of nature in *Leviathan,* where men live in 'that condition called Warre'.[72] He affirms a prior fundamental law of nature to seek peace. The natural law of self-preservation, which he construes innovatively as a right to self-preservation, follows from the law of nature which commands that people are to aim at securing peace:[73]

And consequently it is a precept, or general rule of reason: that every man ought to endeavour peace, as far as he has hope of obtaining it; and when he cannot obtain it, that he may seek and

---

[69]Grotius, *The Law of War and Peace,* bk 2, ch. 1, §§ I, 2–3.
[70]Grotius, *The Law of War and Peace,* bk 2, ch. 1, §I, 4.
[71]Grotius, *The Law of War and Peace,* bk 2, ch. 1, §§I, 3.
[72]Thomas Hobbes, *Leviathan,* ed. Richard Tuck (Cambridge: Cambridge University Press, 1991), ch. 13, p. 86.
[73]Quentin Skinner supports this reading that Hobbes innovates in turning the scholastic doctrine of self-defence into a liberty of human natural power and ability. See *Hobbes and Republican Liberty* (Cambridge: Cambridge University Press, 2008). See Aquinas, who writes that a person is not guilty of murder 'if he kills another in defense of his own life' (*ST,* II–II, q. 64, a. 7 sed contra). He then proceeds to delimit this defence in terms of what has come to be called 'the doctrine of double effect'; the person must intend the saving of their life and not the death of the aggressor.

use all helps and advantages of war. The first branch of which rule containeth the first and fundamental law of nature, which is: to seek peace and follow it. The second, the sum of the right of nature, which is: by all means we can to defend ourselves.[74]

Hobbes affirms the right to self-preservation but only after affirming that the laws of nature, available to all, are aimed primarily at securing peace. Fear of death and desire of those things commodious to living all incline a person to peace.

And consequently it is a precept, or general rule of reason: that every man ought to endeavour peace, as far as he has hope of obtaining it; and when he cannot obtain it, that he may seek and use all helps and advantages of war. The first branch of which rule containeth the first and fundamental law of nature, which is: to seek peace and follow it. The second, the sum of the right of nature, which is: by all means we can to defend ourselves.[75]

The right of self-defence follows from this prior law as a law that nature also commands as a means of providing for peace when people live together in multitudes and are prone to intemperance. The right of self-defence is a dictate of reason, not yet legal, that regulates human co-existence in a moral sense preparatory to law.[76]

The right of self-defence

The innovative aspects of Hobbes's construal of the natural law of self-preservation consists in his view that the liberty of self-defence (*libertas*) is synonymous with *dominium* and thus with legal right (*jus*). Quentin Skinner writes:

Here [Hobbes] cunningly appropriates the scholastic doctrine to the effect that natural right consists of acting in accordance

---

It must also be proportionate to the end of self-defence. It is not lawful for any person to intend to kill another in self-defence; only a public authority acting for the common good may intend to kill a person lawfully.
[74]Hobbes, *Leviathan*, ch. 14.
[75]Hobbes, *Leviathan*, ch. 14.
[76]Hobbes does recognize a natural, moral right to punish evil (*Leviathan*, ch. 28).

with the dictates of reason . . . he is able to twist the scholastic doctrine in such a way as to produce the startling conclusion that the liberty 'of using our own natural power and ability' must therefore be equivalent to the natural right of preserving ourselves at all times.[77]

Despite Hobbes's prioritizing of peace-seeking, there is a significant shift in his philosophy of natural right as compared to the scholastics whereby natural law is a function of reason, 'promulgated by the very fact that God instilled it into man's mind so as to be known by him naturally' wherein any claim to self-defence is conceived judicially and never far from reference to the common good.[78] By contrast, Hobbes's account of the right of self-defence becomes increasingly the right of a person to make their own judgements about what specific actions might be necessary for self-preservation and the avoidance of pain and death. Hobbes moves towards an account of the laws of nature no longer understood with reference to the Eternal Law as the necessary pattern by which God brought the created world into existence and by whose pattern and hierarchy of ends humans may discern what is reasonable but in terms of what is conducive to our self-preservation. 'His final conclusion is thus that the liberty or right of nature must comprehend the right to do anything we may desire to do at any time.'[79] At the least, one has the liberty to act for one's self-preservation.

Hobbes is read more often for his account of individual liberty and influence on national law rather than international law, not least because he is normally thought to have suggested that in war there are no rules; the 'state of nature' is coextensive with the state of war. Larry May has argued recently, however, that Hobbes's discussion of cruelty in *Leviathan* and *Dialogue between a Philosopher and a Student of the Common Laws of England* influenced the development of jus in bello.[80] With May, we are interested in the role that the laws of nature play in Hobbes's understanding of the state of war and how his insight that rationality governs all

[77]Skinner, *Reason and Rhetoric*, pp. 36–37.
[78]Aquinas, *ST*, I–II, q. 90, a. 4.
[79]Skinner, *Reason and Rhetoric*, p. 37.
[80]Larry May, 'A Hobbesian Approach to Cruelty and the Rules of War', passim but esp. pp. 1–4. http://etykapraktyczna.pl/index.php?option=com_mtree&task=att_download&link_id=1575&cf_id=24 [accessed 21 February 2013].

human affairs bears upon his construal of natural law commands with respect to self-defence.[81] Of interest for our purposes is Hobbes's place in the history or ideas and, more specifically, Hobbes's influence on Pufendorf's subsequent prioritizing of self-preservation over all other considerations as commanded by the natural law.

In *On the Duty of Man and Citizen According to Natural Law*, Pufendorf declares that the precepts of the natural law are accessible via examination of the nature and disposition of humankind.[82] This represents a significant shift from the theological methodology of the scholastics whereby the divine will is knowable only by participation, by grace, of the natural law in the eternal law. Pufendorf moves further towards the objectification of the natural law as something independent of God. God is still deemed by Pufendorf to be the author of all life and also of the natural law but he relies for proof on natural reason supported by revelation.[83] The command of the natural law with respect to self-preservation is a matter of a person's duty towards themselves. It turns on the principle of necessity and overrides positive law:

> [S]elf-preservation is so highly regarded, that, if it cannot be obtained otherwise, in very many cases it is thought to exempt from the obligation of the general law. . . . Hence regularly the laws, especially the positive sort, and all human institutions, are considered to except the case of necessity, in other words, not to oblige, when observance of them would be attended by an evil destructive of human nature, or exceeding the common endurance of men . . . It is presumed that the case of necessity is not included under a law conceived in general terms.[84]

Necessity further, says Pufendorf, gives a person the right to expose another indirectly to the danger of death provided that one's purpose is not to harm that person but that this exposure

[81]May, 'A Hobbesian Approach', p. 2.
[82]Samuel von Pufendorf, *De Officio Hominis et Civis Juxta Legem Naturalem Libre Duo*, trans. Frank Gardener Moore (London: Wildy & Sons, 1964), bk I, ch. III, §1, p. 17.
[83]Pufendorf, *De Officio*, bk I, ch. III, §11, p. 19.
[84]Pufendorf, *De Officio*, bk I, ch. V, §39, p. 34.

of another to potential harm is necessary in the interest of self-preservation no other option is available for the mitigation of injury:

> Thus, if a stronger pursues me, with designs upon my life, and somebody happens to meet me in a narrow street, my necessary way of escape, if, though admonished, he does not give way, or the limitations of time or space do not admit of his doing so, I shall have a right to knock him down, and continue my flight over his fallen body, even though it may seem probable that he will be seriously hurt by the blow. All this, unless I am bound to the man by special obligation, so that I ought actually to take the risk for his sake.[85]

Those who suffer injury in such cases ought to bear their misfortune as their destiny. In other words, a subjective right to self-defence governed by the principle of necessity is emerging with increasing clarity. This principle of necessity also provides a limited permission to destroy the property of others, provided that it cannot be removed to a safe place and that we do not destroy another's more valuable item to save our own less precious thing.

Analogous principles apply internationally. The laws of nature do not permit a nation to go to war 'for any cause indifferently' but do permit those instances where no gentler means are available and arbitration has failed. It is to be lamented that human beings to not have more regard for their fellow-citizens and neighbouring nations but even the most cursory observation may convince us that the virtues by which one party will seek the well-being of another exert a very feeble force. The desire to rule over another or acquire property sought by others is more typical than good will. 'For this reason . . . happy is that state regarded which even in peace thinks of war.'[86] Pufendorf's concessions to the perversity of human nature are extensive at the levels of both individual and national conflict. Prudence and humanity should always govern human actions. More harm should not result from an act of war than the good effected.[87] With this proviso, however, the just causes

---

[85]Pufendorf, *De Officio*, bk I, ch. V, §39, p. 35–36.
[86]Pufendorf, *De Officio*, bk II, ch. I, §39, p. 93.
[87]Pufendorf, *De Officio*, bk II, ch. XVI, §1, p. 138.

for which a war may be undertaken are summarized by Pufendorf as follows:

> that we may preserve and protect ourselves and our belongings against the unjust invasion of others; or that we may assert our claim to what is owed us by others who refuse to pay: or to obtain reparations for an injury already inflicted, or a guarantee for the future. A war waged for the first cause is called defensive, if for the other causes, offensive.[88]

The just cause for which a war is fought must be established without question but what counts as a just cause is more extensive than permitted by Grotius. Pufendorf sanctions the possibility of defensive wars as a means of preventive warfare. He recommends recourse to a third-party arbiter. Even so, this acceptance of preventive, pre-emptive attacks is significant. It is permissible, according to Pufendorf, for a nation to launch an attack against a neighbouring state that harbours a fugitive who is planning acts of hostility against the nation he has left.[89]

It was Kant's short essays 'Idea for a Universal History with a Cosmopolitan Purpose' (1784) and 'Perpetual Peace' (1795), however, that reshaped modern debate about the law of nations. His sceptical method swept away the pretensions of both those who still rely upon metaphysical knowledge and those who hold that a just war theory is the best of all possible ways to escape the state of nature, which is a state of war, and further dispenses with the axiom that war is justifiable when there is a failure of ordinary means. Grotius, Pufendorf and Vattel are dismissed as 'sorry comforters' whose conceptual frameworks with their fine talk of 'right' had served only to justify the use of force. Prescient of the evidence-based decision-making that now characterizes medicine, education and politics, Kant challenged those holding to the tradition of Grotius and others to look at what their high-minded reasoning had actually produced. Given that their homage to the concept of 'right' had produced absolutely no evidence of a reduction in warfare but many instances wherein the concept of 'right' is very closely tied to 'might', Kant urges his readers to leave behind the notion that

---

[88]Pufendorf, *De Officio*, bk II, ch. XVI, §1, p. 138.
[89]Pufendorf, *De Officio*, bk II, ch. XVI, §1, p. 140.

warfare can serve the ends of peace and opt instead for 'a pacific federation' (*fœdus pacificum*) in which the aim is to end all wars.[90]

> It is therefore to be wondered that the word *right* has not been completely banished from military politics as superfluous pedantry, and that no state has been bold enough to declare itself publicly in favour of doing so. For Hugo Grotius, Pufendorf, Vattel and the rest (sorry comforters as they are) are still dutifully quoted in *justification* of military aggression . . . Yet there is no instance of a state ever having been moved to desist from its purposes by arguments supported by the testimonies of such noble men.[91]

War, he comments in Hobbesian mode, is after all 'only a regrettable expedient for asserting one's rights by force within a state of nature'.[92] Neither party can be declared the 'unjust enemy' as if with reference to an impartial judge's decision because there can be no such relationship of superior to inferior in international relations. '[O]nly the *outcome* of the conflict, as in the case of a so-called "judgment of God", can decide who is in the right.'[93]

Membership or non-membership of the *fœdus amphictyonum*

Much that is positive can be said about Kant's account of the role of international law in securing freedom as well as about his vision of cosmopolitan justice, not least his exposure of pathologies within the modern just war tradition that allowed it become a justificatory gloss for the exercise of political power. He cites those just war theorists (Gentili, Grotius, Hobbes, Pufendorf) whom Tuck names as part of the humanist tradition as contributors to this problem before outlining his hope for an era when war is increasingly obsolescent as cultures settle their differences through submission to laws that have been mutually agreed, desist from accumulating national debts to pay for wars and concentrate

---

[90]Immanuel Kant, 'Perpetual Peace: A Philosophical Sketch', in H. S. Reiss (ed.), *Political Writings* (Cambridge: Cambridge University Press, 1970), pp. 103–104.
[91]Kant, 'Perpetual Peace', p. 103.
[92]Kant, 'Perpetual Peace', p. 96.
[93]Kant, 'Perpetual Peace', p. 96.

instead on the furtherance of trade. Kant's hope is for a great federation (*fœdus amphictyonum*) that will derive security from the power of legal judgements and 'the law governed decisions of a united will'.[94] This will be a cosmopolitan system of political security in which the barbarous freedoms of established states will progress beyond the chaotic political relations of warfare and find means other than warfare of facilitating the development of human societies.[95] Kant's philosophical project, says Allen Wood, 'is truly cosmopolitan in its intent, not limited by any geographic or cultural borders'.[96] Its articles are means by which to realize this vision not merely as the precepts of a *ius gentium*, applying only to the relations between sovereign states, says Wood, but as principles of a *ius cosmopoliticum*, which regards all the peoples of the earth as a single, universal community, founded on the universal right of humankind and all this entails for mutually regulating laws, the right of hospitality, federal union and so on. This vision is not to the exclusion of the bounds of national sovereignty; national borders will remain. Cosmopolitan law deals with relations across borders and permits war in self-defence.[97]

Kant singles out the significance of economic interchange in establishing a single, enlightened world culture.[98] His hope arose

[94]Immanuel Kant, 'Idea for a Universal History with a Cosmopolitan Purpose', in *Political Writings*, p. 47.
[95]Kant, 'Idea for a Universal History', p. 51.
[96]Allen W. Wood, 'Kant's Project for Perpetual Peace', in Pheng Cheah and Bruce Robbins (eds), *Cosmopolitics: Thinking and Feeling Beyond the Nation* (Minneapolis: University of Minnesota Press, 1998), p. 62.
[97]David Colclasure, 'Just War and Perpetual Peace: Kant on the Legitimate Use of Political Violence', in Elisabeth Krimmer and Patricia Anne Simpson (eds), *Enlightened War: German Theories and Cultures of Warfare from Frederick the Great to Clausewitz* (Woodbridge, Suffolk: Camden House, 2011), pp. 241–57. Conflicting interpretations of Kant's international political theory centre around the extent to which his vision of a great federation was to be a federation of political peoples, as distinct from nation-states, with emphasis given to the rights of individuals over the interests of nation-states, or whether his emphasis was on the congress of states. See John Rawls, *The Law of Peoples, with 'The Idea of Public Reason Revisited'* (Cambridge, MA: Harvard University Press, 1999). Rawls's preference for the term 'peoples' as distinct from 'nations' or 'states' stems from his earlier rejection of the classical conception of state sovereignty found in the doctrines of Bodin and Hobbes. Unlike states, peoples do not have *absolute* internal power over their subjects because their authority is limited by a doctrine of human rights (pp. 23–30).
[98]The theorist who brought the essay 'Perpetual Peace' to the centre stage of recent international law was the political scientist Michael Doyle in his two-part article 'Kant,

from the prospect of leaving behind decades of warfare across Europe as trading links proliferate and individuals realize that peace is the necessary condition of economic prosperity. 'Kant treats international insecurity and competition as the self-perpetuating results of bad counsel, the advice of "political moralists" or "moralising politicians" who pretend that "human nature is not capable of good" and whose advice can lead ultimately only to annihilation, the peace of the graveyard.'[99] Instead, he advocates the advantages of commerce and possibility that, some day, all foreigners arriving at the borders of another country will want only to exchange goods and ideas.

The Kantian vision of the *ius cosmopoliticum* has much to commend it. Indeed, for many theorists, this vision has been realized, in limited respects, in the achievements of the League of Nations at the end of the Second World War and also the faltering achievements of the United Nations to this day. Pauline Kleingeld draws attention to Kant's role in preparing for the establishment of a non-coercive league of states without any highest or legislative authority 'as the only possible road to the ultimate ideal, a state of states'.[100] Kant saw international law as providing the conditions for a lasting, or perpetual, peace among nation-states: '"All politics must bend its knee before right", and this means that "right must

---

Liberal Legacies and Foreign Affairs' (*Philosophy and Public Affairs* 12 [Summer 1983], pp. 205–35; [Autumn 1983], pp. 323–53). Doyle's significance is noted by Richard Falk in his review of Susan Marks, *The Riddle of All Constitutions* (*American Journal of International Law* 96 [January 2002], p. 264). Of related interest is the collection of essays in James Bohman and Matthias Lutz-Bachmann, (eds), *Perpetual Peace: Essays on Kant's Cosmopolitan Ideal* (Cambridge: MIT Press, 1997). Kant, Doyle argued, offers the best guidance for relations between liberal states and the encouragement of non-liberal states to become such, and he lays the groundwork for subsequent theorists to cast discussions about individual freedom under the rubric of cosmopolitan democracy and the capitalist processes of globalization (Doyle, 'Kant, Liberal Legacies and Foreign Affairs', p. 225). Since Doyle, moderate cosmopolitans of diverse neo-Kantian ilk (Kwame Anthony Appiah, Amartya Sen, Henry Shue, Jürgen Habermas, Seyla Benhabib, Allen Buchanan et al.) have written in various ways that endorse the legacy of 'Perpetual Peace' in international relations.

[99] Amanda Perreau-Saussine, 'Immanuel Kant on International Law', in Samantha Besson and John Tasioulas (eds), *The Philosophy of International Law* (Oxford: Oxford University Press, 2010), p. 54.

[100] Pauline Kleingeld, 'Kant's Theory of Peace', in Paul Guyer (ed.), *The Cambridge Companion to Kant and Modern Philosophy* (Cambridge: Cambridge University Press, 2006), p. 485.

never be accommodated to politics, but politics must always be accommodated to right".'[101] He balances between the seeming anarchy whereby the notion of 'right' cannot be held up by one state in judgement against another and the utopian hope of a peaceful federation where every nation subjects itself quietly to rules that it has previously agreed. Herein lies his hope for justice without coercion.[102] The 'cosmopolitan condition' has subsequently been specified in terms of international constitutions, organizations and procedures, based on the assumption that law remains an appropriate medium for realizing the declared goals of peace, security, democracy and the recognition of human rights throughout the world.

I look in Chapter 7 at growing problems with respect to how the discourse of human rights is being subsumed increasingly within diverse ideological frameworks. For present purposes, the (related) point to which I wish to draw attention is how Kant's vision of the *ius cosmopoliticum* potentially expands the justifications for war beyond the overcoming of wrong-doing to include violence against those who live outside the *fœdus amphictyonum*. In a footnote to the section of 'Perpetual Peace' which outlines the definitive articles of peace between states, he writes:

> It is usually assumed that one cannot take hostile action against anyone unless one has already been actively *injured* by them. This is perfectly correct if both parties are living in a *legal civil state*. For the fact that the one has entered such a state gives the required guarantee to the other, since both are subject to the same authority. But man (or an individual people) in a mere state of nature robs me of any such security and injures me by virtue of this very state in which he coexists with me. He may not have injured me actively (*facto*), but he does injure me by the very lawlessness of his state (*statu iniusto*), for he is a permanent threat to me, and I can require him either to enter into a common lawful state along with me or to move away from my vicinity. Thus the postulate on which all the following articles are based

---

[101]Paul Formosa, '"All Politics Must Bend Its Knee before Right": Kant on the Relation of Morals to Politics', *Social Theory and Practice* 34 (2008), pp. 157–81.
[102]Perreau-Saussine, 'Immanuel Kant on International Law', p. 60.

is that all me who can at all influence one another must adhere to some kind of civil constitution.[103]

Kant wrote at a time when it was still possible (conceptually at least) for a person to 'move away from my vicinity' into territories where a lawless state of nature pertained between individuals.[104] Noteworthy for our purposes, however, is that the identity of the problematic party in question is more significant than their actions; the question of why the armed conflict is taking place, or where, is being replaced by the question of the identity of the actor. What matters is not that the problematic party in question has injured a people or member of a nation-state but that, by their very existence in a 'state of nature' they constitute a threat to all members of the *fœdus amphictyonum*. The critical question is no longer whether an injustice has been committed or a wrong done but whether the individual or group operates with a (problematically) different political structure or ideology from the *fœdus amphictyonum*. As Antony Anghie observes: 'What this permits – indeed, requires – then, is the development of a set of ideas relating to how we should understand a legal civil state and the formulation of a set of criteria for distinguishing a civil state from a not-civil state, a task that evolved into the nineteenth-century project of distinguishing civilized states from non-civilized states.'[105]

This kind of formulation of a set of criteria for distinguishing a civil state from a not-civil state is close to what John Rawls offers in *The Law of Peoples* where he distinguishes between liberal and non-liberal societies. Rawls's project in this book is to develop the idea of 'the law of peoples' out of a liberal conception of justice similar to that which he calls 'justice as fairness' in *A Theory of Justice*. The law of peoples is intended as a guideline for the interactions between what Rawls calls liberal peoples and comprises eight principles.[106] Liberal peoples can be considered as well ordered and

---

[103]Kant, 'Perpetual Peace', p. 98.
[104]On Kant and the 'state of nature', see Arthur Ripstein, 'Kant and the Circumstances of Justice' in Elisabeth Ellis, (ed.), *Kant's Political Theory: Interpretations and Applications* (University Park, PN: Penn State University Press, 2012), ch. 2.
[105]Antony Anghie, *Imperialism, Sovereignty and the Making of International Law* (Cambridge: Cambridge University Press, 2005), p. 296.
[106]Peoples are free and independent, and their freedom and independence are to be respected by other peoples. Peoples are to observe treaties and undertakings. Peoples

reasonable because they respect these principles. Rawls extends the guideline to include 'decent', hierarchical peoples whose polity does not recognize reasonable pluralism and whose systems might not be democratic (e.g. women might not be permitted to hold office) yet whose affairs are well ordered enough to warrant a place in international society. They (1) honour human rights, (2) have some mechanism for public consultation over policy decision and (3) do not pursue an aggressive foreign policy. The main difference between liberal and decent hierarchical peoples is that the latter do not run the first Original Position that Rawls described because they are not committed to the moral individualism underlying contemporary liberalism.[107]

Kant's vision of a great federation is minimally adapted by Rawls to become 'new institutions and practices to serve as a kind of confederative center and public forum'.[108] Rawls urges well-ordered peoples to persuade outlaw regimes of the wisdom of changing their ways: 'Gradually over time, then, well-ordered peoples may pressure the outlaw regimes to change their ways . . . backed up by the firm denial of economic and other assistance, or the refusal to admit outlaw regimes as members in good standing in mutually beneficial cooperative practices.'[109] He treats such persuasive methods (whatever merits such methods may have in their own terms) as integral to just war doctrine; the defence of liberal democratic institutions requires it.[110] The narrow, judicial and

---

are equal and are parties to the agreements that bind them. Peoples are to observe a duty of non-intervention. Peoples have a right to self-defence, but no right to instigate war for reasons other than self-defence. Peoples are to honour human rights. Peoples are to observe certain specified restrictions in the conduct of war. Peoples have a duty to assist other peoples living under unfavourable conditions that prevent them from having a just or decent political or social regime. Rawls, *The Law of Peoples*, p. 37.

[107]Rawls, *The Law of Peoples*, pp. 78–83. On this central feature of Rawls's political liberalism, see *A Theory of Justice* (London: Harvard University Press, 1971), p. 454.

[108]Rawls, *The Law of Peoples*, p. 93.

[109]Rawls, *The Law of Peoples*, p. 93.

[110]Consider George W. Bush's inaugural address in 2001, in which he spoke of America's faith in freedom and democracy as 'a rock in a raging sea' and 'seed upon the wind, taking root in many nations'. America, he says, was to lead the cause of freedom. 'The enemies of liberty and our country should make no mistake: America remains engaged in the world by history and by choice, shaping a balance of power that favours freedom. We will defend our allies and our interests' (Inaugural Address,

penal confines of the classic just war tradition are being replaced by an amorphous, less limited ambition to establish the conditions of liberal freedom. Kant's hope of a pacific federation is at risk of becoming an ideological struggle for the realization of a particular construal of individual and political freedom, with this vision of freedom a driver of violence.

Rawls himself stays focused on the need to expose to public view the unjust and cruel institutions of oppressive regimes. Yet his 'guide to foreign policy' includes statements about the long-run aim of free and democratic peoples to bring all societies eventually to honour the Law of Peoples, with human rights 'secured everywhere'.[111] Just war doctrine, which includes both the justification of war and the conduct of war, is part of consensus between decent hierarchical and liberal peoples. In the absence of any defensible appeal to comprehensive metaphysical and moral doctrines of 'right', just war doctrine is open to becoming more about the pursuit of freedom and respect for human rights rather than opposition to injustice. Thus Rawls is clear that any society which is non-aggressive and honours human rights has the right of self-defence.[112] It is not clear under what conditions societies that are non-aggressive and do not honour human rights lose the right of self-defence.[113] Of concern for our purposes is the shift in just war thinking from the questions of what wrong has been committed, and how might this wrong be stopped and remedied, to questions about the non-liberal status of regimes. The identity of an actor is becoming more important than

---

20 January 2001 http://georgewbush-whitehouse.archives.gov/infocus/bushrecord/documents/Selected_Speeches_George_W_Bush.pdf [accessed 8 January 2012]). President Bush spoke of democracy as 'the creed of our country' and 'the inborn hope of our humanity', 'an ideal we carry but do not own, a trust we bear and pass along'. His quasi-religious language stirs believers in democracy to find unity in these principles and 'leave the cause of freedom' internationally.

[111]Rawls, *The Law of Peoples*, p. 93. This discussion is in the section entitled 'Just War Doctrine: The Right to War'.

[112]Rawls, *The Law of Peoples*, p. 92.

[113]I have written elsewhere about how the concept of Responsibility to Protect (RtoP) shifts the focus of debate from the rights of sovereignty to the responsibilities of sovereignty and rights of the civilian population, and about rising levels of violence under the guise of an objective 'to protect'. See Esther D. Reed, 'Responsibility to Protect and Militarized Humanitarian Intervention', *Journal of Religious Ethics* 41 (March 2013), pp. 183–208.

what they have done; armed conflict is becoming an amorphous, non-limited, ideological affair rather than a narrowly judicial and penal proposal for corrective action.

Security and imminent threat

This sketch of the backdrop against which politicians and legal theorists are permitting the lowering of the threshold for IHL is brief but alerts us to some reasons why it is proving possible for politicians to posit the obsolescence, in effect, of jus ad bellum criteria and operate predominantly with the jus in bello principles of discrimination and proportion. In the context of international terrorism, the old concept of 'war' appears increasingly to have been abandoned and replaced with the looser and as yet legally ill-defined concept of 'armed conflict' that is either international or non-international.[114] Traditional jus ad bellum criteria are being replaced by the question of whether the action is necessary for the maintenance of the security of a given state.[115] The need for security in the face of international terrorism has become one of the defining characteristics of our time. Those living in the villages of Afghanistan, Pakistan and elsewhere, where the 'droning' of armed unmanned aerial vehicles – perhaps only on surveillance missions – is experienced as terror will have a different perspective. In the West, however, there is pressing need to clarify what issues and assumptions underlie political use of the concepts of 'national security', 'international security' and 'global security'.

The most significant argument in defence of the choice of armed conflict over law enforcement mechanisms is the imminent terrorist threat. The President's adviser John Brennan told a gathering at Harvard Law School that the Obama Administration had worked to establish a counter-terrorism framework guided by the core values that define Americans, including adherence to the rule of law: 'when we uphold the rule of law it provides a powerful

---

[114]Elzbieta Mikos-Skuza, 'International Law's Changing Terms: "War" becomes "Armed Conflict"', in O'Connell (ed.), *What is War?*, p. 29.
[115]Jutta Brunnée, 'The Meaning of Armed Conflict and the Jus ad Bellum', in O'Connell (ed.), *What is War?*, p. 47.

alternative to the twisted worldview offered by al-Qa'ida'.[116] Brennan emphasized that even covert operations were undertaken with due regard for the rule of law, albeit with a strongly pragmatic outlook based on what would enhance the security of the United States and the safety of the American people. Significantly, however, he commented that changes were under way in the international community with respect to what it means to adhere to the rule of law. In particular, he said: 'We are finding increasing recognition in the international community that a more flexible understanding of "imminence" may be appropriate when dealing with terrorist groups'.[117] This changing understanding is due in part, he observed, to the reality that al-Qaeda does not follow a traditional command structure, wear uniforms, carry its arms openly or mass its troops at the borders of the nations it attacks. Moreover al-Qaeda, and its associated forces, continue to pose a threat to the United States which demands a response. Practically speaking, he said, the question turns principally on how one defines 'imminence'.

The concept of 'imminent threat' has a long history in the traditions of just war ethics. The overtly theological tradition associated with Augustine, Aquinas, Gratian, Molina and others maintained an emphasis on the punitive nature of just war, proper limits on state action and prohibitions against pre-emptive strikes based on fear. The first Christians interpreted the teaching of Jesus as prohibiting the use of any kind of violence.[118] While others found that the same witness to peace in Jesus' teaching demanded judgement on wrongdoing and action on behalf of innocent, injured parties, there was never any escaping Jesus' teaching to turn the other cheek (Matt. 5.39) and put away the sword (Matt. 26.52). The latter way of thinking came to be known as the classic just war tradition and can be traced back to Augustine's engagement with early Roman law, notably Cicero's *De Republica*, through Isidore

---

[116]John O. Brennan, 'Strengthening Our Security by Adhering to Our Values and Laws', Program on Law and Security, Harvard Law School, Cambridge, MA, 16 September 2011 www.whitehouse.gov/the-press-office/2011/09/16/remarks-john-o-brennan-strengthening-our-security-adhering-our-values-an [accessed 21 February 2013].

[117]Brennan, 'Strengthening Our Security by Adhering to Our Values and Laws'.

[118]For a very brief summary of this history, see David Clough and Brian Stiltner, *Faith and Force: A Christian Debate about War* (Washington, DC: Georgetown University Press, 2007), pp. 40–43.

of Seville, the canon lawyers of the eleventh and twelfth centuries, the Salamancan school of moral theology and beyond.[119] At its best, this tradition kept sight of the gospel imperative to peacemaking (Matt. 5.9) while standing alongside political and military leaders in their difficult efforts to effect judgement on wrongdoing and take the measures necessary for future peace. Thus Augustine held that the Christian has no right to self-defence – thereby keeping faith with the witness to non-violence among the earliest Christians – while accepting that the law properly permits this defence because it punishes what it must in order to keep peace among the people.[120] Vitoria is clear that fear of attack does not excuse immoral action: 'no fear, even of death, can excuse an act forbidden in natural law.'[121] Grotius wrote that the danger must be immediate to warrant defensive action. Merely to feel fear is not sufficient justification for pre-emptive slaughter.[122] As we have seen above, Kant's conception of threat is different: 'But man (or an individual people) in a mere state of nature robs me of any such security and injures me by virtue of this very state in which he coexists with me.'[123] The threat to a nation comprises the state of perceived lawlessness among other individuals or peoples rather than actual wrongs committed.

Today, the meaning of imminent threat is unavoidably context-dependent. Those in government and charged with protecting the security of citizens face heavy responsibilities. Few of us have access to high-level intelligence about terrorist plots that have been foiled. Increasingly, however, the question, How much security is enough? as faced by politicians requires an answer from citizens too. No

---

[119]Christoph A. Stumpf, *The Grotian Theology of International Law* (Berlin: de Gruyter, 2006), p. 203.
[120]Augustine, *On Free Choice of the Will*, trans. Thomas Williams (Indianapolis, IN: Hackett, 1993), pp. 8–9; Augustine, *Reply to Faustus the Manichaean*, in Philip Schaff, (ed.), *Nicene and Post-Nicene Fathers*, series 1, vol. 4: *St. Augustine: The Writings against the Manichaeans, and against the Donatists* (New York: Cosimo, 2007), p. 301; *Questions on the Heptateuch*, 6.10. The Christian is free not to defend him- or herself against an assailant because that would entail inordinate desire for one's own life and a loss of love.
[121]Francisco de Vitoria, *Political Writings*, ed. Anthony Pagden and Jeremy Lawrance (Cambridge: Cambridge University Press, 1991), p. 212, citing the *Moralia* of the Paris theologian Jacques Almain.
[122]Grotius, *De iure belli ac pacis*, bk 2, ch. 1, §5, cited by Oliver O'Donovan, p. 133.
[123]Kant, 'Perpetual Peace', p. 98.

one is exempt from the question given that terrorism is a mode of attack calculated to generate fear and anxiety in those unlikely ever to suffer loss of life or limb. The predictions in 1989 in 'The Changing Face of War' with respect to fourth-generation warfare have come true in the sense that fear of attack has found its way onto many streets and systems of public transportation. William Lind et al. wrote: 'Actions will occur concurrently throughout all participants' depth, including their society as a cultural, not just a physical, entity.'[124] In other words, the effects of terror will be felt by ordinary citizens going about their daily activities. A Mike Baldwin cartoon shows a taxi driver passing his prospective passenger through a large security scanner before allowing him into the car.[125] This makes the point with humour. But the implications are far-reaching. If citizens feel an imminent danger from international terrorism every time they travel by public transport such that high-street security becomes the presenting cause for armed conflict overseas, then there is political pressure to replace traditional and proportionate meanings of 'imminent threat' with notions that are far more amorphous and expansive.[126] The challenge for all citizens is not to allow false hopes of total security and the emotion of fear to contribute to electoral pressure on governments to choose armed conflict over law.

Robin Lovin observes in Christian realist perspective that governments maintain power through the use or threat of violence in exchange for the promise of security. Drawing on an Augustinian version of the biblical understanding of human nature in anxiety is

---

[124]Lind et al., 'The Changing Face of War', p. 25.

[125]Mike Baldwin, 'Taxicab Security', 30 November 2004 www.cartoonstock.com/cartoonview.asp?start=&search=main&catref=mba0636&MA_Artist=&MA_C ategory=&ANDkeyword=taxi+security&ORkeyword=&TITLEkeyword=& NEGATIVEkeyword= [accessed 21 February 2013].

[126]There is an obligation under all the 1949 Geneva Conventions to teach the law of war so that the 'entire population' is aware of the rules. Convention I, art. 47 states: 'The High Contracting Parties undertake, in time of peace as in time of war, to disseminate the text of the present Convention as widely as possible in their respective countries, and, in particular, to include the study thereof in their programmes of military and, if possible, civil instruction, so that the principles thereof may become known to the entire population, in particular to the armed fighting forces, the medical personnel and the chaplains.' International Committee of the Red Cross, Convention I, Geneva, 12 August 1949 www.icrc.org/ihl.nsf/full/365?opendocument [accessed 4 March 2013].

more basic than pride, and on which Reinhold Niebuhr relied, he considers political anxiety as a state of affairs in which inadequate power (or the wrong kind of power), uncertain circumstances and the lack of a clear set of goals and ideals leads people to act on the belief that those who are responsible for leadership are no longer in control of events. Lovin asks what characterizes a government that is strong enough, and opens for question what happens when security is treated as something to be supplied according to consumer specifications, when the electorate is always ready to change the supplier if the product does not live up to expectations. His reminder is that some human anxieties cannot be met by the state: 'A government that is strong enough neither offers itself as a faith nor allows a faith to take the place of law.'[127] Anxiety is not evil, says Lovin, but it is morally ambiguous. Citizens should be sceptical of those who exploit the fear of attack for their own ends, and be alert to the politics of security.

The meaning of security in Christian discourse has always meant more than the absence of physical threat and low probability of a successful attack by an enemy. This point is made by Jeremy Waldron:

Christians are also taught that earthly safety is not the be-all and end-all, and that the peace we should look for is not necessarily peace as the world understands it. It is 'the peace of God which passeth all understanding' in the blessing at the end of the Eucharist. Or, again, the peace we pray for at Evensong: '[G]ive unto thy servants that peace which the world cannot give'. Or finally the peace Jesus promised his disciples: 'Peace I leave with you; my peace I give to you. Not as the world gives do I give to you,' a peace that was apparently consistent with his prediction, 'the hour is coming when whoever kills you will think he is offering service to God. . . . have said these things to you, that in me you may have peace. In the world you will have tribulation. But take heart; I have overcome the world'.[128]

---

[127]Robin W. Lovin, 'Security and the State: A Christian Realist Perspective on the World since 9/11', in Esther D. Reed and Michael Dumper (eds), *Civil Liberties, National Security and Prospects for Consensus: Religious and Secular Voices* (Cambridge: Cambridge University Press, 2012), p. 255.
[128]Jeremy Waldron, 'Safety and Security', in Reed and Dumper (ed.), *Civil Liberties*, p. 16.

Christian liturgy associates a worldly quest for security with defence against fear and danger and contrasts this with the peace that is found in the mercy of God and provides opportunity for service of God and neighbour. Worldly fears are not always rational. Fear is a mental state generated not least by terrorists, who calculate how to generate the greatest amount of fear and anxiety to accompany actual loss of life and limb. Pure security is impossible to attain, and the threat from terrorism is often real: 'At the same time, it is worth considering what a richer notion of security involves, if only to see how much we are panicked into losing when we become preoccupied with physical safety under the immediate pressure of events.'[129]

Perceptions of the enemy

Against this backdrop of (problematic) changing conceptions of war and when a person may lawfully be deemed an enemy target, we turn, in this section, to perceptions of the enemy in Christian just war reasoning. Our focus is the threshold at which the 'extraordinary' means of war or non-international armed conflict such that basic human rights are suspended by executive decision for those whom governments (not only that of the United States) deem to be a threat to national security, and the blurring of the traditional distinction between two legal situations: armed conflict and peace. In the remainder of this chapter, I press theological questions about the identity of enemies, and what love of one's enemy might entail with respect to the law. The claim is that the gospel imperatives to peacemaking and love of enemy demand – at least in part – not only a refusal to normalize political violence and a default position in favour of adherence to international law but also by a 'delaying movement' with respect to the lowering of legal thresholds whereby protections afforded to individuals are lost.

So far, we have observed a drift towards identifying an enemy on the grounds of their ideological, religious or otherwise political commitments rather than the injuries that they have inflicted, and implications that include the lowering of legal thresholds whereby

---

[129]Waldron, 'Safety and Security', p. 32.

protections afforded to individuals are lost and something approaching a right to kill is becoming politically and electorally acceptable. Mindful of this drift, I have been attempting to expose why, where and how foci of the narrow, judicial, theological tradition of just war reasoning are becoming blurred – notably, where and how the criteria of whether peace and the restoration of just order are no longer the only valid reasons for resorting to arms, how to distinguish between guilt and innocence, how to effect judgement on wrongdoing, how to ask the question of transformation from death and destruction to life and how these questions might differ from an insatiable need for security. In this section, I attempt to conceive of the concept of 'enemy' theologically and review what is at stake for the church when speaking of enemies of the state.

I draw especially on Karl Barth's treatment of the concept of 'enemy' within his theology of redemption; it is here that the Christian community best learns its ethics and political theology, and learns the meaning of 'enemy' theologically. We learn rapidly that Barth uses the concept and language of 'enemy' in very different ways to that of popular newspapers with respect to 'enemy troops', 'Britain's worst enemy' – which might be anything from non-prescription drugs to a rival newspaper or junk mail. Instead, he is emphatic in teaching that sin makes humankind the enemy of God. Outside of Christ, every person has the status of enemy of God.[130] Even those who acknowledge their status as the elect in Christ must wrestle with God as an enemy if they are to partake of his blessing.[131] Faith seeks to conclude an arbitrary peace to bridge the distance between self and God, when justice demands recognition of enemy status; 'all the time God is really the enemy with whom it must wrestle like Jacob to be blessed anew by Him.'[132]

Barth does not – as far as I am aware – state explicitly that the love of enemies may/should be understood as a way of breaking the cycle of violence, but this has been argued by Timothy Gorringe in an exposition of the implications of Barth's theology of justice for criminal justice: 'The love of enemies, I take it, is a way of breaking

[130]Barth, CD, II/2, p. 347.
[131]Barth, CD, II/2, p. 354.
[132]Barth, CD, II/2, p. 407.

the cycle of violence.'[133] Gorringe argues that, if the command to love our enemies is the sign of the new order inaugurated by Christ, then this should be engaged by Christian people in terms of restorative justice, or 'the restoration of *shalom*'.[134] My purpose in this section is to develop this insight with reference to international law. The thesis is that this imperative may be met, at least in part, through the institutions and machinations of international law, and in responses to terrorism in terms of justice that is restorative of community and wider political relationships.

Who is my enemy?

According to Barth, the mighty enemies to whom God could deliver us are sin and death.[135] If God abandoned us to these enemies, we should be condemned to destruction. Humanity would certainly be excluded from covenantal with God.[136] Of ourselves we can only expire at the hands of death.[137] The gospel is that Christ has taken this death upon himself and gained victory over this last enemy of humankind (1 Cor. 15.24). In Christ, every person is thus elected to salvation and shown to be an enemy of God:

> In His person man is shown to be a recreant and rebel, an enemy and opponent of God, whom God can meet only as such. In this person the case is instigated against him. In this person he is impeached and sentenced and condemned.[138]

The gospel is that by grace alone 'God is our Friend and not our worst enemy'[139] God's grace is given to humanity precisely in our status as enemies of God. It is as his enemies that God bestows grace upon us in Christ, thereby reconciling all to himself. Sin, death and

---

[133]Timothy J. Gorringe, 'Crime, Punishment and Atonement: Karl Barth on the Death of Christ', in Daniel L. Migliore (ed.), *Commanding Grace: Studies in Barth's Ethics* (Grand Rapids, MI: Eerdmans, 2010), p. 160. He further adds: 'and of responding to harm without doing harm in return'.
[134]Gorringe, 'Crime, Punishment and Atonement', p. 152.
[135]Barth, *CD*, II/2, p. 485.
[136]Barth, *CD*, II/2, p. 498.
[137]Barth, *CD*, II/2, p. 637.
[138]Barth, *CD*, II/2, p. 749.
[139]Barth, *CD*, II/2, p. 770.

nothingness are thereby overcome. It is thus God and neither sin nor death who is to be feared.[140] Even our last enemy, death, can do no more than it is ordered to do. The will of God rules among his enemies.[141] His grace is sufficient for all things, even obedience to the command to love our enemies. Here too, and especially here, says Barth, 'is the tenor of New Testament exhortation'.[142]

Barth does not offer a generic definition of 'enemy' as applied to human relationships but maintains a difference in usage between contexts involving believers and non-believers.[143] The latter is treated relatively simply in political with reference to the state; the state determines who the enemy is, or is not, for all its members. The former is defined with reference to the church; the enemy is the person 'who refuses to accept the message of reconciliation'[144] although the Christian 'will refuse to become his enemy' in human terms in any way 'even within the political order' and its necessary fight against evil. The Christian, implies Barth, should be not seduced or slip into a sense of enmity against a non-believer but, to the contrary, should offer communion to them. As Mack Dennis observes, 'Barth moves freely between these two seemingly contradictory terms – neighbor and enemy. . . . The neighbor and the enemy . . . can be one and the same person. The neighbor and the enemy are the same person *especially* when the enemy hates, injures, and persecutes us (the "us" is in reference to Christians).'[145] So, for instance, persecutors of the Confessing Church during the Nazi regime were enemies of the church in their intention to destroy it but remained neighbours of those believers whom they were seeking to destroy. '[The living God] loves man even though he is an enemy (Rom. 5.10), and thus makes him the friend who loves Him in return.'[146] This is the law of the Spirit of life which not only frees believers but binds and engages them to do likewise.

---

[140]Barth, *CD*, III/2, p. 608.
[141]Barth, *CD*, IV/1, p. 171.
[142]Barth, *CD*, IV/1, p. 189.
[143]This point is made by Mack Dennis in a helpful paper written while a PhD student at Duke Divinity School, Durham, NC: 'Toward a Homiletics of Reconciliation: How Karl Barth's Use of Enemy Language in *Church Dogmatics* Models a More Faithful Grammar for Preaching', p. 8 www.georgetowncollege.edu/cdal/files/2011/06/mack_dennis.pdf [accessed 21 February 2013].
[144]Barth, *CD*, IV/1, p. 721.
[145]Dennis, 'Toward a Homiletics of Reconciliation', p. 10.
[146]Barth, *CD*, IV/2, p. 580.

The love of God is to be offered freely and without restriction, says Barth, to all enemies of the church. This takes the particular form of intercession. 'Pray for those who persecute you' (Matt. 5.44b). Barth interprets the injunction to love one's enemy earlier in this verse as a form of love to be expressed in intercession especially 'with its model and original in the prayer of the Crucified in Lk. 23:34'.[147] The enemy is received proleptically into the community of faith when they are loved and not hated. The work of the believer is to pray for and thereby love every enemy of the Church who would seek its destruction. In this sense the believer has no real enemy because divine grace is more weighty than the enmity of humans one to another. I assume with Barth in what follows that the initial and predominant use to which the believer will put the word 'enemy' is to their status before God that is overcome in Christ; the love of God in Christ is for all. The gospel imperative is to love one's enemy is fulfilled primarily in intercessory prayer. Petition and intercession are the fourth element in most liturgies after doxology, thanksgiving and confession. Believers plead for divine assistance not because of divine justice but because of God's love for humankind and all creatures. It is in intercession that one's obligation before God with respect to one's enemies is met.

This theological framework for the definition of, and disposition towards, the enemy does not prevent Barth speaking of the enemy of the state in the course of discussing the problem of war: 'It has always been realised that the main goal in war is to neutralise the forces of the enemy.'[148] The increasing objectivity of military killing, says Barth, is hopeful sign to the extent that the appalling effectiveness and dreadful nature of the methods and instruments of war are restrained. He cites with approval Schleiermacher's contextualized abhorrence of the warfare that has killing as its aim rather than the possession of that which constitutes the power of the enemy, that is, land and people before proceeding to discuss questions that should be put to the state about the necessity of any resort to war and limits to be put upon its conduct.[149] Barth speaks of the criminal as an internal enemy of the state as distinct

---

[147]Barth, CD, IV/2, p. 805.
[148]Barth, CD, IV/2, p. 452.
[149]Barth, CD, IV/2, p. 453.

from external enemies.[150] In other words, he uses the language of 'enemy' with relative ease but does not speak of 'love of enemy' specifically when discussing the problem of war. There is no attempt to interpret discussion of the necessity of, and limits to be placed upon the conduct of, war in the explicit terms of 'love of enemy'.

This leaves unasked and unanswered questions. Barth's remarks on the imperative 'love your enemies' do not obviously hang together well with his discussion of the problem of war and use of lethal force. This might be because he intends readers to interpret 'enemy' narrowly to mean those who would destroy the Christian community. This would follow from a narrow reading of the Sermon on the Mount as intended primarily for the disciples and Jesus' closest followers rather than the crowd at large, but would not fit so well if it were supposed that Jesus would have been speaking to men and women living under occupation. It is scarcely conceivable, however, that some among the crowd would not have associated Jesus' reference to 'enemies' with the occupying forces, as well as individuals from whom they had encountered hatred or hostility. Rather, it seems reasonable to suppose that Jesus' words may be read as having spoken directly to those who might have suffered violence at the hands of Roman soldiers and/ or who felt enmity towards the Roman Empire. Jesus was crucified by order of the empire. R. T. France warns against casuistry of the kind Jesus was sweeping aside but notes that shift from the singular 'enemy' of verse 43 to the plural in verse 44 might point to the comprehensiveness of Jesus' meaning.[151] France then alludes, however, to the example of Stephen in Acts 7.60 thereby drawing attention to the religious officials of Judea rather than Rome. The hermeneutic problem of how to interpret Jesus' command of enemy love in relation to his message as a whole, and wider New Testament teaching too, is beyond the scope of this essay. I opt in what follows for John Piper's suggestion that concentrating on the 'how' of the love command's realization helps readers to uncover the decisive elements of the imperative.

---

[150]Barth, CD, IV/2, p. 444.
[151]R. T. France, The Gospel of Matthew: The New International Commentary on the New Testament (Grand Rapids, MI: Eerdmans, 2007), p. 225.

Enemies of the state?

Church history is too full of examples of faith being used as an excuse to justify attrocities to speak comfortably about love of one's enemy in the context of UK military operations and discussion about types of weaponry. There are simply too many religiously motivated instances for just war, inquisition and other forms of violent coercion for believers to risk thinking that they know what it means to love one's enemy as God wills. This discomfort is felt intensely, viscerally, by many, including myself. I feel equally uncomfortable, however, about supposing that Jesus' imperative may be delimited to the personal and ecclesial spheres of life and not the social and political, national and international. As John Piper observes in his notable study of Jesus' command to love one's enemies, the command to love cannot be delimited by believers to their one for another because they are to do *everything* in love, 'εν 'αγαπη (1 Cor. 16.14).[152] Merely because the verb *agape* is used is insufficient reason to delimit the exercise of love to and for who participate by grace in the eucharistic life of the church.

So the question remains: Should Christians attempt to love enemies who have threatened or shown hostility to them as citizens of a given nation-state and not as disciples of Jesus per se? To avoid the question would be irresponsible. To answer no would suggest that enemies of the state are not 'enemies' in any theologically significant way. Those designated as enemies by a given nation-state attract the same respect from Christians due to every human being as a creature of God but might not be included within the category of 'enemy' referred to by Jesus in Matthew 5.44. Only if and when enemies of the state seek the direct destruction of the Christian community, or express hostility to individual believers, would they become enemies of believers per se and thus objects of love. The import of Jesus' teaching seems elsewhere in the Beatitudes to expand rather than reduce his hearers' expectations of the coming kingdom.

---

[152]John Piper, 'Love Your Enemies': Jesus' Love Command in the Synoptic Gospels and the Early Christian Paraenesis (Cambridge: Cambridge University Press, 1979), p. 130.

To answer yes might suggest that God is on 'our side' and not that of 'the enemy'. If Christians are to love enemies of the state for God's sake and because Jesus instructed them to do so, the inference might easily be drawn that these people have been declared enemies for God's sake too. A more nuanced and adequate answer will take inquirers into a range of issues about human governance in relation to the lordship of Christ that are contentious from almost every conceivable angle.

Building on Piper's exegesis that tends towards an inclusive reading of the imperative, that is, that little, if anything, in the biblical texts suggest that the disciples of Jesus are to exclude enemies of the state from their obligation to love, I adopt his further suggestion of concentrating on the 'how' of Jesus' command in the wider context of the Beatitudes and other New Testament teaching. This practical and constructive way forward can both protect against the risk of arbitrary exclusion of any from the scope of imperative while also bridging the gap between love of one's own personal enemies or enemies of the Christian community, and those declared to be enemies of one's nation-state. Piper observes four characteristics of enemy love in the New Testament:

1   enemy love is ready and willing to meet the *physical* needs of the enemy (Rom. 12.20; 1 Thess. 5.15). The provision of food and drink is required and also the disposition to 'seek to do good' and not let anyone suffer when one has the power to prevent it;

2   enemy love seeks the *spiritual* welfare of the enemy. 'The most common positive admonition concerning the enemy is that the Christian 'bless' him (Rom. 12.14; 1 Pet. 3.9; 1 Cor. 4.12). This form of enemy love is ultimately a desire for the enemy's participation in the 'fullness of Christ's blessing' (Rom. 15.29; see 1 Pet. 2.12);

3   enemy love continues to hate evil while attempting to hold fast to the good (Rom. 12.9). 'If there is no intense hatred of evil, then there will be no intense love for one's enemy because the good which love desires for the enemy is primarily the removal of the cause of enmity which is the evil of unbelief'. Genuine love hangs on 'abhorring evil and holding to the good' (Rom. 12.9);

4   enemy love requires that a person's heart genuinely desires
the enemy's good and not hide a corrupt love that yearns
secretly for their destruction.[153]

Meeting the *physical* needs of the enemy accords with Christian
perspectives on human rights whereby sheer fact of being human
entitles one to certain life-goods.[154] It is the ontology of relationship
between the Creator and creature that makes it possible, indeed,
necessary, theologically for Christian people to affirm the love of
God as the sole constituting basis of every person's inherent rights,
thereby proving a framework for a practically oriented philosophy
and politics of human rights. The believer must therefore welcome
and affirm minimum standards in the humane treatment of every
detainee, whether lawful or unlawful combatant.[155]

Seeking the *spiritual* welfare of the enemy has meant different
things to the Christian community through the centuries. One
need only review accounts of the inquisition or witchcraft trials
to shudder at many interpretations of Matthew 5.44.[156] For the
moment, we need note only that the concept of 'liberty of conscience'
is rooted deeply in Roman Catholic and Protestant thought. For
Aquinas, *synderesis,* the capacity of the human for moral reason
and adaptation to the principles bestowed upon us by nature, is
a special power of the soul that may be likened to light required
for sight.[157] In Protestant tradition, historiographers have traced
similarities between early Protestant affirmations of God's lordship
over the conscience of the individual and early World Council of
Churches support for rights to freedom of religion recognized under
the UN Declaration of Human Rights.[158] For present purposes, we
may thus suppose broad-based support among Christian people
for seeking the spiritual welfare of everyone, including all types

---

[153]Piper, *'Love Your Enemies'*, pp. 129–30.
[154]Nicholas Wolterstorff, *Justice: Rights and Wrongs* (Princeton, NJ: Princeton University Press, 2008).
[155]'Minimum standards indicate *legal* thresholds of behaviour and thus, in this context, guarantee fair court procedures as well as humane treatment of detainees' (Detter, *The Law of War*, p. 1086).
[156]Russell, *The Just War in the Middle Ages*, p. 119.
[157]Aquinas, *ST*, I, q. 79, a. 5 ad 3; q. 79, a. 12, c.
[158]See, for example, James E. Wood, Jr, 'An Apologia for Religious Human Rights', in John Witte, Jr and Johan D. van der Vyver (eds), *Human Rights in Global Perspective: Religious Perspectives* (The Hague: Martinus Nijhoff, 1996), pp. 455–83 (466).

of 'enemies', through the protection of human rights to religious liberty.[159]

Loving one's enemy while *hating evil* may be interpreted in terms of negotiating between the two poles of hating the evils of attacks against the innocent by terrorists and others and hating also the evils of war. Jesus' injunction to love one's enemies intensifies what is already the 'double and contradictory' heritage of this tradition.[160] The tension between hating evil – with all that it entails for doing justice by executing judgement and attempting to delimit abuses against the innocent – and loving those who perpetrate these abuses is irreducible in a world where justice falls short of the truth and mercy of God, and where even the closest approximation to restoring a just legal order and enforcing right in the international area is not 'righteous without qualification'.[161] Even the most justifiable use of lethal force cannot be abstracted from an economic and political hinterland where many corrupt as well as innocent interests are served. There are few simple dividing lines between good and evil when political matters are at issue. Merely deciding where and how to start the conversation is contentious. (To start with the terrorist attacks of 11 September 2001 might be deemed partisan because of failure to engage wider political questions of US and UK foreign policy in the Middle East, Central, South and Southeast Asia, and elsewhere, including policies in Palestine, Iraq and Afghanistan. Not to start with 11 September might be deemed partisan because even self-confessed 'leftists' regard the events of that day as playing a decisive role in shaping subsequent policy.)[162] Yet justice has a chance only if evil is despised.

---

[159]The US Baptist Joint Committee for Religious Liberty has an astonishingly strong track record of working for the religious liberty of prisoners at Guantanamo Bay and elsewhere www.bjconline.org/ [accessed 22 February 2012].

[160]Jacques Derrida, *Aporias*, trans. Thomas Dutoit (Stanford, CA: Stanford University Press, 1993), p. 16.

[161]William Werpehowski, 'Karl Barth and Politics', in John Webster (ed.), *The Cambridge Companion to Karl Barth* (Cambridge: Cambridge University Press, 2000), p. 238.

[162]See Alan Johnson, (ed.), *Global Politics after 9/11: The Democratiya Interviews* (London: Foreign Policy Centre, 2008). This is a collection of interviews with Jean Bethke Elshtain, Martin Shaw, David Held and others, with introductions by Michael Walzer.

Desiring the enemy's good

Genuinely *to desire the enemy's good* is perhaps the most difficult witness for the Christian to bear in the context of terrorism. Applied to our context, this cannot mean failure to punish wrongdoing. Punishment is a proper function of the courts to curtail the perpetrator from committing further crimes, ensuring that laws are obeyed, and providing some opportunity for repentance. Of itself, however, punishment does not provide for the healing of relationships and rebuilding of community. Justice effective of peace requires that all parties desire goods higher than reparation. International criminal law enforcement aims to punish the guilty, give the victims a voice, make an historical record of atrocities committed, draw to the attention of the world community that crimes against peace, and more, do not go unmarked.[163] Injustice comprises not only breaches of the law but of relationships too. Justice, in turn, is the restoration of relationship, 'something that cannot be decreed by statute but only decided by debate and negotiation'.[164] This is as true at the level of international community as at the national or local.

Three summary points may be made:

1   'Terrorists function outside the law. It is vitally important that the UK and its allies do not do so too.'[165] At a time when 'lawfare', or the calculated strategy employed increasingly by states and non-state actors of using or misusing law to achieve military objectives, is common, Christian people and others are obligated to think hard about why, when and how, international law both can delay the state's decision to kill, and about decreasing constraints on the use of force.[166]

---

[163]For a good account of the aims of international criminal trials, see David Luban, 'Fairness to Rightness: Jurisdiction, Legality, and the Legitimacy of International Criminal Law', in Samantha Besson and John Tasioulas (eds), *The Philosophy of International Law* (Oxford: Oxford University Press, 2010), pp. 574–77.
[164]Gorringe, 'Crime, Punishment and Atonement', p. 153.
[165]Public Issues Team Report to the Methodist Conference, 'Drones: Ethical Dilemmas in the Application of Military Force', 5 July 2012 www.methodistconference.org.uk/media/117981/16%20drones.pdf [accessed 21 February 2013].
[166]'Lawfare is not something in which persons engage in the pursuit of justice, and must be defined as a negative phenomenon to have any real meaning. Otherwise, we risk diluting the threat and feeding the inability to distinguish between that which is

2   Political energy is needed to establish and enforce 'ordinary' means under international law by which terrorism can be countered, in an effort to cope better in the 'twilight zone' between conventional war and conventional peace.[167] No one can doubt that the realities of terrorism, which include training camps in remote locations and the exploitation of failing states, demand judgement and action to overcome the doing of wrong. At issue is the comparative neglect of the law enforcement paradigm and law enforcement measures in favour of armed conflict, and the rush to armed conflict as compared to lacklustre attempts to envisage what law can accomplish against war.[168]

3   The politics of security in the West should make us sceptical of reductionist attempts to define national security in relation to threats posed by non-state actors with a global reach. International common good requires more than the paradigm argument, 'Unless we do x, the terrorists win'.[169]

---

the correct application of the law, on the one hand, and that which is lawfare, on the other. Because that is the essence of the issue here: how do we distinguish between that which constitutes a constructive, legitimate legal battle (even if the legal battle is against us and inconvenient) from that which is a counterproductive perversion of the law, which should be allocated no precedent? The delineation is not as simple as some may like to make it; that is, that lawsuits against terrorists are good, and legal actions against democracies are bad. The question is not "Who is the target?" but "What is the intention?" behind the legal action: Is it to pursue justice, to apply the law in the interests of freedom and democracy, or is the intent to undermine the very system of laws being manipulated?' (Brooke Goldstein, The Lawfare Project www.thelawfareproject.org/what-is-lawfare.html [accessed 21 February 2012]). See also Maj. Gen. Charles J. Dunlap, Jr, 'Lawfare Amid Warfare', *Washington Times*, 3 August 2007 www.washingtontimes.com/news/2007/aug/03/lawfare-amid-warfare [accessed 12 January 2012]. I am grateful to Paul Schulte for this reference.

[167]William Banks, 'International Legal Framework for Countering Terrorism', report of conference panel workshop at the International Centre for Counter-Terrorism, The Hague, 12–13 December 2010 www.un.org/en/sc/ctc/specialmeetings/2011/docs/icct-hague-launch-confreport.pdf [accessed 12 January 2012]. See also David Ross Black and Paul D. Williams, (eds), *The International Politics of Mass Atrocities: The Case of Darfur* (Abingdon, Oxon: Routledge, 2010).

[168]O'Connell, Introduction, *What is War?* p. 3.

[169]Lovin, 'Security and the State', p. 247.

5

Responsibility to Protect and Militarized Humanitarian Intervention: Tests and Challenges

In June 1999, US President Bill Clinton said to Jim Lehrer of the Public Broadcasting Service:

> I think the most important thing is we were right to take a stand in Kosovo against ethnic cleansing. . . . We can't stop every fight like the fight between Eritrea and Ethiopia and the struggles in Chechnya. But where we can, at an acceptable cost; that is without risking nuclear war or some other terrible thing, we ought to prevent the slaughter of innocent civilians and the wholesale uprooting of them because of their race, their ethnic background or the way they worship God. I think that's an important principle myself. I think it's a noble thing. I think the United States did a good thing.[1]

Two years later, the International Commission on Intervention and State Sovereignty (ICISS), established by the Canadian government, issued its report, which addressed the complex of legal, moral, operational and political issues surrounding humanitarian

---

[1]'The President on Peacekeeping Efforts and the Morality of the War', *The NewsHour with Jim Lehrer*, 11 June 1999 www.pbs.org/newshour/bb/europe/jan-june99/clinton_6–11b.html [accessed 28 September 2009].

intervention to prevent, inter alia, ethnic cleansing and genocide.[2] Kofi Annan, the then Secretary General of United Nations, commented approvingly that its authors wanted to avert these ills by forging consensus around basic questions of principle and process entailed in humanitarian intervention.[3]

For reasons reviewed below, the Vatican and World Council of Churches (WCC) broadly accepted the central concept of the ICISS report, namely, 'the responsibility to protect' (RtoP), between September 2003 and September 2008. At the latter date the Vatican became more critical; speaking before the General Assembly of the United Nations, Msgr Celestino Migliore implied that the principle had been invoked as a pretext for the arbitrary use of military might.[4] This note of concern was a long time coming, however, and seems barely to have touched upon moral issues concerning the militarization of humanitarian action, the blurring of humanitarian and other security-related or Western liberal political agendas, the authority of customary international law regarding the authorization of force and more. This paper attempts to identify grounds for adequate investigation in Christian perspective of moral challenges associated with its component elements.

Vatican and WCC statements on RtoP

I begin with a brief overview of Vatican and WCC statements on RtoP between September 2003 and September 2008. Prior to Msgr Migliore's address, the thrust of Vatican and WCC statements about RtoP was broadly positive:

- In 2001, a policy document approved by the Central Committee of the World Council of Churches referred

---

[2]*The Responsibility to Protect*, Report of the International Commission on Intervention and State Sovereignty, December 2001 http://responsibilitytoprotect. org/ICISS%20Report.pdf [accessed 28 September 2009].
[3]Kofi Annan, *In Larger Freedom: Towards Development, Security and Human Rights for All*, Report of the Secretary General, United Nations, September 2005 www.un.org/largerfreedom/ [accessed 3 February 2013].
[4]Celestino Migliore, address to the UN General Assembly, 63rd Session, New York, 29 September 2008 www.vatican.va/roman_curia/secretariat_state/2008/documents/ rc_seg-st_20080929_general-debate_En.html [accessed 28 September 2009].

back to WCC work in 1994–95 on criteria for determining
the applicability and effectiveness of sanctions, and was
mindful of serious criticisms of UN peacekeeping.[5] The
paper talked in broad terms about 're-shaping the debate'
and about why '[t]he protection of endangered populations
often requires '"robust" action to stop atrocities . . . restore
the rule of law' and rebuild.[6] I start with this 2001
WCC paper because it includes the subheadings 'The
Responsibility of the International Community for
Prevention of Violent Conflict', 'When Prevention Fails'
and 'Sovereignty and International Law'. In other words,
the WCC was grappling with the same issues as the United
Nations, and the ground was prepared for finding in RtoP
a simple and powerful idea around which Christian people
holding very different ideas about the use of armed force
in any circumstance could potentially unite.

• In 2003, the WCC issued 'The Responsibility to Protect:
Ethical and Theological Reflections' as a follow-up to 'The
Protection of Endangered Populations'. Despite including
in its title the name of the ICISS report and recommending
it for further study, this WCC report is little more than a
list of topics for further work.[7] A book of the same title
was published subsequently in 2005 and comprised papers
from a WCC conference that year at which Gareth Evans,
co-chair of the ICISS, was present.[8]

---

[5]World Council of Churches, Commission of the Churches on International Affairs,
'The Protection of Endangered Populations in Situations of Armed Violence: Toward
an Ecumenical Ethical Approach', policy document submitted to a meeting of the
Central Committee, Potsdam, 6 February 2001 www.oikoumene.org/en/resources/
documents/wcc-commissions/international-affairs/commission-on-international-
affairs-policy/the-protection-of-endangered-populations-in-situations-of-armed-
violence-toward-an-ecumenical-ethical-approach.html [accessed 28 September
2012].
[6]WCC, 'The Protection of Endangered Populations', §20.
[7]World Council of Churches, Commission of the Churches on International
Affairs, 'The Responsibility to Protect: Ethical and Theological Reflections',
report to meeting of the Central Committee, Geneva, 26 August–2 September
2003 www2.wcc-coe.org/ccdocuments2003.nsf/index/pub-3.l-en.html [accessed
28 September 2013].
[8]World Council of Churches, The Responsibility to Protect: Ethical and Theological
Reflections, ed. Semegnish Asfaw et al. (Geneva: WCC, 2005).

- In 2005, UN employment of the concept 'responsibility to protect' was welcomed by the Vatican as affirming the dignity of persons. Cardinal Angelo Sodano spoke during the 60th General Assembly of the principle having arisen from the United Nations' long-standing commitment to the 'pre-eminent dignity of every single man and woman over the State and over every ideological system'. The Cardinal welcomed the continuity of the principle with the Preamble of the Statute of the United Nations, which says specifically that the UN Organization was created 'in order to save future generations from the scourge of war'.[9]

- By 2006, the WCC was using the phrase 'the responsibility to protect' in its own documentation. It did so in the context of Christian teaching that war is never an act of justice. Even so, the phrase was deemed to resonate with Christian commitment to the most vulnerable people beyond one's own state boundaries. The statement issued by the WCC Assembly in 2006 welcomed explicitly how the concept of RtoP shifted the focus of debate from the rights of sovereignty to the responsibilities of sovereignty and rights of the civilian population. It added further:

  The churches are in support of the emerging international norm of the responsibility to protect. This norm holds that national governments clearly bear the primary and sovereign responsibility to provide for the safety of their people. Indeed, the responsibility to protect and serve the welfare of its people is central to a state's sovereignty. When there is failure to carry out that responsibility, whether by neglect, lack of capacity, or direct assaults on the population, the international community has the duty to assist peoples and states, and in extreme situations, to intervene in the internal affairs of the state in the interests and safety of the people.[10]

---

[9]Cardinal Angelo Sodano, address to the Summit of the Heads of State and Government, UN General Assembly, 60th Session, New York, 16 September 2005   www.vatican.va/roman_curia/secretariat_state/2005/documents/rc_seg-st_20050916_onu_En.html [accessed 18 February 2013].

[10]World Council of Churches, statement of the 9th Assembly, Porto Alegre, Brazil, 23 February 2006 www.oikoumene.org/en/resources/documents/wcc-commissions/

The report referred positively to the concept of 'human security' as providing ways of talking about human life compatible with the vision of God's kingdom, and refused to refute absolutely the need to resort to the use of force for the protection of the vulnerable. A key condition was that the use of force must be controlled by international law in accordance with the UN Charter:

> This is an imperative condition. The breach of law cannot be accepted even when this, at times, seems to lead – under military aspects – to a disadvantage or to hamper the efficiency of the intervention in the short term.

This 2006 report was clear also about the need to distinguish humanitarian relief from the use of force for humanitarian purposes, which, in turn, must be distinguished from military war-fighting objectives.

- In 2006, Msgr Migliore used the phrase 'the responsibility to protect' to describe that which is essential to the *raison d'être* of any state. In other words, he opted to treat state sovereignty in these terms.[11] Msgr Migliore closed his address at the United Nations on the phenomenon of genocide with the rhetorically rousing phrase 'never again', having just repeated the growing international consensus that 'when a country cannot or does not want to intervene to protect its population, the international community represented by the UN has not only the right but the duty to intervene.'

- Also in 2006, Msgr Silvano M. Tomasi called for sufficient political will in the international community to interpret the responsibility to protect broadly enough in order to prevent the forced displacement of persons fleeing conflict.[12]

---

international-affairs/responsability-to-protect/vulnerable-populations-at-risk-the-responsibility-to-protect.html [accessed 18 February 2013].

[11] Msgr Celestino Migliore, 'The Phenomenon of Genocide' (debate), United Nations, New York, 6 April 2006 www.vatican.va/roman_curia/secretariat_state/2006/documents/rc_seg-st_20060406_stockholm-forum_En.html [accessed 19 February 2013].

[12] Msgr Silvano M. Tomasi, statement to the Executive Committee, UN High Commissioner for Refugees, Geneva, 4 October 2006 www.vatican.va/roman_curia/secretariat_state/2006/documents/rc_seg-st_20061004_unhcr_En.html [accessed 29 February 2013].

- In 2007, Msgr Migliore extended the concept in Vatican usage to mean not only a responsibility to protect citizens, but 'to promote their welfare' especially through legal means.[13] In an intervention on the rule of law, he spoke of the need to pursue debate about juridical codification of peaceful means in order to promote the rule of law under which sovereignty is not understood as an absolute right. Of significance here is that Msgr Migliore links RtoP to the protection of citizens not only from the International Criminal Court (ICC) provisions against genocide, war crimes, ethnic cleansing and crimes against humanity, but more socio-economic provisions also. This runs counter to United Nations interpretation of RtoP that predominated in Secretary General Ban Ki-Moon's report in 2009[14] and is, to my mind, welcome. Msgr Migliore's intervention had the effect in Vatican usage of keeping the concept relatively broad by including the socio-economic needs of citizens. Elsewhere, Msgr Pietro Parolin called for the concept of RtoP to apply also in the context of climate change.[15]

- Also in 2007, the Executive Committee of the WCC repeated theological support for RtoP:

  > "It is in those who are most vulnerable that Christ becomes visible for us", the Assembly said, "the responsibility to protect the vulnerable reaches far beyond the boundaries of nations and faith traditions. It is an ecumenical responsibility, conceiving the world as one household of God."[16]

---

[13]Msgr Celestino Migliore, address, 'The Rule of Law', UN General Assembly, 62nd Session, New York, 26 October 2007 www.vatican.va/roman_curia/secretariat_state/2007/documents/rc_seg-st_20071026_rule-law_En.html [accessed 18 February 2013].

[14]"Implementing the Responsibility to Protect', report of the Secretary General, UN General Assembly, 63rd Session, 12 January 2009 daccess-dds-ny.un.org/doc/UNDOC/GEN/N09/206/10/PDF/N0920610.pdf?OpenElement [accessed 4 March 2013].

[15]Msgr Pietro Parolin, address, 'The Future Is in Our Hands: Addressing the Leadership Challenge of Climate Change', High-level Panel on Climate Change, United Nations, New York, 24 September 2007 www.vatican.va/roman_curia/secretariat_state/2007/documents/rc_seg-st_20070924_ipcc_En.html [accessed 29 September 2009].

[16]World Council of Churches, minute on Darfur, meeting of the Executive Committee, Etchmiadzin, 28 September 2007 www.oikoumene.org/en/resources/documents/

This minute précised United Nations' understanding of RtoP at the time, urged member churches to bring the people of Darfur to the attention of their governments alongside reference to WCC 9th Assembly policy on the responsibility to protect, and noted with seeming approval that UN Security Council Resolution 1706 on Darfur was the first time the Security Council had referred to the responsibility to protect in a specific crisis: 'we recommend that churches request their governments to pay special attention to its implementation.'

• In April 2008, His Holiness Benedict XVI commented that the 'responsibility to protect'

> is coming to be recognized as the moral basis for a government's claim to authority. It is also a feature that naturally appertains to a family, in which stronger members take care of weaker ones. This Organization performs an important service, in the name of the international community, by monitoring the extent to which governments fulfil their responsibility to protect their citizens.[17]

In a meeting with the members of the UN General Assembly, he rooted the concept of the responsibility to protect in ancient philosophical discourses on governance, notably the ancient concept of *ius gentium* 'as the foundation of every action taken by those in government with regard to the governed' and cited the Dominican friar Francisco de Vitoria, who 'described this responsibility as an aspect of natural reason shared by all nations'.[18] Explicit reference was made to the capacity of the principle to evoke the idea of the person as created in the image of the Creator.

• Not until September 2008 did the Vatican voice a strong public word of caution. In his address to the 63rd Session of the General Assembly, Msgr Migliore stated:

> In the past, the language of 'protection' was too often a pretext for expansion and aggression. In spite of the many

---

executive-committee/etchmiadzin-september-2007/minute-on-darfur.html [accessed 19 February 2013].

[17] Benedict XVI, address, United Nations, New York, 18 April 2008. At: www.vatican.va/holy_father/benedict_xvi/speeches/2008/april/documents/hf_ben-xvI_spe_20080418_un-staff_En.html [accessed 18 February 2013].

[18] Benedict XVI address, 18 April 2008.

advancements in international law, this same understanding
and practice tragically continues today. . . .

Despite the growing consensus behind the responsibility to
protect as a means for greater cooperation, this principle
is still being invoked as a pretext for the arbitrary use of
military might. This distortion is a continuation of past
failed methods and ideas. The use of violence to resolve
disagreements is always a failure of vision and a failure
of humanity. The responsibility to protect should not
be viewed merely in terms of military intervention but
primarily as the need for the international community to
come together in the face of crises to find means for fair
and open negotiations, support the moral force of law
and search for the common good. Failure to collectively
come together to protect populations at risk and to prevent
arbitrary military interventions would undermine the moral
and practical authority of this Organization.[19]

Here a warning was sounded about the use of violence under the
guise of an objective 'to protect'. Hitherto the principle of RtoP, its
component elements and norms, seems to have provided not only
the United Nations but also the churches with a way of holding
together disparate elements of debates about responding ethically
to the humanitarian horrors of the 1990s (Rwanda, Srebrenecia,
Racak and more).

Considerably more critical comment was made on 23 July 2009
by H. E. Father Miguel d'Escoto Brockmann, M. M., president of the
63rd Session of the United Nations General Assembly – albeit not
in his capacity as ordained priest in the Roman Catholic Church.[20]
Referring to the silence and inactivity that had shamed much of the
world after the Khmer Rouge killing fields, the massacres in Rwanda
and the former Yugoslavia, to name just a few. D'Escoto opened to
question the best form of response to these horrors. Significantly, he
noted the prevailing lack of trust from many developing countries

---

[19]Migliore address, 29 September 2008.
[20]Miguel d'Escoto Brockmann, opening statement, 'The Responsibility to Protect'
(thematic dialogue), UN General Assembly, New York, 23 July 2009 www.un.org/
ga/president/63/statements/openingr2p230709.shtml [accessed 19 February
2013].

when it came to the use of force for humanitarian reasons, identifying four tests for RtoP:

1   Do the rules apply in principle, and is it likely that they will be applied in practice equally to all nation-states, or, in the nature of things, is it more likely that the principle will be applied only by the strong against the weak?

2   Will adoption of the RtoP principle more likely enhance or undermine respect for international law?

3   Is the doctrine of RtoP necessary and, conversely, does it guarantee that states will intervene to prevent another Rwanda?[21]

4   Do we have the capacity to enforce accountability upon those who might abuse the right that RtoP would give nation-states to resort to the use of force against other states?

D'Escoto asked difficult and critical questions about the moral and political hazards associated political agenda to require potential interveners to be proactive in the use of force.

While not comprehensive, this review shows that the churches were broadly uncritical in welcoming the RtoP doctrine, even though it moved debate about the use of force towards the requiring of states to be proactive militarily rather than reactive. Between September 2003 and September 2008, the Vatican and WCC both accepted and used the new doctrine called RtoP as a way of expressing that the world could no longer remain inactive in the face of massive human suffering, waiting until the crisis spilled across borders or posed a more conventional threat to international peace and security. The notion of RtoP was deemed to resonate favourably with many of the impulses of Christianity: it directed attention to the vulnerable, affirmed the dignity of every person created in God's image; shifted the focus of debate from the rights of sovereignty to the responsibilities of sovereignty and rights of the civilian population; had features that appertained naturally to a family in which stronger members take care of weaker ones; and had roots in ancient and traditional teaching with respect to *ius gentium*. At issue is whether the churches were too quick to accept

---

[21]D'Escoto's point is that the absence of the doctrine was not what prevented the international community from acting.

humanitarian wars alongside defensive wars as paradigmatically justified, and too slow in developing a sufficiently questioning engagement with the RtoP doctrine in service of the international community.

Of course, when new approaches are adopted, no one can see with the clarity of hindsight what consequences might ensue. Even so, to have 'signed up' to RtoP and continued to endorse it without more adequate attempts to assess the militarization of humanitarian invention in Somalia, Rwanda, Bosnia-Herzegovina and Kosovo, and elsewhere now seems rather too much like heeding only one aspect of the truth; a triumph of optimism over experience. My concern in this chapter is that difficult questions were largely unasked and unaddressed by the churches, at least in public, between September 2003 and September 2008. Where, we must ask, were the questions about perceptions of RtoP from those at the receiving end? Where was the concern that a new customary rule should not develop in international law to legitimize unilateral or regional organization intervention? Where were questions about the widening of the legal grounds on which force may be used against states thereby risking the emergence of a new culture of violence under the guise of church-blessed moral acceptability? What about empirical investigations into whether, on balance, military intervention for humanitarian purposes more often does harm than good? What about evidence to the effect that, since 2001, there has been a frequent merging of humanitarian intervention with broader security concerns and political agendas? What about the concern that the RtoP doctrine, at least in its dominant interpretations, is locked into a particular human rights discourse and promotion of Western liberal values that Christian people might want to question? Where are questions about the correlation between acceptance of RtoP and a new acceptability of war? The churches do not seem to have seen beyond the welcome objectives in RtoP; both the Vatican and the WCC stated their positions rather too enthusiastically without examining fully enough the implications.

On the identity of the authority that can approve intervention

Few member states condemned NATO for violating international law after the decision to use force in Yugoslavia in 1999, and fundamental values underpinning the legitimate authority of the United Nations Security Council remain broadly recognized. Yet few since the Kosovo conflict have supported the argument that NATO and other regional security organizations are no longer bound by the requirements of Security Council authorization.[22] The Outcome document of the 2005 World Summit reiterated the importance of promoting and strengthening the multilateral process 'and of addressing international challenges and problems by strictly abiding by the Charter and the principles of international law, and further stress our commitment to multilateralism'.

> We reaffirm that the relevant provisions of the Charter are sufficient to address the full range of threats to international peace and security. We further reaffirm the authority of the Security Council to mandate coercive action to maintain and restore international peace and security. We stress the importance of acting in accordance with the purposes and principles of the Charter.[23]

Gareth Evans has emphasized that the ICISS did not see its work as trying to find alternatives to the legal authority of the UN Security Council but rather to make it work better.[24] This in contrast to Tony Blair, who in a speech in April 1999 noticeably omitted legitimate authority, that is, approval by the Security Council, from his list of five basic considerations.[25] Evans's multilateralism helps to close the gap that Blair attempted to introduce between law and morality, that is, between the militarized pursuance of humanitarian goals

---

[22]Mary Ellen O'Connell, 'The UN, NATO, and International Law after Kosovo', *Human Rights Quarterly* 22 (2000), p. 88.

[23]World Summit Outcome, UN General Assembly, 60th Session, 24 October 2005, §79 http://unpan1.un.org/intradoc/groups/public/documents/un/unpan021752.pdf [accessed 2 February 2013].

[24]Gareth Evans, *The Responsibility to Protect: Ending Mass Atrocities Once and for All* (Washington, DC: Brookings Institute, 2008), p. 43.

[25]Blair listed right cause ('Are we sure of our case?'); last resort ('Have we exhausted all diplomatic options?'); probability of success ('Are there military options we can sensibly and prudently undertake?'); long-term commitment; and national interest ('The mass expulsion of ethnic Albanians from Kosovo demanded the notice of the rest of the world. But it does make a difference that this is taking place in such a combustible part of Europe'; Tony Blair, address to the Chicago Economic Club, *The NewsHour with Jim Lehrer,* 22 April 1999 www.pbs.org/newshour/bb/ international/jan-june99/blair_doctrine4–23.html [accessed 1 October 2009].

and their Security Council authorization. Even so, NATO's decision to use force in Yugoslavia raised questions about the identity of the authority that can approve intervention.

The legality or otherwise of the NATO authorization of force in Yugoslavia has been debated in detail.[26] Some have (correctly, to my mind) regarded the bypassing of right authority as troubling. Father Miguel d'Escoto Brockmann spoke of 'the extent to which some great powers have recently avoided the strictures of the Charter in resorting to the use of force, and have gone out of their way to denigrate international law'.[27] D'Escoto spoke of 'self-appointed saviours who arrogate to themselves the right to intervene with impunity in the name of overcoming nation-state impunity.' His idiom is inflammatory. Nevertheless, that some member states bypassed the Security Council is insufficient reason to suppose that the principle no long holds, or that the principles of the UN Charter now apply directly to NATO and its members.

D'Escoto is surely correct that bypassing of the principle of right authority should be resisted. Yet the temptation is to freeze political discourse into dismal prospects for reform of the Security Council versus the need to provide security for all peoples in dire humanitarian need, or at risk of becoming caught up in non-international armed conflicts. The temptation to allow this opposition may be illustrated with further reference to Ramsey's essay 'The Ethics of Intervention'. The choice, said Ramsey in 1965, is to side with the Charter and try to strengthen the United Nations, or for the smaller nations to rally in an effort to prevent the UN forum remaining 'an ancillary of luxuriant nationalism'.[28]

---

[26]UN Security Council Resolution 1199 affirmed that the deterioration of the situation in Kosovo constituted a threat to peace and security in the region, yet resolved only to consider further action and additional measures (UN Security Council, Resolution 1199, 23 September 1998 www.un.org/peace/kosovo/98sc1199. htm [accessed 3 February 2013]). Winter was coming and people would die in the mountains if action was not taken. NATO Secretary General Solana made clear that the whole point of NATO action was to support 1199 (Javier Solana, NATO Secretary General press conference, Belgrade, 15 October 1998 www.nato.int/docu/speech/1998/s981015a.htm [accessed 3 February 2013].

[27]D'Escoto, opening statement.

[28]Paul Ramsey, 'The Ethics of Intervention', *The Review of Politics* 27 (July 1965), pp. 287–310, reprinted in *The Just War: Force and Political Responsibility* (1968; Lanham, MD: University Press of America, 1983), ch. 2, p. 26.

Ramsey wrote to a predominantly American audience where the prospect of reform of the veto was unlikely to have been welcome and weighed the balance of interests question regarding intervention in full awareness of the problem with the veto. 'Until higher authorities in the government of mankind are organized, resolute and powerful', he writes, 'the responsibilities of national statesmen in our structurally defective international order must still include possible resort to intervention.'[29]

Ramsey's 1965 essay rehearsed with remarkable prescience many of the arguments that have been in play since the NATO use of force in Yugoslavia. Theoretically, said Ramsey, the principle of state sovereignty in the world community contains within itself at least the possibility of intervention: 'even the principle of non-intervention contains an implied right to intervene to bring protective retribution upon any violation of . . . policy, and to restore the system of non-interventionary states by deterring future non-compliance.'[30] This is not readily accepted because 'we have not properly analyzed the meaning of a commitment to non-intervention as a *political promise*' (emphasis in original). In other words, the system of non-intervention rests in the international community upon states claiming the right to be impermeable. Deterrence rests upon at least the possibility of intervention – the problem being that the people of the world lose out when permanent members of the Security Council exercise their veto thereby putting a stop to interventionary measures that could correct threats and dangers to peace: 'the Assembly seems not to be an organ capable of the radical sort of decision-making this would require.'[31]

Towards the end of 'The Ethics of Intervention', Ramsey pulls back from the seemingly wide-open range of possibilities for intervention presented to the statesperson. His discussion of 'penultimate' justifications of interventions comprises a case-study type consideration of two justifications of intervention: counter-intervention; and intervention by invitation.[32] Nothing in his exposition prohibits in theory unilateral or regional action inconsistent with the UN Charter if justice and order require it. Nor would

---

[29]Ramsey, *The Just War*, p. 25.
[30]Ramsey, *The Just War*, p. 25.
[31]Ramsey, *The Just War*, p. 26.
[32]Ramsey, *The Just War*, pp. 33–38.

anything in Ramsey's discursus necessarily have required member States to accept that such action was exceptional and should have no bearing on the future need for Security Council authorization.[33] Indeed, some sections of the essay read as though they could have been written as a briefing for Tony Blair's April 1999 speech to the Chicago Economic Club, and also for *The Responsibility to Protect* report which proposed a significant departure from the UN Charter in its claim that *subsequent* authorization could be sought from the Security Council by a regional or sub-regional authority.[34] Ramsey is resistant to the legalism that does not give the statesperson room to move in an attempt to effect the best available conjunction of justice and peace, and opts, at the end of the day, for military force. The question is whether his realism hides a way to unfreeze political discourse from the dilemma between dismal prospects for reform of the Security Council versus the need to respond to humanitarian need.

Need for reform of the Security Council is no less urgent today than in 1965. As Ramsey anticipated, states have not obtained the authorization which they sought for the use of force. Yet more can be done than merely lament this impasse. The UN report *A More Secure World* faced up to the bypassing of the Security Council by, inter alia, returning to core principles of the just war tradition, and it acknowledged that the Council had not been very consistent or effective in dealing with humanitarian disasters in Somalia, Bosnia and Herzegovina, Rwanda, Kosovo, Darfur, Sudan and elsewhere.[35] The report also endorsed the emerging norm that the United Nations should exercise a collective responsibility to protect against

---

[33]The issues here about the rules governing the use of force by regional organizations are complex. I draw on O'Connell for her discussion of whether NATO's operations since 1992, in supporting no-fly zones (Resolution 781) and enforcing the embargo (Resolution 787), meant in effect that the Security Council treated NATO as a Chapter VIII organization, that is a regional agency authorized to undertake enforcement action. Her conclusion is that Resolution 1031, which authorized NATO participation in the stabilization of Bosnia-Herzegovina, referred only to Chapter VII: 'From then on, it was clear that the Council would not treat NATO as a Chapter VIII organization' ('The UN, Nato, and International Law', pp. 62–67).
[34]*The Responsibility to Protect*, p. xiii.
[35]*A More Secure World: Our Shared Responsibility*, Report of the High-level Panel on Threats, Challenges and Change, United Nations, 2004 www.un.org/secureworld/report2.pdf [accessed 1 February 2012], §201.

genocidal acts or other atrocities and addressed the issue of the legality of militarized interventions in such contexts.

The Security Council is fully empowered under Chapter VII of the Charter of the United Nations to address the full range of security threats with which States are concerned. The task is not to find alternatives to the Security Council as a source of authority but to make the Council work better than it has.[36]

It acknowledged that the Security Council was far from perfect as an institution but still provided the means for a global collective security system that is subject legally to the UN Charter. Of particular interest, however, was that the question of legality of military measures authorized, or not authorized, by the Security Council was addressed explicitly alongside a relatively detailed exposition of a set of guidelines that should always be addressed by the Security Council or anyone else involved in such decisions: seriousness of threat, proper purpose, last resort, proportional means and balance of consequences. *A More Secure World* appears to be seeking constructive engagement with the orientation of traditional just war thinking about limiting the use of force. At the least, it focuses attention on the principled relation between military action, the identity of the authority that can approve intervention and the rule of law.

RtoP and the protection of human rights

The emerging doctrine of RtoP is associated closely with respect for human rights and promoting confidence in legal institutions that protect human rights. Of foundational significance in the 2001 ICISS report was the role of human rights obligations: 'specific legal obligations under human rights and human protection declarations, covenants and treaties, international humanitarian law and national law.'[37] The report recounts, inter alia, how international organizations, civil society activists and NGOs use international human rights norms and instruments as reference points against

---

[36] *A More Secure World*, §198.
[37] *The Responsibility to Protect*, p. xi.

which to judge state conduct.[38] The 2009 Report of the Secretary General, *Implementing the Responsibility to Protect,* has lengthy sections on the monitoring of human rights and humanitarian norms, education and advocacy.

At issue in this section is the nature of appeal to legal human rights obligations in the doctrine. My concern is that the RtoP doctrine – at least in its dominant interpretations – has been locked into a particular human rights discourse that Christian people and others might want to question. It is important to make clear that I do not have an anti-human rights agenda. To the contrary, I have argued elsewhere that rights-talk can have a pragmatic, justice-related home in Christian tradition and need not be seen as belonging overwhelmingly to a secularizing agenda in the modern era, progressively at odds with older Christian traditions of political right.[39] Yet the question of how the United States/NATO should lend its weight on the international stage in the name of human rights protection remains of high importance. Some kinds of human rights ideology undermine rather than support universality claims for human rights and damage prospects for the sustainability of human rights regimes in the twenty-first century. Politically, it can be argued, for instance, that the UN Mission in Kosovo (UNMIK) and the NATO-led Kovoso Force (KFOR) were too optimistic in assuming that the adoption of minority rights standards under international law would not only be possible but would also transform political practice. As Abdullahi Ahmed An-Na'im has said about religious minorities under Islamic Law: 'It takes more than normative formulation in terms of positive law, even in the domestic context, to achieve compliance.'[40]

Consider briefly the failure of the UN Mission in Kosovo and the Kovoso Force to turn the rhetoric of protecting minority rights into reality. This is especially noteworthy because the so-called doctrine of humanitarian intervention began to take shape shortly after Prime Minister Tony Blair's speech to the Chicago Economic

---

[38]*The Responsibility to Protect*, p. 14.
[39]Esther D. Reed, *The Ethics of Human Rights: Contested Doctrinal and Moral Issues* (Waco, TX: Baylor University Press, 2007).
[40]Abdullahi An-Na'im, 'Religious Minorities under Islamic Law and the Limits of Cultural Relativism', *Human Rights Quarterly* 9 (February 1987), pp. 1–18.

Club in April 1999.[41] In the short term, the consequence of military intervention was to escalate the fighting. In the medium term, the reports from Minority Rights Group International in 2006 and 2009 repeatedly expressed concern about the lack of capacity or legal accountability under the international mission for the protection of minorities. According to Clive Baldwin's report, *Minority Rights in Kosovo under International Rule*, written for Minority Rights Group International, an NGO working to secure rights for minorities and indigenous peoples worldwide, reasons for concern politically clustered around:

- such broad reference to 'minority rights' that the term becomes too unwieldy to be effective;
- casual appeal to 'minority rights' in situations of ethnic conflict readily leads to segregation rather than integration;
- the prioritizing of 'minority rights' used to justify the problematic overturning of other legal standards; and
- for example, Regulation 2000/47 *On the Status, Privileges and Immunities of Kfor and Unmik and Their Personnel* used, in effect, to allow detention without the order of a judge.[42]

More recently, the 2009 report from Minority Rights Group International conveyed disquiet about the accountability deficit for the protection of Kosovo's minorities – Bosnians, Croats, Gorani, Roma, Ashkali and Egyptians. From having been a people in need of international protection, the new Kosovo state was now reportedly failing to protect minority rights within its newly proclaimed independence:

In the new Kosovo state, smaller minorities suffer from lack of access to information or tertiary education in their own languages, and discrimination due to association with the former Serbian majority. Together with a bad economy, these conditions mean that many members of minority communities are now leaving the new Kosovo altogether. Unless reversed, this trend

---

[41] Blair, Address to the Chicago Economic Club, 22 April 1999.
[42] Clive Baldwin, *Minority Rights in Kosovo under International Rule* (London: Minority Rights Group International, 2006), pp. 3–6, 26.

will see the steady migration of minority groups who have other states to migrate to, such as Bosniaks and Turks, who have lived in Kosovo for hundreds of years. For Ashkali, Gorani and Roma, who have no such options of escape, these trends are likely to lead to ingrained poverty and further marginalization for generations to come.[43]

The report analyses the shortcomings of legal protections for minorities under the pre-independence UNMIK international protectorate and under the post-independence Constitution. The focus is on the rule of law, political participation and, crucially, on international accountability with respect to minority rights. The concern in these MRGI reports is that minority rights are not discussed in abstraction from implementation of the rule of law. They discuss in some detail the effects of the absence of effective remedy for human rights abuses before and during the transfer from UNMIK protection to the implementation of the Ahtissari Plan by the International Civilian Office and the European Union Rule of Law Mission in Kosovo. The message that comes through loud and clear is that, in this multi-religious and multi-ethnic context, high-minded and quasi-philosophical abstract talk about minority rights without adequate domestic and international legal mechanisms has been counter-productive.[44]

---

[43]Georgina Stevens, *Filling the Vacuum: Ensuring Protection and Legal Remedies for Minorities in Kosovo* (London: Minority Rights Group International, 2009), p. 6.
[44]Debate about how globalization has affected human rights thinking has been ongoing within the *Journal of Religious Ethics* for nearly two decades. Preston N. Williams warned in 1995 about the need to be watchful for Western biases in human rights discourse and mindful because no talk about human rights is self-evidently neutral. The counter-position, that is, the autonomy of human rights vis-à-vis religion, was argued later by Louis Henkin. David Little's review of human rights literature for the spring 1999 issue questioned the plausibility of Abdullahi An-Na'im's resistance of cultural relativism combined with critique of the assumed universality of rights discourse but heightened sensitivity with respect to his concerns. In both 1998 and 2004, Sumner Twiss laid out the hermeneutical options available to theorists seeking intra- and cross-cultural understanding, with a view to understanding the impact of globalization on the politics and philosophy of human rights. He highlighted the need for practical wisdom alert to the need for cross-cultural dialogue and active search for consensus. One of my concerns in writing this paper is that the ICISS report was inadequately sensitive to such matters and too close to the 'autonomous' position advocated by Henkin. Preston N. Williams, 'Human Rights Thinking in Relationship to African Nation-States: Some Suggestions in Response to Simeon O. Ilesanmi', *Journal of Religious Ethics* 23 (Fall 1995), p. 324; Louis Henkin, 'Religion,

Many things are needed where massive violations continue to occur. It is necessary both to deny violators the pretext of claiming that they need not act in conformity with human rights standards because they are alien to their own cultural standards, and to advance the politics of human rights in a religiously and otherwise plural world. An underlying problem is also that no normative system of morality and politically accountability is culturally neutral; all normative systems are the product somehow of contextual specificities.[45] Even the language of human rights is not neutral. Kosovo shouts to us that this was not adequately recognized. As the cultural critic Mikhail M. Bakhtin reminds readers, we can never find a word in its 'virginal state'; any word is 'always-already' imbued with the evaluations and perceptions of others.[46] Whether used of Cain killing Abel or the Cambodian genocide of 1975–79, the language of human rights cannot be employed as if we were primordial humans existing prior to socio-economic and cultural constructs. Nor can the language of human rights ever grasp the entirety of the event but represent only some aspects to the neglect of others. Bakhtin, Bloch, Gramsci, Adorno and other major twentieth-century analysts of ideology interpreted neglect of this reality with respect to language as a fundamental form of injustice. We must, of course, use words, concepts and identifications in order to talk or think about anything. The point here is not to reject conceptual identification of the injustice suffered by the Cambodians and so many others as violations of human rights but to call attention to the shortcomings of many attempts to shake the a priori universality of human rights into the partiality of culturally shaped positive law. The problem is forgetfulness of the blind spots of all representational thinking, and neglect of how the supposed achieving of unity and identity

---

Religions, and Human Rights', *Journal of Religious Ethics* 26 (1998), pp. 229–39; David Little, 'Rethinking Human Rights: A Review Essay on Religion, Relativism, and Other Matters', *Journal of Religious Ethics* 27 (1999), pp. 149–77; Sumner B. Twiss, 'Moral Grounds and Plural Cultures: Interpreting Human Rights in the International Community', *Journal of Religious Ethics* 26 (1998), 271–82; idem., 'History, Human Rights, and Globalization', *Journal of Religious Ethics* 32 (2004), pp. 39–70.
[45]An-Na'im, 'Religious Minorities under Islamic Law', pp. ix–xiv, 1–32 (3).
[46]Mikhail Bakhtin, *Problems of Dostoevsky's Poetics*, ed. and trans. Caryl Emerson, 2nd edn (1963; rpt Minneapolis: University of Minnesota Press, 1984), p. 231.

in language can suppress or ignore different understandings of the object in question.

The ICISS report is, to my mind, a good example of this forgetfulness of what John Gray calls 'standard or conventional liberal thought' which supposes human rights norms to be rationally derived and therefore insulated from those incommensurabilities that arise within and among religious conceptions. Gray points more effectively than most political theologians to the cultural shifts under way in most, if not all, NATO countries from post-liberalism to pluralism. My concern is that human rights theorists are not keeping up with these developments, and that there is need for Christian people to contribute to this debate. The drafters of the United Nations Declaration of Human Rights were silent on matters of faith and philosophy. More recently, theorists such as Michael Ignatieff have urged those working with human rights to maintain this deliberate silence with respect to substantive beliefs. A 'thin' (describing only the rights themselves) rather than 'thick' (contextualizing rights in the religious, cultural, economic and other complexes of a given society) approach is preferable, he argues, because it tends to keep human rights instruments out of political debates about the relation of rights to traditional, religious and authoritarian sources of power.[47] Significant here is that Ignatieff was one of the human rights specialists on the ICISS when it was launched in 2000. He was, says Gareth Evans, 'particularly closely engaged with the co-chairs' along with Ramesh Thakur. No surprise, therefore, that the ICISS report is characterized by the core values of liberalism: individualism, egalitarianism, universalism and meliorism – to borrow Gray's summary.[48] The report represents something of a low point in this non-sustainable approach to human rights discourse in the twenty-first century.

RtoP and limiting the use of force

In picking up these issues now, I turn to the criteria in *A More Secure World*, the UN report outlining considerations in whether to

---

[47]Michael Ignatieff, *Human Rights as Politics and Idolatry*, ed. Amy Gutman (Princeton, NJ: Princeton University Press, 2003), p. 76.
[48]John Gray, *Enlightenment's Wake: Politics and Culture at the Close of the Modern Age* (London: Routledge, 1995), p. 200.

authorize or apply military force.[49] More specifically, I work from comments on these criteria by Gareth Evans, co-chair of the 2001 International Commission on Intervention and State Sovereignty which informed the 2005 World Summit Outcome document, in which the RtoP doctrine became internal to the United Nations. These tests (seriousness of risk, intention, last resort, proportional means, balance of consequences) have not yet been adopted formally by the General Assembly or Security Council, but debate tends to centre around them (or the six tests proposed initially by the ICISS).[50] This essay is structured in the main by these tests and Evans's comments on them.[51]

A risk with all criteria-centred reasoning is described by Oliver O'Donovan as the reduction of moral reasoning to a checklist which, when applied, renders one armed conflict just and another unjust in a quasi-formulaic manner, whereas the tradition of just war reasoning demands far more rigorous participation in 'a discipline of deliberation, a way of focusing and posing questions of political responsibility to oneself and to others'.[52] A similar point is made by international relations theorist Nicholas Rengger: 'What we tend to get, for the most part, are theories of international *legitimacy* that treat legitimacy as, effectively, "validity"; in the manner in which H. L. A. Hart famously saw a legal system as being valid – that is not self-contradictory without being in itself the subject of moral claims.'[53] While accepting with Hart that many difficulties beset

---

[49]Annan, *A More Secure World*, §207, p. 67.

[50]The original report *The Responsibility to Protect* proposed six criteria for military intervention under the following headings: right authority, just cause, right intention, last resort, proportional means and reasonable prospects. I mentioned issues surrounding 'right authority' in a previous article (Esther D. Reed, 'Responsibility to Protect and Militarized Humanitarian Intervention: When and Why the Churches Failed to Discern Moral Hazard', *Journal of Religious Ethics* 40:2 [2012], pp. 308–34) and, while continuing to maintain that this is a matter of pressing concern, refrain from commenting again here.

[51]Gareth Evans, 'Implementing the Responsibility to Protect: Lessons and Challenges', Alice Tay Lecture on Law and Human Rights, Freilich Foundation, Canberra, 5 May 2011 www.gevans.org/speeches/speech437.html [accessed 24 August 2012].

[52]Oliver O'Donovan, *The Just War Revisited* (Cambridge: Cambridge University Press, 2003), pp. 13, 16.

[53]Nicholas Rengger, review of *Just Wars: From Cicero to Iraq* by Alex J. Bellamy; *Morality and Political Violence* by C. A. J. Coady; *Law, Ethics, and the War on Terror* by Matthew Evangelista, *Perspectives on Politics* 7 (December 2009), p. 938.

the claim that a law is valid when framed for the enforcement of morality per se, there are problems too in supposing that serious moral reasoning can be replaced by quasi-administrative procedure. A longer project would be needed to examine when and how some types of thinking about the criteria that constitute a just war are cut off from their broader hinterland. For the moment, I accept for the purposes of this essay that these tests create a space for discourse and warrant consideration by the churches because they continue to be used in decision-making about delimitating the use of force.

Two interim observations are offered.

On the restraint of others from sin

First, there need be no a priori principled objection in Christian perspective to the resolution adopted by the UN General Assembly in 2005 that '[t]he international community, through the United Nations, also has the responsibility to use appropriate diplomatic, humanitarian and other peaceful means, in accordance with Chapters VI and VIII of the Charter, to help to protect populations from genocide, war crimes, ethnic cleansing and crimes against humanity.'[54] To the contrary, it could be argued from Christian tradition that responsibility for others of this kind is precisely what the churches should be encouraging. Augustine writes: 'If we are to be blameless, therefore, our duty includes not only doing no harm to anyone, but also restraining him from sin or punishing his sin, so that either he who is chastised may be corrected by his experience, or others may be warned by his example.'[55] This passage about equitable rule mainly concerns the 'order of nature' whereby the paterfamilias has a duty to exercise authority over slaves and all in a household to ensure peaceful co-existence. The context of the reflection and its conclusion, however, is the wider harmony of the city's peace and civic rule. Allowing for the patriarchal character of the domestic and civic arrangements of the time, the point remains that some bear a responsibility to punish and restrain the sins of others.

Similarly, Aquinas's teaching about what kind of war is lawful might be understood to mean that a war may be deemed

---

[54]World Summit Outcome, 24 October 2005, §139.
[55]Augustine, *The City of God against the Pagans*, trans. R. W. Dyson (Cambridge: Cambridge University Press, 1998), bk XIX, ch. 16, p. 945.

lawful not in response to an attack against one's own people but against other peoples too because the objective of war is the overcoming of wrongdoing wherever it occurs: 'it is necessary that the belligerents should have a rightful intention, so that they intend the advancement of good, or the avoidance of evil. . . . "True religion looks upon as peaceful those wars that are waged not for motives of aggrandizement, or cruelty, but with the object of securing peace, of punishing evil-doers, and of uplifting the good."'[56] Grotius further discusses war in terms of punishment and the overcoming of wrongdoing and deems it proper that, in certain circumstances, a sovereign power bring force to bear upon another sovereign power not only for injury inflicted against their own subjects but the subjects of other states too: 'It is proper also to observe that kings and those who are possessed of sovereign power have a right to exact punishment not only for injuries affecting immediately themselves or their own subjects, but for gross violations of the law of nature and of nations, done to other states and subjects.'[57] The rationale for punishment arises not only from the civil law that applies in a given area but also from the natural law which has prevailed since before the foundation of any state and is still in force. According to natural law, wrongs done to the innocent are susceptible of punishment. Hence pirates and 'general robbers' and other enemies of the human race are to be punished. Natural law does not determine with any degree of precision who bears the responsibility for such punishment, and there might be questions about degrees of guilt in various parties.[58] Grotius is clear, however, that wrongdoing perpetrated by or against a third party is liable to punishment by others. From this rationale, there is no reason to exclude the severe and systematic wrongdoing of rulers against their peoples. The natural endowment of all humanity includes the knowledge that seizing the property of another against their will and doing violence or injury to another does not make for peace.[59]

---

[56]Aquinas, *ST*, II–II q. 40, a. 1, sed contra.
[57]Hugo Grotius, *On the Law of War and Peace*, trans. A. C. Campbell (London: Boothroyd, 1814), bk II, ch. 20, §XL.
[58]Grotius, *On the Law of War and Peace*, bk II, ch. 20, §III.
[59]Grotius, *On the Law of War and Peace*, Prolegomena, p. 10.

In other words, it could be argued from these authorities that to take up arms in defence of people(s) in a nation-state where those in authority are failing in their responsibilities is potentially more justifiable than an armed response to aggression against a lawful authority's own state. These major sources in Christian tradition allow the possibility that it might be right to prevent a party who has injured another from doing injury to others, and that, if this objective can be accomplished only by disarming the offender of the means of farther injury or otherwise preventing them from committing further harm, the use of force might be necessary.[60]

Realism and mixed motives

Second, mixed motives with respect to armed conflict does not always mean that interventions will fail: 'Military interventions in Sierra Leone, Liberia, East Timor and Bosnia did not solve all problems, but they did improve the lives of the people there. Other interventions – for example, in Somalia – did not.'[61] Indeed, I accept that the debate over RtoP requires Christian ethics and political theology to analyse an insufficiently recognized problem with the way that so-called realists within the discipline have responded to the question of mixed motives. Traditions of political realism influenced heavily by Augustine's warnings against evil in the human heart, pride, lust for power, wickedness and corruption, and more, could be said to dilute the vitality of their contribution to debate when appearing merely to recite warnings that familiar

---

[60]Emerich de Vattel develops different grounds on which the use of force might be deemed necessary for the prevention of further harm to others. Vattel bases his argument more directly than Augustine, Aquinas or Grotius on the concept of humanity *per se* and the solidarity that one human owes to another by virtue this reality: 'The offices of humanity are those succours, those duties, which men owe to each other, as men, – that is, as social beings formed to live in society, and standing in need of mutual assistance for their preservation and happiness, and to enable them to live in a manner conformable to their nature' (*The Law of Nations of the Principles of the Natural Law*, trans. John Chitty [Philadelphia: T. & J. W. Johnson, 1883], bk II, ch. 1, §2) www.constitution.org/vattel/vattel_02.htm [accessed 3 September 2012]). Vattel writes without reference to Christian belief and occupies a significant place in the emergence of the idea of crimes against humanity, where this crime is not understood as an offence primarily against God.

[61]Joseph S. Nye, 'The Intervention Dilemma', *Al Jazeera*, 15 June 2012 www. aljazeera.com/indepth/opinion/2012/06/201261292523651706.html [accessed 24 August 2012].

vices continue to confound and corrupt moral reasoning. Hence the criticism that Hans J. Morgenthau imbibed so much from Augustine that he failed to attend with sufficient detail to what was actually happening, thereby recoiling from treating international affairs in a sufficiently scientific manner: 'Morgenthau's deep pessimism leaves few concrete mechanisms to guide foreign policy except national interest defined as power, which he defends as both moral and practical.'[62] The charge is that his lack of discrimination in this regard produces a brand of realism that is insightful but insufficient as a guide for policy.

I am less critical of Morgenthau than Kaufman but accept that merely to lament and expose the pervasive evil in human nature can render engagement with international affairs so generalized that it cannot speak directly to the situation in hand. While it remains a responsibility of Christian ethics and political theology to denounce evil as a consequence of the wrong use of creaturely freedom and expose the earthly city as marked by discord, opposing interests, murder and deceit, even the most unalloyed neo-Augustinian realist must recognize with respect to RtoP that the initiative is a response, at least in part, to the failures of the international community in response to the 1992 massacres in Somalia, genocide in Rwanda, the UN experience in Bosnia and more. The problem, of course, is that even when the noblest of motivations are present in the mix, even the most genuine political will to end the killing and butchery of innocent people is inadequate if it fails to recognize that baser intentions play a role also in decision-making. Karl Barth writes of wars deemed to be 'just': 'All affirmative answers to this question are wrong if they do not incorporate a recognition that even *in extremis* it is far more difficult to express even a qualified affirmative at this point than when we stand on the outer margin in such matters as suicide, abortion, self-defence, etc.'[63] Barth wished to free contemporaries from the illusion that war was fought for reasons other than economic gain and national interest.[64]

---

[62]Robert Kaufman, 'Morgenthau's Unrealistic Realism', *Yale Journal of International Affairs* 1 (Winter/Spring 2006), p. 29 http://yalejournal.org/wp-content/uploads/2011/01/061202kaufman.pdf [accessed 7 February 2013].

[63]Barth, *CD*, III/4, p. 4.

[64]David Clough, 'Fighting at the Command of God: Reassessing the Borderline Case in Karl Barth's Account of War in the *Church Dogmatics*', in John C. McDowell and Mike Higton (eds), *Conversing with Barth* (Aldershot, Hants: Ashgate, 2004), p. 224.

Christian ethics and political theology needs to revisit its handling of mixed motives in order to meet challenges such as RtoP. The point remains, however, that there are no completely just wars or purely humanitarian interventions, and that the churches and others are foolishly naïve (not dovelike in innocence) when insensitive to the linkages between support for RtoP and broader foreign and domestic policy concerns of those effecting protection. Intervention might be the lesser of evils but decision-makers must reckon always with differences in motivation and degree between the parties.

Given these preliminary considerations, the following areas of concern will be examined in response to Evans's treatment of the five tests:

1 How assessment of 'the seriousness of risk' plays into domestic foreign policy around wider questions of security and risk management.

2 Whether and when with respect to 'right intention' the dice are loaded in favour of a military response on the grounds that larger political programs and projects are served.

3 Why the 'last resort' criterion should be employed not only in situations of extremis but prepared for earlier in negotiations about the development of international legal institutions and mechanisms.

4 Whether and how questions about the *jus post bellum* should be included in decision-making about 'proportionate means'.

5 The extent to which assessment of the 'balance of consequences' is adequately transparent, empirically and contextually based, given the growing significance of capabilities provided by technological advances in the area of so-called precision strikes.

This list of concerns is not comprehensive and cannot be considered with the level of detail warranted. It is indicative, however, of the kind of questioning that Christian people, in dialogue with others, might want to be developing today. I make no apology for a contextually specific attempt to disenthrall the churches from RtoP. The backdrop of this and my previous paper remains the (to my mind) inadequately critical engagement by the churches with the RtoP doctrine and policy. I do not conclude that such action is always and wholly unacceptable; this point must be underlined. I presuppose throughout, however, that killing is alien to the good functioning of a state and the role given by God to governing authorities as servants for good (Rom. 13.1–7). With Barth I affirm a 'detached and delaying movement' for the churches in any assessment of the justifiability of armed force:

> If they do not first and for a long time make this the burden of their message, if they do not throw in their weight decisively on this side of the scales, they have become savourless salt, and must not be surprised if they are freely trampled underfoot on every side.[65]

Five tests

The five tests (seriousness of risk, intention, last resort, proportional means, balance of consequences) look similar to, although are not the same as, the requirements of traditional just war reasoning. I do not delay to examine these differences, even though such an investigation might be illuminating, but work with Evans's summaries of the World Summit Outcome criteria as opening into debate.

Seriousness of risk

The first test is seriousness of risk: is the threatened harm of such a kind and scale as to prima facie justify the use of force?[66]

In commenting on this test, Evans observes that the risk of an imminent civilian bloodbath was 'as real in Benghazi and Abidjan in recent weeks as it was in Rwanda in 1994'. By contrast, he says, 'there was no such imminent risk in Iraq in 2003'. The current situations in Bahrain, Yemen and above all Syria are 'on

---

[65]Barth, CD, III/4, p. 456.
[66]Evans, 'Implementing the Responsibility to Protect'.

the cusp: ugly, but smaller scale and perhaps still retrievable by pressure short of military action (of which the United States and its allies could usefully continue to apply much more)'. I do not pause to comment on variant risk calculations of these situations but focus on how to question the relation between responsibility and risk.

The idea of risk is 'the predominant reality of our times'.[67] War may be understood in terms of risk management. So writes Christopher Coker in *War in an Age of Risk*. Influenced by the sociologist Ulrich Beck's observations on the world at risk from global terrorism, environmental catastrophe, financial crises and more, Coker's thesis is that war is effectively an exercise in risk-management and consequence-management, where the ideal war is 'pre-programmed' or scripted in advance, packaged for cable television, and 'spun as a success'.[68] Coker writes relatively little about RtoP but observes that, '[t]oday, we have begun to acknowledge radically new responsibilities to those far from us, not only in terms of space but also time in what Beck calls our de-bounded world.'[69] Morally it is laudable, he implies, to run risks not only for ourselves but for others. Increasingly, politicians and public are making decisions on the promise that an action will save future lives. This is true with respect to environmental concerns but also of wars: 'The invasion of Iraq was justified, after all, in terms of the precautionary principle.'[70]

Coker's observations illuminate our discussion to the extent that he draws attention to how the assessment of risk plays into decision-making. The idea of 'risk', he says, has relatively few positive connotations.[71] At a time when the big risks of climate change and ecological destruction, hand-held nuclear bombs and suicide terrorists who might infect themselves with a deadly virus to spread the disease in a city, botnets (robot networks) and other such unmanageable risks are prevalent, populations grow anxious because distance no longer offers security and arguably 'the unmanageability of risks has diminished the authority of the

---

[67]Christopher Coker, *War in an Age of Risk* (Cambridge: Polity Press, 2009), p. viii.
[68]Coker, *War in an Age of Risk*, pp. 8–9.
[69]Coker, *War in an Age of Risk*, p. 129.
[70]Coker, *War in an Age of Risk*, p. 130.
[71]Coker, *War in an Age of Risk*, p. 64.

nation-state to which we once looked for our security'.[72] Amidst such predicaments, the social construction of risk management acquires political importance, and risk-based approaches to national (and international) security become the norm. Risk and consequence management 'has become the demand of the hour'.[73]

It is against this backdrop that I suggest we consider the 'seriousness of risk' test proposed by Evans. Coker's point, and mine, is that it is politically impossible to abstract the immediate humanitarian calculus from what Beck calls the 'inescapable structural conditions of the global society' in which some have the capacity to define risk and others do not.[74] The capacity to manage risk is becoming another way of describing power and domination; the politics of risk plays into how societies not only perceive and conduct war but also a growing number of international and domestic considerations too. On the international scene: 'This is especially true of the world risk society in which the Western governments and powerful economic actors determine the risks for others, for the underdogs of the world risk society.'[75] In other words, an RtoP assessment of the seriousness of risk cannot be isolated from the wider assessments of risks that 'mutually refract one another'[76] in the international community. Any armed conflict between the 'world risk society' and others, the new 'West and the rest', will always be to some extent a staged war in which electorates are encouraged to feel that their government is managing risk responsibly in what is, in effect, a staged war where defeat cannot happen.

My point in citing Coker and Beck is not to detract from the desperate plight of those individuals, tribal groups or others under threat, or from the possible justifiability of military action under RtoP, but to observe that there is no such thing as a politics-free or disinterested assessment of the 'seriousness of risk'. RtoP calculations cannot be abstracted from the politics of the risk-management that Western governments are undertaking against the figure of the suicide attacker, and such like. 'In this way', writes Beck, 'a contradictory complementarity develops between the risk-transfer wars and the

---

[72]Coker, *War in an Age of Risk*, p. 75.
[73]Coker, *War in an Age of Risk*, p. 103.
[74]Ulrich Beck, *World at Risk* (Cambridge: Polity Press, 2008), p. 142.
[75]Ulrich Beck, *World at Risk*, p. 142.
[76]Ulrich Beck, *World at Risk*, p. 154.

global political significance of terrorist attacks.'[77] Where precision armed conflict can be conducted against those who would harbour and train the suicide attacker, with relatively few casualties on our side and the 'felt' benefit of protecting peoples at risk, the military imperative is likely to be strong. Hence the criticism from some that selective application is a problem for the RtoP doctrine. 'For example', writes political journalist Jon Western, 'if China were to crack down aggressively with military force against some form of separatist uprising in Tibet or Xinjiang Provinces, the international community could condemn it, but there would be no real military options for a response.'[78] What about the relative indifference towards the atrocities committed by President Robert Mugabe and his regime in Zimbabwe? Risk assessment is undertaken by political agents and must therefore be treated as at least partially self-reflexive.

Jacques Derrida makes the same point about self-interest being inherent in the exercise of responsibility. I cite the passage below because of its call to honesty amidst political life that is never pure or innocent:

And let us not forget that an inadequate thematization of what responsibility is or must be is also an irresponsible thematization: not knowing, having neither a sufficient knowledge or consciousness of what being responsible means, is of itself a lack of responsibility. In order to be responsible it is necessary to respond or to answer to what being responsible means. For if it is true that the concept of responsibility has, in the most reliable continuity of its history, always implied involvement in action, doing, a praxis, a decision that exceeds simple conscience or simple theoretical understanding, it is also true that the same concept requires a decision or responsible action to answer for itself consciously, that is, with a knowledge of a thematics of what is done, of what action signifies, its causes its ends, etc. In debates concerning responsibility one must always take into account this original and irreducible complexity that links

---

[77]Ulrich Beck, *World at Risk*, p. 156.
[78]Jon Western, 'After Libya and Syria: Can R2P Survive?' *Current Intelligence*, 27 September 2011 www.currentintelligence.net/columns/2011/9/27/after-libya-and-syria-can-r2p-survive.html [accessed 1 September 2012].

theoretical consciousness (which must also be a thetic or thematic consciousness) to 'practical conscience' (ethical, legal, political), if only to avoid the arrogance of so many 'clean consciences'.[79]

Derrida's analysis is cast in terms of the impossibility of either a clear conscience with respect to responsible action, or pure responsible action per se. In order even to begin to undertake an assessment of one's responsibility to others given the risks that they face, the responsible subject must understand how their own thoughts and context influence the conditions within which action is undertaken.[80] 'Grace is the axe laid at the root of the good conscience', writes Barth.[81] There is 'no such thing as the "building up" by men of an adequate ethical life, not even if the quality of their moral behaviour were so sublime that it might be claimed that the will of God had been united with the human will.'[82] This critique of confidence in the human to act rightly and responsibly before God is not a negation of the imperative to ask responsibly but a warning against even the thought that we can establish ourselves as having done so.

Right intention

The second test is whether the primary purpose of the proposed military action is to halt or avert the threat in question.[83]

That halting or averting the threat in question should be the (primary) purpose of the proposed military action is not in question. As we saw in Chapter 4, a witness at the heart of the classic just war tradition is that the 'extraordinary' means of war are potentially justifiable when there has been a failure of 'ordinary' means, that is, when wrongdoing cannot be overcome by policing at regional

---

[79]Jacques Derrida, *The Gift of Death*, trans. David Wills (Chicago: University of Chicago Press, 1995), p. 25.

[80]Gregory B. Sadler, 'Responsibility and Moral Philosophy as a Project in Derrida's Later Works', *Minerva* 8 (November 2004) www.minerva.mic.ul.ie//vol8/derrida. html [accessed 31 August 2012].

[81]Barth, *CD*, III/4, p. 430.

[82]Barth, *CD*, III/4, p. 431.

[83]Evans, 'Implementing the Responsibility to Protect'.

and national levels, the processes of criminal international law, and such like.[84] With respect to 'right intention', Evans's second test resonates harmoniously with the overtly theological tradition(s) of just war reasoning associated with Augustine, Aquinas, Gratian, Molina and others, which maintained an emphasis on the punitive nature of just war – as well as the proper limits on state action, and prohibitions against pre-emptive strikes based on fear, and more besides.[85] Evans's formulation of the test of 'right intention' speaks, however, of 'the *primary* purpose of the proposed military action' (emphasis added) allowing potentially for additional secondary purposes. So, for instance, Evans's judgement regarding Libya is that the intervention passed this test because neither oil nor regime change were the primary motivators.[86] Secondary benefits such as favourable treatment by the new Libyan regime of the United States, the United Kingdom and France in relation to the rebuilding of the infrastructure and economy are presumably allowable. My question pertains to what other secondary purposes are allowable and how they play into decision-making. Consider the following observation about the geopolitics of risk management in the face of a world divided into nation-states that rest on order versus those that do not:

> And war must be fitted into this picture too as an organizing or regulating principle. . . . The US often sees itself as a 'facilitator' of globalization; the EU actually claims to be a 'facilitator' of global civil society. Force can be seen as a facilitating factor too. . . . The West is no long in the business of fighting crusades (such as the liberal world's crusade against fascism). . . . Today there is no vision of the 'social' any longer; there is only a very utilitarian understanding of the future: the world is a dangerous place that needs to be policed against a range of enemies from terrorist movements to criminal syndicates and drug cartels.[87]

---

[84]'Judgment in war was extraordinary in that it arose out of the failure of ordinary means, but ordinary in that it was governed by the same principles as the ordinary means. So it held out the promise of extending ordinary means and widening the scope of ordinary judgments to encompass international disputes' (O'Donovan, *The Just War Revisited*, p. 19).

[85]We reviewed above how major figures in the classical, narrow, judicial just war tradition treated the question of pre-emptive strikes.

[86]Evans, 'Implementing the Responsibility to Protect'.

[87]Coker, *War in an Age of Risk*, p. 149.

The concern is that (well-managed) lethal force is a tool in the kit of those seeking to effect 'historical change, or a way of looking at the world and solving some of its problems'.[88]

Hence my plea to the churches at least to be aware that a secondary purpose for the leading proponents of RtoP might well be a struggle for particular values. In his commentary on Blair's speech, Noam Chomsky cites Václav Havel's comments, and also the lead articles in relevant academic journals at the time, to the effect that NATO was fighting the first war in history 'in the name of principles and values'.[89] Chomsky does not have a principled objection to RtoP but calls for awareness of how the UN doctrine plays into wider agendas. Similarly, Richard Falk, professor emeritus of international law at Princeton University, draws attention to 'an unfortunate triumphal spirit' that has surrounded media coverage, in the United States especially, of RtoP and the intervention in Libya especially because some at least are interpreting the intervention as force being used with United Nations backing and in furtherance of human rights and liberal values. Falk cites the celebrated journalist Roger Cohen's conclusion: 'There are no fixed doctrinal answers – a successful Libyan intervention does not mean one in Syria is feasible – but the idea that the West must at times be prepared to fight for its values against barbarism is the best hope for a 21st century less cruel than the 20th.'[90]

Robert Jackson, noted professor of international relations and political science at Boston University, writes of RtoP: 'Behind much if not all of the foregoing is a basic Western predilection, namely that of rationalism or the progressive outlook that grew out of the Enlightenment. Fundamental to this attitude is the

---

[88]Coker, *War in an Age of Risk*.

[89]Noam Chomsky, *A Generation Draws the Line: Humanitarian Intervention and the "Responsibility to Protect" Today* (Boulder, CO: Paradigm, 2012), pp. 1–2, citing Václav Havel, 'Kosovo and the End of the Nation-State', *New York Review of Books*, 19 June 1999.

[90]Richard Falk, 'Preliminary Libyan Scorecard: Acting beyond the UN Mandate', 6 September 2011 http://richardfalk.wordpress.com/2011/09/06/preliminary-libyan-scorecard-acting-beyond-the-un-mandate/ [accessed 2 September 2012]; Roger Cohen, 'Score One for Interventionism', *The New York Times*, 29 August 2011 www.nytimes.com/2011/08/30/opinion/30iht-edcohen30.html?_r=2 [accessed 1 September 2012].

seemingly unquestioned assumption that if we, the enlightened, apply our knowledge and good will, we can solve the problems of human existence – not only for ourselves but for everyone, everywhere.'[91] Wolfgang Krieger says of the intervention in Libya: 'Just look at how the African Union failed to support the UN-mandated intervention in Libya, and how the Arab League only supported the no-fly zone – but nothing else. To speak of an 'international community' being in agreement on the protection of civilians from mass violence carried out by their own governments is simply not in accordance with the facts.'[92] In other words, a substantial body of scholarship is pressing for critical engagement not only with the primary intention of those proposing military action to halt or avert the threat in question but the close-running secondary intentions too.

Last resort

The third [test] is last resort.[93]

Evans's third test looks similar to the traditional principle in classic just war reasoning whereby 'last resort' is bounded by the last practicable moment for effective action[94]. My comments in this section are not intended to take issue with this test *per se* but, rather, to press the question of why – when RtoP is not only a military doctrine but encompasses a wide range of diplomatic measures – relatively little attention has been paid to conceptualizing and responding to the threats as breaches of international criminal law. 'Last resort' test remains a test for whether any other recourse for action to remove the threat is available. At a time when the supposed precision of distance-operated weaponry weighs on the side of a military solution, the

---

[91]Robert Jackson, 'R2P: Liberalizing War', *World Politics Review*, 28 June 2011 www.worldpoliticsreview.com/articles/9308/RtoP-liberalizing-war [accessed 24 August 2012].
[92]Wolfgang Krieger, 'R2P, Corruption and Noble Causes', Kyle Matthews vs. Wolfgang Krieger, *Global Brief: World Affairs in the 21st Century*, 19 October 2011 http://globalbrief.ca/blog/tag/responsibility-to-protect/ [accessed 24 August 2012].
[93]Evans, 'Implementing the Responsibility to Protect'.
[94]O'Donovan, *The Just War Revisited*, p. 60.

question is how to press for longer-term, law-based options to be in place in advance of emergency. Don Hubert and Ariela Blätter write that

> one of the few areas where genuine clarity exists is the circumstance under which the Responsibility to Protect should be invoked. Not only are these crimes relatively well understood, their unique character in generating both state responsibility and individual criminal liability has been widely accepted. Yet surprisingly little attention has been given to how legal standards and jurisprudence might further advance this agenda. This is due in large measure to the fact that the architects of the doctrine of the Responsibility to Protect have not been specialists in either international criminal or human rights law.[95]

Hubert was a member of the International Commission on Intervention and State Sovereignty's research team and co-author of the Commission's research volume. Blätter served recently on the expert working group for Secretaries Albright and Cohen's Genocide Prevention Task Force. In other words, they are well placed to make the judgement that examining the definitions and elements of genocide, ethnic cleansing, other major crimes against humanity and war crimes, as international crimes is an untapped resource for those seeking to more clearly articulate the doctrine of RtoP.

Hubert and Blätter suggest that a greater focus in RtoP discussions on the legal aspects of the threats in question could provide a valuable perspective on how to conceptualize the international responsibility in question and focus on priorities for prevention. To date, as they make plain, Secretary General Ban Ki-Moon's approach has been to focus on three pillars: the responsibilities of the state, international assistance in state capacity building and timely and decisive responses where states are 'manifestly failing'.[96] The argument advanced by Hubert and Blätter is that more

---

[95]Don Hubert and Ariela Blätter, 'The Responsibility to Protect as International Crimes Prevention', *Global Responsibility to Protect* 4 (2012), p. 33.
[96]'Implementing the Responsibility to Protect', Report of the UN Secretary General, 12 January 2009.

specificity with respect to the criminal character of the actions and/ or threats in question would help when assessing the specifics of criminal responsibility among perpetrators, the criminal nature of the prohibited acts and the scale of the crimes. The four crimes in question are: genocide, crimes against humanity, ethnic cleansing and war crimes. The likely outcome of the kind of development they propose would be increased expectation that international criminal proceedings would result from involvement by the international community, and that such proceedings might not be dependent upon the consummation of a crime. So, for instance, Article 3 of the UN Convention on the Prevention and Punishment of the Crime of Genocide makes conspiracy to commit genocide punishable per se, whether or not this conspiracy is followed up by the consummation of the crime.[97]

My reason for citing Hubert and Blätter is to join with them in urging the development of international criminal law measures to deal as far as possible with potential and actual perpetrators of crimes against humanity, their command and control structures, motivations and intentions, plans and stockpiling of weapons, hate media, mobilization of militia and more. With respect to the 'last resort' test, the point is that this test need not be addressed only at the point of highly pressurized decision-making at times of dire emergency but understood to demand that appropriate 'ordinary' means (i.e. institutions of international law and the applications of international law across nation-state borders) are developed when there is no emergency.

The obvious retort is that the International Criminal Court and other institutions of international criminal justice are too much the tool of political interests to perform this role, and that

---

[97]Hubert and Blätter conclude that reference to the four 'crimes' is redundant and that crime against humanity alone provides an appropriate framework for conceptualizing and implementing the RtoP doctrine. More generally, their thesis is that this approach to RtoP through the lens of international crimes yields the basis for a policy framework in terms of the preventing and halting of the crimes that the International Criminal Court was established to prosecute; they emphasize the need to develop and adapt the machinery of international peace and security to address what are essentially human rights crises ('The Responsibility to Protect as International Crimes Prevention', p. 64). Their claim is that a crimes prevention approach can help to sharpen preventive initiatives by specifying those who must be either deterred or coerced to change their behaviour.

the massive issues of law enforcement make such an approach impossible.[98] Perpetrators must be caught and tribunals offer no immediate answer to mass bloodshed. Mary Ellen O'Connell writes: 'the real basis of international law's authority is . . . the international community's acceptance.'[99] Without the support of the international community for the development of institutions of international law and other means by which to prosecute offenders, the criminality of violence against the innocent is inadequately expressed and armed conflict is the 'last resort' because appropriately competent frameworks of international criminal law are not available. International criminal measures mean little without enforcement measures. Equally, however, militarized intervention should not be cut loose, either conceptually or practically, from the criminality of the human rights abuses in question. An understanding of RtoP as an 'extraordinary' response to wrongdoing requires a default position in favour of adherence to international law and the appropriate development of its institutions.

Proportional means

> The fourth test is proportional means: are the scale, duration and intensity of the proposed military action the minimum necessary to meet the threat in question.[100]

Proportionality has long been recognized as a general principle of international law and plays a central role in the laws of armed conflict. There is frequently a need to balance military necessity with humanitarian considerations; proportionality is a standard for weighing or balancing these considerations. Proportion, as O'Donovan summarizes, 'has to do with the rational form which

---

[98]David Luban, 'Fairness to Rightness: Jurisdiction, Legality, and the Legitimacy of International Criminal Law', in Samantha Besson and John Tasioulas (eds), *The Philosophy of International Law* (Oxford: Oxford University Press, 2010), p. 571.
[99]Mary Ellen O'Connell, *The Power and Purpose of International Law: Insights from the Theory and Practice of Enforcement* (Oxford: Oxford University Press, 2011), p. 16.
[100]Evans, 'Implementing the Responsibility to Protect'.

such an act assumes, i.e., with the shape of a successful judgment'.[101] It is not contentious therefore that the United Nations builds into its considerations about RtoP the question of whether the scale and intensity of the proposed military action is necessary to meet the objective.[102] Given the persistent witness in the classic just war tradition to defence of the innocent with only necessary and proportionate levels of force, it is unnecessary to engage Evans on this point.

At issue is the scope of this test and whether, or to what extent, proportionality has a role to play in *jus post bellum* as well as *jus ad bellum* and *jus in bello* considerations. Paragraph 139 of the World Summit Outcome document states the intention of the United Nations

> to commit ourselves, as necessary and appropriate, to helping States build capacity to protect their populations from genocide, war crimes, ethnic cleansing and crimes against humanity and to assisting those which are under stress before crises and conflicts break out.[103]

But to what extent should *jus post bellum* considerations limit the initiation of armed conflict? This question has been discussed most notably in recent years by Larry May and Alex Bellamy. May and Bellamy question variously whether the rules that govern, and the measures that are necessary to achieve, a just and lasting peace when hostilities have ceased should be factored into the proportionality calculus about whether to initiate hostilities. May argues that such factors should be included but acknowledges that proportionality becomes a much more difficult test to apply when the proportionality calculus is extended to include the quality of the *post bellum* peace relative to the peace in the *status quo ante bellum*: 'the *jus post bellum* proportionality principle forces us to confront a larger issue, or the total effects of a war, in ways that the other two proportionality principles do not.'[104] By contrast, Bellamy

---

[101]O'Donovan, *The Just War Revisited*, p. 48.

[102]The inclusion of 'duration' in the criterion might be questioned as playing to domestic audiences rather than being of moral or legal significance, but I do not discuss this here.

[103]World Summit Outcome, 24 October 2005, §139.

[104]Larry May, *After War Ends: A Philosophical Perspective* (Cambridge: Cambridge University Press, 2012), p. 226.

doubts the wisdom of developing *jus post bellum* criteria as limits on the initiation of an otherwise 'just' conflict because, inter alia, it is not often clear to whom postwar duties should fall, different responsibilities emerge from different types of war, and because such duties must be developed through consensus. The justice of the peace, he says, should be evaluated independently of the justice of the war.[105]

The particularities of different contexts typically evade generalized observations but I am sympathetic to May's requirement that what he calls *jus post bellum* considerations are factored into the proportionality calculus about whether to initiate hostilities. It is at least arguable that the broad witness of the classic just war tradition is that the quality of the peace for which a war is fought is relevant to the weighing of *jus ad bellum* considerations. Augustine, says Mattox, treated the question of the quality of peace *post bellum* as integral to whether the war is justifiable or not. Rather than considering the peace likely to result from the war under a separate rubric, Augustine treats the peace for which the war is fought as something to be considered *ante bellum*. Augustine, says Mattox, goes beyond Cicero and Ambrose in recognizing that peace is the indisputable end to which all wars are fought by specifying that the likely quality of this peace is a proper matter of concern. Peace is the indisputable end to which all wars are fought – where peace means more than the mere cessation of the immediate cause of the war or the retribution necessary to bring the wrongdoer to reformation. Augustine's innovation is his conviction that 'a war should not be fought unless the balance of good which reasonably could be expected to result from fighting the war is greater than the evil which can be foreseen to result from the war.'[106] War is fought, at least in part, to obtain a better peace than whatever peace, or lack of peace, it is intended to replace.

This debate is larger than can be addressed adequately here. If May's questions connect to Augustine's teaching, however, as I think they do, then churches that comment favourably on RtoP cannot be indifferent to questions about the quality of peace likely

[105]Alex J. Bellamy, 'Realizing the Responsibility to Protect', *International Studies Perspectives* 10 (2009), p. 127.

[106]John Mark Mattox, *Saint Augustine and the Theory of Just War* (London: Continuum, 2006), p. 81; Augustine, *City of God*, bk XIX, ch. 12.

to result from military intervention, or to assumptions implicit in the discourses and policy literature about peace-building. Helpful in this regard is Oliver Richmond's account of differing conceptions of the peace that is rebuilt after interventions. Richmond's concern is with the quality of the peace that the international community seeks to build in post-conflict situations. At its simplest, his point is that debates about peace-building often suppose liberal modes of governance, economics, polities and development as a logical extension of conflict transformation and peace-building: 'The reform of governance is directed by an alliance of actors, which become custodians of the liberal peace.'[107] Richmond speaks of the 'liberal peace' as comprising democratization, the rule of law, human rights, free and globalized markets and what he calls neo-liberal developments with respect to economic and liberal reform, as sometimes different from those institutions and practices that grow from locally rooted processes.

My point is not that the churches should be opposed necessarily to what Richmond calls 'the liberal peace' but should recognize that broadly uncritical support for the RtoP doctrine involves some kind of positioning with respect to these debates. There is no reason for the churches to adopt a stance of ideological opposition *de rigueur* to all aspects of 'the liberal peace'. Equally, however, it should not be supposed that Christian discipleship equates to support for liberal democracy. While many Christian people (myself included) are comfortable in broad terms with how representative democracy legitimizes a regime by subjecting it somehow to agreed legal conditions, there are no doctrinal links between the gospel of Christ and this particular polity. To suppose as much, even unwittingly, risks sacralizing a particular type of politics rather witnessing to the coming reign of God by exposing and denouncing injustice, feeding the hungry and more.

Rather than unwittingly supporting liberal modes of governance, economics, polity and development as integral to peace-building or enjoining ideological battle against 'the liberal peace', those churches that speak in support of RtoP might want also to support those endeavouring to attend carefully to what is really required to build a sustainable, law-governed peace, in a given region.

---

[107]Oliver P. Richmond, *The Transformation of Peace* (Basingstoke: Palgrave Macmillan, 2005), p. 111.

Richmond et al. have drawn our attention to the need for empirically based examination of the nature of the peace developed through different approaches to, and aspects of, peace-building, that attend to bottom-up requirements as well as top-down.[108] To this end, the shape of a successful judgement about the proportionality of means entailed in 'the responsibility to protect' might be deemed to include a 'responsibility to honour' a range of forms of peace-as-governance – even if different from the protectors' vision of peace, and resulting in much more parochial discourses and infrastructures coloured by local concerns. Those churches that speak in support of RtoP might want to think critically also about the peace that is to be rebuilt – at least when a top-down 'liberal peace' is assumed to be unproblematic in its internal structure, and a sufficient condition for helping states to protect their populations from genocide, war crimes and more.

Balance of consequences

> The final, and usually toughest, test for legitimate military intervention is balance of consequences: will those at risk be overall better or worse off?[109]

Evans's fifth test was not required per se by the classic just war tradition although the 'probability of success' criterion has featured in recent accounts of just war reasoning.[110] I accept for present purposes, however, that Christian people may properly be committed to assessing the balance of consequences not because 'there is no other standard than ends against which to judge and determine acts'[111] but because, following Reinhold Niebuhr, this examination

---

[108]The establishment of the United Nations Peacebuilding Commission in 2005 represents a major step forward that can analyze over time and in a range of contexts whether and/or how to move from a 'one-size-fits-all paradigm' (Richmond, *The Transformation of Peace*, p. 2) to less prescribed theoretical and practical frameworks in post-conflict environments.

[109]Evans, 'Implementing the Responsibility to Protect'.

[110]National Conference of Catholic Bishops, *The Harvest of Justice is Sown in Peace* (Washington, DC: United States Catholic Conference, 1994) http://old.usccb.org/sdwp/harvest.shtml [accessed 1 September 2012].

[111]Mark L. Haas, 'Reinhold Niebuhr's "Christian Pragmatism": A Principled Alternative to Consequentialism', *The Review of Politics* 61 (1999), p. 607.

is necessary for fulfilling the law of love, given the world as it is.[112] Christianity remains incompatible with consequentialism (as a 'total' ethic) because of the belief that God ultimately judges the relative morality or immorality of an act. No relation between responsibility and the balance of consequences is unmediated in Christian ethics because judgement rests ultimately with God. For this reason, any assessment of the balance of consequences in Christian ethics and just war reasoning will be a form of *restricted* consequentialism in the sense that the consequentialism of Christian people is only ever the second step of a two-step process, when the first step is the attempt to grasp what it means, in the context of Creator and creature, to live in response to the Word of God.

At issue, therefore, is not that the churches need be unduly wary of strategic engagement with questions of consequence measurement but whether they are sufficiently committed to what is really entailed in this kind of assessment. The need for this kind of assessment has been underlined recently by an increasing number of international relations theorists concerned about the failings of NATO and UN methods for the recording of casualties, in particular their transparency and systemic adequacy. Consider this claim by Gregory McNeal, School of Law, Pepperdine University:

> In recent years, an entire body of academic literature and policy commentary has been based on an incomplete understanding of how the U.S. conducts military operations. The literature is incomplete because U.S. practices are shrouded in secrecy and largely inaccessible. As a result commentators have lacked a descriptive foundation to analyze and critique U.S. operations.[113]

McNeal's concern is with how collateral damage is estimated in targeted killing operations and other precision-strike attacks. Similar concerns are voiced repeatedly by the Bureau of Investigative

---

[112]Haas, 'Reinhold Niebuhr's "Christian Pragmatism"', p. 608.
[113]Gregory McNeal, 'The US Practice of Collateral Damage Estimation and Mitigation', paper presented at a conference at the Centre for International Intervention, University of Surrey, Guildford, 12–13 July 2012 http://works.bepress.com/gregorymcneal/22/ [accessed 5 September 2012].

journalism, for instance, Chris Woods's recently questioning of CIA figures for civilian deaths in Pakistan drone strikes since 2004. Others focus on how the rhetoric of protecting civilians is manipulated by both sides in a conflict, and on how new weapons technology is being represented to public opinion as facilitating attacks upon the perpetrators of crime while downplaying the harm to civilians.[114] Together these theorists require that the 'balance of consequences' test must include the consequences of actions by the protectors as well as the immediate initiators of threat and violence in question; the evidence base must be as adequate as is possible in the circumstances and open to scrutiny.

My point in this section is not to contest or denounce rigorous evaluation by the international community of how the 'balance of consequences' is assessed, or to downplay how difficult it is for the international community to foresee the consequences of actions. Rather, it is to underline the need for such evaluation to be adequately transparent and empirically based, and not reliant merely on claims about technological advances in the area of so-called precision strikes. The results might not always be palatable.[115] Nor should it ever be forgotten that the irreplaceability of every civilian and soldier lost in conflict puts their death beyond calculation. At the least, however, questions should be put to the repeated

---

[114]See papers presented at the conference Hitting the Target held at the Centre for International Intervention, University of Surrey, Guildford, 12–13 July 2012: Chris Woods, 'Covert Drone Strikes and the Fiction of Zero Civilian Casualties' www. ias.surrey.ac.uk/workshops/intervention/papers/ChrisWoods.pdf [accessed 3 March 2013]; Wali Aslam and Ciaran Gillespie, 'US Drone Strikes in Pakistan and Political Appropriation of Casualties in Threat Construction'; Caglar Kurc, 'How Military Technology Became a Tool for Justification for Military Interventions' www.ias. surrey.ac.uk/workshops/intervention/papers/CaglarKurc.pdf [accessed 3 March 2013].

[115]Recent comparisons of approaches to humanitarian military interventions and their outcomes by the Stockholm International Peace Research Institute make clear, for instance, that a significant factor in success is the level of political interest that the country in question holds for the potential intervener: 'humanitarian intervention is most likely to succeed when the political interests of the intervening states are strongly engaged because only then will other important factors be present, such as adequate resources and the commitment to persevere in the face of adversity' (Taylor B. Seybolt, *Humanitarian Military Intervention: The Conditions for Success and Failure* [Oxford: Oxford University Press, 2007], p. 20).

political discourse that new weapon technologies tip the scales towards intervention because civilian casualties will be low. When the discourse of humanitarian ethics 'intermingles with military technology',[116] the 'balance of consequences' judgement must be as well informed as possible.

Conclusions

The debate over the UN Responsibility to Protect doctrine (RtoP) has a way of dividing opinion. For some, the doctrine means that now, at least in principle, genocide, ethnic cleansing and other major crimes against humanity and war crimes 'are regarded as everyone's business'.[117] Tyrants and governing elites now know that state sovereignty cannot hide behind claims of sovereign impunity with respect to major human rights abuses; it cannot be right that vicious regimes are left to do as they wish without regard to the basic rights of their peoples. For others, coercive military action that is so dependent on the international political context will be overtaken, almost inevitably, by objectives other than the immediate goal of preventing mass atrocity.[118] 'A doctrine of intervention that both claims the moral high ground and clamours its universality but under which the interveners are always from the Global North and the intervened upon always from the Global South is not moral

---

[116]Kurc, 'How Military Technology Became a Tool'.

[117]Evans, 'Implementing the Responsibility to Protect'. See also Samantha Power, Remarks at the International Symposium on Preventing Genocide and Mass Atrocities, Paris, 15 November 2010 www.responsibilitytoprotect.org/index.php/component/content/article/134-americas/3079-samantha-power-remarks-at-the-international-symposium-on-preventing-genocide-and-mass-atrocities [accessed 24 August 2012].

[118]Bellamy gives a history of what he calls the post-2005 'revolt' against the principle of RtoP in which he recounts how a number of states have expressed scepticism about the principle and its use in different settings. He looks especially at comments by Arab and Asian members of the Human Rights Council and evidences frequent concern that RtoP will open the door to abuse and self-interested unilateral interventionism ('Realizing the Responsibility to Protect'). See also Jean Bricmont, foreword to Noam Chomsky, *A New Generation Draws the Line: Humanitarian Intervention and the "Responsibility to Protect" Today* (London: Paradigm, 2012), p. vi; David Chandler, 'R2P or Not R2P? More Statebuilding, Less Responsibility', *Global Responsibility to Protect* 2 (2010), p. 166.

progress; it is geopolitical business as usual.'[119] It is clear, however that a questioning response from the churches to RtoP, rather than merely uncritical affirmation of this doctrine as a way of protecting the vulnerable, is warranted.

This is not to say that delays in providing humanitarian aid and failures to act might not also be morally culpable. Military intervention will sometimes demand our support. Responsibility exercised on behalf of others – even when motives are mixed – is more easily overlooked than acted upon for domestic interests. This chapter is intended, however, as a corrective to inadequately uncritical engagement by the churches with respect to questions about the imposition of Western values and widening of the grounds for military action, and an attempt to identify further pressing questions about why it is an illusion to think that there can be an impartial protector (or protectors) in international relations, how assessment of 'the seriousness of risk' plays into domestic foreign policy around wider questions of security, risk management and more. The churches are not to master Jesus' imperative to be 'wise as serpents' at the expense of 'innocence as doves' (Matt. 10.16). But the wisdom of the serpent is that of keen perception of the environment through a variety of means. May the churches not be negligent in either regard.

---

[119]David Rieff, 'R2P, R.I.P.', *The New York Times*, 7 November 2011 www.nytimes. com/2011/11/08/opinion/r2p-rip.html?pagewanted=all [accessed 24 August 2012].

6

Nation-States, Borders and Love of Neighbour: Impartiality and the *Ordo Amoris*

This chapter is about love of neighbour near and far, given humanity's division into nations. Secularist discourse tends to divide between 'partialists' and 'impartialists'. Partialists work with an ideal of states as distinct cultural communities that justifies priority for the interests of citizens over refugees. Impartialists work with an ideal of states as cosmopolitan agents which take into account equally the interests of citizens and refugees. Yet there is a relative dearth of theological contribution to present-day debate about how to conceive theologically of humanity in its division into nations and/or nation-states, and how to get our loves ordered rightly given this de facto reality. At issue is how to conceive of the priority of our created, common humanity over humanly constructed divisions into nation-states, whether and/or how the cries of neighbours far away require Christian people to downplay the ethical significance of the nation-state and opt instead for a new form of cosmopolitanism. The claim in this chapter is that, despite the considerable and proper challenges from Peter Singer and other new cosmopolitans who challenge readers to count the welfare of individuals impartially, it remains possible and, indeed, necessary at the present time for Christian people to work with an account of territorial borders, nation and nationhood, as permitted within divine providence. This claim is cast in terms of traditional Christian teaching about the order of love (*ordo amoris*).

At its simplest, Singer seeks the best consequences for the largest number of people and, in so doing, cuts across territorial borders and also the ordering of loves according to traditional Christian teaching. His plea is for renewed appreciation of the humane, non-sectarian, non-nationalistic, universal values that were embodied in the greatest writers of ancient and modern times. Having recounted in *Pushing Time Away* what national partiality and its perversion did to his grandparents, Singer looks for a way of thinking in which the whole world rather than nation-states is the starting point for moral reasoning; he seeks an approach to moral reasoning wherein the challenge is to count the welfare of individuals impartially, regardless – or, at least, with far less regard than is often given – of whether they live nearby or at a distance. His preference utilitarianism challenges readers to count the welfare of individuals impartially, regardless of – or, at least, with far less regard than is often given – divisions into nation-states. His new cosmopolitanism cuts across partiality based on culture, history and co-nationality, and requires at least the attempt to regard the suffering of all as equally worthy of relief.[1] At issue for our purposes is what kind of cosmopolitanism, if any, should characterize Christian ethics and political theology.

The bulk of the chapter is given by three sets of issues associated with territorial borders, nation, nationality and the ordering of love:

1   What response is required of Christian people given that the very nature of the post-Westphalian democratic nation-state system makes it unfeasibly difficult to love one's neighbour

---

[1]Some of Singer's most moving descriptions of this type of cosmopolitanism are found in the book in which he tells the life-story of his maternal grandfather, David Oppenheim. Born a Jew in Bruenn (now Brno) in the Czech Republic, Oppenheim fought in the First World War for the Kaiser, worked as a schoolmaster in Vienna and died in the concentration camp at Theresienstadt. In reflections at the close of this book, Singer writes: 'Though the world will remain divided into nation-states for the foreseeable future, the development of a global community at many different levels is beginning to make it possible to think in terms of universal human values and the more open, cosmopolitan world that David always favoured' (Peter Singer, *Pushing Time Away: My Grandfather and the Tragedy of Jewish Vienna* [London: Granta Books, 2003], p. 244).

and especially one's distant neighbour appropriately? At an earlier delivery of this essay a woman asked me if I agreed with Peter Singer's condemnation of the ex gratia, that is, by favour, approach to the reception of refugees which gives more moral weight to the arbitrariness of existing territorial borders than to the immediate needs of those starving or fleeing persecution.[2] She lauded his condemnation of this current political orthodoxy and was disappointed not to hear an equally strong Christian cosmopolitanism from me to the effect that priority is to be given to world-wide principles of distributive justice rather than to society-wide principles. Her point was that global citizens have as much claim upon us as fellow nationals; states should accept binding obligations to grant to persons, not their nationals, a permanent right to settle. My answer to the woman was an unsatisfactory yes and no. Yes, the eschatological hope must surely dispose Christian people to echo Singer's outrage at how the arbitrariness of political borders contributes to the fact that fully one-third of all human beings still die from poverty-related causes. No, dangers beset those cosmopolitan theories that suppose that we can be educated to fraternity, 'whereupon the unfortunate passions that tear societies asunder – greed, aggressiveness, lust for power – will vanish'.[3] What made utopias turn malignant in the nineteenth and twentieth centuries is not far removed from Singer's specifying of positive obligations upon all persons to relieve the suffering of others because states do not have legitimate grounds for the exclusion of foreigners.[4] This optimism relies on dreams of the universal brotherhood of humankind that proved not only unfeasible but suppressive of difference. I still maintain that way forward for Christian ethics in this regard is not a sacralized version of Singer's cosmopolitanism but now attempt a more adequate answer to a very good question.

---

[2]'As far as refugees are concerned . . . the ex gratia approach is the current orthodoxy' (Peter Singer, *Practical Ethics*, 2nd edn [Cambridge: Cambridge University Press, 1993], pp. 255–56).
[3]Leszek Kołakowski, *Modernity on Endless Trial* (Chicago: University of Chicago Press, 1990), p. 139.
[4]Singer, *Practical Ethics*, pp. 255–56.

2 Is it possible and, indeed, desirable to work with an account of territorial borders, nation and nationhood, as permitted within divine providence without falling into aggressive nationalism or immoral partiality? Aggressive nationalism produces a caricatured imitation of theocracy or aleteiocracy where the state instantiates the rule of truth and community. The more difficult question concerns the extent to which a realist Christian ethic of borders allows for national partiality. Again, the response is too often an uneasy yes and no. Yes! The Christian realist must surely recognize that most political choices are made not only in terms of self-interest and power but also with reference to what Roger Scruton calls the personal state, the nation-state which is so governed by a rule of law and procedure that every citizen can adopt political outcomes as their own, and which is characterized by a shared sense of identity and common interests.[5] Not every justification for national partiality smacks of ethnocentrism or even racism such that the believer can do little other than regard it as an evil to be overcome. Yes! as Toni Erskine emphasizes, it is surely right to call attention to local ties and loyalties, community and culture, the profound importance 'of particularity and of passion, in shaping our values and defining who we are' without which it is not possible to further reciprocal interchange between peoples.[6] No – it is not possible to work with an account of territorial borders, nation and nationhood, as permitted within divine providence, if this means a moral partiality or politics of superiority that would deny to others the same human rights as those of its members, is marked by hostility towards and suspicion of other nations, and condones the violence and destruction that results from these attitudes.

3 Keeping these issues in mind, what if anything should be retained from traditional teaching, and in particular the structure of the *ordo amoris,* when addressing the

---

[5]Roger Scruton, *The West and the Rest: Globalization and the Terrorist Threat* (London: Continuum, 2002), pp. 134–44.
[6]Toni Erskine, *Embedded Cosmopolitanism: Duties to Strangers and Enemies in a World of 'Dislocated Communities'* (Oxford: Oxford University Press, 2008), p. 2.

deceptively simple question, Who is my neighbour?
All things being equal, we might suppose that the *ordo
amoris* is relatively uncontentious. The repeated witness in
Christian tradition is that one cannot love everyone equally:
'[A]ll men are to be loved equally. But since you cannot do
good to all, you are to pay special regard to those who, by
the accidents of time, or place, or circumstance, are brought
into closer connection with you'.[7] No individual *can* love
everyone equally and so the question becomes how to love
appropriately. Justice is about getting our loves ordered
rightly. Aquinas writes: 'out of charity, we love more those
who are more nearly connected with us, since we love them
in more ways'.[8] Family, community and co-nationals might
be deemed to have a greater claim upon our consideration
than those far away simply because those distant from
us are in relations of nearness with others who have
corresponding responsibilities as ourselves. All things being
equal, it is better that I care for an elderly relative nearby
and expect those far away to care for their own elderly
relatives rather than me try to care for their relative at a
distance. Similarly with respect to co-citizens. Well-ordered
societies are those in which citizens exercise a politically
mediated duty of care one to another.[9]

The new cosmopolitan concern, of course, is that all
things are *not* equal. The Westphalian system – which has
been inseparable from its inception from the capitalist
market economy security against debt provided by nation-
states – is widely recognized as having failed to create fair
trading agreements between what the neo-Gramscians call
the transnational capitalist class (TCC) and the 'have-nots'
or social underclasses who already reject the idea that
globalization does anything for them. The Westphalian
system has failed to sustain a balance between the need

---

[7]Augustine, *Christian Doctrine*, trans. James Shaw, in *Nicene and Post-Nicene
Fathers*, ed. Philip Schaff, series 1, vol. 2 (Buffalo, NY: Christian Literature Publishing
Co., 1887), bk I, ch. 28.
[8]Aquinas, *ST*, II–II, q. 26, a. 7, c.
[9]To my mind, this includes redress of shocking levels of inequality. See Richard
Wilkinson and Kate Pickett, *The Spirit Level: Why Equality is Better for Everyone*
(London: Penguin, 2010), passim.

for a growing economy and the resulting environmental damage, and to constrain the gap between rich and poor nation-states around the world, and more besides.[10] In other words, this system of nation-states makes the command to love one's neighbour, and especially one's distant neighbour, unfeasibly difficult, when globalization means that every citizen of the world is for the believer the man going down from Jerusalem to Jericho (Lk. 10.25–37). The question is whether it is simply wrong to affirm an *ordo amoris* or hierarchical order of partiality when universal benevolence demands more, and whether such an affirmation is simply a cover for inaction and defence of the status quo.

In arguing that it is possible for Christian people to work with an account of territorial borders, nation and nationhood, as permitted within divine providence, it is necessary to develop an ethic of answerability in which the choice between commitment to everyone universally and the reality of the other person beside me is not experienced as oppositional. The question becomes how it is possible to avoid a dilemma between a commitment to those nearby, including co-citizens, and the equality of all human beings that cuts across all other distinctions to place a burden of responsibility equally on all. Every person encounters and engages the world from a limited perspective and with finite consequences; to act is to be selective.[11] At issue is whether we can seek after a more dialectical relation in which to interrelate and intensify the several modes (L. *pluribus modis*) of love that connect human creatures one to another. Love is not a zero-sum game which highlights that giving something to someone necessarily means not giving it to someone else. Either this, or the ethical life is reduced to a form of solipsism in which the agent is accountable ultimately to themselves for their maximizing of the reduction of suffering and the moral limits (or not) of the utilitarian calculus.

In practical terms, choice is rarely an abstract alternative between a quantitative-based ethic that treats the equality of all persons as

---

[10]Susan Strange, 'The Westfailure System', *Review of International Studies* 25 (1999), p. 346.
[11]I draw on Robert Spaemann, *Happiness and Benevolence*, trans. Jeremiah Alberg, S. J. (London: T&T Clark, 2000), ch. 10, esp. p. 131. The original German edition was published in 1989.

a quasi-numerical value versus love of the person nearby. How we love the person nearby has implications for how we engage the neighbour far away. Singer is undoubtedly correct that money spent on luxury gifts for a relative would achieve more elsewhere. One can obtain the same utility in a poor country, more or less, by spending 10p as you can by spending £1 in the United Kingdom. This is not in dispute. The Christian is challenged to consider how they spend or otherwise dispose of every single penny. The challenge is not to set love of one's immediate neighbour over against love of neighbour far away; to do so fabricates a universality in which the moral responsibility to minimize suffering overall replaces an ontology of love. This cannot be acceptable to Christian ethics if the result is a potentially unsustainable imperative in which benevolence becomes what Roman Catholic ethicist Robert Spaemann calls 'an imagined totality of goodness' in which the self's relationships with others do not grow deeper and more vibrant but tend towards abstraction.[12] The challenge is to learn better how to love the person nearby while responding sacrificially to the needs of those far away and, vice versa, to love one's distant neighbour in a manner informed by love of the person nearby.

It is also necessary to investigate the realities of how territorial borders function. The political choices of today are not between a cosmopolitanism that sees no difference between family relations and responsibility to persons unknown to us and at a distance, or partialism that denies the human rights of non-nationals. The real choice is closer to home and about how to engender an ethic of answerability with respect to territorial borders, not only before God but also the international community, and those like the appellants in our case-study who were refused the right even to speak for themselves by applying for asylum. It is too far to leap from Matthew 25.31–35 and biblical traditions that the nations will be judged to present-day legal and political judgements. The premise that the nations will stand before the Son of Man during the last judgement does not yield necessary truths with respect to the morality of the procedures adopted by governments and applied to appellants; this, in part, because the requirements of an ethic of answerability are complex in liberal Western democracies

---

[12]Spaemann, *Happiness and Benevolence*, p. 120.

where the 'Who?' aspect of the question about answerability is far from simple. Today, every citizen is a policy maker with respect to the function of territorial borders. The moral responsibility with respect to asylum seekers, refugees, overseas aid budget, carbon emissions and more, lies with every citizen and not only elected politicians. Hence the need to look carefully at how borders actually function to effect either social justice and peace or suffering and injustice.

A world without borders?

The idea of a world without borders is a powerful one for Christian people, and for good reason. Christians confess that the lordship of Christ is cosmic rather than merely regional (Eph. 1.10; Phil. 2.9–11; Col. 1.15–20; Rev. 20.11–13). That Jesus taught his disciples to pray 'our Father' construes the entirety of humanity, of all peoples and ethnic backgrounds, colours and gender orientations, learning, rank or social status, as a unity without distinction. The mission of the Church is to the ends of the earth (Matt. 11.28; 28.16–20). The gospel is preached in all tongues (Acts 2.3–11) and not one sacred language. The hope of the coming kingdom of God transcends national boundaries; the gospel is not about lines on maps that may readily be construed as about division and the delimiting of territory and authority. 'Amen!' we must surely agree. As John Paul II wrote, the Catholic Church 'is not confined to a particular territory and she has no geographical borders; her members are men and women of all regions of the world.'[13] The Church's mission is universal because 'the event of Jesus Christ has a universal application'.[14] The gospel of Christ breaks down rather than marks out defensive lines that differentiate between 'us' and 'them'.

---

[13]John Paul II, 'The Freedom of Conscience and Religion', letter on the eve of the Madrid Conference on European Security and Cooperation, 1 September 1980 www.ewtn.com/library/PAPALDOC/JP2FREED.htm [accessed 1 February 2013].
[14]Jan P. Schotte, C.I.C.M, 'Jesus Christ the Saviour and His Mission of Love and Service in Asia', Synod of Bishops, Special Assembly for Asia, 1996 www.vatican.va/roman_curia/synod/documents/rc_synod_doc_01081996_asia-lineam_En.html [accessed 1 February 2013].

A hymn by John Oxenham that many of my generation sang at
school assemblies proclaims:

In Christ there is no east nor west
In Him no south or north
But one great fellowship of love
Throughout the whole wide earth.

This hymn emphasizes the inclusiveness and universal scope of
the gospel and urges believers to 'join hands . . . whate'er your
race may be'. Whereas the ethnic community of Judaism called
upon Abraham as its father (Matt. 3.9; Lk. 3.8), the church is
universal in that it has but one body (1 Cor. 12.12) and is one
people (1 Pet. 2.9). So:

Who serves my Father as His child
Is surely kin to me.

Such doctrinal affirmations are pivotal in Christian thinking about
nations and nationhood, and demand profound indifference at deep
spiritual and existential, theological and philosophical levels to the
national context(s) into which one is born. Nothing matters more
than the orientation of all people and peoples to Christ; the church
views the world and all its societies in light of their common destiny
in Christ.

  This does not mean, however, that an adequate response to global
poverty, the pressing needs of asylum seekers and refugees today, and
more is merely to allude to the eschatological vision of 'a new heaven
and a new earth' (Rev. 21.1). Critical and constructive engagement
is needed with the claim that the answerability of the nations before
God implies something provisionally significant about territorial
borders. The eschatological nature of this hope is no reason to
downplay present-day questions about Christian attitudes to the
democratic nation-state system and whether it facilitates or hinders
love of neighbour near and far. Conscious of Barth's warning against
any supposition that humanity's existence in our various nations
equates to an 'order of creation', I suggest that the answerability of
the nations before God implies something provisionally significant

in Christian ethics about territorial borders.[15] Despite the complex and problematic ways in which borders function politically, what Bakhtin calls 'the unity of answerability' before God, other nations, individual asylum seekers or refugees and more provides a functional framework for responsible action.

Reasons for caution

Many reasons for caution present themselves when addressing theologically the ethico-political question of whether the very nature of the post-Westphalian democratic nation-state system makes it unfeasibly difficult to love one's neighbour. The first is the need to make clear that references to genealogies, peoples and nations throughout the bible cannot be transposed directly onto political discourse about the nation-state today. There is no deductive doctrinal or exegetical chain of links between Christianity and post-Westphalian systems of nation-state relations or late-modern, Western practices of democracy.

A related reason for caution concerns how biblical texts have already, or might yet, be used in this way especially texts which suggest that God set the boundaries of the peoples:

> You have set all the borders of the earth. (Ps. 74.17)

> These are the borders by which you shall divide the land as an inheritance among the twelve tribes of Israel. (Ezek. 47.13)

> He has made from one blood every nation of men to dwell on all the face of the earth, and has determined their preappointed times and the boundaries of their dwellings. (Acts 17.24–6)

> When the Most High apportioned the nations,
> when he divided humankind,
> he fixed the boundaries of the peoples
> according to the number of the gods;

---

[15]It is widely known that Barth retracted his early use of the concept of 'orders of creation', which had been put to tragic use by National Socialism; see Paul Nimmo, 'The Orders of Creation in the Theological Ethics of Karl Barth', *Scottish Journal of Theology* 60 (2007), p. 24.

the Lord's own portion was his people,
Jacob his allotted share. (Deut. 32.8–9)

The passage from Deuteronomy has attracted much attention from
biblical scholars because of textual variants pertaining to the phrase
'according to number of the gods'. A Masoretic text reflected in
some later versions of the Septuagint reads 'according to the sons of
Israel'. Some versions of the Septuagint read 'angels of God', which
reflects two Hebrew manuscripts from Qumran. The New Revised
Standard Version, cited above, reads 'according to the number of
the gods', alluding to the spirit world of Near Eastern cosmology
as reflected in the Old Testament (see also Dan. 10.13–20, 12.1;
Is. 24.21). Whether the verse should be rendered 'according to the
sons of the gods', 'sons of God' or 'sons of Israel', the point is the
same: God has catalogued and allocated to the nations the land that
they should occupy. While we may not sacralize arbitrary historical
occurrences with the sanction of divine intention, there is no
avoiding altogether the suggestion that the nations enjoy territorial
identity at least in part because of divine decision.

From these texts alone, it is easy to suggest that equivalence
may be traced between the boundaries alluded to in Deuteronomy
32.8 and the borders in, say, post-colonial Africa or the disputed
territories of the West Bank and Gaza Strip, Nagorno-Karabakh,
the seabed of Antarctica, the state of Jammu and Kashmir and so
on. Regina Schwartz reminds readers of how easily affirmations
of 'One nation under God' can slip into nationalism as religion.
'Monotheism', she writes, 'is a myth that forges identity
antithetically – against the other.'[16] When used as a manual for
politics, the Bible has authorized nationalism and sanctioned all
manner of violence and the 'cutting' and 'recutting' of identities.[17]
Foundational biblical accounts of the possession and rule of the
promised land and the imagining of the people(s) of God as chosen
determine ways of thinking about secular government that divide
peoples into 'us' versus 'them'. Israel's identity began with the
cutting of three animals and birds for sacrifice (Gen. 15.9–10).
The historian Laura Donaldson exposes how borders featured

---

[16]Regina Schwartz, *The Curse of Cain: The Violent Legacy of Monotheism* (Chicago:
University of Chicago Press, 1997), p. 16.
[17]Schwartz, *The Curse of Cain*, p. 9.

when the supposed superiority of Christianity fuelled European imperialism and was a powerful tool in convincing the colonizers that they were embarked upon activities consistent with God's will. One cannot underestimate the political influence of the Christian tradition in disseminating imperialist ideologies: 'While many countries occupied and dominated foreign territories, only the group of nations claiming Christian identity implemented a global colonial system upon which the sun never set.'[18]

Carl Schmitt further confronts readers with claims about the transfer of the meaning of sovereignty from theology to the modern nation-state: 'All significant concepts of the modern theory of the state are', he says, 'secularized theological concepts . . . not only because of their historical development – in which they were transferred from theology to the theory of the state, whereby for example the omnipotent God became the omnipotent lawgiver – but also because of their *systematic structure*.'[19] Notorious for his Nazi allegiances but with arguments that warrant attention nevertheless, Schmitt's implied claim was that modern attitudes to borders have become quasi-theological. The fetishization of borders and especially the power to exclude became a quasi-theological form of absolutism. Giorgio Agamben has recently employed Schmitt's axiom that the sovereign is the one who decides on the status of friend or foe, the state of exceptionality and so on to expose the innate tendency within some aspects of modern liberalism to engender unrestricted executive policing in the name of a continuous emergency. Like Schmitt, his warning is that something inherent in the secularization of theological notions of sovereignty justifies exercises of the power of exclusion such that people's legal status is erased. Border controls and the like produce 'legally unnameable and unclassifiable beings'.[20] The nation-state claims for itself the powers of a tyrannical god.

---

[18]Laura E. Donaldson, 'God, Gold and Gender', in Laura E. Donaldson and Pui-Lan Kwok, *Postcolonial Feminism and Religious Discourse* (Abingdon, OX: Routledge, 2001), p. 6.

[19]Carl Schmitt, *Political Theology: Four Chapters on the Concept of Sovereignty*, trans. George Schwab (Chicago: University of Chicago Press, 2005), p. 36 (emphasis in original). Published in the original German (rev. ed.) in 1934.

[20]Giorgio Agamben, *State of Exception*, trans. Kevin Attell (Chicago: University of Chicago Press, 2005), p. 3. While critical of Agamben's assumptions regarding the influence of Christian notions of kingship upon modern notions of sovereignty, I

The accuracy of Schmitt's account of Christian history might be challenged but, for present purposes, the nub of his challenge remains with respect to the power of exclusion. Consequently, we need a method of approach which reminds us that any account of political borders and national identities is likely to be constructed from the point of view of those who made it, and that biblical texts about nations and borders must be examined in terms of self-interest and power. Interpretation of contentious biblical passages is vulnerable always to ideological abuse; the risk of falling into aggressive nationalism or immoral partiality is always at hand. Analogous to feminist critical hermeneutics, the methods employed in our investigation must, at the least, be adequate to lay bare some of the most shameful aspects of Christian tradition and to trace how the Bible has been read as enslaver and liberator, for violence and healing, with respect to the nation-state.

Theoretical contexts

To this end, it is not necessary for Christian ethics and political theology to adopt one or more of the theories of the nation-state that inform present-day debates about partialism and impartialism. 'Augustine', says O'Donovan, 'managed altogether without what was later called a theory of sovereignty.'[21] Similarly, I do not think it necessary to 'buy into' any particular theory but attempt to outline major theories about the nation-state because this sets Singer's challenge in context and helps to explain the import of his questions now. There can be no theological supposition that Christian doctrine translates into political theory but a brief review of recent theoretical discussions helps to situate the new cosmopolitan challenge about whether globalization and the inequalities of the post-Westphalian system of nation-states demand of Christian people the dismantling of the traditional *ordo amoris* in favour of unconditional benevolence towards every creature individually.

---

find affinity between his association of human rights with 'bare life', rather than the status of citizenship, and a Christian theology of human rights rooted in a person's creaturely status before God.
[21] I recall Oliver O'Donovan making this observation at the Society for the Study of Theology conference, University of Durham, in 2008 but might be mistaken.

A definition of 'nation' has often proved elusive in much theory and international law. It is notoriously difficult to find a United Nations definition of these terms, but a UNESCO glossary of migration-related terms defines 'nation-state' as 'an area where the cultural boundaries match up with the political boundaries'.[22] Slippage also occurs between 'nation' as a group of people who share the same nationality, that is, the same culture, language and heritage, 'state' as the legal term for a country or geographical region, and 'nation-state' as the legal or political entity where the majority share a common sense of identity and culture. As the legal theorist Shirley V. Scott explains, it is possible to have a nation without a state. The political ideal since the French and American revolutions, however, has been the 'nation-state', that is, the idea that every nation should have its own state.[23]

Relatively few theorists these days treat 'the nation' or nation-state in terms of ethnicity, blood or land or emphasize the etymological roots of nation (L. *na-*, stem of *natio* 'birth') with its links to ethnicity. The trend in political science is away from the ethnic and cultural consciousness of national populations to the democratic political ideals or imaginings that tie people together. Even the strongest accounts of national identity couched in terms of collective responsibility within particular boundaries of distributive justice, notably David Miller's advocacy of a strong nation-state, tend to be built around the liberal ideals of the idea of equal citizenship, the social rights of citizenship and corresponding duties one to another.[24] Yael Tamir's theory of liberal nationalism

---

[22]UNESCO, 'Nation-State' www.unesco.org/new/en/social-and-human-sciences/themes/international-migration/glossary/nation-state/ [accessed 17 February 2013].
[23]Shirley V. Scott, *International Law in World Politics: An Introduction* (Boulder, CO: Rienner, 2004), p. 24.
[24]David Miller defends the state's delivery to its members of 'bundle of rights, opportunities, and resources to its own members, not to outsiders' (*National Responsibility and Global Justice* [Oxford: Oxford University Press, 2007], p. 17). Nationhood gives rise to legitimate attachments on which are founded duties of justice and humanitarian assistance exceeding those of family and friendship; the sense of nationhood is inherited across generations, and those sharing it can rightfully become the occupants of territory (Miller, 'Immigrants, Nations and Citizenship' in *The Journal of Political Philosophy* 16 [2008], pp. 371–90 (381)). Miller argues that cosmopolitanism requires a person to give moral priority to compatriots along with the expectation that all persons should do this – that is, he advocates cosmopolitanism via a moral defence of nationhood.

emphasizes the values of belonging, culture, shared history, loyalty and solidarity together with the liberal values of liberty and equality.[25]

There are, of course, many accounts of the rise of the modern nation-state. Benedict Anderson ties the nation-state to a European reaction to breakaway colonies in the Americas; Anthony D. Smith argues that nation-states are constructed on top of older ethnic identities; Elie Kedourie understands the nation-state as Enlightenment doctrine; Adrian Hastings finds the nation-state's origin in the medieval period; Anthony Giddens ties the nation-state to the gathering up of military power.[26] Ernest Gellner's thesis is that the modern European bureaucratic state is largely a function of the market economy. His *Nations and Nationalism* has been significant in demonstrating that modern societies are essentially economies serviced by the state.[27] Hence nationalism is portrayed by Charles Taylor as a 'call to difference' against the homogenization of economic forces.[28] I am sympathetic to Gellner's thesis that the rise of the modern nation-state is related inseparably to the rise of the modern market economy and note that present-day interest

---

[25]Wanting to define nationalism in positive terms rather than as stemming from irrational fear of the stranger or a desire for power at the expense of others, Yael Tamir renounces the term altogether in favour of the less pejorative 'people' or 'community' (*Liberal Nationalism* [Princeton, NJ: Princeton University Press, 1993], p. 5). Culture in its widest sense, she says, is what holds a nation together (p. 8). National rights rest on the values that individuals attach to their membership in a nation, and so all nations are entitled to equal respect. The liberal concept of distributive justice emerged historically from an amalgamation of liberal, democratic and national ideas.

[26]I am grateful to Robert Heimburger for this useful summary. See variously Benedict Anderson, *Imagined Communities: Reflections on the Origin and Spread of Nationalism*, rev. ed. (London: Verso, 2006), esp. ch. 3; Anthony D. Smith, *Nations and Nationalism in a Global Era* (Cambridge: Polity Press, 1995), p. viii and esp. ch. 3; Elie Kedourie, *Nationalism*, 4th edn (Oxford: Blackwell, 1993), p. xiii et passim; Adrian Hastings, *The Construction of Nationhood: Ethnicity, Religion and Nationalism* (Cambridge: Cambridge University Press, 1997), pp. 2–5; Anthony Giddens, *A Contemporary Critique of Historical Materialism*, vol. 2: *The Nation-State and Violence* (Cambridge: Polity Press, 1985).

[27]Ernest Gellner, *Nations and Nationalism*, 2nd edn (Oxford: Blackwell, 2006), ch. 5. I remain broadly convinced by Gellner's thesis but recognize the complexity of this history.

[28]Charles Taylor, 'Nationalism and Modernity', in Robert McKim and Jeff McMahan (eds), *The Morality of Nationalism* (Oxford: Oxford University Press, 1997), p. 51.

in trans-sovereignty is similarly fuelled by economic and related political factors.

The new cosmopolitan challenge takes different forms in diverse neo-Kantian and utilitarian theory.[29] Thomas Pogge is critical of the centrality of the nation in international affairs and the priority given to proximity as a basis for aiding less what is in fact rather more severe poverty.[30] Allen Buchanan offers a principled account of international legal order built around human rights with a view to bolstering international institutions for the protection of human rights in ways that will inevitably supersede national interest.[31] More important, for Buchanan, than proximity and popular consent as the basis of state legitimacy is the 'natural duty of justice' – a principle that rests on the even more foundational premises that all persons should be treated with equal concern and respect and that basic human rights should not be violated. All argue variously for the legitimacy of states and international law to be measured against international standards. Jürgen Habermas's reconstruction of Kant's theory of cosmopolitan right locates the authority of international law in

---

[29]Witness the plethora of recent books and articles, such as Maryann Cusimano Love, *Beyond Sovereignty: Issues for a Global Agenda*, 4th edn (Boston, MA: Wadsworth, 2010); Alexandros Yannis, 'The Concept of Suspended Sovereignty', *European Journal of International Law* 13 (2002), pp. 1037–52; Kok-Chor Tan, *Justice without Borders: Cosmopolitanism, Nationalism and Patriotism* (Cambridge: Cambridge University Press, 2004); Sibylle Scheipers, *Negotiating Sovereignty and Human Rights* (Manchester: Manchester University Press, 2010) and suchlike. The shift is away from sovereignty conceived as an attribute of military power or legal standing or the locus of decisive political power and towards a definition subject to a variety of trans-sovereign problems and responsibilities that cross borders and entail what cosmopolitans call 'transnational citizenship', which is understood predominantly in economic terms as money flows across borders but which is supported by neo-Kantian notions of universal right and cosmopolitan justice; see Osamu Ieda, (ed.), *Beyond Sovereignty: From Status Law to Transnational Citizenship?* (Sapporo: Slavic Research Center, Hokkaido University, 2006).
[30]Pogge investigates how national borders worsen poverty because citizens and governments tend to show more concern for their own compatriots than others, and he supplements economic arguments with a political proposal for the 'vertical dispersal of sovereignty' or reframing of national identities and democratic practices in ways that cut across Westphalian notions of state sovereignty (Thomas Pogge, *World Poverty and Human Rights*, 2nd edn [Cambridge: Polity Press, 2008], pp. 150, 188–201, 510).
[31]Allen Buchanan, *Justice, Legitimacy, and Self-Determination: Moral Foundations for International Law* (Oxford: Oxford University Press, 2004), p. vii.

the legitimating force of democratic process on the assumption that liberal capitalism, which combines constitutionalism with a strong market sector, is pacifistic. Not yearning for an inevitably illiberal world state, he seeks the visioning of cosmopolitan international law as the law of individuals protected both by international institutions and the internalization of strong protection of individual rights within the many and domestic legal systems of the nations.[32]

The import of this shift for Christian ethics and political theology may be illustrated by means of a comparison between Paul Ramsey's exploration of notions of sovereignty in the 1950s and 1960s and more recent accounts. Ramsey engaged with versions of modern or post-Westphalian doctrines of sovereignty.[33] He spoke of national sovereignty as that which locates the cause of justice 'among the rights and duties of states unless and until supplanted by superior government'.[34] In an essay on human rights in *Basic Christian Ethics*, he contrasted biblical notions of Israel's obligation to God and Grotius's success in putting sovereignty under the concept of natural right. Here, Ramsey declared, is the heart of the modern Hobbesian notion of contracted sovereignty whereby the people retain no rights of 'a governing kind'.[35] Similarly, in *The Just War*, he referred to the inherent attributes of national sovereignty supposed in the encyclical *Pacem in Terris* of 1963 and to the desirability of resolving disputes between nations by diplomacy rather than arms.[36] Albeit alert to the differences between these modern theorists, his discussion of sovereignty is framed by them. Ramsey supposed the familiar range of modern conceptions of sovereignty as attributes that embody force, dominance, legal superiority and so on and which weigh against intervention. Today, the issues are changing and the Christian ethicist must face squarely the cosmopolitan

---

[32] Jürgen Habermas, 'Does the Constitutionalization of International Law Still Have a Chance?' in Ciaran Cronin (ed.), *The Divided West* (Cambridge: Polity Press, 2006), p. 116.
[33] Paul Ramsey, *Basic Christian Ethics* (1950; rpt Louisville, KY: Westminster/John Knox Press, 1993), p. 384.
[34] Paul Ramsey, *The Just War: Force and Political Responsibility* (1968; rpt Lanham, MD: University Press of America, 1983), p. 20.
[35] Ramsey, *Basic Christian Ethics*, p. 383. A footnote expounds differences between Grotius, Rousseau and Hobbes regarding personal liberty in relation to sovereignty.
[36] Ramsey, *The Just War*, p. 192.

challenges concerning the moral failures of Westphalian systems of
international relations.

Nations and divine wrath

Theologically, I work broadly in what follows within the stream
of Western tradition that runs from Augustine to Karl Barth where
the existence of the nations is regarded as within a disposition of
divine blessing but only in conjunction with a work of divine wrath
(Gen. 11.1–9).[37] I draw in particular upon Barth's account of 'Near
and Distant' neighbours in which he assumes that the plurality of
nations, and the history of humanity as a world of nations, is not
part of salvation history until Genesis 10:

> the indisputable intention of Genesis 10 is to give an account of the
> development of the descendants of Noah into a manifold world
> of nations as divinely ordered for the humanity reconstituted by
> the deliverance of Noah. This takes place under the sign of the
> covenant established between God and Noah in Genesis 9.8f.[38]

The separation of humanity into peoples and nations is within
divine providence 'as undoubtedly a work of divine wrath, even
if with an undertone of grace'.[39] Obedience to the evangelical
command cannot be abstracted from the time, place and culture
in which it encounters us. Consequently a person cannot view
their native place, language and the historico-cultural context of
their homeland as only negative in character but must find in these
relations what God requires of them:

> Since God addresses him as the man who exists in these particular
> relationships to the men of his own and other races, they acquire

---

[37]Augustine, *The City of God against the Pagans*, trans. R. W. Dyson (Cambridge:
Cambridge University Press, 1998), bk XVI, ch. 10, p. 711; Barth, *CD*, III/4, p. 311.
[38]Barth, *CD*, III/4, p. 312. Gerhard von Rad advises readers to understand Genesis
10 as an ancient account of nations that were politically and historically distinct
from or related to one another, rather than a family table of humanity as descended
from Noah (*Genesis: A Commentary*, rev. ed. [Philadelphia: Westminster Press,
1972], p. 140).
[39]Barth, *CD*, III/4, p. 313.

for him the character of an allotted framework in which he has to express his own distinctive obedience.[40]

A person properly takes up and shares not only the problems of a nation's present but also 'the problems of its future'.[41] Nevertheless, deep ambivalence besets the history of humanity as a world of nations and any sense of national identity.

This ambivalence recalls Augustine's description of national identity as a 'sort of lot'. When Augustine posed the question of how we decide whom to aid, he was uncompromising in affirming that kinship and ethnicity matter less than our common humanity: 'all men are to be loved equally', he insisted.

> But since you cannot do good to all, you are to pay special regard to those who, by the accidents of time, or place, or circumstance, are brought into closer connection with you. For, suppose that you had a great deal of some commodity, and felt bound to give it away to somebody who had none, and that it could not be given to more than one person; if two persons presented themselves, neither of whom had either from need or relationship a greater claim upon you than the other, you could do nothing fairer than choose by lot to which you would give what could not be given to both. Just so among men: since you cannot consult for the good of them all, you must take the matter as decided for you by a sort of lot, according as each man happens for the time being to be more closely connected with you.[42]

In the fifth-century CE, Augustine knew that it was impossible to do good to all equally and drew the conclusion that it would be just as fair to give of one's limited resources to someone close by than far away; 'you must take the matter as decided for you by a sort of lot'. The Christian cannot despise prima facie any aspect of the network of relations into which one is either born or finds oneself as 'a sort of lot'. A person exists and is a self only in such networks of relation. This is different, however, from affirming that membership of a particular people or nation is subject directly to

---

[40]Barth, CD, III/4, p. 288.
[41]Barth, CD, III/4, p. 295.
[42]Augustine, Christian Doctrine, bk I, ch. 28.

the divine command, 'for when we speak of home, motherland and people, it is a matter of outlook'.[43]

Holding with Augustine and Barth to national identity as 'a sort of lot' helps to guard against fixity or ultimacy in attitudes to the nation. This need to resist any sacralization of territorial borders with the gloss of religion is underlined, I suggest, by Jesus' reconceptualization of Israel's national restoration. Of interest exegetically is what happens in Jesus' reworking of Israel's hope of national restoration. Recall Ezekiel's hope of restoration:

> Thus says the Lord God: These are the boundaries by which you shall divide the land for inheritance, among the twelve tribes of Israel. Joseph shall have two portions. You shall divide it equally; . . . this land shall fall to you as your inheritance. (Ezek. 47.13–14)

The vision of restoration after exile is not only spiritual but also territorial and political. Briefly, Ezekiel was appointed a sentinel or watchman for the people of Israel (Ezek. 3.16–19). He was to warn the people that they would face God's judgement if they returned to sin, and he received a vision of the future temple. Writing from Babylon, the prophet's description of the temple and its rebuilding was for the transformation of the people and their return to God's law.[44] Ezekiel prophesies about the temple and the land of Israel within which it is to be located. Today the borders of the land described by Ezekiel can, more or less, be mapped onto the state of Israel, some of Lebanon, the Golan Heights and arguably into Syria. Our question is how Jesus (re)conceives of Israel's hope of restoration and what happens in his teaching to Ezekiel's talk of borders.

Stephen Bryan suggests that Jesus reconfigures Israel's hope of national restoration: Jesus makes positive use of Israel's restoration traditions, he says, but rejects the anticipated geographical re-establishment of the 12 tribes by Elijah.[45] The continuity of

---

[43]Barth, *CD*, III/4, p. 293.

[44]John W. Schmitt and J. Carl Laney, *Messiah's Coming Temple: Ezekiel's Prophetic Vision of the Future Temple* (Grand Rapids, MI: Kregel, 1997), p. 80.

[45]Steven Bryan, *Jesus and Israel's Traditions of Judgement and Restoration* (Cambridge: Cambridge University Press, 2002), p. 75.

God's commitment to Israel remains firm, but there is a new act of election. Now 'sinners' too may enjoy the blessings of restoration. The eschatological feast is for 'all peoples' (Isa. 25.5). It was widely expected that God's eschatological act would be one of national forgiveness. In the gospels, however, Elijah's expected restoration of Israel is accomplished through the ministry of John the Baptist. Jesus' parables of the vineyard summon Israel to repentance and recall Isaiah 5.1: 'Let me sing a song for my beloved, my love-song concerning a vineyard . . . when I expected it to yield grapes, why did it yield wild grapes?' In other words, divine judgement changes the nature of Israel's restoration. God comes seeking fruit from Israel, and Israel is thus exposed to the impending judgement. From henceforth 'Israel's election must not be seen as the basis for an iron-clad guarantee of God's protection and favour.'[46] The end-time restoration of the 12 tribes is reinterpreted in terms of the calling of 12 disciples. Jesus' table fellowship with sinners is an enacted parable that encapsulates the meaning of the parable of the great banquet. His association with sinners speaks of an interpretation of the eschatological blessings of the kingdom different from those expected by some of his contemporaries. A non-material eschatological temple was to be built by Israel's messiah. Jesus rejects that strand of the tradition that anticipated a re-establishment of the 12 tribes within physical borders; the constitutional shape of the restored Israel is already realized in part.

This exegesis does not mean that Jesus was a supra-nationalist, one who idealized timeless or ahistorical communities, or a post-nationalist, whose project was to create a post-national world. The suggestion, rather, is that Israel's restoration is beyond borders, *yet* the nations will be judged. The challenge again is to live at the point of the impossible *nevertheless*. Some kind of borders belongs to divine providence because divine judgement presupposes some kind of delineation between peoples. Earthly government is integral to the 'all things' that will be subject to Christ (Matt. 25.31–35; 1 Cor. 15.24–28) and are already 'under his feet' (Eph. 1.22). Until he comes again this entails the designation of borders if the nations are to be judged. Yet there is no ultimacy to human borders, and the question is always how they function in the service of God and neighbour. Today, our birthplace is still a matter of 'a sort of

---

[46]Bryan, *Jesus and Israel's Traditions*, p. 235.

lot'. This does not mean Christian people can despise any aspect of the network of relations into which they are born.[47] The moral imperatives that arise within the nation-state we happen to inhabit are not impersonal 'oughts' that can be abstracted from the vagaries of life amidst which one finds oneself; the radical contingency of human existence includes membership of peoples, nations and/or nation-states and is integral to the dignity of human creatureliness.[48] The networks of relation into which a person is born, or that they acquire, are not morally insignificant.[49] Neither, however, are they morally exhaustive. The question is how best to love neighbours both near and far, and whether traditional Christian teaching about the *ordo amoris* still assists or hinders in this task.

Aquinas on the 'Order in Charity'

Aquinas's teaching about the 'order in love' is laid out most clearly in a question regarding the nature of order per se.[50] Aquinas teaches that all love tends towards God as to its origin or first cause. Order belongs to reason and to the appetitive powers therefore order belongs to love. With respect to the general principle of order he writes:

> I answer that, As the Philosopher says, the terms 'before' and 'after' are used in reference to some principle. Now order implies that certain things are, in some way, before or after. Hence wherever there is a principle, there must needs be also order of some kind. But . . . the love of charity tends to God as to the principle of happiness, on the fellowship of which the friendship of charity is based. Consequently there must needs be some order in things loved out of charity, which order is in reference to the first principle of that love, which is God.[51]

---

[47]For these reasons I would develop the argument, if space permitted, that Christian people should lend their support to the political obligation of 'a right to a nationality'.

[48]Barth, *CD*, III/4, p. 312.

[49]'[T]he concept of one's people is not a fixed but a fluid concept . . .' (Barth, *CD*, III/4, p. 291).

[50]Aquinas, *ST*, II–II, q. 26.

[51]Aquinas, *ST*, II–II, q. 26, a. 1, sed contra.

The ultimate reason for loving is God. The notion of 'order', which involves an understanding of what comes 'before' and 'after', is explained with reference to this ultimate end and to how God has ordered human life. In explication of the nature of this order, Aquinas asks in this question whether one should love all neighbours equally or what distinctions should apply. His clear and repeated answer is that an order of charity is included in the divine precept.[52] This order in love may be understood by use of the terms 'before' and 'after', with all love tending towards God as its final end.[53] God is the cause or first reason for love, for whom all things are loved according to their measure of goodness.[54] Hence everyone should love God more than themselves because God is the reason for self-love.[55]

Within the order of love determined by the cause and end of all love which is God, Aquinas asks the further question of whether a person ought to love herself more than her neighbour, and/or her neighbour more than her own body. The answer to the former is yes. A person ought to love herself more than her neighbour because 'the model exceeds the copy'.[56] As Jesus taught his disciples:

> You shall love the Lord your God with all your heart and with all your soul and with all your mind. This is the great and first commandment. And a second is like it: You shall love your neighbor as yourself. (Matt. 28.37–39; Lev. 19.18)

Love of self is a spiritual good pertaining to relation with God and thus a more potent reason for loving than any other consideration. Love takes both its quantity and quality from its object, which is God. Hence a person ought to attend before all things to their spiritual obligation to love God. For Aquinas, this primary attention to one's spiritual nature is expressed as love of self more than neighbour. Significantly, this prioritizing of love of self over neighbour does not result in neglect of neighbour. Aquinas

---

[52]See also Aquinas, *ST*, II–II, q. 88, a. 8, c.
[53]Aquinas, *ST*, II–II, q. 26, a. 1, sed contra.
[54]Aquinas, *ST*, II–II, q. 26, a. 2, ad.1.
[55]Aquinas, *ST*, II–II, q. 26, a. 3, sed contra.
[56]Aquinas, *ST*, II–II, q. 26, a. 4, c.

proceeds to ask whether a person ought to love her neighbour more than her own body and answers:

> Augustine says that 'we ought to love our neighbor more than our own body'.
>
> Out of charity we ought to love more that which has more fully the reason for being loved out of charity . . . Now fellowship in the full participation of happiness which is the reason for loving one's neighbor, is a greater reason for loving, than the participation of happiness by way of overflow, which is the reason for loving one's own body. Therefore, as regards the welfare of the soul we ought to love our neighbor more than our own body.[57]

Giving priority to love of one's own soul and spiritual well-being does not entail neglect of one's neighbour's bodily needs or, indeed, their spiritual health. Each partial good has its place in relation to other goods. Everyone is concerned most immediately with the care of their own body, but perfection in charity entails obligations to others too.[58] Aquinas does not go into detail about how this obligation might be worked out but reminds readers that the common good is more perfect than the good of the part:

> Every man is immediately concerned with the care of his own body, but not with his neighbor's welfare, except perhaps in cases of urgency: wherefore charity does not necessarily require a man to imperil his own body for his neighbor's welfare, except in a case where he is under obligation to do so and if a man of his own accord offer himself for that purpose, this belongs to the perfection of charity.[59]

Every person is to care for their own body while preferring the common good to their private good, and developing an outlook on life where the common good is always 'more loveable' to the individual than their private good.[60]

---

[57]Aquinas, *ST,* II–II, q. 26, a. 5, *c.*
[58]Aquinas, *ST,* II–II, q. 26, a. 5, ad. 3.
[59]Aquinas, ST, II–II, q. 26, a. 5, ad. 3.
[60]Aquinas, *ST,* II–II, q. 26, a. 4, ad. 3.

This brings us to Aquinas's teaching on whether we ought to love one neighbour more than another. The objections that he lists include Augustine's teaching that 'One ought to love all men equally' and the suggestion that there should be no inequality of love.[61] With surprising prescience regarding the questions put to Christian ethics today by the new cosmopolitans today, Aquinas asks directly whether Christians ought to love all neighbours equally because all are created by God, who is the reason for loving all equally. Aquinas appears to feel the force of these questions, but his answer is clear:

> One's obligation to love a person is proportionate to the gravity of the sin one commits in acting against that love. Now it is a more grievous sin to act against the love of certain neighbors, than against the love of others. Hence the commandment (Leviticus 10.9), 'He that curseth his father or mother, dying let him die', which does not apply to those who cursed others than the above. Therefore we ought to love some neighbors more than others.[62]

It is natural, says Aquinas, to have an unequal love for persons. One's encounter with some is more intense than with others. Relations with parents, for instance, are more meaningful than others farther away. Hence it is appropriate to love them more than persons unknown. Should this natural love for parents and others be interpreted to mean affections only but not 'the outward effect'?[63] In other words, should the *ordo amoris* apply only to the experience of love in the affections and not the practicalities of money management and daily affairs? Again, Aquinas's answer is that love should be proportionate to the situation in which one finds oneself. It might be more sinful to neglect the material love of parents than the material well-being of a neighbour far away:

> It is written (1 Timothy 5.8): 'If any man have not care of his own and especially of those of his house, he hath denied the faith, and is worse than an infidel'. Now the inward affection

---

[61]Aquinas, *ST*, II–II, q. 26, a. 6, obj. 1, 2, citing Augustine, *Christian Doctrine*, bk I ch. 28.
[62]Aquinas, *ST*, II–II, q. 26, a. 6, sed contra.
[63]Aquinas, *ST*, II–II, q. 26, a. 6, c.

of charity ought to correspond to the outward effect. Therefore charity regards those who are nearer to us before those who are better.[64]

Every act of love should be proportionate to the situation and correspond to the relations amidst which one finds oneself. It is appropriate to care for one's own parents and children especially, and other members of the household, with more attention than those farther away.

Aquinas does not let matters rest here, however. He does not simply affirm a natural duty to care most for parents, children and those closest to one. Proportionality is a flexible concept that gives different answers in different contexts, but this flexibility is not infinite. Aquinas's answer is not simply to love one's own more than others but to love proportionately to both the object and agent of that love. Given that the object of all human love is God, the diversity with which one loves one's own household as distinct from the neighbour far away depends on one's relation to God. The love of every agent for their neighbour has its place within love of God. It is appropriate out of charity to love more those who are more nearly connected with us, since we love them in more ways. In this respect, natural ties to some flows from divine wisdom. Living in proximity with some provides more opportunities for love than is available to those far away. Critically, however, the love of each has its place within the order of perfection. It is not enough for the believer simply to love those closest to them without regard for distant neighbours. The challenge is always to refer the local, particular love to the good of the whole.

Nation as family?

It is important to clarify that Aquinas does not extend the partiality owed to those connected to us by ties of blood and close proximity to the entirety of one's fellow nationals. This is significant in the debate about partialism and impartialism because it could be argued that Aquinas treats one's fellow nationals in the same terms as family members, that is, with reference to ties of blood.

---

[64]Aquinas, *ST*, II–II, q. 26, a. 7, sed contra.

It would be deeply problematic for reasons noted above if this were so. My reading, however, is that, while Aquinas accepts the realities of human existence as entailing proximity to some and not others – reflecting Aristotle's treatment of partiality, which suggests that it would be appropriate to show partiality towards one's fellow citizens because 'love' of this kind cannot be shown to all people at once[65] – he does not treat the nation as, in effect, an extended family.

Consider the following passage in which Aquinas notes that some people are necessarily nearer to us than others in terms of kinship, affection and *other factors such as being co-nationals*:

> Moreover there is yet another reason for which, out of charity, we love more those who are more nearly connected with us, since we love them in more ways. For, towards those who are not connected with us we have no other friendship than charity, whereas for those who are connected with us, we have certain other friendships, according to the way in which they are connected. Now since the good on which every other friendship of the virtuous is based, is directed, as to its end, to the good on which charity is based, it follows that charity commands each act of another friendship, even as the art which is about the end commands the art which is about the means. Consequently this very act of loving someone because he is akin or connected with us (L. *vel quia coniunctus*), or because he is a fellow-countryman (L. *et vel concivis*) or for any like reason that is referable to the end of charity, can be commanded by charity, so that, out of charity both eliciting and commanding, we love in more ways those who are more nearly connected with us.[66]

A concern is that Aquinas's account of the gradation of primary relations should not be read to justify partiality to co-nationals through an extension of love to family and kin. At issue is how being a co-national or fellow-countryman is conceived vis-à-vis kinship.

---

[65]'One cannot be a friend to many people in the sense of having friendship of the perfect type with them, just as one cannot be in love with many people at once (for love is a sort of excess of feeling, and it is the nature of such only to be felt toward one person)' (Aristotle, *Nichomachean Ethics*, VIII, 6).

[66]Aquinas, *ST*, II–II, q. 26, a. 7, c.

In the passage cited above, particular mention is made of fellow-citizens within a city-state (*concivis*), commonly translated as fellow-citizen or fellow-countryman. Interpretation of the relation of co-nationality in relation to kinship turns on the meaning of the word 'or' (*vel*) in the sentence: 'Consequently this very act of loving someone because he is akin or connected with us (L. *vel quia coniunctus*), or because he is a fellow-countryman . . .'. Used typically to co-ordinate two or more elements in a sentence between which there is an alternative but not necessarily a negation, *vel* could be translated readily as having an inclusive rather than exclusive meaning. According to this reading, one's fellow-citizens would be included in the sequence of love that begins with one's kin and those otherwise 'connected with us' and that extends to one's citizens. In other contexts, the word *vel* could be used to distinguish two words denoting the same thing.[67] At issue for our purposes is the degree of conjunction and/or disjunction between kinship or related affinity and wider relations of co-citizenship, and the risk that Aquinas could be read to the effect that co-citizenship is to be conceived consecutively and within the same order of love as kinship relations. I opt for an interpretation that emphasizes the disjunction between kinship and co-nationality, thereby resisting an understanding of co-nationality as a type of kinship affinity. It is not utterly clear from the text that that reading is required. For Christian ethics and political theology today, however, the choice between co-nationality as based on kinship-type affinity or on proximity is clear.

Proximity and constitutional patriotism

Jeremy Waldron has written powerfully on this choice between co-nationality as a kinship-type of affinity or based on proximity. I adopt his urging of proximity rather than affinity or kinship as the basis of political community while refusing to jettison the connection between proximity and cosmopolitanism but, rather, seeking to keep open the question of what responsibility entails

---

[67]For a good summary of the difficulties associated with translating *vel* and *aut*, see Ray Jennings, 'Disjunction', *Stanford Encyclopedia of Philosophy* http://plato. stanford.edu/entries/disjunction/ [accessed 30 October 2011].

for relations between human beings in our division into nations.[68]
For Waldron, political community based on proximity rather
than affinity accords better with central Christian convictions
regarding love of one's enemy and the possibility of forgiveness.
His account of proximity as the basis for political community
emphasizes (Kantian) duties owed to people in our vicinity.
Drawing upon Kant's conviction that nation-states should be
formed among those who live 'unavoidably side by side', he
underscores that the point of political community is not to affirm
solidarity and quasi-kinship affinity but to prevent the outbreak
of murderous conflict.[69] Drawing also upon Jürgen Habermas's
ideal of constitutional patriotism and cosmopolitanism as the best
available option for a proximity model of political community
mediated only through the rule of law, Waldron claims that the
principle of proximity is not anti-cosmopolitan but dialectic in
its understanding of what it is to be a global citizen through
membership of a particular political community. Christians
and neo-Kantians can (and should) focus on ways of living in
political community with people of different ethnicities, cultures,
religions and so on, dealing with potential conflicts near at hand
rather than avoiding them through distance, differentiation and
hostility.[70]

---

[68]Waldron notes that Hobbes and Kant argue differently for political community
based on affinity or kinship-type love. Both recognize the need for peaceable existence
alongside those to whom one is in close proximity and therefore most likely to fight.
Jeremy Waldron, 'Proximity as the Basis of Political Community', paper presented
at the workshop 'Theories of Territory', King's College, London, 21 February 2009,
p. 5 http://eis.bris.ac.uk/~plcdib/territory/papers/Waldron-Proximity.pdf [accessed 9
September 2011]

[69]Waldron, 'Proximity', p. 5.

[70]I am sympathetic also to Rawls's argument in *The Law of Peoples* that while well-
ordered peoples have a duty to assist burdened societies, it does not follow that
the only way, or the best way, to carry out this duty of assistance is by following a
principle of global distributive justice to regulate economic and social inequalities
among societies. For Rawls, the responsibilities of the international community are
to help a people establish basic institutions for a free, constitutional (democratic)
society, the aim being to establish just institutions rather than raise levels of wealth.
He places much emphasis on the political culture of a nation and supposes that
few societies exist where resources are so scarce that they cannot be organized and
governed such that no one starves. See John Rawls, *The Law of Peoples* (Cambridge,
MA: Harvard University Press, 1999), §16.

Answerability within and beyond territorial borders: Matthew 25.31–35

Having thus defended the broadly traditional claim that there is properly an order in love and argued that it is possible to work with an account of territorial borders, nation and nationhood, as permitted within divine providence, without falling into aggressive nationalism or immoral partiality – albeit with an understanding of 'nation' based on proximity rather than affinity – we once again face the new cosmopolitan challenge. Analogous to the broad acceptance in Christian ethics and political theology of private property, my realist stance assumes that borders are natural to post-fall human beings, considered as a species, since they are meant to serve our bodily needs.[71] Territorial borders do not stem directly from the pre-fall purposes of God. Like private property, the institution of borders may be considered as an 'addition to the natural law . . . to serve the well-being of the human community'.[72] Analogous to private property, territorial borders may be a legitimate addition to the natural law but not significant enough to warrant detailed attention of itself. Borders and national identity may be deemed a relative, not absolute, right permitted within divine providence for the sake of humanity's need, potentially a way of ensuring a peaceable world and of managing the goods of the earth. Borders are not recognized theologically for their own sake but for the social benefits they can bring and are to be judged accordingly, mindful that 'the land shall not be sold in perpetuity, for the land is mine; you are but aliens and tenants' (Lev. 25.23). The problem is that territorial borders serve in deeply problematic ways to justify injustice.[73]

---

[71]Aquinas, *ST*, II–II, q. 66, a. 1; Jean Porter, 'The Virtue of Justice (IIa–IIae, qq. 58–122)', in Stephen J. Pope (ed.), *The Ethics of Aquinas* (Washington, DC: GUO, 2002), pp. 279–84 (280).

[72]Aquinas, *ST*, II–II, q. 66, a. 2. Porter's observation regarding the institution of private property is that it was 'devised by human reason'; a positive rather than natural right that presupposed the existence of social conventions (Aquinas, *ST*, II–II, q. 66, a.1, ad. 1). For Aquinas, private property was important but did not necessarily merit its own discussion. Rather, private property was discussed in the context of an examination of the claims of justice between individuals with respect to material goods.

[73]John Williams, 'The Borders of a Just War', working papers series, School of Government and International Affairs, Durham University (June 2007), p. 9. At: www.dur.ac.uk/resources/sgia/SGIARWP07–03.pdf (accessed 22 February 2013).

How borders function

Christians have long been concerned about refugee rights and immigration, the needs of asylum seekers, aggressive nationalism, xenophobia and more.[74] Yet the majority of reflections in this area tend to be doctrinally selective and limited; we talk freely about personhood in the image of God and the biblical imperative to hospitality but not so freely about the ethics of peoples, nations or territorial borders. The Good Samaritan is cited as calling forth from us personalized responses of generous love to fellow human beings (Lk. 10.25–37). Lot's pleading with the people of Sodom is recounted as encouragement not to abuse the strangers in our midst (Lev. 19.33–34). We talk far less about the answerability of nations before God and of living as a people or nation with corporate responsibility for social affairs. Psychologists of social reasoning inform us that individuals tend to be aroused empathetically by perceived distress that is close at hand.[75] Efficacy in campaigns about the plight of refugees and asylum seekers seek to arouse fellow-feeling motivated by awareness of another's distress. But more is required. Detailed attention is needed to how territorial borders function to exclude and repress, motivate violence, engender apathy to global poverty and more, as well as providing structures of answerability for secular authority, government, power, office and civil polity.

My plea is not for a world without borders but for more attention to how borders function to facilitate social justice and peacemaking, or their opposites. The morally ambiguous reality borders is evident, for instance, in the asymmetry of answerability with respect to issues of climate change. Powerful nations are answerable for their decisions in ways that smaller nations are not similarly answerable. The energy policies of China or the United States, as determined by federal government, have implications for more people around the world than the energy policies of smaller

---

[74]For example M. Daniel Carroll R., *Christians at the Border: Immigration, the Church, and the Bible* (Grand Rapids, MI: Baker Academic, 2008); David Hollenbach, S. J., (ed.), *Refugee Rights: Ethics, Advocacy, and Africa* (Washington, DC: Georgetown University Press, 2008); Nicholas Sagovsky, 'Faith in Asylum: A Theological Critique of the UK's Asylum Policy', Gore Lecture, London, March 2005.

[75]See Martin L. Hoffman, *Empathy and Moral Development: Implications for Caring and Justice* (Cambridge: Cambridge University Press, 2000), p. 4.

developed nations because of the sheer mass of their emissions. 'The road from Rio to Kyoto to Bali to Copenhagen to Cancun is littered with procrastination, obfuscation, and empty promises. For example, all major countries including the United States agreed to the United Nations Framework Convention on Climate Change, which took effect in 1994, and so committed themselves to "protect the climate system for present and future generations". However, global emissions are now up more than 40 percent since 1990, and more than 17 percent in the United States.'[76] The poorest people and the poorest nations are already being hit hardest by climate change.[77] The 2009 Human Impact Report from the Global Humanitarian Forum, Geneva, chaired by Kofi Annan, was clear: 'Least responsible for greenhouse gas emissions are the world's poorest communities who suffer most from climate change.'[78] Answerability extends asymmetrically into the future; present generations are responsible to future generations in non-reciprocal ways.

In the concluding sections of this chapter, I present a case study concerned with immigration and asylum. It represents a reinforcement of familiar and problematic Westphalian notions of territoriality and the power of the sovereign to exclude. The case is *Regina* v. *Immigration Officer at Prague Airport* and the House of Lords ruling that UK obligations under the 1951 Refugee Convention and customary international law were not engaged because the appellants were not outside their country of origin. The case concerned the lawfulness of the pre-entry clearance operations of British immigration officers at Prague airport. In February 2001, the governments of the United Kingdom and Czech Republic agreed to permit British immigration officers to grant or refuse passengers leave to enter the United Kingdom before they boarded planes destined for the United Kingdom. All six appellants in this case who appeared eventually before the House of Lords were

---

[76]Stephen Gardiner, 'The Ethical Dimension of Tackling Climate Change', *Yale Environment 360*, 20 October 2011 http://e360.yale.edu/feature/the_Ethical_dimension_of_tackling_climate_change/2456/ [accessed 22 February 2013].

[77]'Climate Change and Poverty', World Wildlife Fund www.wwf.org.uk/what_we_do/making_the_links/climate_change_and_poverty/ [accessed 22 February 2013].

[78]'Climate Change: The Anatomy of a Silent Crisis', Global Humanitarian Forum, May 2009, p. iii www.ghf-ge.org/human-impact-report.pdf [accessed 22 February 2013].

Czech nationals of Romani ethnic origin, who were refused entry by British immigration officers at the airport. The Court of Appeal framed the question in terms of whether customary international law precluded UK authorities from thwarting asylum applicants from travelling to the United Kingdom without first examining the merits of their asylum case. British immigration procedures were also challenged for unlawfully discriminating against the Roma on racial grounds.

The case illustrates a cluster of issues around the meaning of borders and the urgent need for engagement by Christian people, including the reality that borders shift and are increasingly ubiquitous. The appellants encountered the UK border in their own country. As Alison Kesby recounts for us, Lord Bingham of Cornhill delivered the leading judgement on the asylum issue: 'In summary, he held that the United Kingdom's obligations under the Refugee Convention and customary international law were not engaged as the individual appellants were not outside their country of origin.'[79] No issue of *refoulement* arose under Article 33 of the 1951 UN Convention relating to Refugees. His guiding premise was the sovereign's power to admit, exclude and expel aliens, that is, to control who crosses the border as threshold. 'The court argued that good faith could not be used to expand the United Kingdom's obligations under the Convention and impose an obligation in relation to those expressly excluded from the protection of the Convention, that is, in relation to those who were not outside the state of their nationality.'[80] The Lords judged on the discrimination issue that the Race Relations Act 1976 had been breached.[81] With respect to the asylum issue, the border was deemed to exist at the place where a sovereign power exercises its power of control over people.

This case illustrates the heterogeneity of borders, that is, that borders are increasingly economic, social and cultural, and not merely geographical. Baroness Hale delivered the leading judgement

---

[79]Alison Kesby, 'The Shifting and Multiple Border and International Law', *Oxford Journal of Legal Studies* 27 (2007), pp. 101–19 (104).
[80]Kesby, 'The Shifting and Multiple Border', p. 105.
[81]Thomas Bingham (Lord Bingham of Cornhill), *Opinion of the Lords of Appeal for Judgment in Regina v. Immigration Officer at Prague Airport* [2004] UKHL 55, §10.

of the Lords on the racial discrimination issue. Evidence clearly indicated, she said, that Roma were subjected to more intensive interrogation than non-Roma.[82] Commenting on the concept of the border in this judgement, Kesby observes not only fetishism with respect to lines and their role in separating 'pure identities' but also a 'multiplication' of borders to include not only geopolitical boundaries but procedures that have a socially discriminatory function. 'To draw a border is to establish an identity; and to establish an identity is to draw a border. . . . The status of borders determines the condition of the stranger/foreigner and the very meaning of "being foreign". The focus in international law on the territorial border should not be allowed to render invisible other borders . . . and thereby fail to address the manner in which borders affect lives and determine outcomes.'[83]

Despite the changing meaning of borders to include socio-economic criteria and their location beyond the geographical limits of a nation, some aspects of the meaning of borders remain constant. I refer in particular to the right of nation-states to close borders to immigrants and certain types of refugees. The lead judgement in *Regina v. Immigration Officer at Prague Airport* made clear that external sovereignty, the discharge of the proper responsibility of government as it bears upon relations with all who are not its own people and for matters of global governance, includes the sovereign's power to 'admit, exclude and expel aliens', to control those who cross the threshold of the border.[84] As the judgement intimates, the 1951 Refugee Convention does not provide automatic or permanent protection. The actions of the immigration officers to 'pre-clear' all passengers before they boarded flights were interpreted by Lord Bingham to constitute a border for the purposes of exclusion but not for the purposes of asylum application. The multiplication of national borders and heterogeneous manner in which individuals encounter them means that we cannot suppose the political meaning of border to be stable or fixed – at least in the European context in which I live. Beneath

---

[82]Kesby, 'The Shifting and Multiple Border', p. 107. Bingham, UKHL 55, §11.
[83]Kesby, 'The Shifting and Multiple Border', p. 109, citing Etienne Balibar, *We, the People of Europe? Reflections on Transnational Citizenship*, trans. James Swenson (Princeton, NJ: Princeton University Press, 2004), p. 114.
[84]Bingham, UKHL 55, § 11.

the notion of a clear geographical demarcation lies a multifaceted conception that is variously economic, cultural, metaphorical and ideological. Borders are not, as Balibar intimates, simple edges but more like political barriers that protect rights and prevent interference from others.[85] They still function, however, to exclude and deprive. At the least, we are faced with the morally ambiguous reality of territorial borders.

Particular loves and Catholic benevolence

Singer's new cosmopolitan vision of a world without borders is attractive in the face of such truths, yet I do not believe it to be sufficiently realistic. In arguing, however, that the fundamental structure of the *ordo amoris* should be retained from Christian tradition when addressing the question, Who is my neighbour? and that this structure extends to a proximity-based account of the nation, it is necessary to face the harsh truth that territorial borders often do not bring social benefits either for the residents or non-residents of a given nation. This recognition cannot be placed solely, however, at the feet of politicians. An ethic of answerability is necessarily complex in liberal Western democracies where the 'who?' aspect of the question about answerability is far from simple. As Mikhail Bakhtin knew, the 'who?' question of answerability is deceptively simple. 'The act [of answerability] is like a "two-faced Janus", in which the subject of the action, the "I", is axiological, unique, and unrepeatable in life (being) but its action takes place in a predictable and objective culture.'[86] In modern liberal democracies, minimalist views of what counts as democracy, namely, periodic multiparty elections, are monumentally insensitive to questions of answerability. Answerability entails a complex tension between the representative role of the nations and the personal responsibility of their members. Politicians face electorates hungry for news that the overseas aid budget is modest and immigration figures are down, and more.

---

[85]Balibar, *We, the People*, p. 109.
[86]Greg M. Nielsen, *The Norms of Answerability: Social Theory between Bakhtin and Habermas* (Albany: State University of New York Press, 2002), p. 20, quoting M. M. Bakhtin, *Toward a Philosophy of the Act*, ed. Vadim Liapunov and Michael Holquist (Austin: University of Texas Press, 1993), p. 2.

Taking into consideration Singer's new cosmopolitanism, this chapter has been about how to get loves ordered rightly given humanity's division into nations, and why this ordering is unlikely to be achieved by reducing the experience of love to a calculus based on every individual global citizen. I have begun to argue for the continuing moral relevance of traditional Christian teaching with respect to the *ordo amoris* – albeit with the qualification that the nation-state is not to be understood an extension of the relations of family and kin but a political community based on proximity. The underlying claim is that Christianity is incompatible with preference utilitarian*ism* (as a 'total' ethic) because of its view that God ultimately judges the relative morality or immorality of an act; no relation between self and other is unmediated in Christian ethics, since judgement rests ultimately with God. Yet Singer's provocations remain sharp. As Augustine and Aquinas remind us, love is a political virtue; justice is about ordering loves rightly, and the unity of love of neighbours far and near is found in God. For fear of repeating this too lightly, however, I join with Singer in affirming: 'ye may know them by their fruit'.

7

Human Rights and Ideological Conflict: Threats to the Rule of Law

The drafters of the United Nations Universal Declaration of Human Rights (UNDHR) were silent on matters of cultural difference and faith. More recently, theorists such as Michael Ignatieff have urged those working with human rights to maintain this deliberate silence with respect to substantive beliefs. 'Thin' (describing only the rights themselves) rather than 'thick' (contextualizing rights in the religious, cultural, economic and other complexes of a given society) theories of human rights are preferred because this tends to keep human rights instruments out of political debates about the relation of rights to traditional, religious and authoritarian sources of power.[1] The obvious fear is that, like the proverbial runaway train, there 'ain't no stopping' it once it's started. Once questions are asked about why human rights have moral force, where they are grounded, how they are justified and to what end, rather than how these simple affirmations of human dignity are to be implemented in societies around the world, we are likely to unearth fundamental ethical disagreement with no prospect of consensus about how to act. If no unified philosophical or religious foundation is granted, then

---

[1]Michael Ignatieff, *Human Rights as Politics and Idolatry* (Princeton, NJ: Princeton University Press, 2001), p. 76.

the moral force of appeals to human rights is undermined. As Michael Freeman has said:

> The UN conception of human rights, as expressed in the Universal Declaration, gives rise to a dilemma. If this conception of human rights has a philosophical justification, this will almost certainly be controversial, since all philosophical theories of rights are controversial. However, if the concept of human rights has no philosophical justification, then its claim to have moral force is unfounded.[2]

The astonishing achievement of the human rights movement, as expressed in the Universal Declaration of Human Rights, is that its moral force is contested relatively rarely. One question that arises is whether this achievement is due in part to avoidance of difficult 'why?' questions about the reasons for respect for and protection of these seemingly self-evident truths.

The aim of this chapter is to investigate where and why theorists – from the Abrahamic faiths especially – are challenging Ignatieff's minimalism with respect to the 'why?' of human rights, but also where claims to the supposed neutrality of claims to the universality of human rights are emerging as overblown, ideological notions that hinder rather than help the protection of human rights, with respect to religious freedom especially. Gramsci's theory of hegemony is employed in attempting to distinguish between the role that human rights standards perform beneficially in encouraging the implementation of internationally agreed standards and as a dominant global ideology, given content by Western liberal philosophy and backed by the massive superstructures of the major world powers.

Why attempt to open these questions to debate? Three reasons present themselves:

1   First, if one grants with the Moslem scholar Abdullahi An-Na'im that no normative system is culturally neutral, all normative systems are the product somehow of contextual specificities, then the question becomes whether and/or how

---

[2]Michael Freeman, *Human Rights: An Interdisciplinary Approach* (Cambridge: Polity Press, 2002), pp. 41–42.

to justify human rights across philosophical divides.[3] The language of human rights is not neutral. A Bart cartoon depicts a medieval torture chamber reminiscent of the Inquisition instituted by the Catholic church in the twelfth century to combat heresy. A man lies stretched out on a rack. The caption spoken by the interrogator reads: 'I won't advise it, but you do have the right to remain silent'.[4] The black humour works because of cultural dissonance between the horrors of a medieval torture chamber and the modern language of rights. An-Na'im's point is similar: myth-busting with respect to cultural neutrality extends beyond hamburgers, running shoes and tea-drinking to the very structures of global jurisprudence and law enforcement.

2 Second, refusal to address controversies surrounding the justification of human rights stops moral argument in its tracks. O'Rourke captures this when he asks why we are all equal: 'We hold this truth to be self-evident, which on the face of it is so wildly untrue. . . . are we all equal because we all showed up? . . . Are we all equal because it says so in the American Declaration of Independence and the UN Universal Declaration of Human Rights? Each of these documents contains plenty of half-truths and non-truths as well.'[5] Merely to appeal to a piece of paper, or even to the fact that lots of people have agreed to the words on it, is not ultimately a reason for believing these words to be true. In 'Enlightenment's wake' (to borrow John Gray's phrase) the options are sometimes cast as either disenchantment at attempts by modern philosophers to ground human rights in universal human reason or acceptance that deep cultural diversity is an ineradicable feature of present-day

---

[3]Abdullahi Ahmed An-Na'im, 'Human Rights, Religion, and the Contingency of Universalist Projects', paper presented at the Program for the Advancement of Research on Conflict, Maxwell School of Citizenship and Public Affairs, Syracuse University, September 2000, esp. p. 3.
[4]BART cat. ref. bro0049 www.cartoonstock.com/cartoonview.asp?start=6&search=main&catref=bro0049&MA_Artist=&MA_Category=&ANDkeyword=human+rights&ORkeyword=&TITLEkeyword=&NEGATIVEkeyword [accessed 12 February 2013].
[5]P. J. O'Rourke, Adam Smith's 'On the Wealth of Nations': An Enquiry (New York: Atlantic Monthly Press, 2007), p. 40.

existence – which means that we shall never agree about
the universality of human rights. The tension between these
two positions has historically been about not conceiving of
human rights in terms of the values prevalent in Western
Europe and North America. Today, the tension between
the cosmopolitan norms of human rights and the need for
legal rights that are universal and unconditional is yet more
complex. A fundamental challenge for our times, writes
Robert Post, is the construction of 'a jurisprudential theory
able to reconcile the universality of human rights with the
partiality of positive law'.[6]

3   The major world faiths, Judaism, Christianity and Islam
especially, have relatively under-exploited internal resources
from which to engage debates together about the meaning
of universality. Academic journals and religious newspapers
in the West are bursting with debates about the universal
justification of human rights, or lack of justification, and
whether the human rights corpus as a whole purports to be
non-ideological but derives from Western liberalism.[7] Far
less common are multi-faith conversations about how to
negotiate difference and find common ground.

[6]Robert Post, introduction to Seyla Benhabib, Jeremy Waldron et al., *Another Cosmopolitanism*, ed. Robert Post (Oxford: Oxford University Press, 2006), p. 3.
[7]Academic journals are filled with articles on the tension between the universality of human rights and cultural diversity. See, for example, Christina M. Cerna, 'Universality of Human Rights and Cultural Diversity: Implementation of Human Rights in Different Socio-Cultural Contexts', *Human Rights Quarterly* 16 (1994), pp. 740–52; Sumner B. Twiss, 'Moral Grounds and Plural Cultures: Interpreting Human Rights in the International Community', *The Journal of Religious Ethics* 26 (1998), pp. 271–82; David A. B. Murray, 'Who's Right? Human Rights, Sexual Rights and Social Change in Barbados', *Culture, Health & Sexuality* 8 (2006), pp. 267–81; Jack Donnelly, 'The Relative Universality of Human Rights', *Human Rights Quarterly* 29 (2007), pp. 281–306; David R. Penna and Patricia J. Campbell, 'Human Rights and Culture: Beyond Universality and Relativism', *Third World Quarterly* 19 (March 1998), pp. 7–27; Makau W. Matua, 'The Ideology of Human Rights', *Virginia Journal of International Law* 36 (1996), pp. 589–658; Julia Ching, 'Human Rights: A Valid Chinese Concept?' paper presented at the panel Religious Consultation on Population, Reproductive Health and Ethics, UN World Summit for Social Development, Copenhagen, 11–12 March 1995 www.religiousconsultation.org/ching.htm [accessed 10 February 2012].

Universality in international law

A legal backdrop against which to have these conversations is given by the meaning of 'universality' in international law. For present purposes, I adopt Bruno Simma's account of universality for the practitioner of international law. He proposes three conceptual levels of universality.

At a first, basic level, and corresponding to what he regards as the 'classic' understanding of the universality of international law, Simma describes a working assumption that there exists on the global scale an international law which is valid for and binding on all states.[8]

At a second level, 'wider' and more immediately practical-level understanding, universality responds to the question whether international law can be perceived as constituting an organized whole. Is international law, asks Simma, a coherent legal system, or does it remain no more than 'bric-a-brac', a random collection of norms, or webs of norms, with little interconnection?[9] This question, says Simma, is 'probably best viewed in terms of the "unity" or "coherence" of international law'. It concerns the predictability and legal security of decision-making.

At a third level, universality may be taken as referring to an 'actual or perceived' (changing) nature of the international legal system in line with the tradition of international legal thinking known as 'universalism'. This approach to international law expresses the conviction that it is possible, desirable, indeed urgently necessary (and for many, a process already under way), to establish a public order on a global scale, a common legal order for humankind as a whole: 'International law, according to this understanding, is not merely a tool-box of rules and principles destined to govern interstate coordination and cooperation; rather it constitutes a

---

[8]'Universality thus understood as global validity and applicability excludes the possibility neither of regional (customary) international law nor of treaty regimes which create particular legal sub-systems, nor does it rule out the dense web of bilateral legal ties between states . . . But all of these particular rules remain "embedded", as it were, in a fundamental universal body, or core, of international law. In this sense, international law is all-inclusive' (Bruno Simma, 'Universality of International Law from the Perspective of a Practitioner', *European Journal of International Law* 20 [2009], p. 267).
[9]Simma, 'Universality of International Law', p. 267.

'comprehensive blueprint for social life.'[10] The emphasis at this third level is on international law as expanding beyond the interstate sphere, particularly by endowing individuals with international personality, establishing a hierarchy of norms, including a value-oriented approach, de-emphasizing consent in law-making, introducing international criminal law, building up institutions and procedures for the enforcement of collective interests at the international level, with a view to the emergence of an international community, perceived as a legal community.

We are concerned in this chapter primarily with the third level, that is, with changes afoot to international law such that it no longer consists of only those rules to which states have agreed in treaties, general principles and norms deemed to be *jus cogens* but which extend also to the rights and duties of individuals. The context for our discussion of universality is one in which not only states and intergovernmental organizations are 'subjects' of international law but individuals are too, under humanitarian law and under rules of human rights. Cases tried by the International Criminal Tribunal for the Former Yugoslavia and the International Criminal Tribunal for Rwanda illustrate the point. While the jurisdiction of these tribunals was limited, they tried individuals accused of committing crimes in violation of international humanitarian law under the UN Charter, Chapter 7, Article 48. The Yugoslavia tribunal indicted 80 individuals including the former president of Yugoslavia, Slobodan Milosovic, and the former president of the Republika Srpska, Radovan Karadzic. The meaning of universality in international law has been changing for some time.

Enriching human rights?

Alongside this trend whereby individuals as well as states are the subjects of international law has been a more contentious trend that the leadership of the Organization of the Islamic Conference (OIC) has called 'enriching human rights'. The discussion may be deemed for our purposes to have started with the seminar held jointly under the auspices of the Office of the then High Commissioner on Human Rights, Mary Robinson, and the Organization of the Islamic Conference in November 1998,

---

[10]Simma, 'Universality of International Law', p. 268.

on the fiftieth anniversary of the UN Declaration of Human Rights. Entitled 'Enriching the Universality of Human Rights: Islamic Perspectives on the Universal Declaration of Human Rights', the seminar was representative of the intention of the Islamic Conference to take more initiative in the articulation and formation of norms of conduct in international affairs, with papers presented by 20 Islamic experts from the 56 OIC countries, including participants from Iran, Saudi Arabia and Sudan.[11] A much larger body of observers from various states, UN bodies and non-governmental organizations observed the proceedings.

Mary Robinson opened the seminar with reference to how the half-century anniversary of the UNDHR had encouraged people all over the world to reflect on the meaning of the Declaration for them and on the contribution that their own civilization and traditions could bring to a better understanding and a fuller realization of the rights proclaimed in it. 'The search for unity in cultural diversity', she said, 'is a particular responsibility of the United Nations.'[12] She further commented in personal reflections that she had learned much of the fundamental principles of Islam relating to the dignity of the human person, the search for justice and the protection of the weak as well as to solidarity and respect for other cultures and beliefs: 'The principles of Islam relating to human dignity and social solidarity are a rich resource from which to face the human rights challenges of today.'[13]

Robinson has been vilified for her efforts and dubbed 'a signal booster and key apologist for sharia (Islamic law)'. Right-wing journalist Diana West quotes from Robinson's statement to a symposium hosted by the Organization of the Islamic Conference in 2002:

No one can deny that at its core Islam is entirely consonant with the principles of fundamental human rights, including human dignity, tolerance, solidarity and quality. Numerous passages

---

[11]Mary Robinson, opening address, 'Enriching the Universality of Human Rights: Islamic Perspectives on the Universal Declaration of Human Rights', Geneva, 9 November 1998 www.arabworldbooks.com/HC_speech.html [accessed 12 February13].
[12]Robinson address, 9 November 1998.
[13]Mary Robinson, *A Voice for Human Rights*, ed. Kevin Boyle (Philadelphia: University of Pennsylvania Press, 2006), p. 75.

from the Qur'an and sayings of the Prophet Muhammad will testify to this. No one can deny, from a historic perspective, the revolutionary force that is Islam, which bestowed rights upon women and children long before similar recognition was afforded in other civilisations. Custom and tradition have tended to limit these rights, but as more Islamic States ratify the Convention for the Elimination of Discrimination against Women, ways forward for women are being found and women are leading the debate. And no one can deny the acceptance of the universality of human rights by Islamic States.

Having cited Robinson in this manner, however, West makes a stylistic volte-face by moving to compare Islamic viewpoints and Robinson's defence of a plurality of worldviews with respect to human rights with Nazism: 'I'm sorry, but in a different context, Goebbels couldn't have put it over it better.'[14] Less extreme commentators have criticized Robinson for bordering in some of her comments on the legitimizing of repression by Islamic states.[15] Witness Paul Marshall and Nina Shea's measured but nevertheless critical stance vis-à-vis Robinson's support for the notion of human rights in Islamic perspective, where Islam is understood in terms of *shari'ah* (Qur'an and Hadith) and not in terms of traditions or practices that may vary and mix with historical heritages.[16] Marshall and Shea's assessment of the 1998 seminar was that it provided a platform for government-approved 'experts' to promote *shari'ah* while shutting out UN-registered non-governmental organizations. They condemn the same comments by Mary Robinson cited above as ignoring the reality that sponsors of the seminar actually wanted to oppose, that is, a separate, culturally specific rights regime in which universal human rights are denied.[17]

---

[14]Diana West, 'Mary Robinson: Obama's Medal of Sharia Winner', 4 August 2009 www.dianawest.net/Home/tabid/36/EntryId/973/Mary-Robinson-Obamas-Medal-of-Sharia-Winner.aspx [accessed 12 February 2013].
[15]Paul Marshall and Nina Shea, *Silenced: How Apostasy and Blasphemy Codes are Choking Freedom Worldwide* (New York: Oxford University Press, 2011), p. 209.
[16]This clarification is recorded by the historian and human rights activist David Littman in 'Universal Human Rights and "Human Rights in Islam"', *Midstream* (February–March 1999), pp. 2–7 www.dhimmi.org/Islam.html [accessed 12 February 2013].
[17]Marshall and Shea, *Silenced*, p. 209.

Against this backdrop, the issue for our purposes is whether and/ or how to welcome plural foundations for human rights, how to engage critically with examples of human rights documents – such as the Universal Islamic Declaration of Human Rights (UIDHR) and the Cairo Declaration, and how to avoid both wide-eyed naivety and liberal bigotry with respect to these issues. The claim is made that the universality of human rights is better understood not as an a priori philosophical construct but a project to be undertaken in the twenty-first century. Global discourse about human rights is characterized appropriately by diverse perspectives on the promotion, application and evolution of human rights; this is an inevitable feature of the formulation of common demands as claims to human dignity arising from a sense of shared human identity across different cultures and experiences. This claim is time- and context-specific in that these questions are only necessary and available for investigation now because the promise at the heart of the UNDHR has met with widespread acceptance around the world. It is possible to have this conversation only because the human rights movement has achieved so much since 1948. Nevertheless, sustainability for human rights in the twenty-first century is not likely to be achieved without 'thick' rooting in diverse cultural and religious context. That this will open the door to contention and disagreement is unavoidable. Given, however, that asserting human rights across philosophical and religious divides is also problematic because no normative system is culturally and/or religiously neutral, theorists of human rights must pay their proverbial money and take their choice.

Human rights in Christian perspective(s)

Christian ethics and political theology is familiar with doctrine-informed approaches to human rights. Pope John XXIII wrote in the encyclical *Pacem in Terris* that '[e]very basic human right draws its authoritative force from the natural law, which confers it and attaches to it its respective duty'.[18] To the extent that the

---

[18]John XXIII, *Pacem in Terris*, 11 April 1963, §30 www.vatican.va/holy_father/john_xxiii/encyclicals/documents/hf_j-xxiii_enc_11041963_pacem_En.html [accessed 13 February 2013].

jus gentium or the Law of Nations and the UNDHR are founded upon the objective moral order as given by God and discerned by right reason, they arise indestructibly from the natural law. 'Thus, for example, the right to live involves the duty to preserve one's life; the right to a decent standard of living, the duty to live in a becoming fashion; the right to be free to seek out the truth, the duty to devote oneself to an ever deeper and wider search for it.'[19] The natural law may be understood to mean humankind's participation in the eternal law, through reason and will; its first precept is that good is to be done and pursued, and evil is to be avoided.[20] Natural law reflects the divine reason and/or will of God that conserves the natural order and is a way of expressing God's relationship with creation; a function of reason, 'promulgated by the very fact that God instilled it into man's mind so as to be known by him naturally'.[21] *Pacem in Terris* – which serves for our purpose as representative of Roman Catholic teaching in this respect – makes no direct equation of natural law with human rights. Rather, human rights discourse is integrated into Roman Catholic social teaching to the extent that it facilitates the kind of order and relations between persons that are consistent with what we know of God's purposes for all creation.

In 1975 the World Council of Churches affirmed: 'All human beings are created in the image of God, equal, and infinitely precious in God's sight and ours. Jesus Christ has bound us to one another by his life, death and resurrection, so that what concerns one concerns us all.'[22] The Orthodox scholar Vigen Guroian, who rejects much modern rights theory, accepts 'that the deepest inspiration of the doctrine of human rights has roots in Christian convictions. God is person, and so are human beings, who are created in God's image and likeness. Every human *hypostasis* has needs and makes legitimate claims to certain advantages necessary

---

[19]John XXIII, *Pacem in Terris*, §29. For definitions of the natural law in Roman Catholic tradition, see *Catechism of the Catholic Church*, pt III, §I, ch. 3, art. 1.1 www.vatican.va/archive/ENG0015/__P6U.HTM [accessed 13 February 2013].
[20]Aquinas, *ST*, I–II, q. 94, a. 1–2.
[21]Aquinas, *ST*, I–II, q. 90, a. 4.
[22]World Council of Churches, 5th Assembly, Nairobi, 23 November–10 December 1975, quoted in 'Together on the Way: A Statement on Human Rights', 8th Assembly, Harare, 3–14 December 1998 www.wcc-coe.org/wcc/assembly/hr-e.html [accessed 20 February 2013].

for human flourishing.'[23] Roger Ruston's book *Human Rights and the Image of God* traces historically how Christian confession of creation *imago Dei* morphed into a defence of human rights. I have written elsewhere about how, for the disciple of Christ, He is the mediator through whom, and in whom, they meet their neighbour: 'There is no way from us to others than the path through Christ, his word, and our following him. Immediacy is a delusion.'[24] It is for Christ's sake, and the sake of his coming kingdom, that the rights of every person are to be recognized and respected; for his sake Christians affirm the human body has a claim to food and shelter. The human body has a claim to joy because God created and wills it for joy.[25]

There is no single, monochrome Christian engagement with human rights. Modern rights-talk, with its notion of *inalienable* rights, says Stanley Hauerwas, is tied inextricably to the belief that individuals can do whatever they want to do with their own property including their own bodies: 'The body is then a piece of property

---

[23]Vigen Guroian, *Rallying the Really Human Things: The Moral Imagination in Politics, Literature, and Everyday Life* (Wilmington, DE: ISI Books, 2005), p. 214. *Hypostasis* is the Greek word adopted by the Council of Nicaea (325 CE) to designate personal existence.

[24]Dietrich Bonhoeffer, *Discipleship*, ed. Martin Kuske and Ilse Tödt (German ed.); Geoffrey B. Kelly and John D. Godsey (English ed.), trans. Barbara Green and Reinhard Krauss, vol. 4 of *Dietrich Bonhoeffer Works* (Minneapolis, MI: Fortress Press, 2003), p. 95.

[25]*Ecce Homo!* 'Behold the man!' (Jn 19:5) was Dietrich Bonhoeffer's starting point for his discussion of natural rights. The claim to joy, or to food and shelter, is not grounded in mutual obligation but in God's will and purpose. *In Christ* believers know that natural life has been formed and given by God, and is to be preserved and protected for God's sake; bodily life contains within itself the right to its own preservation because God has willed the continuation of life. See Esther D. Reed, *The Ethics of Human Rights: Contested Doctrinal and Moral Issues* (Waco, TX: Baylor University Press, 2007), p. 71. See also Dietrich Bonhoeffer, *Ethics*, ed. Ilse Tödt, Heinz Eduard Tödt et al. (German ed.); Clifford J. Green (English ed.), trans. Reinhard Krauss, Charles C. West and Douglas W. Stott, vol. 6 of *Dietrich Bonhoeffer Works* (Minneapolis, MN: Fortress Press, 2005), p. 82. This is also noted by Michael L. Westmoreland-White in 'Contributions to Human Rights in Dietrich Bonhoeffer's Ethics', *Journal of Church and State* 39 (1997), pp. 67–83 (69). The claim to joy, or to food and shelter, is not grounded in mutual obligation but in God's will and purpose. *In Christ* believers know that natural life has been formed and given by God and is to be preserved and protected for God's sake; bodily life contains within itself the right to its own preservation because God has willed the continuation of life.

in a capitalist sense.'[26] Joan Lockwood O'Donovan is similarly
alert to the extent to which modern talk about rights, including the
language and conceptuality of human rights, is tied up with modern
notions of self-ownership, property rights, market exchange and
the unrestrained liberty of the individual whereby liberty is an end
in itself.[27] In particular, she identifies a major change in fourteenth-
century Europe from older Christian traditions of political right
in which justice (*justitia*) was synonymous with objective right
(*jus*) to the association of justice with an individual's claim-right

---

[26]Stanley Hauerwas, 'Abortion, Theologically Understood', lecture presented at the
invitation of the Evangelical Fellowship, North Carolina Methodist Conference,
Durham, 14 June 1990 http://lifewatch.org/abortion.html [accessed 16 April 2012].
[27]Joan O'Donovan, 'Rights, Law and Political Community: A Theological and
Historical Perspective', *Transformation* 20 (January 2003), pp. 30–32 www.ocms.
ac.uk/transformation/free_articles/2001.030_odonovan.pdf [accessed 13 February
2013]. The point for present purposes, however, is simply that it would be impossible for many Christians, myself included, to refrain from the seeking and testing
of international human rights against the tests of faith, and it would moreover be
hypocritical to deny this freedom to others because the conclusions they reach might
not be to my liking. In defending the Franciscans' poverty as Christ-like against
the Pope, William of Ockham gave birth to a notion of subjective natural right
that broke with previous notions of right as an objective reality, for example, that
which is right according to the divine ordering of the universe. The process began
innocently enough when controversy arose over whether the friars' use of food, that
is, the eating of it, amounted to property rights (as claimed by John XXII) or simple
factual use or natural right (as claimed by Ockham). O'Donovan claims, however,
that, in the hands of seventeenth-century philosophers, Ockham's theological model
of natural right became the basis for another major shift to the effect that the first
natural right is that of self-preservation. Hobbes, for instance, wrote in 1647 of the
first foundation of natural right as 'that *each man protect his life and limbs as much
as he can*' (emphasis in original) (Thomas Hobbes, *On the Citizen*, ed. Richard Tuck
and Michael Silverthorne [Cambridge: Cambridge University Press, 1998], p. 27).
The theoretical construct of the 'state of nature' became his starting point for natural law teaching. 'Right' is defined as 'the liberty that each man has of using his
natural faculties in accordance with right reason,' from which it follows that, in the
first instance, he has the right to use any means and to do any action by which he
can preserve himself. Locke builds his ideas of political society on the basis of the
'Rights and Privileges of the Law of Nature . . . not only to preserve his Property,
that is, his Life and Estate, against the Injuries and Attempts of other Men; but to
judge of, and punish the breaches of that Law in others' (John Locke, *Two Treatises
of Government* [Cambridge: Cambridge University Press, 1988], p. 324. His arguments are theological to the extent that the argument in the *Second Treatise* starts
from God's creation of Adam, the dominion that God gave Adam over the world at
the time, and the analogous state of perfect freedom to order their actions that all
persons have as a matter of natural right.

to something. O'Donovan draws attention to the increasing assimilation of notions of subjective right to private property and to how the modern discussion, with its notion of *inalienable* rights, is tied inextricably to the belief that individuals can do whatever they want with their own property, including their bodies.

Wherever we stand in these debates, the point for present purposes is that it would be unacceptable for many Christians to be required to refrain from the seeking and testing of international human rights against the tests of faith, and hypocritical to deny this freedom to others because the conclusions they might reach would not be to our liking.

Islamic views on the meaning of 'Universality'

As in Christianity, there is no single Islamic engagement with human rights. Our focus in this chapter will be a selection of widely known theologically rooted Islamic declarations of human rights, notably the Universal Islamic Declaration of Human Rights (1981), the Cairo Declaration on Human Rights in Islam (1990) and the contributions to the seminar 'Enriching the Universality of Human Rights' (1998). All continue to attract considerable controversy among secularist Western audiences and those whom Paola Bernardini terms Enlightened Islamic scholars.[28] While

---

[28]I accept Paola Bernardini's broad categorization of so-called Enlightened Islamic scholars, who urge a distinction between the public law of the state and Islam as a personal matter of faith. Bernardini cites Hasan al-Bannā (1906–79), Abu al-'Ala al-Mawdudī (1903–79) and Ruhollah Musavi Khomeini (1900–89) as examples of traditionalist Islam; the second caliph of Islam and some of the Malikite school as examples of orthodox liberal Islam; and Abdullahi An-Na'im as an example of Enlightened Islam. We might add Tariq Ramadan as an example of present-day orthodox liberal Islam. His efforts to convey to non-Islamic audiences Qur'anic themes of justice, respect and more in ways that are reconcilable with the views of citizens of modern liberal democracies are widely known. Publications such as the *Muslim World Journal of Human Rights* also serve as a forum in which human rights issues are related not only to Islam and Islamic law but equally to those human rights issues found in Muslim societies that stem from various other sources, such as socio-economic and political factors, as well from the interaction and intersections of the two areas. Of relevance also are those whom Bernardini dubs traditionalist Islamic

there is broad consensus in the Islamic world that the UNDHR is an important human achievement, traditionalist Islamic voices are increasingly explicit in their criticism of the doctrine of secularization in the West that stretches broadly from John Locke's *A Letter Concerning Toleration* (1689), through Kant to the present-day French doctrine of *laïceté* and support in the United States for the constitutionally protected separation of church and state,[29] and thence to the modern (non-Islamic) notions of the right to freedom from government interference with respect to religious belief and freedom of expression. Traditionalist Islamic scholar Sheikh Mohammed Ali Al-Taskhiri puts the matter as follows:

This concept [of secularism] saw light on Western grounds and was the result of conflicts between champions of liberalism and Church radicalism. These conflicts culminated in the almost total isolation of the Church from social life, and the ensuing separation between the spheres of religion and public life.

But the nature of Islam, its teachings on life, its definition of governance style and its rational applications are at odds with this idea and we see no possibility of agreement on this point.[30]

---

scholars, who believe that *shari'a* is the only authoritative source of positive law; orthodox liberal Islamic scholars, who do not exclude *shari'a* from the public forum but distinguish between its general principles and some instances of specific norms (e.g. delimiting the application of penalties for theft in certain circumstances).

[29]The First Amendment to the US Constitution reads: 'Congress shall make no law respecting an establishment of religion, or prohibiting the free exercise thereof; or abridging the freedom of speech, or of the press; or the right of the people peaceably to assemble, and to petition the government for a redress of grievances.'

[30]Abdulaziz Othman Altwaijri, 'Entrenching the Concept of the Alliance of Civilizations', *Islam Today* 26 (2009), pp. 15–27 www.isesco.org.ma/templates/isesco/Islamtoday/en/26/26.pdf [accessed 3 March 2013]. I draw deliberately on scholars choosing to publish work with ISESCO, established by the Organization of the Islamic Conference in May 1979. According to the ISESCO website, its objectives include strengthening and promoting and consolidating cooperation among OIC member states in the fields of education, science, culture and communication, developing applied sciences and use of advanced technology within the framework of Islamic values and ideals, consolidating understanding among Muslim peoples, and contributing to the achievement of world peace and security, particularly through education, science, culture and communication www.isesco.org.ma/ [accessed 20 February 2013].

Al-Taskhiri criticizes the secular 'West' that relegates not only ethics but also religion to the realm of inner freedom, and views Christianity and Islam as fundamentally at odds with respect to the relation of faith to public life because, in effect, Christians in the West have accepted Kant's notion of 'Right' and conceived of the right to religious freedom in ways that render Christianity private and interior, with the concomitant separation of church and state. In a manner curiously similar to that of some Christian theologians who are also critical of the neo-Kantian heritage, Al-Taskhiri observes the church's retreat from public life to the point where freedom of religion is, in effect, meaningless. He describes the church's foolish complicity with modern ideas of right, universality and secularity that appear superficially to protect religious freedom but, in reality, render powerless any words that the church might speak because they reflect merely inner convictions and matters of private concern.[31]

There is a growing sense in some traditionalist Islamic quarters that human rights discourse globally requires more careful attention to cultural diversities – with a view to empowering various cultures and religions to participate in the further enrichment and development of human rights law. Hence, for instance, the succession of conferences on human rights planned by the Organization of the Islamic Conference.[32] The December 1980 Colloquium arranged

---

[31]A similar point was made by Stanley Hauerwas as long ago as 1993 when he challenged the foundationalism of modern philosophical claims for knowledge – that is, the idea that critical philosophy can give reliable access to transcendental truth – and traced connections between this kind of philosophy and affirmations of the law's autonomy from community and tradition. Like Al-Taskhiri, Hauerwas contended that modern liberal notions of the law – human rights law especially – presuppose an account of rationality that is invidiously individualistic and linked to modes of political life that run counter to Christian living, not least with respect to the restriction of religion to the private lives of individuals: 'America', he wrote, 'is the first society that has had the disadvantage of being founded as a philosophical mistake – namely, the notion of inalienable rights. Rights are the trumps we believe protect our freedom to have no story except the one I have chosen. That project undermines significant practices on which the law has drawn to give it moral direction – that is, to make the practice of the law a service to those who embody the practices without which the law is unintelligible' ('Christian Practice and the Practice of Law in a World without Foundations', *Mercer Law Review* 44 [1993], p. 748).

[32]For a history of these colloquiums, see Jacques Waardenburg, *Islam: Historical, Social and Political Perspectives* (Berlin: de Gruyter, 2002), esp. pp. 167–75.

by Kuwait appointed the Islamic Conference to prepare a text on human rights and Islam. According to Jacques Waardenburg, the document was intended for discussion at the Mecca-Ta'if summit meeting in January 1981, but lack of time prevented its presentation. In the meantime, the Islamic Council of Europe had been working on a similar initiative. In September 1981, an International Conference on Human Rights and Islam was held in Paris, where the Universal Islamic Declaration of Human Rights (UIDHR) was proclaimed on the same day.[33] As Waardenburg notes, the declaration was formulated by a private body and did not commit or even involve the governments of Muslim countries.[34] Of interest for our purposes are similarities and differences between the UNDHR and the UIDHR with respect to the concept of universality as well as liberal non-religious reactions to the latter.

In the UIDHR, the concept of universality when applied to rights derives from the universality of Islam for all humanity. As the Foreword to the document states:

> O men! Behold, We have created you all out of a male and a female, and have made you into nations and tribes, so that you might come to know one another. Verily, the noblest of you in the sight of God is the one who is most deeply conscious of Him. Behold, God is all-knowing, all aware. (The Qur'an, Al-Hujurat 49.13)

That there will be no further Prophet is considered to be support for this claim to universality. Human rights in Islam are rooted firmly in the belief that God, and God alone is the Law Giver and Source of all human rights. 'Due to their Divine origin, no ruler, government, assembly or authority can curtail or violate in any way the human rights conferred by God, nor can they be surrendered.'[35] The Universal Islamic Declaration of Human Rights is based on the Qur'an and the Sunnah. The universality of human rights in Islam is to be realized within an Islamic order. The authors of the declaration

---

[33]Waardenburg, *Islam*, p. 171.
[34]Universal Islamic Declaration of Human Rights (UIDHR), 19 September 1981 www1.umn.edu/humanrts/instree/islamic_declaration_HR.html [accessed 20 February 2013].
[35]UIDHR, Foreword.

affirm that the Vicegerency (Khilafah) has been created on earth to fulfil the Will of God; it is to establish the conditions wherein all human beings shall be equal, none shall enjoy a privilege or suffer a disadvantage or discrimination by reason of race, colour, sex, origin or language; wherein all human beings are born free; wherein slavery and forced labour are abhorred; wherein the rulers and the ruled alike are subject to and equal before the Law; wherein all worldly power shall be considered as a sacred trust, to be exercised within the limits prescribed by the Law and in a manner approved by it, and with due regard for the priorities fixed by it; wherein all economic resources shall be treated as Divine blessings bestowed upon mankind, to be enjoyed by all in accordance with the rules and the values set out in the Qur'an and the Sunnah; wherein everyone shall undertake obligations proportionate to his capacity and shall be held responsible pro rata for his deeds; and more.

The notion of right constitutes a focal point of legislation in Islamic *shari'ah,* wherein the universality of rights is co-extensive with the universality of the Islamic message: 'And no reward dost thou ask of them for this: it is no less than a message for all creatures' (Yussuf, v. 104); 'We sent thee not, but as a Mercy for all creatures' (Al-Anbia, v. 107); 'Blessed is He who sent down the criterion to His servant, that it may be an admonition to all creatures' (Al-Furqan, v. 1).[36] As the Muslim scholar Mohamed Amara says, the universality of rights in this doctrinal perspective permeates the teachings, culture and values of Islam. This does not imply the monopoly of Islamic civilization over the whole world, to the exclusion of others: 'It means interaction and competition with the other in the full respect of civilizational plurality, cultural diversity and the colour, race, custom and creed as well as racial linguistic, cultural, philosophical and civilizational peculiarities of peoples, nations and tribes. . . . These diversity peculiarities are a law of nature, of the creation and of the divine providence which can never be altered.'[37] Islam recognizes that humanity comprises diverse cultures, peoples, languages and tribes. 'If Allah had so willed, He would have made you a single people, but (His plan

---

[36]Mohamed Amara, 'Between Islamic Universality and Western Globalization', *Islam Today* 26 (2009), pp. 73–88 www.isesco.org.ma/templates/isesco/Islamtoday/en/26/26.pdf [accessed 3 March 2013].
[37]Amara, 'Between Islamic Universality and Western Globalization'.

is) to test you in what He hath given you: so strive as in a race in all virtues. The goal of you all is to Allah; it is He that will show you the truth of the matters in which ye dispute' (Al-Maida, v. 48). In other words, the notion of universality is derived from Islamic belief. Doctrinal convictions permit appeals to humanity's innate nature as a guide to specific rights, but only as interpreted within an account of the truths of Islam.

This Islamic concept of universality includes an awareness of diversity, plurality and difference among all humanity, and is open to interaction with other faiths. According to Al-Taskhiri, there might be shared ground with the Universal Declaration of Human Rights with respect to the concept and types of limitations that should govern human rights and make them reasonable, but there is a difference in the source of these rights. There are, he says, substantial difference between the West and Islam in determining these rights, but this does not mean that a great deal of common ground cannot be reached when comparing the United Nations with the Islamic declaration. For many of these scholars, a faith-based approach to human rights demands critical engagement with the effects of global capitalism on human well-being because the ideology of rights is deemed to be intimately related to the modern evolution of capitalism:

> [G]lobalization exposes the cultures of peoples in various parts of the world to the threat of invasion and crises. The entire world is being steered towards a unified culture, a culture guided by the principles of materialism and secularity and where there is no room for concepts such as faith, hope, morality, inspiration and piety. In such culture, the measure of all things is productivity, materialism and competitive growth in the universal slave market built around demand/offer criteria.[38]

For Mariam Ait Ahmed Ouaali, this requires critical focus on three major facets of the dominating culture of globalization: consumerism, materialism and secularity. He sees evidence of the current moral weakness of the West in the prevalance of pornography,

---

[38]Mariam Ait Ahmed Ouaali, 'Globalization and the Future of Inter-Faith Dialogue', *Islam Today* 26 (2009), pp. 117–26 www.isesco.org.ma/templates/isesco/Islamtoday/en/26/26.pdf [accessed 3 March 2013].

abortion, homosexuality and a weakening of attachments to faith. Similarly, an editorial in *Islam Today* – a journal sponsored by Islamic Education, Scientific and Cultural Organization (ISESCO), set up by members of the Organization of the Islamic Conference – suggests that Islam is more accepting of diversity than many Western empires, whether the Romans who massacred Christians, or present-day Western nations holding hegemonic notions of 'self' and the 'other'.[39] Islamic acceptance of diversity is contrasted with religious, nationalistic and then colonialist wars to spread Western worldviews; today's so-called globalization is seen as the West's attempt to spread the unbridled dysfunctionality of capitalism that yields unprecedented levels of social injustice. In practice, globalization is said to deny to many the human rights that it promises. These scholars call for interrelationship between the religions, so that believer may talk to believer in full respect of each other's religion and in sensitivity to their creeds, and a strong critique of the secularism that produces a rights discourse focused on individual autonomy.

Freedom of religion

Regarding freedom of religion especially, Article X of the UIDHR on Rights of Minorities cites the Qur'anic principle: 'There is no compulsion in religion' and says that, 'in a Muslim country, religious minorities shall have the choice to be governed in respect of their civil and personal matters by Islamic Law or by their own laws. Article XII on Right to Freedom of Belief, Thought and Speech states:

No one shall hold in contempt or ridicule the religious beliefs of others or incite public hostility against them; respect for the religious feelings of others is obligatory on all Muslims.

Article XIII on Right to Freedom of Religion states: 'Every person has the right to freedom of conscience and worship in accordance

---

[39]'Culture in the Battlefield of International Relations', *Islam Today* 27 (2011), pp. 11–14 www.isesco.org.ma/templates/isesco/Islamtoday/en/27/27.pdf [accessed 3 March 2013].

with his religious beliefs.' Article XIV, entitled 'Right to Free Association', states:

> Every person is entitled to participate individually and collectively in the religious, social, cultural and political life of his community and to establish institutions and agencies meant to enjoin what is right (*ma'roof*) and to prevent what is wrong (Ar. *munkar*).

Abdullah Saeed and Hassan Saeed note that the Arabic and English versions of the declaration differ on significant points and comment that a number of the articles on freedom of religion are 'rather vague and over qualified'.[40] An explanatory note states that 'the term "Law" denotes the *Shari'ah*, that is, the totality of ordinances derived from the Qur'an and the Sunnah and any other laws that are deduced from these two sources by methods considered valid in Islamic jurisprudence.' Significantly, the explanatory notes further specify:

> In the exercise and enjoyment of the rights referred to above every person shall be subject only to such limitations as are enjoined by the Law for the purpose of securing the due recognition of, and respect for, the rights and the freedom of others and of meeting the just requirements of morality, public order and the general welfare of the Community (*Ummah*).

The phrases used in the UIDHR and the rights identified are all subject to the limits prescribed by the *shari'ah* and are to be respected provided that, in so doing, one remains within the limits of the *shari'ah*.

The Cairo Declaration on Human Rights in Islam, adopted in 1990 by the Organization of the Islamic Conference, states at the outset:

> Believing that fundamental rights and universal freedoms in Islam are an integral part of the Islamic religion and that no one as a matter of principle has the right to suspend them in whole or in part or violate or ignore them in as much as they are binding

---

[40]Abdullah Saeed and Hassan Saeed, *Freedom of Religion, Apostasy and Islam* (Aldershot, Hants: Ashgate, 2004), p. 17.

divine commandments, which are contained in the Revealed Books of God and were sent through the last of His Prophets to complete the preceding divine messages thereby making their observance an act of worship and their neglect or violation all abominable sin, and accordingly every person is individually responsible – and the Ummah collectively responsible – for their safeguard.[41]

This document reaffirms the civilizing and historical role of the Islamic Ummah and describes its purpose as contributing 'to the efforts of mankind to assert human rights, to protect man from exploitation and persecution, and to affirm his freedom and right to a dignified life in accordance with the Islamic Shari'ah'. Article 24 is clear that '[a]ll the rights and freedoms stipulated in this Declaration are subject to the Islamic Shari'ah'. Article 25 states: 'The Islamic Shari'ah is the only source of reference for the explanation or clarification of any of the articles of this Declaration.' In other words, the Islamic approach to human rights that is propounded here emphasizes that all aspects of human existence are to be considered under the divine prescriptions of Islam. In this respect they are universal in character because the anthropology proposed is theological. Regarding religion, Article X states:

Islam is the religion of unspoiled nature. It is prohibited to exercise any form of compulsion on man or to exploit his poverty or ignorance in order to convert him to another religion or to atheism.

Freedom of religion is interpreted yet more explicitly than the UIDHR in subordination to the precepts of Islam. Significantly, the Cairo Declaration has no article which corresponds to Article 18 of the UN Declaration of Human Rights: 'Everyone has the right to freedom of thought, conscience and religion; this right includes freedom to change his religion or belief, and freedom, either alone or in community with others and in public or private, to manifest his religion or belief in teaching, practice, worship and observance.'

---

[41]Cairo Declaration on Human Rights in Islam, 19th Islamic Conference of Foreign Ministers, 31 July–5 August 1990 www.oic-oci.org/english/article/human.htm [accessed 24 February 2013].

The Cairo Declaration makes no reference to the freedom of conscience.

Others have considered the possible implications of such a plural, religiously rooted approach to human rights more widely than is possible here. Ann Elizabeth Mayer writes of women's rights in the declaration:

> The UIDHR does not admit that women are to be accorded second-class status, and it takes a careful reading of the UIDHR to uncover what is intended, However, many of the provisions assigning women to a subordinate role do so only indirectly and are written in such a convoluted style that their significance may not be obvious to readers – and especially not readers of the English version of the document.[42]

She compares Article 19a of the English version of the Universal Islamic Declaration, which reads: 'Every person is entitled to marry, to found a family and to bring up children in conformity with his religion, traditions and culture. Every spouse is entitled to such rights and privileges and carries such obligations as are stipulated by the Law', with Article 16.1 of the UN document, which reads: 'Men and women of full age, without any limitation due to race, nationality or religion, have the right to marry and to found a family. They are entitled to equal rights as to marriage, during marriage and at its dissolution.' The latter is unqualified, whereas the former could be interpreted as restricting rights under the UN declaration, such as the right to choose a spouse freely and the right not to be compelled to marry while very young.[43] Her point is that superficially dialogic documents that invite comparison with the international human rights discourse are, under the surface, well-financed initiatives by conservative forces committed to delegitimizing international

---

[42]Ann Elizabeth Mayer, *Islam and Human Rights: Tradition and Politics*, 4th edn (Oxford: Westview Press, 2006), p. 123.
[43]See also Chris Jones-Pauly with Abir Dajani Tuqan, *Women under Islam: Gender, Justice and the Politics of Islamic Law* (London: Tauris, 2011); Mahnaz Afkami, ed., *Faith and Freedom: Women's Human Rights in the Muslim World* (London: Tauris, 2000). For a reading of the Qur'an that finds radical egalitarianism and an anti-patriarchal nature in its teachings, see Asma Barlas, *'Believing Women' in Islam: Unreading Patriarchal Interpretations of the Qur'an* (Austin: University of Texas Press, 2002).

human rights and discrediting Muslim critics of international human rights.

My purpose is not to defend the charges of blasphemy and apostasy. Violence in response to blasphemy or apostasy is to be abhorred. Rather, I want to establish that problems regarding respect for freedom of religion pertain not only to traditionalist Islam but to secularist Western ideologies too. Each is violent in its own way and restrictive of public freedoms. Islam can be violently restrictive of religious freedom in the name of religion. Modern liberal democracies are at least seen as perpetuating the brutality of war for political ends: 'Warfare is presented, regretfully, as a mode of killing and dying in the name of one's nation or of national human redemption.'[44] To this end, the bulk of the chapter below is an account of a different set of problems that beset the meaning of universality and efforts to protect religious freedom associated with a recent tendency at the United Nations and in European Court of Human Rights jurisprudence to treat religion as something private that should not encroach upon the neutral public square. This set of problems arises from the assumptions that human rights discourse as we know it today is a predominantly (albeit not exclusively) Euro-American tradition and that, 'like many other European traditions, it imagines itself as universal',[45] and that human rights discourse is deemed by many to be 'secularist' in the sense of presupposing a distinction between private belief and public reason, and the delimitation of the former by a principled understanding of 'the secular' as that which constrains as well as protecting rights to religious freedom.

In preparation, I note Talal Asad's critique of what the West understands blasphemy to be. He contrasts the liberal notion of the free human within an ideology of universality where every individual is 'substitutional' for another. The idea of universalizability central to Western liberal politics and economics accepts the 'substitutionality' of one individual for another. Electoral politics count each voter as one; each is 'the exact equivalent of every other

[44]Talal Asad, Wendy Brown et al., *Is Critique Secular? Blasphemy, Injury, and Free Speech* (Berkeley: University of California Press, 2009), p. 29.
[45]Martti Koskenniemi, 'International Law in Europe: Between Tradition and Renewal', *European Journal of International Law*, vol. 16, no. 1 (2005), pp. 113–24, at p. 113.

voter – no more, no less, no different'.[46] 'Substitutionality' extends beyond electoral politics, however, to the market economy and the mechanisms of bureaucratic control. Western ways of thinking are essentially statistical, with modes of representation that reduce the person to a replaceable unit. Laws against blasphemy and apostasy might be deeply problematic in how they are enacted physically. In contrast to the Western worldview, however, such laws can be seen as valuing the person as person. The pain of apostasy and blasphemy to the religious community is that the particular person in question cannot be substituted for another. Islam has laws against this. Western liberal democracies have laws against different modes of free speech that violate laws – for example, laws of copyright, patent and trademark – that protect the quasi-property rights in these works. Asad is fully aware of differences between these systems of law and points precisely to these differences: 'My point here', he says, 'is not that there is no difference, but that there are legal conditions that define what may be communicated freely, and how, in liberal democratic societies, and that consequently the flow of public speech has a particular shape by which its "freedom" is determined.'[47]

Like Asad, I am concerned to learn more about how Muslims think (variously) about the limits to free speech inherent within Islamic ideas of blasphemy and why the locus of concern about blasphemy is not the private, inner realm of the mind, that is, correctness of belief per se, but a social relationship that is being openly repudiated.[48] Disbelief incurs no legal punishment in Islam. 'In the classical law, punishment for apostasy is justified on the grounds of its political and social consequences, not of entertaining false doctrine itself.'[49] This does not, to my mind, justify violence against those who blaspheme or convert from Islam to another religion, but explains that blasphemy and apostasy in Islam might be very different from popular Western conceptions: 'what matters is the Muslim subject's social practices – including verbal publication – not her internal thoughts, whatever these might be. In contrast, the Christian tradition allows that thoughts can

---

[46]Asad, Brown et al., *Is Critique Secular?* p. 24.
[47]Asad, Brown et al., *Is Critique Secular?* p. 28.
[48]Asad, Brown et al., *Is Critique Secular?* p. 43.
[49]Asad, Brown et al., *Is Critique Secular?* pp. 42–43.

commit the sin of blasphemy'.[50] Leaving aside questions of how Christian tradition has shaped modern Western liberalism or is, to use Asad's phrase, 'the seed that flows into secular humanism', subsequent sections show there to be merit in Asad's reading of differences between Islamic and modern, secularist liberal understanding of religion as, respectively, social and private or spiritual. My purpose is not to approve one and disapprove the other but point to where the meaning of universality is contested, and to where human rights discourse at the United Nations, the Organization for Security and Co-operation in Europe, the Council of Europe and other such institutions is becoming increasingly and unnecessarily dogmatic. A plea is made to recall human rights discourse at the United Nations and the European Court of Human Rights to its primary (and original) purpose – namely, not to advocate an ideology but to provide for human rights protection at law.

Neo-Kantian theory and the meaning of universality

There are many secularist ways of thinking about why human rights are to be respected universally. It is predominantly the Kantian heritage, however, that bequeathes a discourse of rights as universal in the sense that all people, in all times and all places, should have and enjoy the same rights, and that these rights should be available to all individuals as moral and legal standards whether or not recognized by the nation-state in which they live. This tradition of moral universalism is sometimes said to have its roots in Aristotle and the Stoics, or the Judaeo-Christian tradition. It was Kant who spelled out more fully than anyone before him why and how external relations between persons should be dealt with under the concept of Right, and who gave to international human rights discourse the idea of a potentially universal cosmopolis of rational individuals whose exercise of reason should satisfy tests of universality capable of being recognized by all rational agents.

---

[50]Asad, Brown et al., *Is Critique Secular?* p. 40.

To the extent that modern human rights discourse owes its origin to these philosophical ideas of the seventeenth- and eighteenth-century European Enlightenment, it is a mode of philosophical discourse that claims to hold true independent of context and does not contain any admixture of sensibility or knowledge derived from experience. In other words, Kant sets out to establish the limits to what can be known, the conditions of that knowledge, the conditions of the possibility for establishing universal moral laws, and the duty beholden on every individual to elevate themselves to the ideal of moral perfection. His philosophy is all encompassing and universal in its reach. So too are some versions of modern human rights discourse. The UN Declaration of Human Rights is seen by many as a culmination of Kant's philosophical revolution whereby philosophy is the search for ultimate categories that can demonstrate the universal principles of understanding and it is our duty as human beings to elevate ourselves to an ideal of moral perfection whereby each person wills freely to agree with that to which they ought to subject themselves. It is the duty of all rational persons to commit themselves to necessity and universality as the criteria used to determine an a priori judgement or element of morality. 'Many of the central themes first expressed within Kant's moral philosophy', writes Andrew Fagan of the University of Essex, 'remain highly prominent in contemporary philosophical justifications of human rights.'[51] Foremost among these are the ideals of equality and the moral autonomy of rational human beings. Kant's moral philosophy has yielded various declarations, conventions and covenants which comprise the contemporary human rights doctrine and embody both the belief in the existence of a universally valid moral order. This heritage, which includes a particular way of thinking about human rights, is not historically, culturally or religiously neutral.

The problem of hegemony

In traditionalist Islam and at both the United Nations and the European Court of Human Rights there are diverse reasons why human rights discourse ceases to be a legal tool and becomes an

---

[51]Andrew Fagan, 'Human Rights', Internet Encyclopedia of Philosophy, 10 January 2003 www.iep.utm.edu/hum-rts/ [accessed 24 February 2013].

ideological statement. The pressing question at the close of this chapter is whether it remains possible to distinguish between the role that human rights can perform beneficially in encouraging the implementation of internationally agreed standards, and human rights as a dominant global ideology given content by a very particular philosophy and backed by the massive superstructures of the major world powers. I draw attention to how problems arise when the properly protective function of human rights as legal (or quasi-legal) instruments becomes a discourse manipulated by some for the advancement of particular interests, whether religious or secularist, and suggest that distinguishing between the protective, legal role performed by human rights and the manipulation of the concept of human rights for other purposes may be assisted by critical points of engagement forged from a Gramsci-influenced analysis of the problem of hegemony.

Gramsci's theory of hegemony was never systematized to produce a coherent theory or method but is dispersed throughout his *Prison Notebooks* like pieces in a jigsaw puzzle. Repeatedly, however, he attempts to distinguish between the power of ideas used to dominate by means of repression, exclusion and the manipulation of consent, and instruments of government used for concrete egalitarian purposes:

> The conception of law will have to be freed from every residue of transcendentalism and from every absolute; in practice, from every moralistic fanaticism. However, it seems to me that one cannot start from the point of view that the State does not 'punish' (if this term is reduced to its human significance), but only struggles against social 'dangerousness'. In reality, the State must be conceived of as an 'educator', in as much as it tends precisely to create a new type or level of civilisation.[52]

The distinction here is between law used by the state for 'civilizing' or other purposes in ways that eliminate certain customs and attitudes while disseminating others, rather than for the more limited purposes of punishing crime and so on. It might be, says Bates, that, for Gramsci, every state is ultimately a

---

[52]*Selections from the Prison Notebooks of Antonio Gramsci*, ed. Quentin Hoare and Geoffrey Nowell Smith (London: Lawrence & Wishart, 1971), p. 508.

dictatorship and that domination of one sort or another is always present in any political arrangement.[53] The differences between hegemony and strong political leadership are difficult to discern. Dictatorship is not the sole form of political rule described by Gramsci. Government can be exercised – not least through the exercise of law – to better ends. He still alerts us, however, to the problem of hegemony as a conceptual apparatus that is coercive in hidden ways, based on the consent of the many but secured by the diffusion and popularization of a worldview that serves interests that may not be immediately obvious. His theory of hegemony has important implications for critical thinking about how to retrieve the protective function of human rights by reclaiming their delimited legal and quasi-legal role as distinct from human rights as an ideological current of thought that bolsters political manifestos and creates a cultural apparatus of its own, backed by the threat of force.

As Thomas Bates observed in his study of Antonio Gramsci and the theory of hegemony, '[t]he term "hegemony" is certainly not new to western political discourse, and has traditionally signified domination of one sort or another'.[54] Writing from his very particular context of early twentieth-century Italian fascism, Gramsci was concerned with how members of societies lose critical awareness of the problems hidden within the ruling ideas of their age. Having observed the failure of left-wing politicians to confront fascism effectively, he knew the importance of being able to distinguish analytically between the necessary rule of law and forms of political rule that exercise undue control. It is necessary, he says, for societies to be governed by law:

there exist social and state laws which are the product of human activity, which are established by men and can be altered by men in the interests of their collective development. These laws of the State and of society create that human order which historically best enables men to dominate the laws of nature, that is to say which most facilitates their work. For work is the specific mode by which man actively participates in natural life

[53]Thomas R. Bates, 'Gramsci and the Theory of Hegemony', *Journal of the History of Ideas* 36 (April–June 1975), p. 352.
[54]Bates, 'Gramsci and the Theory of Hegemony', p. 352.

in order to transform and socialise it more and more deeply and extensively.[55]

The need for legal order is not in dispute; human work cannot be properly creative and productive outside of a realistic legal order. Gramsci looks for a legal order that commands consent and regulates human life in common: 'Men must respect this legal order through spontaneous assent, and not merely as an external imposition – it must be a necessity recognized and proposed to themselves as freedom, and not simply the result of coercion.'[56] Problems develop, however, when the entire social complex loses the ability to question the legal system and social norms, when individuals become merely passive inculcators of social attitudes and psycho-physical habits, losing the ability to think abstractly and then plunge back into everyday life, to distinguish between social systems that provide for liberty and creativity and those that repress.

The problem of imperialism

Today, the neo-Kantian model of rights discourse is perceived increasingly as problematic because it supposes there to be one notion of universality accessible to all and applicable to all, and because it presents itself as commanding the meaning of 'universal' in ways that sit uneasily with other perspectives and traditions, and voices. William Twining's collection *Human Rights, Southern Voices* made this point clearly, drawing together scholars including Francis Deng of the Ngok Dinka people in Sudan, Yash Ghai of Kenya, Upendra Baxi of India and more, all of whom are variously sceptical of claims to the universality of human rights but affirmative of the core values of the discourse and open to their interpretation in different contexts.[57] For the Dinka, says Deng, respect for one another is an important practice that extends after death through living memory. Failure to recognize this would mean that human rights could not be instantiated successfully in Dinka culture. An abstract affirmation of the universality of human rights

---

[55]Bates, 'Gramsci and the Theory of Hegemony', p. 177.
[56]Bates, 'Gramsci and the Theory of Hegemony', p. 178.
[57]William Twining, (ed.), *Human Rights, Southern Voices* (Cambridge: Cambridge University Press, 2009).

that fails to appreciate their culture and also the inferior status that it seems to be accorded by radical Arab-Islamic elements means little to these people.[58] A decade ago, prominent theorists in human rights discourse were optimistic about grappling with the plurality of ethical commitments and how to maintain a presumed universal moral ethic among cultures and traditions that are in disagreement over ethical norms and how they are practised.[59] Today, disenchantment appears to be growing as the UN Security Council stutters between inactivity and politicized military interventions in situations of conflict. Costas Douzinas's *Human Rights and Empire* has become a landmark in the growing literature examining the relationship between human rights and the politics, including armed conflict, carried out in their name.[60] Michael Hardt and Antonio Negri's *Empire* (2000) made similar points and has become an international bestseller, bearing the whiff of controversial, Marxist-inspired polemic. Douzinas's *Human Rights and Empire* has come to be regarded as a seminal study in human rights that should be in the library not only of every activist but of every human rights scholar too.

---

[58]Francis Deng, 'The Cow and the Thing Called "What": Dinka Cultural Perspectives on Wealth and Poverty', in William Twining (ed.), *Human Rights, Southern Voices*, p. 12.

[59]See William M. Sullivan, 'Ethical Universalism and Particularism: A Comparison of Outlooks', in William M. Sullivan and Will Kymlicka (eds), *The Globalization of Ethics* (Cambridge: Cambridge University Press, 2007), p. 192. Jack Donnelly posed the issues more clearly than many in *Universal Human Rights in Theory and Practice*, 2nd edn (Ithaca, NY: Cornell University Press, 2003), in which he attempted to negotiate a path between recognition that human rights discourse after the Second World War is historically specific and contingent and yet can be held universally in the contemporary world on the grounds of shared humanity.

[60]Costas Douzinas, *The End of Human Rights* (Oxford: Hart, 2000), ch. 1. Douzinas listed the many achievements of human rights discourse, not least a contribution around the globe to a sense of shared human identity. He also examined instances, however, where human rights discourse had become heavily politicized to become an instrument used by governments for the maintenance of the status quo and tools for the operation of power (p. 209). See also Costas Douzinas, *Human Rights and Empire: The Political Philosophy of Cosmopolitanism* (Abingdon, OX: Routledge-Cavendish, 2007) which emphasizes the interconnectedness of the unregulated political economy of globalization, 'Washington' policies adopted by the World Bank, attitudes to the Iraq and Iran wars, the intervention in Kosovo and more (p. 8).

I do not accept unquestioningly the extent to which these diverse culturally-rooted and Marxist-inspired polemics condemn human rights discourse as shaped already by a particular, Western political and cultural hegemony, but point to a growing problem that demands the critical attention of political theology and Christian ethics.[61] Human rights and their accompanying discourses can be diverted from their purpose to protect human beings from tyranny and oppression to means of defending Islamic and/or western, liberal values. Hence the concluding sections of this chapter look critically at the way(s) in which human rights are commonly understood in western countries (as evidenced in the judgements and reports cited below) bear the marks of particular schools of thinking and can be seen as part of a wider socio-philosophical, economic project. At issue is where and why the legal protections offered by human rights degenerate into ideological projects, and what is necessary if the original vision of defence against tyranny protected by the rule of law is to be reclaimed.

Kant's concept of right

Philosophically, at least some of the roots of this (problematic) politics are found in Kant's philosophy of right. Consider how Kant's concept of 'Right' from which law is derived concerns external freedom only and not the inner freedom of individuals. Law does not address inner freedom. Inner freedom depends, however, upon freedom from external compulsion. Ethics is confined to the inner realm of freedom that is, for Kant, where enlightened individuals direct their own lives autonomously in accordance with the requirements of reason. External freedom is governed by a formal condition not to infringe on another's freedom. The task of law is not to be concerned with virtue or the character of one's relationship with others but with the protection of an individual's freedom to act. 'I can never be constrained by others *to have an end*.'[62] Only individual duty to live in accordance

---

[61]See also Slavoj Žižek, 'The Obscenity of Human Rights: Violence as Symptom' (2005) www.lacan.com/zizviol.htm [accessed 28 April 2013].

[62]Immanuel Kant, *The Metaphysics of Morals*, trans. Mary Gregor (Cambridge: Cambridge University Press, 1996), §381, p. 146. (Emphasis in original).

with the requirements of reason can motivate ethical freedom. The coercion of law cannot promote virtuous ends but only create the conditions for autonomously moral action. Law is about external coercion and is thus stripped of the ethics that, for Kant, concern inner freedom. Ethics and law have been separated into the inner and outer divisions of human life. 'Legality, therefore, is a respect only for each other's external freedom.'[63] The first duty of government is to establish those institutions that provide the conditions for juridical law that prevent infringement upon another's freedom. The need for positive law is satisfied with the establishment of the state.[64] At the root of the notion of 'Right' is Kant's division of freedom into internal and external.

On the Principle that Distinguishes the Doctrine of Virtue from the Doctrine of Right

This distinction, on which the main division of the *doctrine of morals* as a whole also rests, is based on this: that the concept of *freedom*, which is common to both, makes it necessary to divide duties into duties of *outer freedom* and duties of *inner freedom*, only the latter of which are ethical.[65]

Freedom is placed in bold by Kant himself and reminds us that, for Kant, freedom is a metaphysical concept that is 'the only original right belonging to every man by virtue of his humanity'.[66] Freedom means 'independence from being constrained by another's choice . . . insofar as it can coexist with the freedom of every other in accordance with a universal law.'[67] Everything that Kant says about morality and ethics depends upon this notion of freedom that, as the citation above indicates, results in the division of duties into inner and outer. Only the duties of inner freedom are ethical. Ethical duties are found exclusively in the exercise of inner freedom.

---

[63]Robert Gibbs, 'Jurisprudence is the Organon of Ethics: Kant and Cohen on Ethics, Law, and Religion', in Reinier Munk (ed.), *Hermann Cohen's Critical Idealism* (Dordrecht: Springer, 2005), p. 198.
[64]Amanda Perreau-Saussine, 'Immanuel Kant on International Law', in Samantha Besson and John Tasioulas (eds), *The Philosophy of International Law* (Oxford: Oxford University Press, 2010), pp. 53–78.
[65]Kant, *The Metaphysics of Morals*, §407, p. 165.
[66]Kant, *The Metaphysics of Morals*, §237, p. 63.
[67]Kant, *The Metaphysics of Morals*, §237, p. 63.

External relations between persons are dealt with under the concept of Right:

> The concept of Right . . . has to do, *first*, only with the external and indeed practical relation of one person to another, insofar as their actions, as facts, can have (direct or indirect) influence on each other. . . . Any action is *right* if it can coexist with everyone's freedom in accordance with a universal law, or if on its maxim the freedom of choice of each can coexist with everyone's freedom in accordance with a universal law.[68]

What matters at law is the possibility that one person's free actions can exist alongside another's free actions. The concept of Right from which law is derived concerns only external freedom and not the inner freedom of individuals. Law does not address inner freedom. But inner freedom depends upon freedom from external compulsion. So, explains Robert Gibbs, Kant's doctrine of Right says that a shopkeeper is within the law if they tempt a customer with low prices for junk food, trying to corrupt their ethical duty to themselves to eat well, but she may not ban the customer from the High Street or market place because this would delimit lawful use of his external freedom. 'Legality . . . is a respect only for each other's external freedom.'[69]

In Kant's language, external freedom is governed by a formal condition not to infringe on other's freedom. The task of law is not to be concerned with your virtue or the character of your relationship with others but with the protection of your freedom to act. Ethics is confined to the inner realm of freedom which is, for Kant, where enlightened individuals direct their own lives autonomously in accordance with the requirements of reason. Only duty to live in accordance with the requirements of reason can motivate ethical freedom. There is no place in the inner life for the coercion or external freedom. Ethics (whether religiously inspired or not) belongs to the true inner court of freedom and not the external realm of coercion. Thus 'Kant does not conceive of moral social relations except in the categories of law' that prevent infringement upon another's freedom.[70] Law is about external

---

[68]Kant, *The Metaphysics of Morals*, §230, p. 56.
[69]Gibbs, 'Jurisprudence is the Organon of Ethics', p. 198.
[70]Gibbs, 'Jurisprudence is the Organon of Ethics', p. 202.

coercion and is thus stripped of ethics which, for Kant, concerns inner freedom. Ethics and law have been separated into the inner and outer divisions of human life.

Implications for the restraint of religious liberty

Implications for the understanding of religious freedom have become apparent in the recent tendency of the European Court of Human Rights jurisprudence to treat religion as something private that should not intrude upon the neutral public square. Note especially comments made by Asma Jahangir, UN Special Rapporteur on freedom of religion or belief (2004–10), on religious symbols.

Since 1986, the work of the Special Rapporteur has been to examine incidents and government measures in all parts of the world that are incompatible with the provisions of the UN declaration of 1981 on eliminating intolerance and religious discrimination. Nothing in this declaration was to be construed as restricting or derogating from any right defined in the Universal Declaration of Human Rights and the International Covenants on Human Rights but rather as explication of it. The declaration was made by signatories '[c]onvinced that freedom of religion and belief should also contribute to the attainment of the goals of world peace, social justice and friendship among peoples and to the elimination of ideologies or practices of colonialism and racial discrimination'.[71] During her six years as Rapporteur, Jahangir made in situ visits, communicated concern about alleged violations to states, and addressed more general questions of how the freedom of religion is to be understood. I welcome her work in reporting violations and raising the profile of such concerns at the United Nations – this is not at issue – but am interested more critically in the underlying assumptions that inform her understanding of the freedom of religion, which are most readily apparent in her comments on

---

[71]Asma Jahangir, UN General Assembly, Declaration on the Elimination of All Forms of Intolerance and of Discrimination Based on Religion or Belief, 25 November 1981 www.un.org/documents/ga/res/36/a36r055.htm [accessed 24 February 2013].

symbols of religious identity such as the Islamic headscarf worn in public schools and similar places, other distinctive clothing or head covering and the like.

According to Jahangir, manifestations of religion are deemed to include customs such as the wearing of distinctive clothing or head coverings, and these are 'susceptible of limitation' when displayed in public because they belong properly to the inner freedom of individuals. Jahangir's language is redolent of Kant's division of freedom into internal and external:

> From a human rights law perspective, the Special Rapporteur notes that most international judicial or quasi-judicial bodies have considered that the display of religious symbols is a 'manifestation' of religion or belief falling within the purview of the second part of article 18, paragraph 1, of [the International Covenant on Civil and Political Rights] and therefore susceptible of limitation rather than an element of the *'forum internum'*, which is protected by the first part of article 18, paragraph 1, of ICCPR and hence not susceptible of any limitation.[72]

The inner life of religion is not to be restrained whereas external manifestations of religion are subject to limitation. The European Court of Human Rights has typically been appropriately reluctant to allow consideration of the *forum internum* but has ruled on several occasions that state neutrality can require an absolute ban on the wearing or display of certain religious symbols. Of concern in this chapter is not that external manifestations of religion should be delimited where harm is done to others or even, potentially, where offence caused to others is great, but that this neo-Kantian model has come to be interpreted in the name of 'neutrality' in ways that are unnecessarily restrictive of individuals' right to the freedom of religion or belief.[73]

---

[72]*Rapporteur's Digest on Freedom of Religion or Belief. Excerpts of the Reports from 1986 to 2011 by the Special Rapporteur on Freedom of Religion or Belief.* Report submitted by Asma Jahangir. Citing from E/CN.4/2005/61 20 December 2004. Citing from E/CN.4/2006/5. Freedom of Religion or Belief. III, Religious Symbols, paras. 36–60 www.ohchr.org/Documents/Issues/Religion/RapporteursDigestFreedomReligionBelief.pdf [accessed 24 February 2013], p. 22.

[73]For a brief review of what counts for the European Court of Human Rights as a 'manifestation' for the purposes of Article 9 and the court's approach

Especially noteworthy are landmark rulings at the European Court of Human Rights (e.g. *Şahin* v. *Turkey* and *Dahlab* v. *Switzerland*) about the role of the state in reconciling the interests of various groups. The Court used the 'margin of appreciation' widely and in ways that have been seen by some as an arbitrary rather than equitable tool.[74] The details of these cases are sufficiently well known for them to be repeated here at length. Briefly stated, in *Şahin* v. *Turkey* the Court decided that Turkey's banning of headscarves (and beards) did not violate Article 9 of the European Convention on Human Rights. The applicant, Leyla Şahin, was a Turkish national born in 1973 who considered it her religious duty to wear the Islamic headscarf. She was a fifth-year medical student at the University of Istanbul where, in February 1998, the vice chancellor of the university issued a circular directing that students with beards and students wearing the Islamic headscarf would be refused admission to lectures, courses and tutorials. In March 1998, Şahin was denied access to a written examination on one of the subjects she was studying because was wearing the Islamic headscarf. Subsequently the university authorities refused on the same grounds to enrol her on a course or to admit her to various lectures and a written examination. The faculty issued her with a warning for contravening the university's rules on dress and suspended her from the university for a term for taking part in an unauthorized assembly that had gathered to protest against them. All disciplinary penalties imposed on Şahin were subsequently revoked under an amnesty law, and the policy on headscarves has been reversed in universities throughout Turkey. To date, however, the Court's decision remains in place and judges throughout states

---

to determining whether an offence which has been caused by an expression of religion is sufficient to warrant legal intervention in the interests of tolerance and respect, see Malcolm D. Evans, 'From Cartoons to Crucifixes: Current Controversies concerning the Freedom of Religion and the Freedom of Expression before the European Court of Human Rights', in Esther D. Reed and Michael Dumper (eds), *Civil Liberties, National Security and Prospects for Consensus: Legal, Philosophical and Religious Perspectives* (Cambridge: Cambridge University Press, 2012), pp. 83–113. I acknowledge indebtedness to Malcolm Evans's insight with respect to issues discussed in this section.

[74] Malcolm Evans and Peter Petkoff, 'A Separation of Convenience? The Concept of Neutrality in the Jurisprudence of the European Court of Human Rights', *Religion, State and Society* 36 (September 2008), pp. 205–23.

subject to the court have to consider the ruling when looking at similar cases, unless and until another case is brought on sufficiently different grounds for it to be heard and yet on sufficiently similar grounds for any fresh ruling to have bearing on the practice.[75]

The applicant in the Dahlab case was a primary schoolteacher prohibited from wearing an Islamic headscarf in the performance of her duties. (She wished for religious reasons to wear a jilbab to school, whereas the school required her to wear a kameez and a shalwar. The school had a uniform policy and tolerated no exceptions to it.) The ruling emphasized the impact of the 'powerful external symbol' conveyed by her wearing the headscarf and indicated concern that it might have a proselytizing effect – noting that wearing the scarf appeared to be imposed on women by a precept laid down in the Qur'an and that this principle was hard to reconcile with gender equality. The Court stated that the margin of appreciation left to states is particularly appropriate when it comes to the regulation of the wearing of religious symbols in teaching institutions, since the rules vary from one country to another depending upon national traditions. There is no uniform European conception of the requirement of 'the protection of the rights of others' and of 'public order'. In both the *Dahlab* and *Şahin* cases, the court ruled that there had been no violation of Article 9 by the prohibitions.

---

[75]"[T]he Court finds that the University of Istanbul's regulations imposing restrictions on the wearing of Islamic headscarves . . . were justified in principle and proportionate to the aims pursued and, therefore, could be regarded as "necessary in a democratic society"' (*Leyla Şahin* v. *Turkey*, no. 44774/98, European Court of Human Rights, judgement, 29 June 2004, §114. At: www.minorityrights.org/download.php?id=386 [accessed 24 February 2013]. As Evans notes, 'Moreover, the prohibition was considered to be compatible with Convention values since it was designed to uphold the principle of secularism which the Court considered "consistent with the values underpinning the Convention system" and that "where the values of pluralism . . . are being taught and applied in practice, it is understandable that the relevant authorities should wish to preserve the secular nature of the institution concerned and so consider it contrary to such values to allow religious attire to be worn"' ('From Cartoons to Crucifixes', p. 92). Finally, in one of the most sparsely reasoned sections of the judgement, the Court decided that the restrictions were proportionate to the aim pursued and so did not violate Article 9 (*Şahin* v. *Turkey*, Grand Chamber judgement, 10 November 2005, §§117–23 hudoc.echr.coe.int/sites/eng/pages/search.aspx?i=001–22643#{"fulltext":["Sahin%20v.%20Turkey"],"itemid":["001–70956"]} [accessed 22 February 2013].

The rulings in both cases were made to uphold the neutrality of the state.[76] Granted that the Dahlab case raised the question of whether children could potentially have been influenced negatively by religious garb deemed by some to be repressive of women, the Court ruled in favour of the supposed values that derive from the Convention system rather than heeding the voices of Islamic feminists and others who argued that Dahlab was an example of an empowered Muslim woman performing a role in public life that contributed directly to the well-being of her society.[77] Supporting the idea that the state has a duty to remain neutral and impartial when exercising regulatory power, the Court accepted that, in Turkey, the headscarf was interpreted as a religious symbol and that it was within the scope of the state to prohibit it in public places as anti-constitutional and contrary to the principle of equality between women and men. No account was taken of the wearer's intention.

Imposing limitations on freedom in this sphere may, therefore, be regarded as meeting a pressing social need by seeking to achieve those two legitimate aims [of secularism and gender equality], especially since, as the Turkish courts stated, this religious symbol has taken on political significance in Turkey in recent years.[78]

The determining concern was the state's role as neutral and impartial in overseeing the exercise of various religions, faiths and beliefs. No issues of harm to others were at stake in the Şahin case. In the Dahlab decision, it appears that the Court took the view that the scarf was not only a religious symbol but contrary to Western values; this, rather than potential harm to children, appears to have been the deciding factor:[79]

It . . . is difficult to reconcile the wearing of a headscarf with the principle of gender equality, which is a fundamental value

---

[76]See, for example, Şahin v. Turkey, 29 June 2004, §§105–107.
[77]See Anicée Van Engeland, 'Are Muslim Feminists at Odds with International Feminism? The Search for a Dialogue', on file with author, c/o SOAS, University of London. At: www.soas.ac.uk/staff/staff78622.php [accessed 24 February 2013].
[78]Şahin v. Turkey, Grand Chamber Judgement, 10 November 2005, §115.
[79]'The Court accepts that it is very difficult to assess the impact that a powerful external symbol such as the wearing of a headscarf may have on the freedom of conscience and religion of very young children. The applicant's pupils were aged

of our society enshrined in a specific provision of the Federal Constitution (Article 4 §2) and must be taken into account by schools.[80]

As Evans writes: 'the call for "impartiality" and "neutrality" has increasingly been taken to mean that the state must present itself, through its servants, in a neutral fashion, where neutral means non-religious and the mere presence of the religious is seen as a threat to the perception of neutrality.'[81] Evans questions the necessity of this interpretation of 'impartiality' and 'neutrality', both of which could be preserved, he says, by ensuring non-discrimination in the recruitment of state servants permitted to wear what they wish, in accordance with more generally applicable rules relating to health and safety and so on or other relevant functional criteria. Human rights legislation appears to be being used not to protect the vulnerable from harm but to defend a particular set of values and notion of state neutrality that is close to religion-phobic.

Appointed to the post of UN Special Rapporteur on freedom of religion or belief in 2010, Heiner Bielefeldt has more recently commented directly on allegations of public manifestations of religious intolerance, stigmatization of persons based on their religion or belief and public announcements of disrespectful acts.[82] He has recognized the concerns above and also the multi-dimensional complexity of the topic. In some constellations of circumstances, he says, restrictions on the freedom to manifest religion or belief by wearing religious symbols may be justifiable in order to protect

---

between four and eight, an age at which children wonder about many things and are also more easily influenced than older pupils. In those circumstances, it cannot be denied outright that the wearing of a headscarf might have some kind of proselytizing effect, seeing that it appears to be imposed on women by a precept which is laid down in the Koran and which, as the Federal Court noted, is hard to square with the principle of gender equality' (*Dahlab* v. *Switzerland*, no. 42393/98, European Court of Human Rights, 15 February 2001 http://hudoc.echr.coe.int/sites/eng/pages/search.aspx?i=001-22643#{"itemid":["001-22643" [accessed 22 February 2013].
[80]*Dahlab* v. *Switzerland.*
[81]Evans, 'From Cartoons to Crucifixes', p. 112.
[82]Heiner Bielefeldt, Special Rapporteur on freedom of religion or belief, 'Report on the Promotion and Protection of All Human Rights', UN Human Rights Council, 19th session, Geneva, 22 December 2011 www.ohchr.org/Documents/HRBodies/HRCouncil/RegularSession/Session19/A-HRC-19-60_En.pdf [accessed 22 February 2013].

minority students from pressure exercised by schoolmates or their community.

[A] teacher wearing religious symbols in the class may have an undue impact on students, depending on the general behaviour of the teacher, the age of students and other factors. In addition, it may be difficult to reconcile the compulsory display of a religious symbol in all classrooms with the State's duty to uphold confessional neutrality in public education in order to include students of different religions or beliefs on the basis of equality and non-discrimination.[83]

Bielefeldt repeats the Jahangir position in this regard. At the same time, however, he maintains that the goal must always be to protect equally the positive and the negative aspects of freedom of religion or belief, 'i.e. the freedom positively to manifest one's belief, for instance by wearing religious clothing, and the freedom not to be exposed to any pressure, especially from the State or within State institutions, to perform religious activities'.[84] Any restrictions on the freedom to observe religious dress codes deemed necessary in that context must be formulated in a non-discriminatory manner. Bielefeldt proceeds to explicate the issues at length, redressing the balance somewhat between respect for the right not to receive religious instruction inconsistent with one's conviction and eradicating prejudices and conceptions incompatible with freedom of religion or belief.[85] The more recent *Lautsi and Others* v. *Italy* judgement of the European Court of Human Rights accepts that the state enjoys a considerable margin of appreciation with respect to the places within which education is provided, and that the display of crucifixes in classrooms falls within this margin.[86] In other

---

[83]Heiner Bielefeldt, Special Rapporteur on freedom of religion or belief, statement, Human Rights Council, 16th session, Geneva, 10 March 2011 www.ohchr. org/Documents/Issues/Religion/HRC16statement_March2011.pdf [accessed 22 February 2013].

[84]Bielefeldt statement, 10 March 2011.

[85]He also begins to address the attribution of legal personality status to religious groups as necessary for the protection of individual freedom of religion or belief.

[86]*Lautsi and Others* v. *Italy*, no. 30814/06, European Court of Human Rights, Grand Chamber judgement, 18 March 2011, §§ 64–69 http://hudoc.echr.coe.int/sites/eng/ pages/search.aspx?i=001–22643#{"fulltext":["Lautsi%20v.%20Italy"],"itemid": ["001–104040" [accessed 22 February 2013]. '[T]he central issue in *Lautsi* was

words, the classroom as public space need not be religiously neutral provided that this does not lead to indoctrination.

Despite recent signs of a less ideologically driven approach in both UN documentation and at the European Court of Human Rights, there have been instances when the Kantian heritage has been applied to the problems of religious fanaticism, religious intolerance and hostility against the manifestation of religion in public places in ways that are highly prejudicial to what believers understand their religion to entail. The legacy of the Enlightenment is being applied in the twenty-first century to delimit and restrict. For this reason, I am inclined to be sympathetic to attempts to reclaim public spaces – whether on the body or elsewhere – for the expression of religion in ways that disrupt the neo-Kantian assumption that religion belongs properly to the *forum internum* and that the proper responsibility of the state is to require neutrality in its treatment of individuals rather than action, to ensure the freedom of individuals from religious discrimination.[87] There is something going on beyond the legal defence of individual rights to the freedom of religion or belief; the delimitation of religion in these cases is both the restrictive interpretation of the right to freedom of religion or belief, for varying political purposes, but also the application of a normative framework in ways that exclude and suppress.

In other words, the obligation of states under the Charter of the United Nations to promote universal respect for and observance of human rights and freedoms, including the right to freedom of thought, conscience and religion, has been invoked to prevent states from imposing brutal punishments for blasphemy, apostasy and

---

whether the presence of a crucifix in an Italian state-school classroom breached the right of a parent to have her children (who were aged between 11 and 13) to be educated in accordance with her religious or philosophical convictions, a right provided for in Article 2 of the First Protocol to the Convention, taken in conjunction with Article 9' (Evans, 'From Cartoons to Crucifixes', p. 95). The initial ECHR decision in 2009 had been that 'the compulsory display of a symbol of a particular faith . . . in classrooms, restricts the right of parents to educate their children in conformity with their convictions and the right of schoolchildren to believe or not believe' (*Lautsi v. Italy*, 3 November 2009, § 57 http://hudoc.echr.coe.int/sites/eng/pages/search. aspx?i=001–22643#{"fulltext":["Lautsi%20v.%20Italy"],"itemid": ["001–95589" [accessed 22 February 2013].

[87]All expressions of religion in public are subject to limitation (which is not in dispute).

political dissidence. Sometimes, however, the manner in which rights to religious freedom and belief are asserted at the United Nations and the European Court of Human Rights creates an environment in which the protection of religious freedom becomes an ideological battleground rather than a legal tool to protect against human rights violations.

Critical accommodation

There is no ideology-free politics or politically neutral construction of the rule of law. But there are more and less peaceable ways of accommodating difference. Three points may be made in conclusion:

1   To demand silence of religious persons with respect to the 'why?' and 'how?' of human rights equates to advocating a particular kind of neo-Kantian ideology that is suspicious of the social function of religion and wants to confine religion to the private or spiritual aspects of life. Such blinkered adherence to a particular ideology is no basis for sustainable discussion in the twenty-first century about religious freedom and liberty of expression. It has long been recognized that the global community can tolerate wide differences in the specific practices by which human rights are respected, provided that the struggle is towards the enhanced protection of basic rights by the processes of law in different countries. This process is made more difficult, however, when the properly protective function of human rights legislation becomes part of the philosophical apparatus in an ideological battle between Islam and secularist liberalism. This chapter has voiced unease at how secularist liberal human rights discourse has contributed to portrayals of Islam as the alien Other, and ventured suggestions about how better understanding of Islam yields critical insight into so-called liberal Western notions of rights.

2   Theoretically, the question of universality has been at the heart of international human rights debates since

1948 and before. With Jack Donnelly, I affirm the real issue is not *whether* human rights are universal or relative but rather *how* they both are and are not universal, and are and are not relative, and how these universalities and relativities interact in theory and in practice. Donnelly usefully identifies three different senses in which human rights may be understood as universal: 'international legal universality', 'functional universality' and 'overlapping consensus universality'. He further identifies two senses in which human rights are not essentially universal: 'ontological universality' and 'historical (or anthropological) universality'.[88] This chapter has added a third sense in which human rights are not essentially universal: 'philosophico-ideological universality' while advocating all three of Donnelly's three senses in which human rights may be understood as universal.

3 Faith traditions of the world, the Abrahamic faiths especially, have the scriptural resources and liturgical practices required for constructions of 'international legal universality', 'functional universality' and 'overlapping consensus universality'. If, with John Howard Yoder and Stanley Hauerwas, we suppose that the confusion of tongues at Babel was not a punishment or a tragedy but a benevolent act that brought blessing through dispersion and diversification, then constructed universalities such as that of human rights must be striven for, and sought, like the understanding between the peoples after the scattering. Like the 'one language' spoken by the whole earth in Genesis 11.1, ideologies of modern human rights could become attempts to resist the post-Babel diversity of cultures; this would be to conceive of human rights in absolute terms as a kind of foundationalist body of theory from which

---

[88]Jack Donnelly, 'International Human Rights: Universal, Relative or Relatively Universal?', in Mashood Baderin and Manisuli Ssenyonjo (eds), *International Human Rights Law: Six Decades after the UDHR and Beyond* (Farnham, Surrey: Ashgate, 2010), pp. 31–48.

all uncertainty has been removed.[89] To my mind, the struggle for 'international legal universality', 'functional universality' and 'overlapping consensus universality' in a multi-cultured and multi-faith world is preferable to enforced uniformity.

Amongst the Abrahamic faiths (and potentially amongst other faith traditions too) this approach to pursuing the diverse meanings of the universality of human rights across difference may be construed methodologically as an extension of the Scriptural Reasoning movement.[90] Scriptural Reasoners are typically Jews, Christians and Muslims who meet, read and reason together around the sacred scriptures for the healing of our separate communities and repair of the world.[91] An extension of Scriptural Reasoning to the reading of shared extra-Scriptural texts is, in some respects, a re-posing of familiar Christian theological questions about natural law. To the extent that natural law reasoning is ethical thinking that supposes a divinely sanctioned, morally lawful universe and has moral and political content, then multi-faith, practically oriented Scriptural Reasoning that extends to extra-scriptural texts is an exercise of this kind. The same biblical and traditional arguments by which Christians advocate natural law reasoning apply (for example, the natural law is universal, that is, 'in all human persons'; despite the devastating effects of sin, the natural law still gives true knowledge of the moral law; humans have the ability to fulfil the natural law but this ability is seriously flawed by the effects of sin; the content of the natural law is the law

---

[89]On this, see Nicholas Wolterstorff, *Reason within the Bounds of Religion*, 2nd edn (Grand Rapids, MI: Eerdmans, 1984), pp. 28–30.

[90]By Scriptural Reasoning, I understand the movement that has developed from conversations between Peter Ochs, a Jewish scholar based at the University of Virginia, Steven Kepnes of Colgate University, David Ford of the University of Cambridge and others; see the *Journal of Scriptural Reasoning* http://etext.lib.virginia.edu/journals/ssr/ [accessed 23 February 2009].

[91]See Steven Kepnes, 'A Handbook of Scriptural Reasoning' http://etext.lib.virginia.edu/journals/jsrforum/writings/KepHand.html [accessed 23 February 2009]. Published as 'A Handbook for Scriptural Reasoning' in *Modern Theology* 22 (June 2006), pp. 367–83.

of God for humankind and has often been identified with the Decalogue and/or with the Logos or reason present by the Spirit of God in humanity; the natural law is part of the natural endowment of all people and can reasonably be expected to be deduced; it is commonly associated with the claim that civil government is part of God's continuing care and a corrective for sin). The task is to hold together the reading of sacred texts – as, in some important ways, constitutive of moral reasoning in the various faith traditions – with moral reasoning about human rights and *ideologiekritik*.

8

Concluding Theses

The following theses are ventured as a summary of the findings of this book and framework for future discussion:

1 *The dogmatic location of questions about all human law, including international law, is in the saving economy of the triune God.*

Everything that the believer might venture to say about the purposes of law within divine providence is consequential upon logically prior confession of God's saving dealings with creation. The origin and end of all things, including human law, is in God. The source of truth about human law is pre-eminently the person of Jesus Christ. Human attempts to think theologically about law cannot be disconnected from Trinitarian, Christological and eschatological doctrine; theological talk about law is a corollary of Christian faith in Christ crucified and risen. The task of thinking ethically and morally about international law is about identifying the consequences of knowledge of God and Father, Son and Spirit, for how humanity lives answerably before God and one another, with the non-human created order, and in ways oriented towards justice and peace. Thinking about international law in Christian theological perspective cannot be separated from questions of the identity and purposes for creation of the self-manifesting God revealed in Jesus.

2   *There is no ontological connection between the eternal law,*
    the divine law, natural law and the human law.

Human law has no metaphysical or other line of connection
that allows us to speak of direct links or conduits from the
eternal law, through the natural law, to the human. There
is no conduit that runs directly from the content, precepts
and principles of the natural law to human law. This does
not mean that Christian ethics and political theology today
should abandon its task of thinking theologically about
human law in relation to divine and natural law, but that
human law *de simplicitur* is never the bearer of divine law
per se. The making, promulgation, revision and enforcement
of law is required by God of human societies. According
to Jewish traditions, the seven laws of Noah included a
prohibition against failing to establish courts of justice. The
human community, in all its diversity, has responsibility
before God for the exercise of justice; the responsibility
is upon all people(s) and not only Israel. Given this, the
question is how to think appropriately about the dynamic
of human engagement with the natural law when asking
about the purpose and characteristics of good human law,
including international law.

3   *The work of natural law reasoning may be considered as a*
    hermeneutical endeavour.

In addition to careful, doctrinal specification of the
purpose of human law in relation to the creating and
redeeming work of God, the theological activity of
thinking about human law, including international law,
may be understood appropriately (that is, theologically) as
a matter of interpreting the scriptures and making sense
for today of the revealed will of God for humankind. The
effect of recasting natural law reasoning as a hermeneutic
activity is to shift the centre of gravity away from the fixed
precepts and precepts of the natural law (whether those
of the Decalogue or Aquinas's instruction to pursue good
and avoid evil)[1] to the work understanding on our part.
This is not to deny the initiating grace of God or priority

---

[1] Aquinas, *ST*, I–II, *q.* 109 *a.* 8, reply obj. 3.

of the divine Word but to recognize the fallibility of human reason and impossibility of instantiating in human affairs the perfections of divine justice. As participant in the contingencies of historical existence, the human interpreter of the precepts of the natural law is an agent amidst complex webs of events and political pressures. The natural law is not a property of human law itself but a capacity and requirement for reasoning.

4   *Only the sheer gratuity of divine grace and sovereign freedom over all creation permits the believer to expect that the requirements of God's will can be known – at least in part – by every person and society.*

Conscience errs and lies in the believer and non-believer alike, and assessment of the requirements of conscience will reflect somehow the complexities of the theological, socio-political and economic contexts from which they arise. Yet the believer may assume moral consciousness in every fellow human being because of the reality throughout the created order of the reconciling power of Jesus Christ and the presence of the Holy Spirit. General human reason and the demands of conscience upon every human being are never separable, in Christian doctrine, from the prevenient grace of God. The believer knows no basis for hope outside of Jesus Christ – including the hope that members of the major world faiths, and more besides, might engage constructively together around issues of international law and politics. This is not to assume a natural order or theory of natural law independent of revelation but to affirm, on the basis of revelation, that human beings know by nature to act in accordance with the divine will even when this knowledge is not obtained with reference to Christ (Rom. 2.14–16).

5   *The importance of international law in Christian tradition may be understood in terms of what good order entails.*

Natural law reasoning with respect to international law is not informed to any degree of precision by the general precepts and principles of the natural law but requires the development of criteria pertaining to just peace and good order, oriented towards common good. All things are ordered by God to their end in various ways. This ordering is integral to the goodness and providential care of creation; the believer confesses that the love of God holds together every other love in creation within a cosmic continuity oriented towards the perfection of powers. Keeping in mind these dogmatic presuppositions and following Aquinas, I deem a 'law' to be a rule relative to the common good of a given community. The common good has primacy over the particular good because of its greater completeness. The substance of the common good might not be knowable in advance or in detail but may yet be posited as entailing substance that can be sought minimally. In contrast to modern liberal theorists who posit the common good as unknowable except as the aggregate of individual goods, natural law reasoning in Protestant Thomist perspective requires a central place for the questions of what makes for just peace and good order for the sake of the commonweal.

6   Ideologiekritik *must be established from the outset as an integral aspect of natural law reasoning about human law, including international law.*

Human law is never far removed from politics and violence, and so questions about whose interests are aided by the constitution and/or enforcement of a law must be asked continuously. No human law effects true justice. The peculiar challenge of neo-Thomist natural law reasoning, however, is to take into account not only national interest but the unity and common vocation of the international community too. As John Paul II made clear, renewal of the international legal order in every generation requires attention to the common good of nation-states within the common vocation of humanity, where international law serves primarily as a pledge of peace.[2] In the Thomist tradition where the

[2]John Paul II, 'An Ever Timely Commitment: Teaching Peace', World Day of Peace, 1 January 2004, §§5, 9 www.vatican.va/holy_father/john_paul_ii/messages/peace/documents/hf_jp-iI_mes_20031216_xxxvii-world-day-for-peace_En.html [accessed 3 February 2013].

relation between virtue and reasonability is inseparable, *ideologiekritik* is not just a form of moralizing criticism but a practically oriented way of thinking, or constructive cognitive endeavour, focused on the requirements of both particular and common good. Consequently, the approach propounded in this book refuses to dissolve questions such as, What is law? What is law for? and By what criteria do we judge between good and bad law?, into strategies of power but brings into play questions about whether actions are oriented towards international justice and peace.

7 *Natural law reasoning in Protestant Thomist perspective focuses attention away from questions about the normativity of law per se and towards the politics, use and abuse of law.*

Natural law reasoning in Protestant Thomist perspective leaves relatively unexplored questions about the precise relationship of the law in question to the revealed law of God and the content of the natural law. While assuming that the Word of God has practical content, this approach recognizes the gap between the natural law and the command of God, and the conclusions of practical reason. False dichotomies between the content and purpose of a law, substance and function, must be avoided, and the formulation and application of any human law must be seen in socio-political, historical perspective. Such an approach in theological perspective always presupposes the givenness of divine revelation and requirements of God upon all humanity but recognizes that individuals and societies make sense of these demands within the concrete events of national and international affairs. It is the retelling of the politics, use and abuse of law that typically exposes when valid actions in the national self-interest become dangerously inattentive to the international commonweal, usually for domestic political purposes.

8 *Constructively critical attention is required to the relation between custom, consent and political authority in*

international law, not least with a view to exposing some of the limits of present-day statism.

Natural law reasoning in Protestant Thomist perspective about international law is sympathetic to the claim that custom can obtain the force of law. The authority of law is measured by its power to restrain evil and cause an increase in the commonweal, and more merely because it reflects the will of an appropriate authority or tyrant. This recognition of a customary basis for law is not made in opposition to treaty- or convention-based approaches to theorizing the authority of international law but in acknowledgement that the consent of free people(s) to laws over time is generative of political and legal authority. There is no guarantee that customary laws will be constructive rather than destructive of the commonweal but neither is the authority of law exhausted by democratic legitimacy. The democratic deficit of international law is not reason enough for governments to override laws that have roots that stretch back for centuries. It is at least possible that something higher (or deeper) than the agreement of states or individuals, positive law whether national or international, has given rise to these norms that have somehow attracted, and continue to attract, widespread accord. What matters more than the treaty and/or custom distinction per se, is Aquinas's question about the reasonability of law. The critical question always is whether a law pertains to the common good, and serves the ends of just peacemaking and good order.

9   *Divinely given order in the universe is incomplete without order in and between human beings, including between 'peoples' and 'nations'. Believers should resist vigorously, however, any identification of the creator's stamp of order on the universe with the laws of a nation-state or elemental forces of the universe.*

The existence of 'peoples' or 'nations' may be regarded as within a disposition of divine blessing but only in conjunction with a work of divine wrath at Babel in Genesis 11. Overly individualistic readings of the human condition are not supported by the biblical texts. In Genesis 9.6 and 10.32, the meaning of creation *imago Dei* makes little sense apart from membership of a family and people with shared language, land and sense of belonging one to another. Yet the fundamental equality of all persons in sin renders all other distinctions meaningless in comparison. National distinctions and the distinctions of language, custom, place and history, are de facto distinctions contingent upon matters 'decided for you by a sort of lot'.[3] That the command of God encounters people in these distinctions means, however, that they cannot be regarded in entirely negative terms. While the idea of a world without borders is a powerful one for Christian people, this does not require believers to be unrealistically cosmopolitan or to accept ideologies that reduce humanity to an abstract principle. The many 'peoples' or 'nations' of the earth are destined to appear before the throne of judgement at the end of time (Is. 16.5; Jer. 25.9; Zech. 8.22; Rev. 1.7; Rev. 21:5–15).

10 *Peculiar obligations rest upon members of the Abrahamic faiths to reason together about the authority, normativity and obligations of international law, including international humanitarian law and human rights legislation.*

Historical, doctrinal and moral reasons combine to demand ever-increasing efforts across the Abrahamic faiths for mutual understanding and shared endeavours for peacemaking and justice. To this end, the Scriptural Reasoning movement and the impetus around *A Common Word* offer models of hope.[4] Both are scripturally rooted movements oriented pragmatically towards reconciliation

---

[3]Augustine, *On Christian Doctrine*, trans. James Shaw, *Nicene and Post-Nicene Fathers*, First Series, vol. 2, bk I, §28.

[4]*A Common Word* began as 'An Open Letter to Pope Benedict XVI' after his controversial Regensburg address of September 2006. Thirty-eight Islamic authorities and scholars joined together to deliver a response to His Holiness in a spirit of open intellectual exchange. One year later, in September 2007, 138 Muslim scholars, clerics and intellectuals wrote *A Common Word between Us and You* www.acommonword.com/ [accessed 12 February 2013].

and healing. Both have enormous potential at local and international levels to promote co-operation and collaboration between members of the major world faiths, especially the Abrahamic, to contribute to public debate about attitudes to and the development of international law. The sustainable future of human rights, for instance, is more likely to depend upon the accessing of claims to their *universality via engagement with one another in and through our deepest differences* rather than upon universality conceived as an ideology or abstract philosophical concept. Scripturally pragmatic ways of thinking urge upon believers negotiation of the gap between the oft-times distorted and corrupt nature of rights talk and the ongoing work of human rights legislation in the service of justice and peace – fallible responses to problems in everyday practice oriented towards repair and corrective activity.

11 *Three strategic moral priorities may be affirmed in matters pertaining to the politics of international law: the needs of the poor, dominated and marginalized must be affirmed as taking priority over the wants of the rich, powerful and those who exclude;[5] the force of law not the law of force must be affirmed as making for justice and peace; the churches are still called to make what Barth calls a detached and delaying movement in any assessment of the justifiability of armed force.*

Whether Aquinas's realism per se is adequately equipped to see international affairs through the eyes of the oppressed, and whether his account of custom, consent and political authority is sufficiently rooted in the experiences of ordinary people rather than the existing structures of power, remains an open question. But that natural law reasoning in Protestant Thomist perspective should be challenged to the core by the poverty and inhuman misery

---

[5]These priorities were penned by David Hollenbach, S. J., *Claims in Conflict: Retrieving and Renewing the Catholic Human Rights Tradition* (New York: Paulist Press, 1979), p. 42.

in which the majority of the world's population lives is not in doubt. Our common humanity and the demands of the gospel make ignorance and apathy both immoral and sinful. Attention is required with some urgency to uncovering the profound and powerful relationships between international law and global financial systems, capitalism and the law and also the use of force. Theological perspectives, with voices from all the Abrahamic faiths and more, are needed to analyze the juridico-economic structure of the contemporary state of international affairs and future developments in international law.

BIBLIOGRAPHY

Aaken, Anne van, 'To Do Away with International Law? Some Limits to "The Limits of International Law"', *European Journal of International Law* 17 (2006), pp. 289–308.

Afkami, Mahnaz (ed.), *Faith and Freedom: Women's Human Rights in the Muslim World* (London: Tauris, 2000).

Agamben, Giorgio, *State of Exception* (trans. Kevin Attell, Chicago: University of Chicago Press, 2005).

Ait Ahmed Ouaali, Mariam, 'Globalization and the Future of Inter-Faith Dialogue', *Islam Today* 26 (2009), pp. 117–26 <www.isesco. org.ma/templates/isesco/Islamtoday/en/26/26.pdf> [accessed 3 March 2013].

Altwaijri, Abdulaziz Othman, 'Entrenching the Concept of the Alliance of Civilizations', *Islam Today* 26 (2009), pp. 15–27 <www.isesco. org.ma/templates/isesco/Islamtoday/en/26/26.pdf> [accessed 3 March 2013].

Amara, Mohamed, 'Between Islamic Universality and Western Globalization', *Islam Today* 26 (2009), pp. 73–88 <www.isesco.org. ma/templates/isesco/Islamtoday/en/26/26.pdf> [accessed 3 March 2013].

American Law Institute, *Restatement of the Law, Third: The Foreign Relations Law of the United States*, 2 (1987), §702, p. 161.

Anderson, Benedict, *Imagined Communities: Reflections on the Origin and Spread of Nationalism* (rev. ed., London: Verso, 2006).

Anghie, Antony, *Imperialism, Sovereignty and the Making of International Law* (Cambridge: Cambridge University Press, 2005).

An-Na'im, Abdullahi Ahmed, 'Human Rights, Religion, and the Contingency of Universalist Projects', paper presented at the Program for the Advancement of Research on Conflict, Maxwell School of Citizenship and Public Affairs, Syracuse University, Syracuse, NY, September 2000.

— 'Religious Minorities under Islamic Law and the Limits of Cultural Relativism', *Human Rights Quarterly* 9 (February 1987), pp. 1–18.

Appiah, Kwame Anthony, *Cosmopolitanism: Ethics in a World of Strangers* (Princeton, NJ: Princeton University Press, 2007).

Aquinas, Thomas, *Summa Contra Gentiles*, book three: *Providence*, part I (trans. Vernon J. Bourke, Notre Dame: University of Notre Dame Press, 1975).

— *Summa Theologiæ*, 60 vols. (London: Eyre & Spottiswoode, 1963–74).

Araujo, Robert John, SJ, 'John Paul II and the Rule of Law: Bringing Order to International Disorder', *Journal of Catholic Legal Studies* 45 (2007), pp. 293–319.

Armstrong, R. A., *Primary and Secondary Precepts in Thomistic Natural Law Teaching* (Leiden: Martinus Nijhoff, l966).

Asad, Talal et al., *Is Critique Secular? Blasphemy, Injury, and Free Speech* (Berkeley: University of California Press, 2009).

Aslam, Wali and Ciaran Gillespie, 'US Drone Strikes in Pakistan and Political Appropriation of Casualties in Threat Construction', paper presented at a conference at the Centre for International Intervention, University of Surrey, Guildford, 13 July 2012.

Athanasius, *On Luke X. 22* (Matt. XI. 27), in *Nicene and Post Nicene Fathers*, series 2, vol. 4: *Athanasius: Select Writings and Letters* (ed. Philip Schaff and Henry Wace, Edinburgh: T&T Clark, 1891).

Augustine, 'Christian Doctrine', in Philip Schaff (ed.) (1887), *Nicene and Post-Nicene Fathers*, series 1, vol. 2 (rpt Edinburgh: T&T Clark, 1989. Buffalo, NY: Christian Literature Publishing Co., 1887), pp. 519–597.

— *The City of God against the Pagans* (trans. R.W. Dyson, Cambridge: Cambridge University Press, 1998).

Augustine, *On Free Choice of the Will* (trans. Thomas Williams, Indianapolis, IN: Hackett, 1993).

— *On Order* (trans. Silvano Burruso, Chicago: St. Augustine's Press, 2007).

— 'Reply to Faustus the Manichaean', in Philip Schaff (ed.) (1887), *Nicene and Post-Nicene Fathers*, series 1, vol. 4: *St. Augustine: The Writings against the Manichaeans, and against the Donatists* (rpt Edinburgh: T&T Clark, 1989), pp. 155–345.

Badiou, Alain, *Saint Paul: The Foundation of Universalism* (trans. Ray Brassier, Stanford, CA: Stanford University Press, 2003).

Bakhtin, Mikhail, *Problems of Dostoevsky's Poetics* (ed. and trans. Caryl Emerson, 2nd edn (1963), rpt Minneapolis: University of Minnesota Press, 1984).

Baldwin, Clive, *Minority Rights in Kosovo under International Rule* (London: Minority Rights Group International, 2006).

Balibar, Etienne, *We, the People of Europe? Reflections on Transnational Citizenship* (trans. James Swenson, Princeton, NJ: Princeton University Press, 2004).

Bamforth, Nicholas C. and David A. J. Richards, *Patriarchal Religion, Sexuality and Gender: A Critique of New Natural Law* (Cambridge: Cambridge University Press, 2008).

Banks, William, 'International Legal Framework for Countering Terrorism', report of conference panel workshop at the International Centre for Counter-Terrorism, The Hague, 12–13 December 2010 <www.un.org/en/sc/ctc/specialmeetings/2011/docs/icct-hague-launch-confreport.pdf> [accessed 12 January 2012].

Barcelona Traction, Light and Power Co., Ltd. (Belg. v. Spain), I.C.J. 3, 14 (5 February 1970), §§ 33–34

BART cat. ref. bro0049 www.cartoonstock.com/cartoonview.asp?start= 6&search=main&catref=bro0049&MA_Artist=&MA_Category=& ANDkeyword=human+rights&ORkeyword= &TITLEkeyword=& NEGATIVEkeyword [accessed 12 February 2013].

Barlas, Asma, *'Believing Women' in Islam: Unreading Patriarchal Interpretations of the Qur'an* (Austin: University of Texas Press, 2002).

Barth, Karl, *Church and State* (trans. G. Ronald Howe, London: SCM, 1939).

— *Church Dogmatics*, 13 vols. (ed. G. W. Bromiley and T. F. Torrance, Edinburgh: T&T Clark, 1956–75).

— *The Epistle to the Romans* (trans. E. C. Hoskyns (1933), rpt Oxford: Oxford University Press, 1968).

— *Ethics* (trans. G. W. Bromiley, Edinburgh: T&T Clark, 1981).

Bates, Thomas R., 'Gramsci and the Theory of Hegemony', *Journal of the History of Ideas* 36 (April–June 1975), pp. 351–66.

Bauckham, Richard, *The Theology of the Book of Revelation* (Cambridge: Cambridge University Press, 1993).

Beck, Ulrich, *The Cosmopolitan Vision* (Cambridge: Polity Press, 2006).

— *World at Risk* (Cambridge: Polity Press, 2008).

Bellamy, Alex J., 'Realizing the Responsibility to Protect', *International Studies Perspectives* 10 (2009), pp. 111–28.

Benedict XVI, Address, United Nations, New York, 18 April 2008 <www. vatican.va/holy_father/benedict_xvi/speeches/2008/april/documents/ hf_ben-xvI_spe_20080418_un-staff_En.html> [accessed 18 February 2013].

Berkman, John, 'Towards a Thomistic Theology of Animality', in Celia Deane-Drummond and David Clough (eds), *Creaturely Theology: On God, Humans and Other Animals* (Norwich: SCM Press, 2009), ch. 1.

Black, David Ross and Paul D. Williams (eds), *The International Politics of Mass Atrocities: The Case of Darfur* (Abingdon, Oxon: Routledge, 2010).

Blair, Tony, Address to the Chicago Economic Club, *The NewsHour with Jim Lehrer*, 22 April 1999 <www.pbs.org/newshour/bb/international/ jan-june99/blair_doctrine4–23.html> [accessed 1 October 2009].

Bohman, James and Matthias Lutz-Bachmann (eds), *Perpetual Peace: Essays on Kant's Cosmopolitan Ideal* (Cambridge: MIT Press,1997).

Bond, Helen K., *Pontius Pilate in History and Interpretation* (Cambridge: Cambridge University Press, 1998).

Bonhoeffer, Dietrich, *Discipleship* (ed. Martin Kuske and Ilse Tödt (German ed.); Geoffrey B. Kelly and John D. Godsey (English ed.), trans. Barbara Green and Reinhard Krauss, vol. 4 of *Dietrich Bonhoeffer Works*, Minneapolis, MN: Fortress Press, 2003).

— *Ethics* (ed. Ilse Tödt, Heinz Eduard Tödt et al. (German ed.); Clifford J. Green (English ed.), trans. Reinhard Krauss, Charles C. West and Douglas W. Stott, vol. 6 of *Dietrich Bonhoeffer Works*, Minneapolis, MN: Fortress Press, 2005).

Bowlin, John, 'Contemporary Protestant Thomism', in Paul van Geest, Harm Goris and Carlo Leget (eds), *Aquinas as Authority* (Leuven: Peeters, 2002), pp. 235–51.

Boyd, John R., 'Patterns of Conflict' (1982) <www.dnipogo.org/fcs/pdf/4GW_wilson-wilcox_boyd_conf_2002.pdf> [accessed 20 February 2013].

Brennan, John O., 'Strengthening Our Security by Adhering to Our Values and Laws', Program on Law and Security, Harvard Law School, Cambridge, MA, 16 September 2011 <www.whitehouse.gov/the-press-office/2011/09/16/remarks-john-o-brennan-strengthening-our-security-adhering-our-values-an> [accessed 21 February 2013].

Bricmont, Jean, Foreword to Noam Chomsky, *A New Generation Draws the Line: Humanitarian Intervention and the 'Responsibility to Protect' Today* (London: Paradigm, 2012), pp. i–xv.

'Britain Drops "War on Terror" Label', *Daily Mail*, 28 December 2007 www.military.com/NewsContent/0,13319,159067,00.html [accessed 20 February 2013].

Brown, O. J., *Natural Rectitude and Divine Law in Aquinas: An Approach to an Integral Interpretation of the Thomistic Doctrine of Law* (Toronto: Pontifical Institute of Medieval Studies, 1981).

Brunnée, Jutta, 'The Meaning of Armed Conflict and the Jus ad Bellum', in Mary Ellen O'Connell (ed.), *What is War? An Investigation in the Wake of 9/11* (Leiden: Martinus Nijhoff, 2012), ch. 4.

Bryan, Steven, *Jesus and Israel's Traditions of Judgement and Restoration* (Cambridge: Cambridge University Press, 2002).

Buchanan, Allen, *Justice, Legitimacy, and Self-Determination: Moral Foundations for International Law* (Oxford: Oxford University Press, 2004).

— 'The Legitimacy of International Law', in Samantha Besson and John Tasioulas (eds), *The Philosophy of International Law*, Oxford: Oxford University Press, 2010), ch. 3.

Bull, Hedley, 'The Importance of Grotius in the Study of International Relations', in Hedley Bull, Benedict Kingsbury and Adam Roberts (eds), *Hugo Grotius and International Relations* (Oxford: Clarendon Press, 1990), pp. 65–93.

Bush, George W., address to Joint Session of Congress, 20 September 2001 <http://georgewbush-whitehouse.archives.gov/news/releases/2001/09/20010920-8.html> [accessed 20 February 2013].

— Inaugural Address, 20 January 2001 <http://georgewbush-whitehouse.archives.gov/infocus/bushrecord/documents/Selected_Speeches_George_W_Bush.pdf> [accessed 8 January 2012]. Declaration on Human Rights in Islam, 19th Islamic Conference of Foreign Ministers, 31 July–5 August 1990 <www.oic-oci.org/english/article/human.htm> [accessed 24 February 2013].

Calvin, John, *Commentary on Isaiah*, Grand Rapids, MI: Christian Classics Ethereal Library, 1958, vol. 1 <www.ccel.org/ccel/calvin/calcom13.toc.html> [accessed 16 February 2013].

— *Institutes of the Christian Religion* (ed. John T. McNeill, 2 vols., Louisville, KY: Westminster/John Knox Press, 2001).

Carroll R. and M. Daniel, *Christians at the Border: Immigration, the Church, and the Bible* (Grand Rapids, MI: Baker Academic, 2008).

Carter, T. L., 'The Irony of Romans 13', *Novum Testamentum* 46 (2004), pp. 209–28.

Cassese, Antonio, *International Law*, 2nd edn (Oxford: Oxford University Press, 2005).

Catechism of the Catholic Church <www.vatican.va/archive/ENG0015/_INDEX.HTM> [accessed 3 March 2013].

Cerna, Christina M., 'Universality of Human Rights and Cultural Diversity: Implementation of Human Rights in Different Socio-Cultural Contexts', *Human Rights Quarterly* 16 (1994), pp. 740–52.

Chandler, David, 'R2P or Not R2P? More Statebuilding, Less Responsibility', *Global Responsibility to Protect* 2 (2010), pp. 161–66.

Charlesworth, Hilary and Christine Chinkin, *The Boundaries of International Law: A Feminist Analysis* (Manchester: Manchester University Press, 2000).

Ching, Julia, 'Human Rights: A Valid Chinese Concept?' paper presented at the panel Religious Consultation on Population, Reproductive Health and Ethics, UN World Summit for Social Development, Copenhagen, 11–12 March 1995 <www.religiousconsultation.org/ching.htm> [accessed 10 February 2012].

Chomsky, Noam, *A Generation Draws the Line: Humanitarian Intervention and the 'Responsibility to Protect' Today* (Boulder, CO: Paradigm, 2012).

Chrysostom, John, *Homilies on the Gospel of Saint Matthew*, in *Nicene and Post-Nicene Fathers*, series 1, vol. 10 (ed. Philip Schaff, Grand Rapids, MI: Eerdmans, 1952).

Cicero, *De Officiis*, (trans. Walter Miller, Cambridge, MA: Harvard University Press, 1913).

— *On the Nature of the Gods* (trans. Francis Brooks, London: Methuen, 1896).

Clement of Alexandria, 'Exhortation to the Heathen', in Philip Schaff (ed.) (n.d.), *Ante-Nicene Fathers*, vol. 2: *Fathers of the Second Century* (rpt Edinburgh: T&T Clark, 1994), pp. 163–206.

— 'The Paedagogus', in Philip Schaff (ed.) (n.d.), *Ante-Nicene Fathers*, vol. 2: *Fathers of the Second Century* (rpt Edinburgh: T&T Clark, 1994), pp. 207–298.

Clinton, Bill, 'The President on Peacekeeping Efforts and the Morality of the War', *The News Hour with Jim Lehrer*, 11 June 1999 <www.pbs. org/newshour/bb/europe/jan-june99/clinton_6–11b.html> [accessed 28 September 2009].

Clough, David, *Ethics in Crisis: Interpreting Barth's Ethics* (Aldershot, Hants: Ashgate, 2005).

— 'Fighting at the Command of God: Reassessing the Borderline Case in Karl Barth's Account of War in the *Church Dogmatics*', in John C. McDowell and Mike Higton (eds), *Conversing with Barth* Aldershot, Hants: Ashgate, 2004), pp. 214–26.

Clough, David and Brian Stiltner, *Faith and Force: A Christian Debate about War* (Washington, DC: Georgetown University Press, 2007).

Cohen, Roger, 'Score One for Interventionism', *The New York Times*, 29 August 2011 <www.nytimes.com/2011/08/30/opinion/30iht-edcohen30.html?_r=2> [accessed 1 September 2012].

Coker, Christopher, *War in an Age of Risk* (Cambridge: Polity Press, 2009).

Colclasure, David, 'Just War and Perpetual Peace: Kant on the Legitimate Use of Political Violence', in Elisabeth Krimmer and Patricia Anne Simpson (eds), *Enlightened War: German Theories and Cultures of Warfare from Frederick the Great to Clausewitz* (Woodbridge, Suffolk: Camden House, 2011), pp. 241–57.

Cole, David, 'Killing Citizens in Secret', *New York Review of Books* blog, 9 October 2012 <www.nybooks.com/blogs/nyrblog/2012/nov/28/its-time-stop-killing-secret/> [accessed 20 February 2013].

A Common Word between Us and You, September 2007 <www. acommonword.com/> [accessed 12 February 2013].

Cuddon, J. A., 'Deconstruction', in *A Dictionary of Literary Terms and Literary Theory*, 3rd ed., (London: Blackwell, 1991), p. 189.

Cullen, Anthony, 'The Threshold of Non-International Armed Conflict', in idem, *The Concept of Non-International Armed Conflict in International Humanitarian Law* (Cambridge: Cambridge University Press, 2010), pp. 117–57.

'Culture in the Battlefield of International Relations', *Islam Today* 27 (2011), pp. 11–14 <www.isesco.org.ma/templates/isesco/Islamtoday/en/27/27.pdf> [accessed 3 March 2013].

Dahlab v. *Switzerland*, no. 42393/98, European Court of Human Rights, 15 February 2001 <http://hudoc.echr.coe.int/sites/eng/pages/search.aspx?i=001-22643#{"fulltext":["Dahlab%20v.%20Switzerland"],"itemid":["001-22643"]}> [accessed 22 February 2013].

d'Amato, Anthony, 'Customary International Law' (2009), Audiovisual Library of International Law, UN Office of Legal Affairs <http://untreaty.un.org/cod/avl/ls/D-Amato_IL.html> [accessed 20 February 2013].

Deng, Francis, 'The Cow and the Thing Called "What": Dinka Cultural Perspectives on Wealth and Poverty', in William Twining (ed.), *Human Rights, Southern Voices* (Cambridge: Cambridge University Press, 2009), pp. 9–29.

Dennis, Mack, 'Toward a Homiletics of Reconciliation: How Karl Barth's Use of Enemy Language in *Church Dogmatics* Models a More Faithful Grammar for Preaching', PhD student paper, Duke Divinity School, Durham, NC, 1 March 2010 <www.georgetowncollege.edu/cdal/files/2011/06/mack_dennis.pdf> [accessed 21 February 2013].

Derrida, Jacques, 'Faith and Knowledge: The Two Sources of "Religion" at the Limits of Reason Alone', in idem., *Acts of Religion*London: Routledge, 2002), ch. 1.

— 'Force of Law: The "Mystical Foundation of Authority"', in idem, *Acts of Religion* (ed. Gil Anidjar, London: Routledge, 2002), ch. 5.

— *The Gift of Death* (trans. David Wills, Chicago: University of Chicago Press, 1995).

— *Of Hospitality* (Stanford, CA: Stanford University Press, 2000).

d'Escoto Brockmann, Miguel, opening statement, 'The Responsibility to Protect', UN General Assembly, New York, 23 July 2009 <www.un.org/ga/president/63/statements/openingr2p230709.shtml> [accessed 19 February 2013].

Detter, Ingrid, *The Law of War*, 2nd edn (Cambridge: Cambridge University Press, 2000).

Donaldson, Laura E., 'God, Gold and Gender', in Laura E. Donaldson and Pui-Lan Kwok, *Postcolonial Feminism and Religious Discourse* (Abingdon, Oxon: Routledge, 2001), pp. 5–6.

Donnelly, Jack, 'International Human Rights: Universal, Relative or Relatively Universal?' in Mashood Baderin and Manisuli Ssenyonjo (eds), *International Human Rights Law: Six Decades after the UDHR and Beyond*, pp. 31–48 (Farnham, Surrey: Ashgate, 2010).

— 'The Relative Universality of Human Rights', *Human Rights Quarterly* 29 (2007), pp. 281–306.

— *Universal Human Rights in Theory and Practice*, 2nd edn (Ithaca, NY: Cornell University Press, 2003).

Douzinas, Costas, *The End of Human Rights* (Oxford: Hart, 2000).

— *Human Rights and Empire: The Political Philosophy of Cosmopolitanism* (Abingdon, Oxon: Routledge-Cavendish, 2007).

Doyle, Michael, 'Kant, Liberal Legacies and Foreign Affairs', *Philosophy and Public Affairs* 12 (Summer 1983), pp. 205–35; (Autumn 1983), pp. 323–53.

Dunlap, Charles J., Jr, 'Lawfare amid Warfare', *Washington Times*, 3 August 2007 <www.washingtontimes.com/news/2007/aug/03/lawfare-amid-warfare> [accessed 12 January 2012].

Elshtain, Jean Bethke, *Just War against Terror: The Burden of American Power in a Violent World* (New York: Basic Books, 2003).

Epiphanus the Latin, *Interpretation of the Gospels*, 38 in A. Hamman, (ed.), *Patrologia Latinae Supplementum* (Paris: Garnier Frère, 1958), 33, p. 899.

Erskine, Toni, *Embedded Cosmopolitanism: Duties to Strangers and Enemies in a World of 'Dislocated Communities'* (Oxford: Oxford University Press, 2008).

Evans, Gareth, 'Implementing the Responsibility to Protect: Lessons and Challenges', Alice Tay Lecture on Law and Human Rights, Freilich Foundation, Canberra, 5 May 2011<www.gevans.org/speeches/speech437.html> [accessed 24 August 2012].

— *The Responsibility to Protect: Ending Mass Atrocities Once and for All* (Washington, DC: Brookings Institute, 2008).

Evans, Malcolm D., 'From Cartoons to Crucifixes: Current Controversies concerning the Freedom of Religion and the Freedom of Expression before the European Court of Human Rights', in Esther D. Reed and Michael Dumper (eds), *Civil Liberties, National Security and Prospects for Consensus: Legal, Philosophical and Religious Perspectives*, Cambridge: Cambridge University Press, 2012), pp. 83–113.

Evans, Malcolm and Peter Petkoff, 'A Separation of Convenience? The Concept of Neutrality in the Jurisprudence of the European Court of Human Rights', *Religion, State and Society* 36 (September 2008), pp. 205–23.

Fagan, Andrew, 'Human Rights', Internet Encyclopedia of Philosophy, 10 January 2003 <www.iep.utm.edu/hum-rts/> [accessed 24 February 2013].

Falk, Richard, 'Preliminary Libyan Scorecard: Acting beyond the UN Mandate', 6 September 2011 <http://richardfalk.wordpress.com/2011/09/06/preliminary-libyan-scorecard-acting-beyond-the-un-mandate/> [accessed 2 September 2012].

— Review of *The Riddle of All Constitutions* by Susan Marks, *American Journal of International Law* 96 (January 2002), pp. 264–68.

Fieser, James, 'The Logic of Natural Law in Aquinas's "Treatise on Law"', *Journal of Philosophical Research* 17 (1992), pp. 147–64.

Fine, Robert, *Cosmopolitanism* (London: Routledge, 2007).

Finnis, John, *Natural Law and Natural Rights* (Oxford: Clarendon Press, 1980).

Formosa, Paul, '"All Politics Must Bend Its Knee Before Right": Kant on the Relation of Morals to Politics', *Social Theory and Practice* 34 (2008), pp. 157–81.

Fortin, Ernest L., *Classical Christianity and the Political Order: Reflections on the Theologico-Political Problem*, vol. 2 of *Collected Essays* (ed. J. Brian Benestad, Lanham, MD: Rowman & Littlefield, 1996).

— *Human Rights, Virtue, and the Common Good: Untimely Meditations on Religion and Politics*, vol. 3 of *Collected Essays* (ed. J. Brian Benestad, Lanham, MD: Rowman & Littlefield, 1996).

France, R. T., *The Gospel of Matthew: The New International Commentary on the New Testament* (Grand Rapids, MI: Eerdmans, 2007).

Freeman, Michael, *Human Rights: An Interdisciplinary Approach* (Cambridge: Polity Press, 2002).

Frei, Christoph, *Hans J. Morgenthau: An Intellectual Biography* (Baton Rouge, LA: Louisiana State University Press, 2001).

Gadamer, Hans-Georg, *Truth and Method*, 2nd edn, rev. (trans. Joel Weinsheimer and Donald G. Marshall, London: Continuum, 2004).

Gardiner, Stephen, 'The Ethical Dimension of Tackling Climate Change', *Yale Environment 360*, 20 October 2011 <http://e360.yale.edu/feature/the_Ethical_dimension_of_tackling_climate_change/2456/> [accessed 22 February 2013].

Gellner, Ernest, *Nations and Nationalism*, 2nd edn (Oxford: Blackwell, 2006).

Gibbs, Robert, 'Jurisprudence is the Organon of Ethics: Kant and Cohen on Ethics, Law, and Religion', in Reinier Munk (ed.), *Hermann Cohen's Critical Idealism* (Dordrecht: Springer, 2005), pp. 193–230.

Giddens, Anthony, *A Contemporary Critique of Historical Materialism*, vol. 2: *The Nation-State and Violence* (Cambridge: Polity Press, 1985).

Global Humanitarian Forum, 'Climate Change: The Anatomy of a Silent Crisis', May 2009 <www.ghf-ge.org/human-impact-report.pdf> [accessed 22 February 2013].

Goldsmith, Jack L., *The Terror Presidency: Law and Judgment inside the Bush Administration* (New York: Norton, 2009).

Goldsmith, Jack L. and Eric A. Posner, *The Limits of International Law* (New York: Oxford University Press, 2007).

— 'The New International Law Scholarship', *Chicago Public Law and Legal Theory Working Paper*, no. 126 (May 2006), University

of Chicago Law School, pp. 463–83 <www.law.uchicago.edu/files/
files/126.pdf> [accessed 17 February 2013].
— 'A Theory of Customary International Law', *John M. Olin Law
& Economics Working Paper*, no. 63, 2nd ser. (November 1998),
University of Chicago Law School <www.law.uchicago.edu/files/
files/63.Goldsmith-Posner.pdf> [accessed 17 February 2013].
Goldstein, Brooke, The Lawfare Project <www.thelawfareproject.org/
what-is-lawfare.html> [accessed 21 February 2012].
Gorringe, Timothy J., 'Crime, Punishment and Atonement: Karl Barth on
the Death of Christ', in Daniel L. Migliore (ed.), *Commanding Grace:
Studies in Barth's Ethics*, Grand Rapids, MI: Eerdmans, 2010), ch. 8.
Gosztola, Kevin, 'In YouTube Event, Obama Defends Government's Use
of Drones', BBC World News, 30 January 2012 <http://dissenter.
firedoglake.com/2012/01/30/president-obama-says-us-must-be-
judicious-in-drone-use/> [accessed 3 March 2013].
Gramsci, Antonio, *Selections from the Prison Notebooks of Antonio
Gramsci* (ed. Quentin Hoare and Geoffrey Nowell Smith, London:
Lawrence & Wishart, 1971).
Gratian, 'Decretum Magistri Gratiani', in Emil Friedberg (ed.), *Corpus
Iuris Canonici* (1879), rpt Graz: Akademische Druck- u. Verlagsanstalt,
1959 <www.columbia.edu/cu/lweb/digital/collections/cul/texts/
ldpd_6029936_001/index.html> [accessed 20 February 2012].
Gray, Christine, 'The Meaning of Armed Conflict: Non-International
Armed Conflict', in Mary Ellen O'Connell (ed.), *What is War? An
Investigation in the Wake of 9/11* (Leiden: Martinus Nijhoff, 2012),
ch. 6.
Gray, John, *Enlightenment's Wake: Politics and Culture at the Close of
the Modern Age* (London: Routledge, 1995).
Greenwood, Christopher, 'The Development of International
Humanitarian Law by the International Criminal Tribunal for the
Former Yugoslavia', *Max Planck Yearbook of United Nations Law*
2 (1998), pp. 97–140 <www.mpil.de/shared/data/pdf/pdfmpunyb/
greenwood_2.pdf> [accessed 19 February 2013].
Greggs, Tom, *Barth, Origen, and Universal Salvation: Restoring
Particularity* (Oxford: Oxford University Press, 2009).
Gregory, Eric, 'The Spirit and the Letter: Protestant Thomism and Nigel
Biggar's "Karl Barth's Ethics Revisited"', in Daniel L. Migliore (ed.),
Commanding Grace: Studies in Karl Barth's Ethics, Grand Rapids, MI:
Eerdmans, 2010), ch. 3.
Grotius, Hugo, *On the Law of War and Peace*, (trans. A. C. Campbell,
London: Boothroyd, 1814), bk II, ch. 20, §XL.
— *The Law of War and Peace* (trans. Francis W. Kelsey, Indianapolis, IN:
Bobbs-Merrill, 1925).

Guroian, Vigen, *Rallying the Really Human Things: The Moral Imagination in Politics, Literature, and Everyday Life* (Wilmington, DE: ISI Books, 2005).

Guthrie, Charles and Michael Quinlan, *Just War: The Just War Tradition: Ethics in Modern Warfare* (London: Bloomsbury, 2007).

Haakonssen, Knud, *Natural Law and Moral Philosophy: From Grotius to the Scottish Enlightenment* (Cambridge: Cambridge University Press, 1996).

Haas, Mark L., 'Reinhold Niebuhr's "Christian Pragmatism": A Principled Alternative to Consequentialism', *The Review of Politics* 61 (Fall 1999), pp. 605–36.

Hart, Trevor, 'The Barth-Brunner Debate Revisited', *Tyndale Bulletin* 44 (November 1993), pp. 289–305.

Habermas, Jürgen, *Between Facts and Norms: Contributions to a Discourse Theory of Law and Democracy* (Cambridge: Polity Press, 1996).

— 'Does the Constitutionalization of International Law Still Have a Chance?' in Ciaran Cronin (ed.), *The Divided West*, pp. 115–93 (Cambridge: Polity Press, 2006).

— 'Kant's Idea of Perpetual Peace: At Two Hundred Years' Historical Remove', in Ciaran Cronin and Pablo De Greiff (eds), *The Inclusion of the Other: Studies in Political Theory* (Cambridge, MA: MIT Press, 1998), pp. 165–202.

— *Legitimation Crisis* (London: Heinemann, 1976).

Hall, Stephen, 'The Persistent Spectre: Natural Law, International Order and the Limits of Legal Positivism', *European Journal of International Law* 12 (2001), pp. 269–307.

Hardt, Michael and Antonio Negri, *Empire* (Cambridge, MA: Harvard University Press, 2000).

Hastings, Adrian, *The Construction of Nationhood: Ethnicity, Religion and Nationalism* (Cambridge: Cambridge University Press, 1997).

Hauerwas, Stanley, 'Abortion, Theologically Understood', lecture presented at the invitation of the Evangelical Fellowship, North Carolina Methodist Conference, Durham, 14 June 1990 <http://lifewatch.org/abortion.html> [accessed 16 April 2012].

— 'Bonhoeffer: The Truthful Witness', 2011 <www.homileticsonline.com/subscriber/interviews/hauerwas.asp> [accessed 20 February 2013].

— 'Christian Practice and the Practice of Law in a World without Foundations', *Mercer Law Review* 44 (Spring 1993), pp. 743–51.

— *War and the American Difference: Theological Reflections on Violence and National Identity* (Grand Rapids, MI: Baker Academic, 2011), ch. 3.

Hayek, Friedrich A., *The Road to Serfdom* (London: Routledge, 1944).

Hegel, George W. F., *Natural Law* (Philadephia: University of Pennsylvania Press, 1975).

Held, David, 'Principles of Cosmopolitan Order', in Gillian Brock and Harry Brighouse (eds), *The Political Philosophy of Cosmopolitanism* (Cambridge: Cambridge University Press, 2005), pp. 10–27.

Heller, Agnes, *Can Modernity Survive?* (Cambridge: Polity Press, 1990).

Henkin, Louis, 'Religion, Religions, and Human Rights', *Journal of Religious Ethics* 26 (Fall 1998), pp. 229–39.

Henle, R. J., SJ, *The Treatise on Law: ST, I-II, qq. 90–97* (Notre Dame, IN: University of Notre Dame Press, 1993).

Hessler, Stephanie, 'Presidential Power to Kill? Obama's Assassination Orders Deface the Constitution', *Washington Times*, 16 March 2012 <www.washingtontimes.com/news/2012/mar/16/presidential-power-to-kill/> [accessed 20 February 2013].

Hick, John and Paul F. Knitter (eds), *The Myth of Christian Uniqueness: Toward a Pluralistic Theology of Religions* (Maryknoll, NY: Orbis Press, 1987).

Hobbes, Thomas, *Leviathan* (ed. Richard Tuck, Cambridge: Cambridge University Press, 1996).

— *On the Citizen* (ed. Richard Tuck and Michael Silverthorne, Cambridge: Cambridge University Press, 1998).

Hobsbawm, E. J., *Nations and Nationalism since 1780: Programme, Myth, Reality* (Cambridge: Cambridge University Press, 1990).

Hoffman, Martin L., *Empathy and Moral Development: Implications for Caring and Justice* (Cambridge: Cambridge University Press, 2000).

Holder, Eric, Speech at Northwestern University School of Law, Chicago, 5 March 2012 <www.northwestern.edu/newscenter/stories/2012/03/attorney-general-holder.html> [accessed 20 February 2013].

Holland, G., 'Paul's Use of Irony as a Rhetorical Technique', in S. E. Porter and T. H. Olbricht (eds), *The Rhetorical Analysis of Scripture: Essays from the 1995 London Conference*, Sheffield: Academic Press, 1997), pp. 234–48.

Hollenbach, David, SJ, *Claims in Conflict: Retrieving and Renewing the Catholic Human Rights Tradition* (New York: Paulist Press, 1979).

— *The Common Good and Christian Ethics* (Cambridge: Cambridge University Press, 2002).

Hollenbach, David, SJ (ed.), *Refugee Rights: Ethics, Advocacy, and Africa* (Washington, DC: Georgetown University Press, 2008).

Horton, Scott, 'Six Questions for Mary Ellen O'Connell on the Power of International Law', *Harper's Magazine*, 6 December 2008 <www.harpers.org/archive/2008/12/hbc-90003966> [accessed 3 February 2013].

Hubert, Don and Ariela Blätter, 'The Responsibility to Protect as International Crimes Prevention', *Global Responsibility to Protect* 4 (2012), pp. 33–66.

Hudson, Walter M., Review essay, *The Limits of International Law* by Jack Goldsmith, *The Army Lawyer*, pamphlet 27–50–400 (September 2006), pp. 31–38 <www.loc.gov/rr/frd/Military_Law/pdf/09–2006. pdf> [accessed 20 April 2011].

Ieda, Osamu (ed.), *Beyond Sovereignty: From Status Law to Transnational Citizenship?* (Sapporo: Slavic Research Center, Hokkaido University, 2006).

Ignatieff, Michael, *Human Rights as Politics and Idolatry* (Princeton, NJ: Princeton University Press, 2001).

Inazumi, Mitsue, *Universal Jurisdiction in Modern International Law: Expansion of N Jurisdiction for Prosecuting Serious Crimes under International Law* (Utretcht: G.J. Wiarda Institute, 2005).

International Commission on Intervention and State Sovereignty, *The Responsibility to Protect*, December 2001 <http:// responsibilitytoprotect.org/ICISS%20Report.pdf> [accessed 28 September 2009].

International Committee of the Red Cross, Convention I, Geneva, 12 August 1949 <www.icrc.org/ihl.nsf/full/365?opendocument> [accessed 4 March 2013].

— 'The Relevance of IHL in the Context of Terrorism', 1 January 2011 <www.icrc.org/eng/resources/documents/misc/terrorism-ihl-210705.htm> [accessed 20 February 2013].

International Theological Commission, *In Search of a Universal Ethic: A New Look at the Natural Law* (2009) <www.vatican.va/roman_curia/ congregations/cfaith/ctI_documents/rc_con_cfaith_doc_20090520_ legge-naturale_En.html> [accessed 11 February 2013].

Irenaeus, 'Against Heresies', in ed. Philip Schaff (1884), *Ante-Nicene Fathers*, vol. 1: *The Apostolic Fathers with Justin Martyr and Irenaeus* (rpt Edinburgh: T&T Clark, 1994), pp. 309–567.

Jackson, Robert, 'R2P: Liberalizing War', *World Politics Review*, 28 June 2011 <www.worldpoliticsreview.com/articles/9308/RtoP-liberalizing-war> [accessed 24 August 2012].

Jennings, Ray, 'Disjunction', *Stanford Encyclopedia of Philosophy* <http:// plato.stanford.edu/entries/disjunction/> [accessed 30 October 2011].

Jennings, Theodore W., Jr., *Reading Derrida/Thinking Paul: On Justice* (Stanford, CA: Stanford University Press, 2006).

John of Damascus, *The Sacred Parallels*, in *Patrologia Graeca* (ed. Jacques Paul Migne, Paris: Garnier Frères et J.-P. Migne, 1864).

John XXIII, *Pacem in Terris*, 11 April 1963 www.vatican.va/holy_father/ john_xxiii/encyclicals/documents/hf_j-xxiiI_enc_11041963_pacem_ En.html> [accessed 13 February 2013].

John Paul II, Address to the 9th World Conference on Law, Madrid, 24 September 1979 <www.vatican.va/holy_father/john_paul_ii/speeches/1979/september/documents/hf_jp-iI_spe_19790924_ix-conference-on-law_En.html> [accessed 3 February 2013].
— Centesimus Annus, 1 May 1991 <www.vatican.va/holy_father/john_paul_ii/encyclicals/documents/hf_jp-iI_enc_01051991_centesimus-annus_En.html> [accessed 22 February 2013].
— 'Do Not Be Overcome by Evil but Overcome Evil with Good', World Day of Peace, 1 January 2005 <www.vatican.va/holy_father/john_paul_ii/messages/peace/documents/hf_jp-iI_mes_20041216_xxxviii-world-day-for-peace_En.html> [accessed 3 February 2013].
— 'An Ever Timely Commitment: Teaching Peace', World Day of Peace, 1 January 2004 <www.vatican.va/holy_father/john_paul_ii/messages/peace/documents/hf_jp-iI_mes_20031216_xxxvii-world-day-for-peace_En.html> [accessed 3 February 2013].
— 'The Freedom of Conscience and Religion', letter on the eve of the Madrid Conference on European Security and Cooperation, 1 September 1980 <www.ewtn.com/library/PAPALDOC/JP2FREED.htm> [accessed 1 February 2013].
— 'Peace on Earth for Those Whom God Loves!' World Day of Peace, 1 January 2000 <www.vatican.va/holy_father/john_paul_ii/messages/peace/documents/hf_jp-iI_mes_08121999_xxxiii-world-day-for-peace_En.html> [accessed 3 February 2013].
— Veritatis Splendor, 6 August 1993 <www.vatican.va/holy_father/john_paul_ii/encyclicals/documents/hf_jp-iI_enc_06081993_veritatis-splendor_En.html> [accessed 11 February 2013].
Johnson, Kevin, 'Holder: Constitution Doesn't Cover Terrorists', USA Today, 3 March 2012 <http://usatoday30.usatoday.com/news/washington/story/2012-03-05/eric-holder-killing-us-citizens-terrorist-threat/53374776/1> [accessed 20 February 2013].
Jones-Pauly, Chris, with Abir Dajani Tuqan, Women under Islam: Gender, Justice and the Politics of Islamic Law (London: Tauris, 2011).
Justin Martyr, 'Dialogue with Trypho', in Philip Schaff (ed.) (1884), Ante-Nicene Fathers, vol. 1: The Apostolic Fathers with Justin Martyr and Irenaeus (rpt Edinburgh: T&T Clark, 1994), pp. 194–270.
— 'The First Apology', in Philip Schaff (ed.) (1884), Ante-Nicene Fathers, vol. 1: The Apostolic Fathers with Justin Martyr and Irenaeus (rpt Edinburgh: T&T Clark, 1994), pp. 159–187.
Kant, Immanuel, 'Idea for a Universal History with a Cosmopolitan Purpose', in H. S. Reiss (ed.), Kant: Political WritingsCambridge: Cambridge University Press, 1970), pp. 41–53.
— The Metaphysics of Morals (trans. Mary Gregor, Cambridge: Cambridge University Press, 1996).

— 'Perpetual Peace: A Philosophical Sketch', in H. S. Reiss (ed.), *Kant: Political Writings*, Cambridge: Cambridge University Press, 1970), pp. 93–130.

Käsemann, Ernst, *Commentary on Romans* (Grand Rapids, MI: Eerdmans, 1980).

Kaufman, Robert, 'Morgenthau's Unrealistic Realism', *Yale Journal of International Affairs* 1 (Winter/Spring 2006), pp. 24–38 <http://yalejournal.org/wp-content/uploads/2011/01/061202kaufman.pdf> [accessed 7 February 2013].

Kedourie, Elie, *Nationalism*, 4th ed. (Oxford: Blackwell, 1993).

Keener, Craig S., *A Commentary on the Gospel of Matthew* (Grand Rapids, MI: Eerdmans, 1999).

Kellogg, Davida E., 'International Law and Terrorism', *Military Review* (September–October 2005), pp. 50–57.

Kelsen, Hans, *Principles of International Law* ((1952), rpt Clark, NJ: The Lawbook Exchange, 2003).

Kempshall, M. S., *The Common Good in Late Medieval Political Thought: Moral Goodness and Political Benefit* (Oxford: Clarendon Press, 1999).

Kepnes, Steven, 'A Handbook for Scriptural Reasoning' *Modern Theology* 22 (June 2006), pp. 367–83.

Kesby, Alison, 'The Shifting and Multiple Border and International Law', *Oxford Journal of Legal Studies* 27 (2007), pp. 101–19.

Kleingeld, Pauline, 'Kant's Theory of Peace', in Paul Guyer (ed.), *The Cambridge Companion to Kant and Modern Philosophy*, Cambridge: Cambridge University Press, 2006), pp. 477–504.

Koh, Harold H., 'The Obama Administration and International Law', paper presented at the annual meeting of the American Society of International Law, Washington, DC, 25 March 2010 <www.state.gov/s/l/releases/remarks/139119.htm> [accessed 20 February 2013].

Kołakowski, Leszek, *Modernity on Endless Trial* (Chicago: University of Chicago Press, 1990).

Koskenniemi, Martti, 'International Law in Europe: Between Tradition and Renewal', *European Journal of International Law* 16 (2005), pp. 113–24.

Krieger, Wolfgang, 'R2P, Corruption and Noble Causes', Kyle Matthews vs. Wolfgang Krieger, *Global Brief: World Affairs in the 21st Century*, 19 October 2011 <http://globalbrief.ca/blog/tag/responsibility-to-protect/> [accessed 24 August 2012].

Kurc, Caglar, 'How Military Technology Became a Tool for Justification for Military Interventions', paper presented at a conference at the Centre for International Intervention, University of Surrey, Guildford, 12 July 2012 <www.ias.surrey.ac.uk/workshops/intervention/papers/CaglarKurc.pdf> [accessed 3 March 2013].

Lautsi and Others v. *Italy*, no. 30814/06, European Court of Human
Rights, Grand Chamber judgement, 18 March 2011, §§ 64–69
http://hudoc.echr.coe.int/sites/eng/pages/search.aspx?i=001–
22643#{"fulltext":["Lautsi%20v.%20Italy"],"itemid":["001–
104040" [accessed 22 February 2013].

Lind, William S. et al., 'The Changing Face of War: Into the Fourth
Generation', in Terry Terriff, Aaron Karp and Regina Karp (eds),
*Global Insurgency and the Future of Armed Conflict: Debating
Fourth-Generation Warfare* (London: Routledge, 2008), pp. 13–20.

Linderfalk, Ulf, 'The Effect of Jus Cogens Norms: Whoever Opened
Pandora's Box, Did You Ever Think about the Consequences?'
European Journal of International Law 18 (2007), pp. 853–71 <www.
ejil.org/pdfs/18/5/248.pdf> [accessed 17 February 2013].

List, Christian, 'Republican Freedom and the Rule of Law', *Politics,
Philosophy and Economics* 5 (June 2006), pp. 201–20.

Little, David, 'Rethinking Human Rights: A Review Essay on Religion,
Relativism, and Other Matters', *Journal of Religious Ethics* 27 (Spring
1999), pp. 149–77.

Littman, David, 'Universal Human Rights and "Human Rights in Islam"',
Midstream (February–March 1999), pp. 2–7 <www.dhimmi.org/Islam.
html> [accessed 12 February 2013].

Livy, *History of Rome*, vol. 2 (ed. Ernest Rhys, London: Dent,
1905) <http://mcadams.posc.mu.edu/txt/ah/livy/livy09.html> [accessed
5 February 2012].

Locke, John, *Two Treatises of Government* (Cambridge: Cambridge
University Press, 1988).

Love, Maryann Cusimano, *Beyond Sovereignty: Issues for a Global
Agenda*, 4th ed. (Boston, MA: Wadsworth, 2010).

Lovin, Robin W., *Christian Realism and the New Realities* (Cambridge:
Cambridge University Press, 2008).

— *Reinhold Niebuhr and Christian Realism* (Cambridge: Cambridge
University Press, 1995).

— 'Security and the State: A Christian Realist Perspective on the World
since 9/11', in Esther D. Reed and Michael Dumper (eds), *Civil
Liberties, National Security and Prospects for Consensus: Religious
and Secular Voices*, Cambridge: Cambridge University Press, 2012),
pp. 241–56.

Luban, David, 'Fairness to Rightness: Jurisdiction, Legality, and the
Legitimacy of International Criminal Law', in Samantha Besson and
John Tasioulas (eds), *The Philosophy of International Law*, Oxford:
Oxford University Press, 2010), ch. 28.

Luz, Ulrich, 'The Final Judgment (Matt. 25:31–46): An Exercise in
"History of Influence" Exegesis', in David R. Bauer and Mark Allan

Powell (eds), *Treasures New and Old: Recent Contributions to Matthean Studies*, Atlanta, GA: Scholars Press, 1996), pp. 271–310.

— 'The Son of Man in Matthew: Heavenly Judge or Human Christ', *Journal for the Study of the New Testament* 15 (October 1992), pp. 3–20.

McCorquodale, Robert, 'International Community and State Sovereignty: An Uneasy Symbiotic Relationship', in Colin Warbrick and Stephen Tierney (eds), *Towards an International Legal Community? The Sovereignty of States and the Sovereignty of International Law*, London: British Institute of International and Comparative Law, 2006), pp. 241–65.

McNeal, Gregory, 'The US Practice of Collateral Damage Estimation and Mitigation', paper presented at a conference at the Centre for International Intervention, University of Surrey, Guildford, 12–13 July 2012 <http://works.bepress.com/gregorymcneal/22/> [accessed 20 February 2013].

Mangina, Joseph L., *Karl Barth: Theologian of Christian Witness* (Aldershot, Hants: Ashgate, 2004).

Marga, Amy, *Karl Barth's Dialogue with Catholicism in Göttingen and Münster* (Tübingen: Mohr Siebeck, 2010).

Marshall, Paul and Nina Shea, *Silenced: How Apostasy and Blasphemy Codes are Choking Freedom Worldwide* (New York: Oxford University Press, 2011).

Mattox, John Mark, *Saint Augustine and the Theory of Just War* (London: Continuum, 2006).

Matua, Makau W., 'The Ideology of Human Rights', *Virginia Journal of International Law* 36 (1996), pp. 589–658.

May, Larry, *After War Ends: A Philosophical Perspective* (Cambridge: Cambridge University Press, 2012).

— 'A Hobbesian Approach to Cruelty and the Rules of War' <http://etykapraktyczna.pl/index.php?option=com_mtree&task=att_download&link_id=1575&cf_id=24> [accessed 21 February 2013].

Mayer, Ann Elizabeth, *Islam and Human Rights: Tradition and Politics*, 4th ed. (Oxford: Westview Press, 2006).

Mechels, Eberhard, *Analogia bei Erich Przywara und Karl Barth: Das Verhältnis von Offenbarungstheologie und Metaphysic* (Neukirchen-Vluyn: Neukirchener Verlag, 1974).

Methodist Church, 'Drones: Ethical Dilemmas in the Application of Military Force', public issues team report to the Methodist Conference, 5 July 2012 <www.methodistconference.org.uk/media/117981/16%20 drones.pdf> [accessed 21 February 2013].

Methodist Church and United Reformed Church, *Peacemaking: A Christian Vocation* (London: Trustees for the Methodist Church and the United Reformed Church, 2006).

Migliore, Celestino, Address to the UN General Assembly, 63rd Session, New York, 29 September 2008 <www.vatican.va/roman_curia/ secretariat_state/2008/documents/rc_seg-st_20080929_general-debate_ En.html> [accessed 28 September 2009].

— 'The Phenomenon of Genocide' (debate), United Nations, New York, 6 April 2006 <www.vatican.va/roman_curia/secretariat_state/2006/ documents/rc_seg-st_20060406_stockholm-forum_En.html> [accessed 19 February 2013].

— 'The Rule of Law', address to the UN General Assembly, 62nd Session, New York, 26 October 2007 <www.vatican.va/roman_curia/ secretariat_state/2007/documents/rc_seg-st_20071026_rule-law_ En.html> [accessed 18 February 2013].

Mikos-Skuza, Elzbieta, 'International Law's Changing Terms: "War" becomes "Armed Conflict"', in Mary Ellen O'Connell (ed.), *What is War? An Investigation in the Wake of 9/11* (Leiden: Martinus Nijhoff, 2012), ch. 3.

Miller, David, 'Immigrants, Nations and Citizenship', *The Journal of Political Philosophy* 16 (2008), pp. 371–90.

— *National Responsibility and Global Justice* (Oxford: Oxford University Press, 2007).

Mondin, Battista, *The Principle of Analogy in Protestant and Catholic Theology* (Leiden: Martinus Nijhoff, 1963).

Morgenthau, Hans J., *Dilemmas of Politics* (Chicago: University of Chicago Press, 1958).

— 'The Evil of Politics and the Politics of Evil', *Ethics: An International Journal of Social, Political and Legal Philosophy* 56 (January 1945), pp. 1–18.

— *Political Theory and International Affairs: Hans J. Morgenthau on Aristotle's 'The Politics'* (ed. Anthony F. Lang, Jr., Westport, CT: Greenwood, 2004).

— 'Positivism, Functionalism, and International Law', *American Journal of International Law* 34 (April 1940), pp. 260–84.

— 'The UN in Crisis', *The New York Review of Books*, 25 March 1965.

Morgenthau, Hans J. and Kenneth Thompson, *Politics among Nations: The Struggle for Power and Peace*, 6th ed. (New York: McGraw-Hill, 1985).

Mouffe, Chantal, *On the Political* (London: Routledge, 2005).

Murphy, Mark C., 'Consent, Custom, and the Common Good in Aquinas's Account of Political Authority', *The Review of Politics* 59 (Spring 1997), pp. 323–50.

Murray, David A. B., 'Who's Right? Human Rights, Sexual Rights and Social Change in Barbados', *Culture, Health & Sexuality* 8 (2006), pp. 267–81.

Nanos, M. D., *Irony in Galatians* (Minneapolis, MN: Augsburg/Fortress Press, 2002).

Plank, K. A., *Paul and the Irony of Affliction* (Atlanta, GA: Scholars Press, 1987).

Nielsen, Greg M., *The Norms of Answerability: Social Theory between Bakhtin and Habermas* (Albany: State University of New York Press, 2002).

Nimmo, Paul T., *Being in Action: The Theological Shape of Barth's Ethical Vision* (Edinburgh: T&T Clark, 2011).

— 'The Orders of Creation in the Theological Ethics of Karl Barth', *Scottish Journal of Theology* 60 (February 2007), pp. 24–35.

Norton-Taylor, Richard, 'MI5 former chief decries "war on terror"', *The Guardian*, 2 September 2011 <www.guardian.co.uk/uk/2011/sep/02/mi5-war-on-terror-criticism> [accessed 29 January 2012].

Novak, Michael, *Free Persons and the Common Good* (New York: Madison Books, 1989).

Nussbaum, Martha C., *Love's Knowledge: Essays on Philosophy and Literature* (New York: Oxford University Press, 1990).

Nye, Joseph S., 'The Intervention Dilemma', *Al Jazeera*, 15 June 2012 <www.aljazeera.com/indepth/opinion/2012/06/20126129252365 1706.html> [accessed 24 August 2012].

Obama, Barack, 'Your Interview with the President', 30 January 2012 <www.whitehouse.gov/blog/2012/01/30/watch-live-president-obama-answers-your-questions-google-hangout> [accessed 20 February 2013].

O'Connell, Mary Ellen, 'Affirming the Ban on Harsh Interrogation', *Ohio State Law Journal* 66 (2005), pp. 1231–67.

— 'Defining Armed Conflict', *Journal of Conflict and Security Law* 13 (Winter 2008), pp. 393–400.

— *The Power and Purpose of International Law: Insights from the Theory and Practice of Enforcement* (Oxford: Oxford University Press, 2011).

— 'The UN, NATO, and International Law after Kosovo', *Human Rights Quarterly* 22 (February 2000), pp. 57–89.

— 'Unlawful Killing with Combat Drones: A Case Study of Pakistan, 2004–2009', Notre Dame Legal Studies Research Paper, no. 09–43, 9 November 2009 <http://papers.ssrn.com/sol3/papers.cfm?abstract_id=1501144> [accessed 4 December 2011].

O'Connell, Mary Ellen (ed.), *What is War? An Investigation in the Wake of 9/11* (Leiden: Martinus Nijhoff, 2012).

O'Donovan, Joan, 'Rights, Law and Political Community: A Theological and Historical Perspective', *Transformation* 20 (January 2003), pp. 30–38 <www.ocms.ac.uk/transformation/free_articles/2001.030_odonovan.pdf> [accessed 13 February 2013].

O'Donovan, Oliver, *The Just War Revisited* (Cambridge: Cambridge University Press, 2003).
— *The Ways of Judgment* (Grand Rapids, MI: Eerdmans, 2005).
Orakhelashvili, Alexander, *Peremptory Norms in International Law* (Oxford: Oxford University Press, 2008).
O'Rourke, P. J., *Adam Smith's 'On the Wealth of Nations': An Enquiry* (New York: Atlantic Monthly Press, 2007).
Owens, Patricia, 'Hannah Arendt and the Public Sphere: Model for a Global Public?' paper presented at a conference of the International Studies Association, New Orleans, 24–7 March 2002.
Parker, Tom, 'Eric Holder Unveils "The Cake Doctrine"', Human Rights Now blog, Amnesty International, 6 March 2012 <http://blog.amnestyusa.org/us/eric-holder-unveils-the-cake-doctrine-2/> [accessed 20 February 2013].
Parolin, Pietro, 'The Future Is in Our Hands: Addressing the Leadership Challenge of Climate Change', High-level Panel on Climate Change, United Nations, New York, 24 September 2007 <www.vatican.va/roman_curia/secretariat_state/2007/documents/rc_seg-st_20070924_ipcc_En.html> [accessed 29 September 2009].
Passerin d'Entrèves, Alexander, *Natural Law: An Introduction to Legal Philosophy*, 3rd ed. (New Brunswick, NJ: Transaction, 1994).
Penna, David R. and Patricia J. Campbell, 'Human Rights and Culture: Beyond Universality and Relativism', *Third World Quarterly* 19 (March 1998), pp. 7–27.
Perez, Celestino, 'Jürgen Habermas and Pope John Paul II on Faith, Reason and Politics in the Modern World', PhD thesis, Indiana University, Bloomington, 2008 <http://gradworks.umi.com/33/19/3319921.html> [accessed 24 February 2013].
Perreau-Saussine, Amanda, 'Immanuel Kant on International Law', in Samantha Besson and John Tasioulas (eds), *The Philosophy of International Law*, Oxford: Oxford University Press, 2010), ch. 2.
Pettit, Philip, *Republicanism: A Theory of Freedom and Government* (Oxford: Oxford University Press, 1997).
Piper, John, '*Love Your Enemies': Jesus' Love Command in the Synoptic Gospels and the Early Christian Paraenesis* (Cambridge: Cambridge University Press, 1979).
Pius XII, 'Conditions for a New World Order', Christmas message 1940, reprinted in *The Major Addresses of Pope Pius XII*, 2 vols. (ed. Vincent A. Yzermans, St. Paul, MN: North Central Publishing, 1961).
Pogge, Thomas, *World Poverty and Human Rights*, 2nd edn (Cambridge: Polity Press, 2008).
Porter, Jean, *Moral Action and Christian Ethics* (Cambridge: Cambridge University Press, 1995).

— *Natural and Divine Law: Reclaiming the Tradition for Christian Ethics* (Grand Rapids, MI: Eerdmans, 1999).

— *The Recovery of Virtue: The Relevance of Aquinas for Christian Ethics* (Louisville, KY: Westminster/John Knox Press, 1990).

— 'The Virtue of Justice (IIa-IIae, qq. 58–122)', in Stephen J. Pope (ed.), *The Ethics of Aquinas* (Washington, DC: GUO, 2002), pp. 279–84.

Post, Robert (ed.), *Another Cosmopolitanism* (Oxford: Oxford University Press, 2006).

Power, Samantha, Remarks at the International Symposium on Preventing Genocide and Mass Atrocities, Paris, 15 November 2010 <www. responsibilitytoprotect.org/index.php/component/content/article/134-americas/3079-samantha-power-remarks-at-the-international-symposium-on-preventing-genocide-and-mass-atrocities> [accessed 24 August 2012].

Pufendorf, Samuel von, *De Officio Hominis et Civis Juxta Legem Naturalem Libre Duo* (trans. Frank Gardener Moore, London: Wildy & Sons, 1964).

Rad, Gerhard von, *Genesis: A Commentary*, rev. ed. (Philadelphia: Westminster Press, 1972).

Ramsey, Paul, *Basic Christian Ethics* ((1950), rpt Louisville, KY: Westminster/John Knox Press, 1993).

— *The Just War: Force and Political Responsibility* ((1968), rpt Lanham, MD: University Press of America, 1983).

Rawls, John, *The Law of Peoples, with 'The Idea of Public Reason Revisited'* (Cambridge, MA: Harvard University Press, 1999).

— *A Theory of Justice* (Cambridge, MA: Harvard University Press, 1971).

Reed, Esther D., *The Ethics of Human Rights: Contested Doctrinal and Moral Issues* (Waco, TX: Baylor University Press, 2007).

— '"Let All the Earth Keep Silence": Law, Religion and Answerability for Targeted Killings', *Oxford Journal of Law and Religion* 1 (2012), pp. 496–509.

— 'Responsibility to Protect and Militarized Humanitarian Intervention', *Journal of Religious Ethics* 41 (March 2013), pp. 183–208.

— 'Responsibility to Protect and Militarized Humanitarian Intervention: When and Why the Churches Failed to Discern Moral Hazard', *Journal of Religious Ethics* 40:2 (June 2012), pp. 308–34.

Regina v. Immigration Officer at Prague Airport, Thomas Bingham (Lord Bingham of Cornhill), *Opinion of the Lords of Appeal for Judgment* [2004] UKHL 55.

Rengger, Nicholas, review of *Just Wars: From Cicero to Iraq* by Alex J. Bellamy; *Morality and Political Violence* by C. A. J. Coady; *Law, Ethics, and the War on Terror* by Matthew Evangelista, *Perspectives on Politics* 7 (December 2009), p. 937–39.

Richmond, Oliver P., *The Transformation of Peace* (Basingstoke: Palgrave Macmillan, 2005).
Ricoeur, Paul, 'Hermeneutics and the Critique of Ideology', in Kathleen Blamey and John B. Thompson (trans.), *From Text to Action: Essays in Hermeneutics II* (Evanston, IL: Northwestern University Press, 1991), pp. 270–306.
— *Oneself as Another* (Chicago: University of Chicago Press, 1995).
Rieff, David, 'R2P, R.I.P.', *The New York Times*, 7 November 2011 <www.nytimes.com/2011/11/08/opinion/r2p-rip.html?pagewanted=all> [accessed 24 August 2012].
Ripstein, Arthur, 'Kant and the Circumstances of Justice' in Elisabeth Ellis, Ed., *Kant's Political Theory: Interpretations and Applications* (University Park, PN: Penn State University Press, 2012), ch. 2.
Robinson, Mary, opening address, 'Enriching the Universality of Human Rights: Islamic Perspectives on the Universal Declaration of Human Rights', Geneva, 9 November 1998 <www.arabworldbooks.com/HC_speech.html> [accessed 12 February13].
— *A Voice for Human Rights* (ed. Kevin Boyle, Philadelphia: University of Pennsylvania Press, 2006).
Rommen, Heinrich, *The Natural Law: A Study in Legal and Social History and Philosophy* (trans. Thomas R. Hanley (1936); rpt Indianapolis, IN: Liberty Fund, 1998).
Rorty, Richard, *Philosophy and Social Hope* (London: Penguin, 1999).
Rosenfeld, Michael, *Just Interpretations: Law between Ethics and Politics* (Berkeley: University of California Press, 1998).
Rourke, Thomas R., 'Michael Novak and Yves R. Simon on the Common Good and Capitalism', *The Review of Politics* 58 (Spring 1996), pp. 229–58.
Russell, Frederick H., *The Just War in the Middle Ages* (Cambridge: Cambridge University Press, 1977).
Sadler, Gregory B., 'Responsibility and Moral Philosophy as a Project in Derrida's Later Works', *Minerva* 8 (November 2004), pp. 194–230 <www.minerva.mic.ul.ie//vol8/derrida.html> [accessed 31 August 2012].
Saeed, Abdullah, and Hassan Saeed, *Freedom of Religion, Apostasy and Islam* (Aldershot, Hants: Ashgate, 2004).
Sagovsky, Nicholas, 'Faith in Asylum: A Theological Critique of the UK's Asylum Policy', Gore Lecture, London, March 2005.
Şahin v. Turkey, no. 44774/98, European Court of Human Rights, Grand Chamber judgement, 10 November 2005 <http://hudoc.echr.coe.int/sites/eng/pages/search.aspx?i=001–22643#{"fulltext":["Sahin%20 v.%20Turkey"],"itemid":["001–70956"]}> [accessed 22 February 2013].

— no. 44774/98, European Court of Human Rights, judgement, 29 June 2004 <www.minorityrights.org/download.php?id=386> [accessed 24 February 2013].

Sands, Philippe, QC, 'Rules Did Nothing to Stop Detainee Abuse', *The Guardian*, 18 June 2009.

Saunders, Jason L. (ed.), *Greek and Roman Philosophy after Aristotle* ((1966), rpt New York: Free Press, 1994).

Savage, Charlie, 'Secret U.S. Memo Made Legal Case to Kill a Citizen', *New York Times*, 8 October 2011 <www.nytimes.com/2011/10/09/world/middleeast/secret-us-memo-made-legal-case-to-kill-a-citizen.html?pagewanted=all&_r=0> [accessed 20 February 2013].

Scheipers, Sibylle, *Negotiating Sovereignty and Human Rights* (Manchester: Manchester University Press, 2010).

Schmitt, Carl, *Political Theology: Four Chapters on the Concept of Sovereignty* ((Ger. rev. ed., 1934), trans. George Schwab, Chicago: University of Chicago Press, 2005).

Schmitt, John W. and J. Carl Laney, *Messiah's Coming Temple: Ezekiel's Prophetic Vision of the Future Temple* (Grand Rapids, MI: Kregel, 1997).

Schotte, Jan P., CICM, 'Jesus Christ the Saviour and His Mission of Love and Service in Asia', Synod of Bishops, Special Assembly for Asia, 1996 <www.vatican.va/roman_curia/synod/documents/rc_synod_doc_01081996_asia-lineam_En.html> [accessed 1 February 2013].

Schulte, Paul, 'Going Off the Reservation into the Sanctuary: Cross-Border Counter-Terrorist Operations, Fourth Generation Warfare and the Ethical Insufficiency of Contemporary Just War Thinking', in David Fisher and Brian Wicker (eds), *Just War on Terror? A Christian and Muslim Response* (Farnham, Surrey: Ashgate, 2010), pp. 151–74.

Schwartz, Regina, *The Curse of Cain: The Violent Legacy of Monotheism* (Chicago: University of Chicago Press, 1997).

Scott, Shirley V., *International Law in World Politics: An Introduction* (Boulder, CO: Rienner, 2004).

Scruton, Roger, *The West and the Rest: Globalization and the Terrorist Threat* (London: Continuum, 2002).

Seton-Watson, Hugh, *Nations and States: An Inquiry into the Origins of Nations and the Politics of Nationalism* (London: Methuen, 1977).

Seybolt, Taylor B., *Humanitarian Military Intervention: The Conditions for Success and Failure* (Oxford: Oxford University Press, 2007).

Shamsi, Hina, 'White House in First Detailed Comments on Drone Strikes', BBC World News, 1 May 2012 www.bbc.co.uk/news/world-us-canada-17901400 [accessed 20 February 2013].

Shklar, Judith N., *Legalism: Law, Morals, and Political Trials* (Cambridge, MA: Harvard University Press, 1964).

Simma, Bruno, 'Universality of International Law from the Perspective of a Practitioner', *European Journal of International Law* 20 (2009), pp. 265–97.

Simmons, Beth A. and Lisa L. Martin, 'International Organizations and Institutions', in ed. Walter Carlsnaes, Thomas Risse and Beth A. Simmons, *Handbook of International Relations*, (London: Sage, 2001), pp. 192–211.

Simon, Yves R., *The Tradition of Natural Law: A Philosopher's Reflections* (New York: Fordham University Press, 1965).

Simonetti, Manlio (ed.), *Ancient Christian Commentary on Scripture, New Testament 1b: Matthew 14–28* (Downers Grove, IL: Intervarsity Press, 2002).

Singer, Peter, *Practical Ethics*, 2nd edn (Cambridge: Cambridge University Press, 1993).

— *Pushing Time Away: My Grandfather and the Tragedy of Jewish Vienna* (London: Granta Books, 2003).

Sivakumaran, Sandesh, *The Law of Non-International Armed Conflict* (Oxford: Oxford University Press, 2012).

Skinner, Quentin, *Hobbes and Republican Liberty* (Cambridge: Cambridge University Press, 2008).

Smith, Anthony D., *Nations and Nationalism in a Global Era* (Cambridge: Polity Press, 1995).

Smith, Rupert, *The Utility of Force: The Art of War in the Modern World* (London: Penguin, 2005).

Smith, Wilfred Cantwell, *The Meaning and End of Religion* (Minneapolis, MI: Fortress Press, 1962).

Sodano, Angelo, address to the Summit of the Heads of State and Government, UN General Assembly, 60th Session, New York, 16 September 2005 <www.vatican.va/roman_curia/secretariat_state/2005/documents/rc_seg-st_20050916_onu_En.html> [accessed 18 February 2013].

Solana, Javier, NATO Secretary General press conference, Belgrade, 15 October 1998 <www.nato.int/docu/speech/1998/s981015a.htm> [accessed 3 February 2013].

Spaemann, Robert, *Happiness and Benevolence* (trans. Jeremiah Alberg, SJ, London: T&T Clark, 2000), ch. 10.

Spencer, A. B., 'The Wise Fool (and the Foolish Wise): A Study of Irony in Paul', *Novum Testamentum* 23 (1981), pp. 349–60.

Steiner, Henry J., Philip Alston and Ryan Goodman, *International Human Rights in Context: Law, Politics, Morals*, 3rd ed. (Oxford: Oxford University Press, 2008).

Stendahl, Krister, 'The Apostle Paul and the Introspective Conscience of the West', in idem, *Paul among Jews and Gentiles and Other Essays*, Philadelphia: Fortress Press, 1976), pp. 78–96.

Stevens, Georgina, *Filling the Vacuum: Ensuring Protection and Legal Remedies for Minorities in Kosovo* (London: Minority Rights Group International, 2009).

Strange, Susan, 'The Westfailure System', *Review of International Studies* 25 (July 1999), pp. 345–54.

Stumpf, Christoph A., *The Grotian Theology of International Law* (Berlin: de Gruyter, 2006).

Sullivan, William M., 'Ethical Universalism and Particularism: A Comparison of Outlooks', in William M. Sullivan and Will Kymlicka (eds), *The Globalization of Ethics*, Cambridge: Cambridge University Press, 2007), pp. 191–212.

Tamir, Yael, *Liberal Nationalism* (Princeton, NJ: Princeton University Press, 1993).

Tan, Kok-Chor, *Justice without Borders: Cosmopolitanism, Nationalism and Patriotism* (Cambridge: Cambridge University Press, 2004).

Taylor, Charles, 'Nationalism and Modernity', in Robert McKim and Jeff McMahan (eds), *The Morality of Nationalism*, Oxford: Oxford University Press, 1997), pp. 31–55.

Terriff, Terry, Aaron Karp and Regina Karp (eds), *Global Insurgency and the Future of Armed Conflict: Debating Fourth-Generation Warfare* (London: Routledge, 2008).

Tierney, Brian, *The Idea of Natural Rights: Studies on Natural Rights, Natural Law and Church Law 1150–1625* (Atlanta, GA: Scholars Press, 1997).

Tomasi, Silvano M., statement to the Executive Committee, UN High Commissioner for Refugees, Geneva, 4 October 2006 <www.vatican.va/roman_curia/secretariat_state/2006/documents/rc_seg-st_20061004_unhcr_En.html> [accessed 29 February 2013].

Trebilcock, Michael J. and Ronald Joel Daniels, *The Political Economy of Rule of Law Reform in Developing Countries* (Cheltenham: Edward Elgar, 2009).

Tuck, Richard, *Natural Rights Theories: Their Origin and Development* (Cambridge: Cambridge University Press, 1982).

— *The Rights of War: Political Thought and the International Order from Grotius to Kant* (Oxford: Oxford University Press, 2001).

Twining, William (ed.), *Human Rights, Southern Voices* (Cambridge: Cambridge University Press, 2009).

Twiss, Sumner B., 'History, Human Rights, and Globalization', *Journal of Religious Ethics* 32 (March 2004), pp. 39–70.

— 'Moral Grounds and Plural Cultures: Interpreting Human Rights in the International Community', *Journal of Religious Ethics* 26 (Fall 1998), pp. 271–82.

United Nations, Charter of the United Nations, 26 June 1945 <www.un.org/en/documents/charter/> [accessed 19 February 2013].

— 'Implementing the Responsibility to Protect', Report of the Secretary General (Ban Ki-moon), UN General Assembly, 63rd Session, 12 January 2009 <http://daccess-dds-ny.un.org/doc/UNDOC/GEN/N09/206/10/PDF/N0920610.pdf?OpenElement> [accessed 4 March 2013].

— *In Larger Freedom: Towards Development, Security and Human Rights for All*, Report of the Secretary General (Kofi Annan), September 2005 <www.un.org/largerfreedom/> [accessed 3 February 2013].

— *A More Secure World: Our Shared Responsibility*, Report of the High-level Panel on Threats, Challenges and Change, 2004 <www.un.org/secureworld/report2.pdf> [accessed 1 February 2012].

— Security Council, Resolution 1199, 23 September 1998 <www.un.org/peace/kosovo/98sc1199.htm> [accessed 3 February 2013].

— Special Rapporteur on Extrajudicial, Summary or Arbitrary Executions (Philip Alston), 28 May 2010 <www2.ohchr.org/english/bodies/hrcouncil/docs/14session/A.HRC.14.24.Add6.pdf> [accessed 4 December 2011].

— Special Rapporteur on Freedom of Religion or Belief (Asma Jahangir), 'Declaration on the Elimination of All Forms of Intolerance and of Discrimination Based on Religion or Belief', UN General Assembly, 25 November 1981 <www.un.org/documents/ga/res/36/a36r055.htm> [accessed 24 February 2013].

— Special Rapporteur on Freedom of Religion or Belief (Asma Jahangir), *Rapporteur's Digest on Freedom of Religion or Belief* (1986–2011), <www.ohchr.org/Documents/Issues/Religion/RapporteursDigestFreedomReligionBelief.pdf> [accessed 24 February 2013].

— Special Rapporteur on Freedom of Religion or Belief (Heiner Bielefeldt), Human Rights Council, 16th session, Geneva, 10 March 2011 <www.ohchr.org/Documents/Issues/Religion/HRC16statement_March2011.pdf> [accessed 22 February 2013].

— Special Rapporteur on Freedom of Religion or Belief (Heiner Bielefeldt), 'Report on the Promotion and Protection of All Human Rights', UN Human Rights Council, 19th session, Geneva, 22 December 2011 <www.ohchr.org/Documents/HRBodies/HRCouncil/RegularSession/Session19/A-HRC-19-60_En.pdf> [accessed 22 February 2013].

— World Summit Outcome, General Assembly, 60th Session, 24 October
    2005 <http://unpan1.un.org/intradoc/groups/public/documents/un/
    unpan021752.pdf> [accessed 2 February 2013].
UNESCO, 'Nation-State' <www.unesco.org/new/en/social-and-human-
    sciences/themes/international-migration/glossary/nation-state/>
    [accessed 17 February 2013].
US Catholic Conference, National Conference of Catholic Bishops, *The
    Harvest of Justice is Sown in Peace*, Washington, DC: United States
    Catholic Conference, 1994 <http://old.usccb.org/sdwp/harvest.shtml>
    [accessed 1 September 2012].
Universal Islamic Declaration of Human Rights, 19 September
    1981 <www1.umn.edu/humanrts/instree/islamic_declaration_
    HR.html> [accessed 20 February 2013].
Van Engeland, Anicée, 'Are Muslim Feminists at Odds with International
    Feminism? The Search for a Dialogue', on file with author, School of
    Oriental and African Studies, University of London.
Vattel, Emerich de, *The Law of Nations of the Principles of the
    Natural Law* (trans. John Chitty, Philadelphia: T. & J.W. Johnson,
    1883) <www.constitution.org/vattel/vattel_02.htm> [accessed 3
    September 2012].
Vienna Convention on the Law of Treaties, 23 May 1969 <http://untreaty.
    un.org/cod/avl/ha/vclt/vclt.html> [accessed 17 February 2013].
Villey, Michael, *Questions de saint Thomas sur le droit et la politique*
    (Paris: Presses universitaires de France, 1987).
Vitoria, Francisco de, *Political Writings* (ed. Anthony Pagden and Jeremy
    Lawrance, Cambridge: Cambridge University Press, 1991).
von Arnim, J., *Stoicorum Veterum Fragmenta*, 4 vols. (Leipzig: Teubner,
    1905–34).Waardenburg, Jacques, *Islam: Historical, Social and Political
    Perspectives* (Berlin: de Gruyter, 2002).
Waldron, Jeremy, 'Proximity as the Basis of Political Community', paper
    presented at the workshop 'Theories of Territory', King's College,
    London, 21 February 2009 <http://eis.bris.ac.uk/~plcdib/territory/
    papers/Waldron-Proximity.pdf> [accessed 9 September 2011]
— 'A Religious View of the Foundations of International Law', Charles
    E. Test Lectures, Princeton, NJ, March 2011.
— 'Safety and Security', in Esther D. Reed and Michael Dumper (eds),
    *Civil Liberties, National Security and Prospects for Consensus:
    Religious and Secular Voices*, Cambridge: Cambridge University Press,
    2012), pp. 13–34.
Weber, Max, *Economy and Society: An Outline of Interpretive Sociology*
    (New York, Bedminster Press, 1968).
Webster, John, *Barth's Moral Theology: Human Action in Barth's
    Thought* (Edinburgh: T&T Clark, 1998).

Wenham, David, review of *When Will These Things Happen? A Study of Jesus as Judge in Matthew 21–25* by Alistair I. Wilson, *Journal for the Study of the New Testament* 28 (July 2006), pp. 53–54.

West, Diana, 'Mary Robinson: Obama's Medal of Sharia Winner', 4 August 2009 <www.dianawest.net/Home/tabid/36/EntryId/973/Mary-Robinson-Obamas-Medal-of-Sharia-Winner.aspx> [accessed 12 February 2013].

Western, Jon, 'After Libya and Syria: Can R2P Survive?' *Current Intelligence*, 27 September 2011 <www.currentintelligence.net/columns/2011/9/27/after-libya-and-syria-can-r2p-survive.html> [accessed 1 September 2012].

Westmoreland-White, Michael L., 'Contributions to Human Rights in Dietrich Bonhoeffer's Ethics', *Journal of Church and State* 39 (1997), pp. 67–83.

Wilkinson, Richard and Kate Pickett, *The Spirit Level: Why Equality is Better for Everyone* (London: Penguin, 2010).

Williams, John, 'The Borders of a Just War', working papers series, School of Government and International Affairs, Durham University, June 2007 <www.dur.ac.uk/resources/sgia/SGIARWP07–03.pdf> [accessed 22 February 2013].

Williams, Michael C., 'Why Ideas Matter in International Relations: Hans Morgenthau, Classical Realism, and the Moral Construction of Power Politics', *International Organization* 58 (October 2004), pp. 633–65.

Williams, Preston N., 'Human Rights Thinking in Relationship to African Nation-States: Some Suggestions in Response to Simeon O. Ilesanmi', *Journal of Religious Ethics* 23 (Fall 1995), pp. 323–31.

Williams, Rowan, *On Christian Theology* (Oxford: Blackwell, 2000).

— *Sergii Bulgakov: Towards a Russian Political Theology* (Edinburgh: T&T Clark, 2000).

Wolterstorff, Nicholas, *Justice: Rights and Wrongs* (Princeton, NJ: Princeton University Press, 2008).

— *Reason within the Bounds of Religion*, 2nd edn (Grand Rapids, Mich.: Eerdmans, 1984).

Wood, Allen W., 'Kant's Project for Perpetual Peace', in Pheng Cheah and Bruce Robbins (eds), *Cosmopolitics: Thinking and Feeling Beyond the Nation* (Minneapolis: University of Minnesota Press, 1998), pp. 59–76.

Wood, James E., Jr., 'An Apologia for Religious Human Rights', in John Witte, Jr. and Johan D. van der Vyver (eds), *Human Rights in Global Perspective: Religious Perspectives* (The Hague: Martinus Nijhoff, 1996), pp. 455–83.

Woods, Chris, 'Covert Drone Strikes and the Fiction of Zero Civilian Casualties', paper presented at a conference at the Centre for

International Intervention, University of Surrey, Guildford, 12 July 2012 <www.ias.surrey.ac.uk/workshops/intervention/papers/ ChrisWoods.pdf> [accessed 3 March 2013].

— 'Covert Drone War: A Question of Legality', Bureau of Investigative Journalism, 4 February 2012 <www.thebureauinvestigates. com/2012/02/04/a-question-of-legality/> [accessed 12 December 2012].

World Council of Churches, Commission of the Churches on International Affairs, 'The Protection of Endangered Populations in Situations of Armed Violence: Toward an Ecumenical Ethical Approach', policy document submitted to a meeting of the Central Committee, Potsdam, 6 February 2001 <www.oikoumene.org/ en/resources/documents/wcc-commissions/international-affairs/ commission-on-international-affairs-policy/the-protection-of- endangered-populations-in-situations-of-armed-violence-toward-an- ecumenical-ethical-approach.html> [accessed 28 September 2012].

— Commission of the Churches on International Affairs, 'The Responsibility to Protect: Ethical and Theological Reflections', report to meeting of the Central Committee, Geneva, 26 August–2 September 2003 <www2.wcc-coe.org/ccdocuments2003.nsf/index/pub-3.1-en. html> [accessed 28 September 2013].

— Minute on Darfur, meeting of the Executive Committee, Etchmiadzin, 28 September 2007 <www.oikoumene.org/en/resources/documents/ executive-committee/etchmiadzin-september-2007/minute-on-darfur. html> [accessed 19 February 2013].

— The Responsibility to Protect: Ethical and Theological Reflections (ed. Semegnish Asfaw et al., Geneva: WCC, 2005).

— Statement of the 9th Assembly, Porto Alegre, Brazil, 23 February 2006 <www.oikoumene.org/en/resources/documents/wcc-commissions/ international-affairs/responsability-to-protect/vulnerable-populations- at-risk-the-responsibility-to-protect.html> [accessed 18 February 2013].

— 'Together on the Way: A Statement on Human Rights', 8th Assembly, Harare, 3–14 December 1998 <www.wcc-coe.org/wcc/assembly/hr-e. html> [accessed 20 February 2013].

World Health Organization, 'Food Security', World Food Summit, Rome, 13–17 November 1996 <www.who.int/trade/glossary/story028/en/> [accessed 3 February 2013].

World Wildlife Fund, 'Climate Change and Poverty' <www.wwf.org. uk/what_we_do/making_the_links/climate_change_and_poverty/> [accessed 22 February 2013].

Worsnip, Patrick, 'U.N. Urged to Set Up Panel on Ethics of Robot Weapons', 22 October 2010 <www.reuters.com/article/2010/10/22/ us-un-rights-robots-idUSTRE69L5RL20101022> [accessed 10 December 2011].

Yannis, Alexandros, 'The Concept of Suspended Sovereignty', *European Journal of International Law* 13 (2002), pp. 1037–52.

Zemanek, Karl, *Introduction*, Vienna Convention on the Law of Treaties, 23 May 1969 http://untreaty.un.org/cod/avl/ha/vclt/vclt.html [accessed 17 February 2013].

Žižek, Slavoj, 'The Obscenity of Human Rights: Violence as Symptom' (2005) <www.lacan.com/zizviol.htm> [accessed 28 April 2013].

INDEX OF BIBLICAL REFERENCES

INDEX OF NAMES

INDEX OF SUBJECTS